ENLIGHTENMENT AND VIOLENCE

Other Volumes in the Series:

Volume 1: *Independence and Partition: The Erosion of Colonial Power in India* by Sucheta Mahajan

Volume 2: *A Narrative of Communal Politics: Uttar Pradesh, 1937–39* by Salil Misra

Volume 3: *Imperialism, Nationalism and the Making of the Indian Capitalist Class, 1920–1947* by Aditya Mukherjee

Volume 4: *From Movement To Government: The Congress in the United Provinces, 1937–42* by Visalakshi Menon

Volume 5: *Peasants in India's Non-Violent Revolution: Practice and Theory* by Mridula Mukherjee

Volume 6: *Communalism in Bengal: From Famine to Noakhali, 1943–47* by Rakesh Batabyal

Volume 7: *Political Mobilization and Identity in Western India, 1934–47* by Shri Krishan

Volume 8: *The Garrison State: Military, Government and Society in Colonial Punjab, 1849–1947* by Tan Tai Yong

Volume 9: *Colonializing Agriculture: The Myth of Punjab Exceptionalism* by Mridula Mukherjee

Volume 10: *Region, Nation, "Heartland": Uttar Pradesh in India's Body-Politic* by Gyanesh Kudaisya

Volume 11: *National Movement and Politics in Orissa, 1920–29* by Pritish Acharya

Volume 12: *Communism and Nationalism in Colonial India, 1939–45* by D.N. Gupta

Volume 13: *Vocalising Silence: Political Protests in Orissa, 1930–32* by Chandi Prasad Nanda

Volume 14: *Nandanar's Children: The Paraiyans' Tryst with Destiny, Tamil Nadu 1850–1956* by Raj Sekhar Basu

ENLIGHTENMENT AND VIOLENCE
Modernity and Nation-Making

Tadd Fernée

SAGE Series in Modern Indian History—XV

Series Editors:
Bipan Chandra
Mridula Mukherjee
Aditya Mukherjee

$SAGE   www.sagepublications.com
Los Angeles • London • New Delhi • Singapore • Washington DC

Copyright © Tadd Fernée, 2014

All rights reserved. No part of this book may be reproduced or utilized in any form or by any means, electronic or mechanical, including photocopying, recording or by any information storage or retrieval system, without permission in writing from the publisher.

First published in 2014 by

SAGE Publications India Pvt Ltd
B1/I-1 Mohan Cooperative Industrial Area
Mathura Road, New Delhi 110 044, India
www.sagepub.in

SAGE Publications Inc
2455 Teller Road
Thousand Oaks, California 91320, USA

SAGE Publications Ltd
1 Oliver's Yard, 55 City Road
London EC1Y 1SP, United Kingdom

SAGE Publications Asia-Pacific Pte Ltd
3 Church Street
#10-04 Samsung Hub
Singapore 049483

Published by Vivek Mehra for SAGE Publications India Pvt Ltd, typeset in 10/12 Palatino Linotype by RECTO Graphics, Delhi, and printed at Saurabh Printers Pvt Ltd, New Delhi.

Library of Congress Cataloging-in-Publication Data

Fernée, Tadd Graham, 1971– author.
  Enlightenment and violence : modernity and nation-making / Tadd Fernée.
    pages cm.— (Sage series in modern Indian history ; XV)
  Includes bibliographical references and index.
  1. India—Politics and government. 2. Enlightenment. 3. Political violence. I. Title.
  DS445.F47   954.03'5—dc23   2014   2014001968

ISBN: 978-81-321-1319-5 (HB)

The SAGE Team: Supriya Das, Archa Bhatnagar, Anju Saxena and Dally Verghese

This book is dedicated to Kyoko Mifune. Without her courageous actions and persistent questions, the book would never have been written. This book has attempted to answer the questions I never could answer.

Thank you for choosing a SAGE product! If you have any comment, observation or feedback, I would like to personally hear from you. Please write to me at contactceo@sagepub.in

—Vivek Mehra, Managing Director and CEO,
SAGE Publications India Pvt Ltd, New Delhi

Bulk Sales

SAGE India offers special discounts for purchase of books in bulk. We also make available special imprints and excerpts from our books on demand.

For orders and enquiries, write to us at

Marketing Department
SAGE Publications India Pvt Ltd
B1/I-1, Mohan Cooperative Industrial Area
Mathura Road, Post Bag 7
New Delhi 110044, India
E-mail us at marketing@sagepub.in

Get to know more about SAGE, be invited to SAGE events, get on our mailing list. Write today to marketing@sagepub.in

This book is also available as an e-book.

Contents

Series Editors' Preface		ix
Acknowledgements		xi
Introduction		xiii
1.	Akbar's "Universal Peace" (*Sulh-i Kul*): Relevance to the Enlightenment	1
2.	The European Enlightenment: Between Revenge and Reconciliation	52
3.	Early Indian Nationalism: Between Liberty and Authenticity	106
4.	The Indian National Movement and Gandhi: The Ethic of Reconciliation as Mass Movement	147
5.	The Ottoman–Turkish Experience of the Enlightenment: Mass Movement and Programme	196
6.	The Heritage of Non-violence in the Nehru Period: The Ethic of Reconciliation in Nation-Making	244
7.	Iranian Enlightenment: Struggle for Multi-Cultural Democracy and Its Demise	270
Conclusion		340
Bibliography		364
Index		378
About the Author		386

Series Editors' Preface

The SAGE Series in Modern Indian History is intended to bring together the growing volume of historical studies that share a very broad common historiographic focus.

In the 50 years since independence from colonial rule, research and writing on modern Indian history has given rise to intense debates resulting in the emergence of different schools of thought. Prominent among them are the Cambridge School and the Subaltern School. Some of us at the Jawaharlal Nehru University, along with many colleagues in other parts of the country, have tried to promote teaching and research along somewhat different lines. We have endeavoured to steer clear of colonial stereotypes, nationalist romanticization, sectarian radicalism and rigid and dogmatic approach. We have also discouraged the "flavour of the month" approach, which tries to ape whatever is currently fashionable.

Of course, a good historian is fully aware of contemporary trends in historical writing and of historical work being done elsewhere, and draws heavily on the comparative approach, i.e. the historical study of other societies, states and nations, and on other disciplines, especially economics, political science, sociology and social anthropology. A historian tries to understand the past and make it relevant to the present and the future. History thus also caters to the changing needs of society and social development. A historian is a creature of his or her times, yet a good historian tries to use every tool available to the historian's craft to avoid a conscious bias to get as near to the truth as possible.

The approach we have tried to evolve looks sympathetically, though critically, at the Indian national liberation struggle and other popular movements such as those of labour, peasants, lower castes, tribal peoples and women. It also looks at colonialism as a structure and a system, and analyzes changes in economy, society and culture in the colonial context as also in the context of independent India. It focuses on communalism and casteism as major features of modern Indian development. The volumes in the series will tend to reflect this approach as also its changing and developing features. At the broadest plane our approach is committed to the Enlightenment values of rationalism, humanism, democracy and secularism.

The series will consist of well-researched volumes with a wider scope, which deal with a significant historiographical aspect even while devoting meticulous attention to detail. They will have a firm empirical grounding based on an exhaustive and rigorous examination of primary sources (including those available in archives in different parts of India and often abroad); collections of private and institutional papers; newspapers and journals (including those in Indian languages); oral testimony; pamphlet literature; contemporary literary works. The books in this series, while sharing a broad historiographic approach, will invariably have considerable differences in analytical frameworks.

The many problems that hinder academic pursuit in developing societies—e.g., relatively poor library facilities, forcing scholars to run from library to library and city to city and yet not being able to find many of the necessary books, inadequate institutional support within universities, a paucity of research-funding organizations, a relatively underdeveloped publishing industry and so on—have plagued historical research and writing as well. All this had made it difficult to initiate and sustain efforts at publishing a series along the lines of the Cambridge History Series or the history series of some of the best US and European universities.

But the need is there because in the absence of such an effort, a vast amount of work on Indian history being done in Delhi and other university centres in India as also in British, US, Russian, Japanese, Australian and European universities, which shares a common historiographic approach, remains scattered and has no *voice*. Also, many fine works published by small Indian publishers never reach the libraries and bookshops in India or abroad.

We are acutely aware that one swallow does not make a summer. This series will only mark the beginning of a new attempt at presenting the efforts of scholars to evolve autonomous (but not indigenist) intellectual approaches in modern Indian history.

Bipan Chandra
Mridula Mukherjee
Aditya Mukherjee

Acknowledgements

I researched and wrote this book as a visiting Fellow at the Jawaharlal Nehru University Institute of Advanced Study in New Delhi, India, in 2010. I am grateful to the university for this opportunity to live in India and reflect upon these questions. I would like to thank the Institute director, Aditya Mukherjee, for his intellectual support and generous help during my stay. I would also like to thank Mridula Mukherjee and Bipan Chandra, both of whom offered intellectual guidance and inspiration. I received the help of a community of colleagues and friends while writing this book. I would like to thank Anindo Sahar for long conversations that helped shape the direction of this book, and for his many fruitful research suggestions. At an early stage in the research, Katerine Neal-Phleng and the late Paul Fletcher provided important inputs. My long-time collaborator and friend, Ali Mirsepassi, was an important inspiration and source of ideas in writing this book. He provided important encouragement. The comments and suggestions of all of these people gave the book its shape. I would like to thank Sandy Casado for her patience and kind support during the time of writing this book.

Introduction

INTERPRETING THE ENLIGHTENMENT AS A HERITAGE

This study investigates the Enlightenment heritage as a problem in the history of ideas, an interconnected web spanning debates on nationalism, revolution and post-structuralism. Within this context, the value of progress, science and political organization has been interrogated. The heterogeneous experiences of modern nation-making provide the material for visualizing the historical patterns and collective social institutions that demonstrate the often conflicting kinship patterns of the Enlightenment heritage. The central historical thesis departs from certain comparative reflections of the historian Bipan Chandra.[1] The Gandhi–Nehru paradigm in India's National Independence Movement achieved Enlightenment objectives and advanced the nation-making process through a notion of immanent truth as opposed to transcendental truth. This necessarily entailed a nation-making course of non-violence based upon an ethic of reconciliation. The Indian experience, in this respect, differed from the predominant paradigmatic experience embodied in the Russian or Chinese Revolutions, which claimed a historical–ontological link to the French revolutionary precedent. In the revolutionary aftermath, the Indian people did not become the victims of the means they had used to obtain emancipation.[2] This historical precedent paved the way for the American Civil Rights Movement, the Polish Solidarity Movement and the Jasmine Revolution in Tunisia.

There are, in this, implications for the Enlightenment heritage as a philosophical problematic. The tradition, at its best, transcends the dichotomous and teleological metaphysics defining it

---

[1] For example, Bipan Chandra, *Indian National Movement: The Long-Term Dynamics* (New Delhi: Vikas, 1989) argues that the national movement offers the world lessons in social transformation in comparable fashion to the British, French, Russian, Chinese and other modern revolutions.

[2] See Mridula Mukherjee, *Peasants in India's Non-Violent Revolution: Practice and Theory* (New Delhi: SAGE, 2004) for the theory of the National Independence Movement as a non-violent revolution.

in conventional philosophical discourses. Its 20th-century cumulative and interactive formations suggest neither *alternative modernity* nor history as a single unbroken line hinting at hidden transcendental intent. Nor do Romantic constructions of Enlightenment as an imprisoning and invasive alien discourse—or valorizations of the *fragment*—survive historical scrutiny. The Enlightenment heritage is not manufactured uniquely by a catalogue of verbally constructed rules ("the rules of the 'language' of post-Enlightenment rational thought"), but coloured by the tacit and cumulative habitus patterns of phenomenal lifeworlds.[3] Each modern experience embedded within the Enlightenment heritage is plural, tension-laden and a context-specific universal—requiring a temporal rather than totalizing analytic. It resembles John Dewey's centerless environment of multiple histories, or "non-recurring temporal sequence": "a thing of histories, each with its own plot, its own inception and movement toward its close, each having its own particular rhythmic movement."[4] Dewey articulated an ideal of public action involving "modified institutions" based on "possibilities" and "imagination" of "old things in new relations serving a new end which the new end aids in creating."[5] The central means-ends issue concerns—as far as nation-making prospects for a democratic modernity—the political construction of violence.

The Enlightenment heritage is analyzed through variable elements in the diverse and interactive nation-making experiences of Western Europe (modernity and Enlightenment between England and France) and in three situations of colonial and semi-colonial domination and national struggle: the Ottoman Empire, Turkey, British India, the Indian Republic and Iran leading through the Constitutional Revolution to the mid-20th-century National Front coalition. This book is the study of these different moments—and possible horizons—in the Indian, Turkish and Iranian Enlightenment formations: both the specific historical

---

[3] Partha Chatterjee, *Nationalist Thought and the Colonial World: A Derivative Discourse* (Minnesota: University of Minneapolis Press, 1993), 39.

[4] John Dewey, *The Philosophy of John Dewey* (Chicago: University of Chicago Press, 1973), 410/555.

[5] John Dewey, *A Common Faith* (New Haven: Yale University Press, 1962), 48–49.

contexts in a common globalizing space, and the discursive–practical components operating at the level of transferable power mechanisms.

The Enlightenment, however tacitly, is a heritage which profoundly shaped 20th-century nation-making developments. It is a broadly discursive–practical—rather than specifically religious or cultural—heritage. The 20th century manifested its power and self-contradiction in momentous world revolutions fusing its disparate elements in varied combinations. The century's highly violent Russian and Chinese revolutions (socialist ideology merged with nationalist mobilization) culminated in the largely bloodless Eastern European and Russian revolutions (democratic aspiration merged with nationalist mobilization). Decolonization—in varying discursive–practical constructions of violence—highlighted the power of multi-class mass political participation motivated by opposition to existing conditions and widespread goal consensus in the French Revolutionary pattern. Traditional solidarity values integrated with socialist frameworks, i.e. in the avowedly Marxist Vietnamese Revolution, indicating an underlying fact–value entanglement on the practical level despite official discursive constructs.[6] The 20th-century Enlightenment heritage therefore transcended religious and cultural divisions—yet in a multi-centred flux of participation that exploded the conventional dualistic metaphor of a modernity–tradition frontier.

The Enlightenment is therefore not—despite dominant claims to the contrary in the 18th-century French experience—a unified or contained ontology or epistemology. It has the living reality of a problem, or assemblage of problems, and not the singular inanimate reality of a stone—or the lifeworld terrain of meaning production rather than merely immutable natural law. The problems are universal: world space transformations produced by expanding capitalism, irreversible conditions of human interconnectedness vulnerable to cyclic destabilization, hazardously altering geopolitical landscapes, deepening resource restraints, climate change, colonial legacies of subordinating metropolitan integration and neo-colonial authoritarian modernization. These elements relate, in turn, to a heritage of cumulative struggle for

---

[6] James DeFronzo, *Revolutions and Revolutionary Movements* (Boulder: Westview Press, 1996), chapter 4.

freedom requiring unceasing protection; and a universal if hierarchally apportioned vulnerability providing the underlying logic for non-violence.

The 20th-century practical experience of the Enlightenment heritage undermined many of the Enlightenment's own received discursive assumptions about modernity, i.e. Universal History grounded within the closed logic of a metaphysically dichotomous time horizon. The death of such vivid metaphors signals the more subtle and fundamental demise of an underlying dichotomy between evaluation and description with implications for political action and the rank-ordering of social goods.[7] The existentially ubiquitous fact–value entanglement provides an analytical key for interpreting 21st-century modernity in terms of the central importance of the lifeworld—i.e. embeddedness in basic solidarities of family, work and belonging—as a defining criterion of dignity for development processes. The major lessons of the 20th-century Enlightenment heritage were: the dominant development paradigm based upon purely *objective* forces—supposedly external to human imagination—is tantamount to a politics of authoritarianism; and that—if a free society is to be built—being and becoming must interact practically as a creative ensemble rather than be dichotomized based on rigidly imposed intellectual schema. As ideal types, the alternatives are the immanent–reconciliation or the transcendental–totalization horizons.

Revolution is a moment in development, unless it is envisioned as a golden gate to heaven or "leap in the open air of history."[8] The 20th-century Enlightenment heritage was defined by world revolution, while the 21st-century should be shaped by democratic rather than authoritarian material development. The core Enlightenment problem concerns immense global wealth–poverty disparities, hierarchic class dynamics and the problematic of development between authoritarian and democratic discursive–practical legacies. Democratic development constitutes collectively empowering human interaction systems and generates new existential–ethical understandings of the

---

[7] Hilary Putnam, *The Collapse of the Fact/Value Dichotomy and other essays* (2002) for an in-depth examination of this issue linking John Dewey and Amartya Sen.

[8] Walter Benjamin, *Illuminations* (New York: Schocken, 2007), 261.

human place in the world. The authoritarian development mode is exemplified in Kemal Ataturk's nation-wide imposition of a rigidly homogenous cultural code supposedly representing *universal modernity*, and public purge of traditional ideas, values and identities through violent means. The ideal of democratic development, by contrast, was embodied in Jawaharlal Nehru's critical reserve regarding state power, principle of non-violence and context-specific logic of modernization. The driving principle of Nehruism linked economic development and political freedom in democratic nation-making. In Nehru's policy the Gandhian ethic of reconciliation was implemented through pluralist and non-interventionist solutions to the myriad centre–state and civil society dilemmas of the early Indian republic. Both Ataturk and Nehru derived their politics—in profoundly differing manifestations—from the secular Enlightenment heritage. They highlight the diverging transcendent–authoritarian and immanent–pluralist potentialities of the heritage.

The Nehruvian paradigm demonstrates that development harbours a wider practical potentiality than merely a nihilistic and absurd mass uprooting of populations. It discloses a *meaningful* development mode: immanently invested with multiple cultural meanings and values, and democratically constrained rather than *transcendentally* positing the universal infallibility of the ruling elite. It recognizes the value of the lifeworlds, embeddedness and the everyday within the development process, rather than forcing these elements into a secondary category where they may be sacrificed to a so-called *higher* end.

The theoretical resources for rearticulating the Enlightenment heritage in light of 20th-century learnings were largely produced during the 20th century, and require a synthetic re-interpretation of radical pluralist innovators in Enlightenment interpretation like John Dewey, Max Weber, Hannah Arendt, Michael Polanyi, Mohammed Arkoun, Abdul An-Naim and Amartya Sen. All of these thinkers have confronted the lifeworld-meaning dimension, or embeddedness, as a central problem in modern development experiences. Methodologically, we must interpret Enlightenment patterns and structures employing heterogeneous multiplicities—the pluralistic production of order, irreducible to a pre-established unity—rather than dualistically opposed pairs bounded within closed and homogenous frames (structuralism) or an essence–object correspondence (metaphysics).⁹

The Enlightenment, as an open historical field of contingently radiating threads, never the less requires analysis in terms of the structuring power of an analogical central knot. This region of density shows the Enlightenment heritage as predominantly linked—in a violence–practice discursive compound—to nationalism through the paradigmatic experience of the French Revolution. It is here, in relation to this compound, that the Indian nation-making experience created through its successful practices an alternate region of discursive–practical density in horizon-possibilities for mass political mobilizations.

The historical memory of the French Revolution as a national mass movement has produced an enormous concentration of imaginative power, so that "ever since 1789, there has been one magic word which contained within itself all imaginable futures, and is never so full of hope as in desperate situations—that word is revolution."¹⁰ The French Revolution is described as being an "extraordinary novelty" and "a religion without religion."¹¹ Hegel wrote that "It has been said that the French Revolution resulted from philosophy" and that it let us perceive that "man's existence centers in his head, i.e., in Thought, inspired by which he builds up the world of reality."¹² This was what Walter Benjamin meant when he wrote that modern revolutionary politics—evoking a messianic horizon—tacitly "enlists the services of theology."¹³ It is a transcendental imagining of a historical event, rather than its immanent practical analysis.

---

⁹ This derives from Henri Bergson's contribution to analyzing historical time, in rejection of Heidegger's unified and closed *being* and the Hegelian deduction of existence from an absolute concept. See Henri Bergson, *Essai sur les données immédiates de la conscience* (1888), chapter two. It inspired Gilles Deleuze's theory of the "rhizome" and non-linear "becomings."

¹⁰ Simone Weil, *Oppression and Liberty* 1958. (London: Routledge, 2001), 37.

¹¹ Les Collections de L'Histoire. No.25. La Revolution Francaise. Oct.–Dec. 2004. Interview with F. Furet. "Apres Robespierre, Lenine…".

¹² Georg Wilhelm and Friedrich Hegel, *The Philosophy of History*. (New York: Dover, 1956), 436–37.

¹³ Benjamin, *Illuminations*, 253.

This suggests the total and ontological character of the interpretation that has largely prevailed of this seminal historical event ("the birth of modernity"), its seductive promise of entry into an entirely new political and intellectual space as a mode of imagining.[14] This ontology of inside-out identity and homogeneous linear time in nation-making, the imaginative analysis of the French Revolution by its own leading actors, requires re-evaluation with reference to new historical learnings—above all concerning the naturalness or inevitability of violence in mass-based political change. It should be emphasized, however, that the future is not already written on some determined discursive level, as if the French Revolution were merely a "language" whose adoption guarantees a fixed end.[15] A history of ideas should not merely trace a succession of ideas, but demonstrate idea formation within the historically destabilizing conditions of modernity and the crises which have defined it.

Methodologically, neither Arthur Lovejoy's "history of ideas" nor Michel Foucault's "history of systems of thought" correspond precisely to this analysis of the Enlightenment heritage as a history of ideas. It is, however, partly indebted to both methodological innovators. Foucault employed two methodologies in the history of ideas. He initially employed a "broadly Heideggerian framework of historical ontology" where "he sets himself up as the prophet of the end of one epistemic age and the beginning of another" in "eschatological" fashion.[16] The present analysis corresponds to Foucault's methodological shifting of the Kantian Transcendental Aesthetic (Time–Space) from *a priori* objective knowledge boundaries to the historical contingency of *necessary* ideas. Also, there is some affinity with Foucault's employment of the "unthought" (the "silent horizon [of] the sandy stretches of the non-thought") where the "necessary judgements" of a "science of

---

[14] Ferenc Fehér ed., *The French Revolution and the Birth of Modernity* (1990).

[15] This would be the weakness in Francois Furet's otherwise important interpretation of the French Revolution.

[16] Gary Cutting, "Introduction. Michel Foucault: A User's Manual," in *The Cambridge Companion to Foucault*, Gary Cutting ed. (Cambridge: Cambridge University Press, 2005), 16–20.

nature" are of secondary order to the problem of "existence."[17] Such diverse figures as John Dewey, R. G. Collingwood, Max Weber and Amartya Sen—in varying but related ways—have also emphasized the lifeworld meaning-dimension over *natural laws* in social science and historical methodology. However, Foucault's breaking up and repackaging of totalized modern European history as colourfully distinct units—each defined by a dominant episteme floating in the oceanic unthought— presents a curiously inhuman and non-participatory vision of historical transformation that doubtlessly adopted a tacit Heideggerian intellectual authoritarianism. Secondly, Foucault employed the methodology of "discursive formations" where "discursive rules govern statements" with "no suggestion that language as such has undergone any fundamental transformation from the Classical to the modern age."[18] The present history of ideas—although concerned with discourses—has no special affinity with this *structuralist* methodology in its cold suppression of the phenomenological subject. The agentative subject should be embedded within the wider material world of everydayness, but need not evaporate like a structure puppet imprisoned within intermeshing frameworks of theoretical discourse.

There is affinity, by contrast, with Lovejoy's focus upon the unthought, *"unconscious mental habits,"* and "metaphysical pathos" within the lifeworld space of a transitional historical horizon continuously adding to itself, and where "unit ideas" recombine in new combinations.[19] However, the focalization upon "unit ideas" as the enduring element in Lovejoy's analysis tends to view social actions as "growths from seed scattered by great philosophical systems."[20] Both Foucault and Lovejoy undertake the history of ideas within the limits of Eurocentrism, perhaps precisely in neglecting to theorize capitalism as a global phenomenon of defining linkages. For the present analysis of the

---

[17] Michel Foucault, *The Order of Things: An Archaeology of the Human Sciences* (New York: Vintage, 1973), 322–23.

[18] Cutting, *Cambridge Companion*, 16–20.

[19] Arthur O. Lovejoy, *The Great Chain of Being* (Cambridge: Harvard University Press, 1978), 7–11.

[20] Ibid., 17.

Enlightenment heritage, such analytical limits are methodologically impossible.

The central analytical framework, therefore, is neither "unit ideas" nor "episteme" but discursive–practical regions of density. The only feasible basis for a history of ideas linked to mass social movements are the material realities (poverty, ignorance, gender subordination and other subjugating experiences) that have moved the dispossessed majority in modern mass movements. The material is not *external* to imagination, but a meaningfully full reality only as embedded within human and cultural contexts. While these phenomena constrain human empowerment and progress, they have also moved historical change from below. But, as the subaltern methodological intervention emphasized, these powers remain unrecorded except as residual traces of silenced, fractured and damaged experiences of disempowered majorities.[21] As self-representation through writing implies a heightened level of social power, a history of ideas is necessarily elitist compared to the darkness of historically erased populations. Embedding a history of ideas within social movements entails breaking away from conventions focused exclusively on the central state, elite terminologies and elite perceptions of modernization.[22]

Focus should shift to the meaning for populations undergoing the modernization process, the interaction of those phenomena with the lifeworlds, or the relation between respective discursive–practical formations and greater or lesser achievements of human freedom. The historical record shows important and meaningful differences in how varying discursive–practical formations have emerged and interacted with mass movements to produce alternative social and political realities. Discursive–practical formations require analysis of their multi-centred relational significance (not god-like causality) for workers' right to organize, i.e. in releasing human capabilities, or population expulsions or massacres, i.e. constructions of violence, and how they negotiated the public memory of collective traumas. While accordingly rejecting a dichotomous modernization discursively

---

[21] Ranajit Guha, *Elementary Aspects of Peasant Insurgency in Colonial India*.

[22] Bernard Lewis, *The Emergence of Modern Turkey*.

constructed as History's irresistible March, it is mistaken to condemn in Heideggerian fashion modernization and even *modernity* as a homogeneous universal violence with identical consequences everywhere. The modern world—far from an ethical void—contains meaningful differences.

Discursive–practical regions of density—as analytical tools for historicizing ideas through their immanent and material formations—should divest social movement theory of the atemporal textures of Judgement Day. Mass movements and revolutions enshrine the unique revolutionary status of nationalism because—as a unique historical horizon—it involves an ensemble of temporally compatible motivations among classes, status groups, communities, etc. These historical moments continuously re-constitute regions of density in combining levels of elite self-consciousness and the invisible vistas of the popular in ever new forms. The articulation of regions of density, therefore, requires an analytic of temporal horizons, not totality. There is no *final revolution* with the aura of Judgement Day. The ensemble of temporally compatible motivations that create national revolutions are merely temporal horizons upon a larger and relatively unforgettable scale, but blend into the multitude of historically invisible and intimate temporal horizons of phenomenological everyday life, i.e. those infinite impulses of struggle and self-preservation keeping populations alive in the ordinary everydayness of a desperate world.

The French Revolutionary heritage is the central region of discursive–practical density because the radically violent deterritorialization inflicted upon the global majority by expanding capitalism—a mass of bodies reduced to worthlessness by overabundance, labour disembedded and forced into migration, curtailed capacities, exclusion from representation—has pulled them towards its vortex with the force of a black hole. The French Revolution, from this perspective, is a material rather than merely discursive problematic of embeddedness, embodiment and the unthought. Great pressure is required to force populations to risk violent death in revolt against authority. Following Karl Polanyi, the Enlightenment heritage as a political phenomenon—inevitably linked to its other manifestations in science, war, technology, culture, etc.—is above all a matter of self-protection by populations suffering the impact of multiple modernizations.[23] Like Polanyi, the argument is for a democratic modernization rather than a romantic call to preserve the fragment from modernity's effects. What should be avoided, in this connection, are fanciful methodological tendencies to ontologically sublimate either violence or community—i.e. that community has either some inherent higher value *in itself* or was lacking in violent hierarchy prior to *modernity*, or that political mass violence has some inherent link to the rising of a future new dawn where hierarchy will cease forever to exist.[24]

The trials of 20th-century historical practice have revealed the Enlightenment heritage in manifold and conflicting ways, and distinctive empirical residua stand in tension with the dominant French Revolutionary paradigm. We may identify tacit and self-reproducing discursive–practical patterns. These patterns contain shared and differing discursive–practical components, the specific combination of which produces a distinctive discursive–practical balance of forces in historical time. The discursive–practical formation in sublimated authoritarian violence as means—epitomized in Stalin's Soviet Union—was shared tacitly and to degrees by dominant discursive patterns in the Turkish and Iranian modern nation-making experiments. Simultaneously, they contained significant but minor—i.e. they did not overturn the balance of forces—discursive–practical currents grounded in non-violence and reconciliation. The Indian nation-making experience—while containing important minor currents grounded in sublimated authoritarian violence as means—ultimately saw the balance tilt to favour non-violence and reconciliation as a sustained mass movement leading to a democratic national independence.

No *ultimate* origins can explain these differing paths (i.e. cultural, structural etc.), for there are no homogenous wholes at any national or civilizational level. There is only the context-specific interaction of discursive–practical components patterned through mobile and semi-stable historical-temporal structures

---

[23] Karl Polanyi, *The Great Transformation* (Boston: Beacon, 1957).

[24] For the best example of defending pre-modern innocence, see Ashis Nandy; see Ranajit Guha *Elementary Aspects of Peasant Insurgency in Colonial India* for a recurrent pathos linking mass violence to intimations of a new dawn.

(i.e. economies, technologies, institutions, populations, discourses and languages). These sociologically constitute modern societies and personal experiences everywhere. They do so in the temporal manner of a problem, i.e. without guaranteeing any determinate outcome in advance. India could have taken a different path. Had the British assassinated Gandhi, for example, it is possible that a Left-style violent revolution might have gained ascendency by drawing mass support from out of the vacuum. The 1877–78 Russo-Turkish War, by contributing to the suppression of the Young Ottoman movement, almost certainly changed the Ottoman discursive–practical horizon from a democratic ethic of reconciliation to a totalizing politics in the emerging public sphere.

Methodologically, this approach derives interpretively from Sen's "components," replacing ontological ideational and identity claims with the "unthought." The inside-out identity paradigm—i.e. a prior existing and discoverable whole (West, the Orient)—yields to the constructivist logic of choice over ontological discovery. Any tradition is constituted temporally of variable, heterogeneous and overlapping "components" rather than existing as a premade whole.[25] Community members—passively or actively—construct any tradition discursively and practically through the interaction of explicit and tacit dimensions in time. All traditions are temporal interplays of presence and absence (i.e. of components).[26] Sen invests "embeddedness" and "unthought" with material significance by centering freedom as "capabilities" linked to culture as constitutive and mobile "components." "Capabilities"—essentially a theory of "embeddedness"—emphasizes the importance of *being at home* within the large nation-making processes of state centralization, industrialization and secularization.

The lifeworld—interrelated "functionings," or "beings and doings"—constitutes a person's personal–collective being (i.e. health, security, self-respect, belonging, etc.). Freedom involves the "capability to do things (the person) has reason to value."[27] The setting for struggles over meaning and values are context-providing

---

[25] Amartya Sen, *The Argumentative Indian* (London: Penguin, 2005).
[26] Amartya Sen, *Development as Freedom* (New Delhi: Oxford, 2000), 234.
[27] Amartya Sen, *The Idea of Justice* (Cambridge: Belknap, 2009), 231.

relations for the reproduction of social existence (distribution of material resources, means of appropriation of scarce goods, etc.). The varying interplays of circulation and production (of goods, money)—for all of the coercion, inequality and violence endemic to class conflict—do not conceptually represent an *absolute reality*. The ethical and political problem of capitalism is constituted of multiple elements subject to limit, degree, contingency and interrelation of means and ends, without the mythic conception of an absolute historical process binding social actors teleologically to a single absolute objective. We must avoid totalizing conceptions. For example, the "logic of universal capitalist expansion" in the case of Ottoman manufacture, was context specific: instead of disappearing with incorporation into the periphery of the capitalist world system, it adapted and resisted European onslaught through cost control, use of imported commodities and products and exploitation of niche markets.[28]

Sen's paradigm of a decentred world contextualizes modernity locally. He, thus, sees methodological error in absolute focus on conceiving *perfect institutions* as the foundation for the just society (i.e. Ataturk's transcendental blueprint of *universal modernity*), rather than focusing on the plurality of real lives that people are able to lead (i.e. diverse experiences, traditions and valuings of doing and being).[29] Rather, various "combinations of functionings" are evaluated comparatively.[30] Sen's comparative methodology has affinities with the comparative—rather than metaphysical—analytics introduced by important 20th-century thinkers such as Saussure and Wittgenstein who similarly dismantled totalizing transcendent thought constructs to favour more pluralistic investigative horizons. No single *hidden reality* will provide the conceptual key once and for all, evading the limits imposed by the pluralistic qualities of existence in time.

Nation-making experiences, through this lens, suggest the permanent interaction of agency with a historical unthought where multiple discursive–practical frontiers are expanded and transformed. The height of the mountain depends on how one climbs it.

---

[28] Eric J. Zurcher, *The Young Turk Legacy and Nation Building: From the Ottoman Empire to Ataturk's Turkey* (London: I.B. Taurus, 2010), 46.
[29] Sen, *Justice*, 232.
[30] Ibid., 233.

Viewed through this framework, important 20th-century experiences suggest alternate emergent temporalities to the French Revolutionary paradigm. They embody novel discursive–practical assemblages produced in pragmatic response (i.e. learnings) to the specific limits of the historically dominant paradigm with its imagined spatiotemporal frontiers.

TOWARDS A MULTI-CENTRED INTERPRETATION OF THE ENLIGHTENMENT HERITAGE

The historical problem of Enlightenment is divided into four segments: *(a)* the relation of nation-making to Enlightenment (an *impact–response* colonial epistemic imposition vs. placeless summons to broad human emancipation rooted in multi-centred, cultural-historical and self-protective impulses). *(b)* The vision of modernity (a fixed universal structure vs. plural modes of conceiving power and meaning within mutating institutional-population ensembles). *(c)* The politics of nationalism (modes of constructing an inside-out vs. open identity framework for modern belonging–public values). *(d)* The nature of the national movement and the national revolution (seizure of state power vs. prolonged grassroots public transformation, these violence and non-violence alternatives linked to specific temporal horizons). These opposed inside-out and multi-centred modes of imagining inscribe national modernization (primitive accumulation leading to industrial transformation) between democratic and authoritarian alternatives, and between composite cultural constructions of modernity and cultural *Westernization*.

The Enlightenment, when viewed concretely, is always plural, emerging discursively and practically within the broader field of tensions produced between globalizing capitalisms, nation states and populations in distinctive circulatory processes. Each of these national experiences, however, faced universal problems: of nation-making with a religiously and ethnically diverse population, the struggle of new democratic political configurations against older hierarchic orders invested with *traditional* sacred value, and the need to create new *imaginary* foundations for legitimacy in the wake of radical and unprecedented change. Thus they also faced the issue of forced assimilation of minorities to create a unified national culture, the prospect of a war of modern ideas and values against the traditional past, and attempts to lay absolute intellectual claims corresponding to the new power of the modern state. The three countries outside of Europe faced the additional issue of long term struggle with the economic and political intervention of European colonial power. The distinctive means employed in engaging this crisis in its political and economic dimensions as independence movements was a powerful deciding factor in shaping the road to nation-making they ultimately followed at the level of the post-colonial state. This was especially significant in relation to the plural terrain of emergent civil society.

The context-specific collective deployment of any discursive–practical combination constructs a specific temporal horizon. The thinkable–unthought interaction entails that possibility stands higher than a given axiomatic ground taken for the limits of historical reality. Tacit and self-reproducing discursive formations interact with agents in conflict situations (i.e. independence struggles) and civil society building and institutional organization (i.e. development), the two of which contain multiple overlapping dimensions.

TOWARDS A NON-EUROCENTRIC INTERPRETATION OF THE ENLIGHTENMENT HERITAGE

Epistemically, the Enlightenment heritage represents adaptive coping with a shift in the "social center of gravity" provoked by rapidly emerging secular scientific and technologically conditioned social forms.[31] It is—as Foucault suggested—a "permanent critique of ourselves" linking "elements of social transformation, types of political institution, forms of knowledge, projects of rationalization of knowledge and practices [and] technological mutations."[32] It is Eurocentric only within the provincially imagined limits of a specific historical construction of Enlightenment. Within the limits of this study, it is multiple nation-making

---

[31] Dewey, *Common Faith*, 62.
[32] Michel Foucault, *The Foucault Reader* (New York: Pantheon, 1984), 43.

patterns analyzable through variable discursive–practical formations in their interplay of means to ends.

The study opens with an analysis of the Akbar period in the Mughal Empire (1556–1605) and the political experiment in Universal Peace (*Suhl-i Kul*), identifying significant Enlightenment discursive–practical elements. The purpose, rather than to identify a prior *origin* for the *birth* of the Enlightenment tradition (this time in Asia), is to break away from the homogeneous paradigm of Origins and employ Sen's multi-centred and molecular concept of cultural or ideational "components."[33] Although chronologically prior to what is known as the European age of Enlightenment, Universal Peace merely illustrates one example of many possible moments in the early modern interaction of state formation and population.

The idea of a fountainhead for Enlightenment, grounded in European civilization and spread historically via colonialism, is deconstructed as a Platonic myth grounded in an inside and out metaphysic.[34] There is, instead, a multi-centred historical temporality where modern democratic ideas reside in "constitutive elements" rather than a "whole." The methodological point is not to belittle the classical Greek heritage that grounded the modern giants of European thought such as Hegel, but to emphasize that the "highest good" or "ideal unity" (underlying Orientalist claims to Western uniqueness) is one possible mode of imagining rather than a scientifically defensible *reality*.

The totalizing mode of imagining is critiqued by Sen for its reductive forms of analysis: democracy is reduced to a material or legal basis ("institutional fundamentalism"), or justice is reduced to an economic basis. Sen's analysis emphasizes freedoms (i.e. "capabilities") as irreducibly heterogeneous and requiring maintenance rather than a "single all-purpose remedy" (note the two temporalities). Freedoms, for Sen, requiring complementarity between state and civil society institutions, include existential issues of self-respect linked to variable conventions and customs, and protection from violence. It concerns the temporal and many-sided texture of emergent civil society or the lifeworld as

---

[33] Sen, *Development*, 232–34.
[34] Gaston Bachelard, *La poétique de l'espace* (Paris: Quadrige, 1957), 9; La dialectique du dehors et du dedans.

the long-term condition for building stable democratic political organization and sustainable modes of non-violent conflict resolution. "Components," as elements of a tacit–explicit discursive interaction, are constitutive of the pre-theoretical and proximate lifeworld of "capabilities" blending into our intimate everyday being (unconscious awareness, memories, visual imagination, language, believing and belonging).

As a historical study in ideas, then, Sen's notion of traditions is used to map political movements and developments in terms of "constitutive elements" or "selected components" instead of the *essential blocks* and *unbroken lines* typified by—for example—Bernard Lewis' conception of Islam or Hegel's conception of the West in his *Philosophy of History*.[35] The epistemological ground of Sen's thought embraces not the "whole" but "components": the dialectic of the thinkable and the unthought suggested in Michael Polanyi's theory of the "tacit dimension."[36]

Historical thought, in its imaginative construction of potentially infinite patterns based on assembled observations, and lacking the inner compulsion of mathematical necessity, requires recourse to Polanyi's concept of the "tacit dimension" if it is not to extrapolate its own pattern indefinitely as a dogma of metaphysical grounds in the quest for certainty (i.e. Comtean positivism, Hegelian historicism, vulgar Marxism).[37] This temporal terrain promises not final answers but an "inexhaustible source of new, promising problems," i.e. epistemic non-closure structured through possibilities of existing knowledge.[38] The tacit dimension invests scientific value not in "metaphysics derived from first principles" but the bearing of scientific facts and values upon

---

[35] This is notably in "The Roots of Muslim Rage" (*Atlantic Magazine*, September 1990) and less in classics like *The Emergence of Modern Turkey* (London: Oxford University Press, 1961) at least at the level of detailed empirical analysis.

[36] Sen's introduction to Michael Polanyi, *The Tacit Dimension* (New Delhi: Penguin, 2010), where he identifies the importance of Polanyi's theory in his view.

[37] For Hegel, this seems to occur in efforts to transfer the dialectic from the *Phenomenology* to a concrete historical narrative in *The Philosophy of History*.

[38] Polanyi, *Tacit Dimension*, 61.

"a still unrevealed reality."[39] This directs us methodologically—to borrow from Wittgenstein—from ideal unity to temporal horizons: "you will not see something that is common to *all*, but similarities, relationships," "a concept not closed by a frontier," entailing the task of identifying interactions between the thinkable and the unthought.[40]

It is difficult to overstate the importance of the "unthought" as a theme for 20th-century thought. Foucault, identifying in the Kantian revolution a defining methodological "temporality," argued for the embeddedness of all modern thought within an "unthought" (existing, working, speaking etc.).[41] The sometimes obscure but ubiquitous methodological dilemma of the "unthought" (in Bachelardian or Husserlian phenomenology, Saussurian structuralism, Foucauldian "episteme," Deweyan pragmatism, Weberian "elective affinities," Michael Polanyi's "tacit dimension" and Nietzschean "genealogy") has produced highly variable modes of interpreting the Enlightenment as a non-linear phenomenon. These sea changes in 20th-century thought provide the ground for dismantling the often tacit colonial paradigm which dominated or erased non-Western viewpoints, and incorporating the much wider human experiences of modernity, development, progress, scientific achievement, secularism, the nation, justice, ethics and aesthetics.[42]

We need to think in terms of difference and not sameness. The non-European national struggles embracing the democratic principles of Enlightenment drew deeply from indigenous cultural resources in ideas, values and mobilizing ideologies. They did not simply derive epistemic or political structures from Western resources (as in the inside-out mode of imagining)—even despite greatly uneven relations of global power and sometimes elite aspirations to reproducing artificially closed ideals of *Western*

---

[39] Ibid., 70.

[40] Ludwig Wittgenstein, *Philosophical Investigations* (Malden: Blackwell, 2001), 27–28.

[41] Michel Foucault, *The Order of Things: An Archaeology of the Human Sciences* (New York: Vintage, 1973).

[42] Aditya Mukherjee, "What Human and Social Sciences for the 21st Century: Some Perspectives from the South." Paper read at National Congress on "What Human and Social Sciences for the 21st Century?" 7th December, 2012, University of Caen, France.

INTRODUCTION   xxxi

modernity. The historical reality was multi-centred. This is the history of ideas that the following chapters aim to map out: where the pattern in nation-making significantly tatters and yields new forms that offer substantive political lessons for us today.

THE ENLIGHTENMENT AS EMBODIED MEANS AND THE PROBLEM OF VIOLENCE

What this task must make explicit—within the Habermasian problematic of changing attitudes to authority and power within a historically reconstructed public space—is the emergent unthought relationship to, firstly, violence and, secondly, to time. Neither—upon the social plane—is any way *natural*. The distinct yet interconnected national experiences in this analysis are elucidated in terms of the means. The means, i.e. discursive–practical limits, are studied within the framework of political violence upon the nation-making path following the paradigmatic moment of the French Revolution. At the core of these comparisons in modern nation-making are the distinctively opposed temporal horizons—embedded in the violence and non-violence alternative—of closed ontological totality and an open ethic of reconciliation. Both tendencies are manifested in each of the cases examined here, with one or the other gaining ascendance through the heterogeneous context of movements acting upon bodies and minds.

In contrast to the classical problematic of Enlightenment, centring the spread of philosophical ideas to a population's minds, the temporal point of departure must be everyday life (habitus, values, public gaze and representations unrelated necessarily to writing and reading) as prior to *pure* ideas. It is the pre-epistemic relation to others, the world lived together and shared, defined materially and spiritually by belonging, and necessarily limited by dynamic horizons where the future is either not *remembered* or has yet to happen (i.e. a temporal horizon). This is linked to the broader problematic of *embodiment* encompassing themes of the lifeworld and the body while challenging the Cartesian model of the "subject" contained within its own bubble-like consciousness (i.e. Schopenhauer, Nietzsche, Marx's theory of labour, Deweyan pragmatism, Polanyi's "indwelling" and Foucauldian "ethical substance"). Moral virtue, in the struggle for a non-violent and democratic modernity, precedes totalizing claims of intellectual virtue.[43] The actions and ideas of intellectuals, from civil servants to clerics, become relevant viewed within the everyday lifeworld context as the site of nation-making. From this perspective we may identify certain Enlightenment values in political liberty and social equality, communication over violence, and tolerance in situations of diversity. These ideals have often been negated by the violent means used, ostensibly, to attain them. But if the End is ultimately justified by an omniscient perspective—and this was the worst thing to emerge from the Marxist tradition among some of his followers—then any amount of violence is justified to get there.[44] This was the meaning of Benjamin's comment, the "puppet called *historical materialism* is to win all the time."[45]

The practical principle of non-violence must be linked to temporal horizons of everyday life. The Enlightenment heritage is not a single doctrine or idea complex but is grounded within specific geographic or historical moorings, and there is no single metaphysical identity underlying it. In light of this, we may conceive secularism as two distinctive and potentially opposed practical possibilities linked to violence and non-violence. It stands between a substantive *modern* ideology claiming to supersede older truths (a feature of important moments in the Turkish and Iranian experiences) and as an open conceptual space permitting multiple worldviews based on tolerance (as was critical to the Gandhi–Nehru periods in India). The first variant on secularism can ultimately negate the democratic principle on the road to a professed *ideal unity* or *highest good*, a dilemma with visible roots in the French Revolutionary experience and its Comtean intellectual afterlife. The second, rather than seeking to supersede the everyday, endeavours its transformation while embedded within its own resources of power and meaning. At stake are degrees of autonomy for civil society vis à vis the state, or the pluralism and

---

[43] These terms are used as in Aristotle's *Ethics*.

[44] The broad and heterogeneous Marxist tradition constitutes— notably in 19th-century workers' rights struggles—one of the crucial dimensions of the democratic Enlightenment as a human heritage.

[45] Benjamin, *Illuminations*, 253.

self-reliance tacit in the ethic of reconciliation ("holes")[46] versus a totalizing programme of violence from above in a univocal claim to the future ("ideal unity"). At stake is the political construction of violence and unique ontological claims to truth.

By historically analyzing the multiple interacting expressions of the Enlightenment heritage, foreseeable events may be avoided. A case is made for an Enlightenment ideal as based on a set of identifiable values committed to non-violent conflict resolution rather than any single cognitive worldview claiming a *new* monopoly on *truth*. It follows that the region of density for the Enlightenment heritage should shift to the ethical core of Enlightenment in non-violence. Where claims to total truth or moral certitude justify mass murder—even on grounds of modern secular ideologies—we can say the Enlightenment has been fundamentally betrayed. From this perspective, this book is an auto-critique of the many-sided universal Enlightenment heritage. While historical experience provides learnings, the heritage guarantees nothing if we do not make it happen ourselves (i.e. it does not refer to a single transcendent reality guaranteeing victory). In a case for Enlightenment as immanence and against transcendence, the corresponding discursive–practical formations are highlighted historically in their ethical and political consequences.

The Enlightenment as a heritage–value complex is conceived following Tzvetan Todorov's mapping in terms of autonomy, secularism, truth, humanity and universalism.[47] Todorov sees perpetual ambiguity between rational autonomy and received traditions rather than the transcendence of all traditions in favour of a modern essence. He also recognizes that violent means to achieve Enlightenment democratic ends negates those ends, and urges that this unthought terrain be elucidated critically. The strength of the democratic Enlightenment, Todorov maintains against the grain of substantialist or essentialist thinking, is the absence of identity as a kind of presence (following the tradition

---

[46] This refers to Gaston Bachelard's phenomenology of the lifeworld in *La poétique de l'espace* where the relation of the "productive imagination" to "values" cannot be reduced to geometric terms but involves multiple cominglings of memory, imagination and forgetting.

[47] Tzvetan Todorov, *L'Esprit des Lumières* (Paris: Laffont, 2006).

of Hume, Adorno, Wittgenstein, Sen and more ancient thinkers such as Nagarjuna): a tacit critique of the inside–outside logic that has sometimes defined modernity as a unique identity (the *modern self* as a de facto Protestant, rationalist, European, etc.). Such bounded identities necessarily exclude countless people who fall outside of the definition and yet live in and experience the material and spiritual stakes of the modern world in everyday life interactively (roughly, the new environment created by modern science, technology, scholarship and social life, not least in its negative aspect of deprivation).

ELEMENTS OF A MATERIAL ANALYSIS OF ENLIGHTENMENT "HISTORY OF IDEAS"

As a history of ideas, integrating a limited history of practices and institutional carriers, this study undertakes a mapping of the frontier between the thought and the unthought. While the political memory of the French Revolution dominated the horizon choices made by nationalist movements in the Turkish and Iranian cases—despite impressive experimental moments in alternative temporalities—it was the Indian national movement under Gandhi that expanded the frontiers of the unthought to reveal a temporal choice grounding nation-making in the ethic of reconciliation. The experience of the Indian National Movement, founded on the technique of Satyagraha and non-violence, questions the self-evidence of historically received ideas about national mass movements, revolution and the heritage of Enlightenment.

The Indian national experience—a historical memory yet to be caught up with theoretically—dialectically shares multiple aspects with earlier moments in modern Enlightenment and nation-making. Simultaneously, it initiated an alternative epistemic and political paradigm of nation-making, political struggle and social conflict resolution. The Indian struggle against European imperialism diverged discursively from the metaphysical framework of expectation where violence is a politically natural or inevitable *process*. It diverged practically from state power seizure as the privileged threshold moment for rupturing national modernity from the traditional past. Following independence, national development was undertaken under unprecedented democratic conditions of universal suffrage. There is a demonstrable continuity between these two moments in terms of a specific mutation in the political tradition of democratic Enlightenment upon the discursive–practical plane.

The positing of temporal horizons for modern mass movements and regimes forms the basis for this comparative study. The inside-out temporal horizon of the French Revolutionary heritage may be counter posed to the multi-centred tradition of Husserl's phenomenological time, where the lifeworld is prior to totalizing cosmic time. A three-dimensional *thickened* present imbricates the past and the future in an irreversible interplay of presence and absence (implying the interactive thinkable and unthought components of the tacit dimension).[48] Enlightenment from whichever source across the globalized terrain is always highly selective and reinterpreted, and differs significantly in its outcome in consequence of the ideational framework adopted and linked directly to the means.[49]

On the level of practices, following Weber, the study locates ideas within the practical context of institutional carriers. It identifies their role in a *struggle* among status groups, classes and individuals over power (opportunities), *instrumental rationality* interacting with *traditional action*, altering relationships of *power and meaning*, and the problem of *legitimacy*.[50] Weber's ethical insight, that "the more that action elevates ... absolute values, the less it reflects upon the consequences of ... action" — or "ethics of conviction" versus "ethics of responsibility" — is a recurring and central mode of mapping political developments as the relation of means to ends.[51]

The broader context for these experiences, following Norbert Elias, is the logic of state formation as a matter of survival with the emergence of a European multi-state matrix and its extending

[48] Edmund Husserl, *On the Phenomenology of the Consciousness of Internal Time* (1893–1917).

[49] The French Revolution itself presents such a mixed-bag of forces and traditions. François Furet, *Penser la Révolution française* (Paris: Folio, 1978), 200.

[50] Max Weber, "Basic Sociological Concepts," in *The Essential Weber* (London: Routledge, 2004), 341–42.

[51] Ibid, 331.

colonial appendages. There were universal experiences in organization of population for taxation, administrative and military purposes, scientific and technical development, moments of state consolidation and state collapse: the rapidity of modernization itself inducing conflict and instability.[52]

We also see smaller struggles inside of expanding state territory, following Karl Polanyi. These show resistance and self-protection from among groups or communities within the population to state-capital processes, in dispersed instances that can potentially constitute a unified national revolution with the appropriate level of organization and favourable objective conditions.[53] By this logic everyday life (including the individual *soul*) is the site of struggle, in multi-centred fashion, and not the historical totality as the unfolding of a linear essence (i.e. Hegelian historicism, Herbert Spencer or Auguste Comte).

Political developments are mapped using Antonio Gramsci's distinction between the moment of frontal assault "insurrection" and the long and diffused "ideological and political preparation, organically devised in advance to reawaken popular passions." This suggests the overlapping planes of power and meaning as "the matrix of new changes," or the "war of movement" as distinct from the "war of position" — yet assuming "war of position" has its own value beyond merely a prerequisite to the "war of movement" despite their dialectical relation.[54]

This serves to distinguish the logic of the Indian national movement under Gandhi as a self-conscious hegemonic project from other experiences of power seizure in this study, although the potential for this hegemonic politics is visible at the civil society level (if not leadership) to varying degrees in each instance (notably Iran showed powerful historical instances, and indeed does today). The Gramscian concept of hegemony is used in two senses: of the value of leadership preceding the winning of governmental power, and this struggle significantly occurring upon the "front of cultural struggle," or the irreducible world

---

[52] Norbert Elias, *The Civilizing Process* (New Jersey: Wiley-Blackwell, 2000).

[53] Polanyi, *Great Transformation*.

[54] Antonio Gramsci, *Selections from the Prison Notebooks* (Hyderabad: Orient Longman, 2004), 109–10.

of meanings. Here "hegemony as a complement to the theory of the State-as-force" implies that consent may be wrested from the dominant group by opposition forces over an extended temporal duration.[55]

As Braudel also notes, the site of everyday life is a struggle over values, complicity and consent.[56] In these processes, following Weber, dealings with meaning—as opposed to pure causality—always contain a degree of ambiguity linked to multiple options and their unforeseeable ethical consequences in context-specific practice.[57] Any totalizing historicism is inadequate for dealing with meanings, and in turn values and imaginings that constitute lifeworlds. Solutions are "necessarily indeterminate" in that "the solution of an unsolved problem is indeterminate."[58] Movements—embedded partially within contingent realities and material interests—create horizons of reception for new ideas and affective disinvestment in authority through multiple interpretative radials that transcend the symbolic constructions of discourse.

PRIORITY OF ANALYZING VIOLENCE IN NATION-MAKING

Why violence as a central focus? The defining moments of modernity concern emergent forms of political violence—let us take (as conventional examples) the English Civil War, the American, French and Industrial Revolutions (and Napoleonic Wars), the Russian and Chinese Revolutions, decolonization and the project of a new global juridical order following World War II. Each was an experience of traumatic violence, bringing into question the relation between rapidly changing existence and traditions of value, requiring radical adjustments in institutional accretions, the authority of ideals, imaginings and thought over choice and

---

[55] Gramsci, *Prison Notebooks*, 56.
[56] Fernand Braudel, *La Dynamique du Capitalisme* (Paris: Flammarion, 2008), 67.
[57] Weber, *Essential Weber*, 329.
[58] Polanyi, *Tacit Dimension*, 87.

conduct.⁵⁹ Each had a profound family relation to the heritage of Enlightenment.⁶⁰ If these various moments in the history of capitalism as a site of struggle do not represent a teleological advance towards Condorcet's "true perfection of mankind" through "reason," they certainly represent crucial experiences of learning.

If we define historical modernity in terms of the disappearance of traditionally established authorities (hierarchies directly implying violence), we are on more stable empirical ground than if we talk about any fundamental rupture with traditional *culture* (concerning meanings).⁶¹ Yet the interaction of *institutions* and *lifeworlds*, in all of its ambiguity, constitutes an integral dimension in the problematic of modern violence. The lifeworld is the oldest theoretical-historical problem in the Enlightenment: it is found in the Vico-Descartes debate.⁶² For a long time the lifeworld was swallowed in the aggressive theoretical polemics between Enlightenment *universal* historicism and Romanticist iconoclasm and defence of the fragment. At the lifeworld level of everydayness, however, the dilemma of modern power is a matter of *protection*. This refers to a condition of *vulnerability* at once universal and appallingly unequally divided, in a world where growth and dynamism have their counterpart in violence and deprivation.

The problem of transforming traditional-hierarchic institutionalized and sacralized violence into democratic-egalitarian forms of political interaction has been at the core of European Enlightenment from its beginnings in 17th-century natural right theory through John Locke to Immanuel Kant. The *universal*

---

⁵⁹ This is how John Dewey defines modernity and its dilemmas.

⁶⁰ This is used in Wittgenstein's sense of "family relations." *Philosophical Investigations*, 27–28.

⁶¹ The ideal of destroying all "false meanings" to create a better world is articulated in Richard Dawkins, *The God Delusion*. As an information war conducted through civil society, it contains nothing objectionable in any free society but promises to be very slow. As a state politics, it promises a disastrous authoritarian nightmare.

⁶² Vico denied that the sources of certainty and knowledge are found in "clear and distinct ideas" (i.e. pure geometry omitting history and ordinary experience), but rather in the variegated complex of our multiple activities, practices, embodidness and imagination. While Descartes rejected history as a mass of errors, Vico emphasized history as the world of the humanly made and bearer of values.

undertaking of Enlightenment should be to consolidate and provide momentum for these democratic instances within a sustainable and independent institutional framework, while placing constraints on historically inherited systems of social and political oppression.

This is also why we find many historical Enlightenments, or actual and potential historical moments of democratic practice (in Sen's sense of "components"), in the tension-laden mutations of lifeworlds everywhere. The Enlightenment heritage should imply the tradition of independent growth for scientific research, as of multi-centred civil society in general, and a secular conception of truth as linked to tangible evidence in matters of social justice and historical memory.[63] Yet this has often not been the case, and we have seen recurrent authoritarian modernities under varying ideological banners claiming Enlightenment (in the form of regimes, imperial conquest and wars of aggression).

These different faces of modernity are central in an analysis of political violence as a discursive–practical history rather than a natural force, and where the Enlightenment is conceived as many proliferating roads with differing ethical consequences—or multiple temporal horizons. The political work of Gandhi took up the mantle of democratic Enlightenment values—using a rich composite of Indian and non-Indian influences—and extended its practical implications on the everyday plane of non-violent mass political mobilization, as a self-conscious practical alternative to a transformative politics of violence based on a professed monopoly on truth.

The Enlightenment conception of "'Reason,' in the traditional sense, was, above all, a faculty by means of which human beings were supposed to be able to arrive at one or another set of immutable truths."[64] Almost from the historical beginnings of Enlightenment (at least as it has been so named), violence has too often retained the role of the commanding force of social

---

[63] The problem of creating public memory—itself a "temporal horizon"—is clearly important in this comparative study, following the groundwork prepared by Paul Ricoeur, *La mémoire, l'histoire, l'oubli* (Paris: Seuil, 2009).

[64] Hilary Putnam, *Ethics without Ontology* (Cambridge: Harvard University Press, 2004), 98.

change in a seeming echo of the ancient Greek coupling of *bios* and *bia*, "life" and "force," which in the *Iliad* was expressed in the spectacle of the Trojan War as the human collective unconscious.[65]

The overwhelming region of discursive–practical density for the Enlightenment heritage among democratic social movements has been the French Revolutionary tradition. It happened only yesterday, in historical terms, even as today the Second World War begins gradually to fade from human memory as a personal experience. This study is aimed at expanding on-going researches into a broader and more pluralistic conception of democratic Enlightenment. The Enlightenment heritage is not a moment in European history, but a human aspiration for dignity and security under all of the modern world's dangers.

The study focuses historically upon discursive constructions of organized violence as the means to an ideal end. The biggest leak of classified material in US history by American soldier Bradley Manning—to unmask the American military's "bloodlust" in Iraq and Afghanistan—testifies once more to the inherent terrorism and fundamental incoherence of acts of so-called liberation employing organized mass murder and domination. These still remain buried as an unconscious framework of assumptions in dominant modern political worldviews like a poisonous flower— beautiful promises that lead only to the production of dead bodies and all of the ghosts of bitterness they unleash over generations. We do not have to choose between a politics of such organized violence—claiming to uphold *modern* or *enlightened* ideals—and the fate of a 13-year-old girl like Aisho Ibrahim Dhuhulow who was tried in a Somalian Sharia court for adultery and stoned to death after being gang raped by three men.[66] There are other roads in existence between such extremes of violence, and we have the obligation of making such heritages self-conscious and explicit.

---

[65] Yse-Tardan Masquelier. *De la violence a la non-violence*. Le Monde des Religions. September–October 2007, No. 25, 50.

[66] "Somalia: Girl stoned was a child of 13," Amnesty International, retrieved 31 October 2008.

AN OVERVIEW

Chapter 1 discusses Enlightenment discursive–practical formations for the early modern period in the 16th-century reign of Emperor Akbar. The Mughal Empire under Akbar belonged to the Islamic Triumvirate of South and South West Asia, including the Ottomans and the Safavids. This geo-political entity with its abundant linkages forms one basis for the present historical comparison.

Akbar's public policy was linked to court politics, changing political alliances, and transformations in the broader world of everyday life. The Akbar period saw the flowering of ideas significantly comparable to the later ideas of the West European Enlightenment: centring reason over inherited belief, freedom of thought as the condition of social-political wellbeing, envisioning progress of contemporary people over the ancients, a valuing of secular ethics of general compassion over religious dogma, and the positing of an epistemic limit to human knowledge in the name of pluralism and non-violence.

This is an amazing if coincidental parallel with the Cusa, natural right and Lockean discursive formations implying the logical correlation of thought in historical action. As in the European case, the epistemic limit was the guarantee of non-violent conflict resolution. This non-violent mode of political imagining in state-making was produced in dialectical conflict with powerful monotheistic social forces. These upheld an ontological link between sectarian truth and violence as the means to crisis resolution in early modernity. The Akbarian counter-tendency—embodied the "modesty of thought"—constitutes a discursive–practical formation. Similarly, the political mission of purity proclaimed by conservative forces was linked to power bids. Inflated ontological claims were linked to violence and power, and sought specific power-constructions in changing times.

Non-violence in Akbar's time was a self-consciously adopted contribution of the Chishti Sufi tradition. It expanded the compass of moral consideration to include non-human animals. We see the rejection of proselytization, slavery and widow burning. The Ibn Arabi tradition is affirmed over al-Ghazali, in rejection of ontological precedence for one religion over others. This humanist temporal horizon, incorporating all faiths, grew from political efforts to integrate and unify the multiple ethnic-religious population under the self-consolidating Mughal state. These intellectual developments grew in patterns of changing political alliances in a multi-centred struggle for power within the expanding spatio-temporal state consolidation process.

We see institution building during the Akbar period as the selective affirmation of values, or institutional ethics. It was partly pragmatism, partly value-driven, and only partly conscious in the selective construction of a political horizon from a multi-threaded template of Indo-Islamic traditions. These sources included the humanism of Amir Khusrau, the *pantheism* of al-Arabi, Jain ethics, aspects of the *Mahabharata*, and the political legacy of Emperor Ashoka, among others. The patronage of Chishti saints had importance in terms of the values they upheld, i.e. respect for all religious communities within a tradition of non-violence.

We see neither unique truth claims nor appeals to fabulist causality in the rationality of Universal Peace (*sul i kuhl*), and claims to moral over coercive power. The experience poses the questions: is the truth whole, or temporal? Is it better to force, or to dialogue, with others holding different views? The Akbar period upheld a dialogic reason rather than "pure" reason based on ontological certitude. It, hence, differed from the 18th-century mechanical conception of reason, which often excluded choice among alternatives in favour of conformity to Laws of Nature. Universal Peace was articulated within the context of an unprecedented Mughal state formation process, bids for hegemony (dawn meetings, etc.) and an integrated public (via translation bureaus, etc.), which transpired within an international complex of early modern pressures including innovations in artillery, the influx of silver from the New World, and growing awareness of scientific and geographic progress in Europe.

The traditional conservative *ulama* were marginalized by the centralizing state, with patronage transferred to a new group of secular-oriented philosophers appealing to moral universalism. The Akbarian court conceived a policy for expanding state centralization based on the principle of composite nobility, which in turn required an ideological reordering of the regime towards a secular rationality (i.e. to encompass varying Muslim, Hindu and other worldviews). The House of Worship saw open debate among Hindus, Shi'i and Sunni Muslims, Jains, Christians and Zoroastrians, where the dialogic process undid the limits of the discursive universe of Revelation—creating both consternation and new horizons. This joint development of independent reason, explicitly opposed to the reason of one's upbringing, was linked to genuine conflicts of power in the state-making process. We also see the acknowledgement of the need for institutional defences of freedom, at least at the elite level, and the forging of linkages between the centralizing state and popular movements of Bhakti–Sufi professing religious and human equality.

At the international level, new possibilities of violence in the state-formation process produced new conceptualizations of violence—Spain's Philip II saw the state as an instrument of Providence, while for Akbar a multi-religious state could be built on dialogic principles as a more effective mode. Akbar corresponded with both Philip II and Shah Abbas of Persia, urging them to undertake state consolidation through a policy of tolerance and universal religious equality rather than the truth–violence–dogma triangle of intolerance. During this period a number of Persian refugees, victims of Shah Abbas' religious policy, arrived in India and significantly participated in the intellectual and practical formation of *sul i kuhl*.

The intellectuals of Akbar's court transformed their universal Pantheist mysticism into a coherent state policy of religious tolerance. These experiences indicate two descending levels of bid for hegemony: the experiment in composite nobility, and the interaction with Bhakti–Sufi saints in a domain of popular attitudes with far more radically egalitarian consequences for ideas.

A complex intellectual re-conceptualization shaped Akbar's policy, articulated by court philosophers led by Abul Fazl. Within the dialectical interaction of agentative and structural dimensions in early modernity, the court of Akbar displays identity as a choice rather than a fixed inheritance. Out of the rich discursive multi-verse of Indian traditions, and the complex constraints of early modern political conditions, Akbar chose—in response to a specific conjuncture of events detailed in the chapter—a line of non-violent and humanist thought. We see a central concern with the question of violence in a reimagined temporal horizon linked to state centralization policy where secular science, art and multi-religious equality were promoted. The predominance of this new political tendency was definitively ended in favour of an exclusive politics of religious purism in the War of Succession (1657–59), which also saw the writing of Dara Shikoh's *The Mingling of Two Oceans* as a philosophical plea for the unity of the Hindu and Muslim religions.

Chapter 2 analyzes the internal pluralism and composite construction of the European Enlightenment as a discursive tradition and mode of imagining, and seeks to refute the notion of its monolithic character.[67] The European Enlightenment is analyzed in terms of two competing temporal horizons in nation-making practice. There was totality, focused on the transcendental absolute, and the ethic of reconciliation, focused on the everyday. These alternative discursive–practical formations governed struggles to cope with dilemmas of public meaning and public conflict resolution in early modern European state-formation. Four seminal experiences are analyzed in terms of their discursive construction of violence in nation-making. These include the 17th-century Natural Rights movement and the 18th-century French Enlightenment as discursive formations, and the English Civil War and the French Revolution as practical–discursive formations. The interaction of state-formation, post-Reformation religious war and European global expansion provides the political background. Four interrelated patterns are shown through analysis of these early modern experiences.

Firstly, at the centre of the European Enlightenment was the 17th-century Scientific Revolution. It interacted with state formation and inter-class dynamics, in a newly expanding frontier of secular-scientific knowledge that contrasted with existing ideals of religious knowledge in stasis. This conflict between being and becoming entailed the dialectical transformation of temporal horizons and modes of imagining time—notably historical time in relation to contemporaneous crisis. The primary discursive–practical formation was a contested yet persistent ontological

---

[67] This follows a growing tendency in Enlightenment studies: Dorinda Outram, *The Enlightenment* (Cambridge: Cambridge University Press, 2005); Gertrude Himmelfarb, *The British, French and American Enlightenments* (New York: Knoph, 2004). Unfortunately, in "The Illusions of Cosmopolitanism," *For Love of Country* (Boston: Beacon Press, 1996), Himmelfarb articulated a narrow and essentialist Eurocentrism.

conviction of *total reconciliation*, usually grounded in a complex fabrication of the imagination dubbed *Nature* (i.e. as a counterpart to growing scientific discoveries about nature, and intended to create their equivalent in certitude within the social-political sphere).

These new Enlightenment modes of imagining provoked two principle ethical responses in *(a)* the relative character of knowledge, or *pluralism-acknowledgement* and *(b)* the claim to ontological certainty in *system, laws, Nature, History*, or *substance*, eliminating the difference between natural law and socio-political experience within a totalizing purview, or *totality-assimilation*. Both of these modes of imagining were bound up either consciously or unconsciously in specific attitudes to the problem of political violence. Historically, these two modes of imagining interacted with state-formation and primitive accumulation processes, and other nation-making and revolutionary projects, as emergent discursive–practical formations.

Each mode of imagining is embedded in different valuations. The *pluralism–acknowledgement* mode of imagining tends to tolerance, pluralism, learning, self-reliance and an everyday temporal horizon, demonstrating a profound linkage between intellectual pluralism and practical non-violence. It tends to emphasize the importance of institutional limits to power as a guarantee of non-violent conflict resolution on an ongoing and provisional basis, rather than totalizing visions of final resolution claiming ontological legitimacy (i.e. a temporal ethic rather than absolute vision of reconciliation). In this way, the *pluralism-acknowledgement* mode of imagining constitutes a break from Plato's powerful dualistic metaphor of the cave.

By contrast, the *totality–assimilation* mode of imagining, as an epistemic totalization claiming privileged access to reality, demonstrates the linkage of epistemic totalization and political violence. As the heir of the temporal-historical imagining of Providence, violence goes from being providential to natural, i.e. conforming to fixed historical laws and guaranteeing the victory of one side over the other in a conflict because of their privileged access to the Truth. Thus, the *totality–assimilation* mode of imagining extends the Platonic dualistic metaphor of the cave with its anti-democratic implications.

From these two modes of imagining within merely the European Enlightenment tradition, it follows firstly that there are multiple paths to Enlightenment where neither means nor ends are identical; secondly, that Enlightenment is dialectical (i.e. rather than conforming to a principle of identity or definition); thirdly, that when viewed uniquely as an *objective* process (enclosed within known rules), modernization excludes broad public participation and so ceases to be democratic—it becomes the imagined project of a state elite laying claim to transcendent historical truth.

Secondly, modes of imagining are constituted in *immanent* material history which is multi-centred and temporal. Democracy is not grounded in the *unified* or *atemporal* nature of the universe, or the Will of God (the *transcendent*). It is a human mode of imagining politics non-violently. The Enlightenment—because of transcendental pretensions—has not always been democratic. In its *teleological* self-imagining, usually linked to totality-assimilation, it has often been anti-democratic and elitist as an intellectual worldview. The predominant tendency in the 18th-century French Enlightenment was a dualistic mode of imagining temporality, or temporal horizon. The future makes war on the past in a transcendental moment of *rupture*.

Historically and sociologically, democratization was *multi-centred* rather than *teleological* (the unfolding of an *idea, reason, or a cultural essence*). This multi-centred history involved the everyday interaction of self-protection, hegemony and violence within the state formation processes of early modernity. Within this context, there were turning points in the mode of imagining and public articulation of the limits and possibilities of democracy (discursive formations). The discourse of the Levellers in 1647 was one such precedent-making moment. These interactive struggles, in their give and take, produced institutionalized modes of political participation, raising the important question of institutional ethics.

Along similar lines, the political discourse of *foundation* (i.e. Machiavelli) is an imaginary construction linked to primitive accumulation and the rivalry of the interstate matrix. It is a mode of imagining time teleologically from pure beginnings, vesting the state with identity continuity. Violence on behalf of this unifying narrative of assimilation is pitted against the plurality of memory. This new imaginary construction interacted dialectically with the old truth–sacred–violence triangle of Providence. The resulting discursive compound, in turn, interacted with the new scientific imaginary construct of mechanistic *continuity* in a conflict between *being* and *becoming*. Discursive–practical components cross religious-secular boundaries, often by way of tacit transmissions.

In these processes, we see the *creation*, and not the *discovery*, of meanings. They are created upon the immanent plane (usually in piecemeal fashion by many people), not discovered upon the transcendent plane (following the pattern of Revelation). There was no underlying democratic teleology (i.e. linked to ancient Greece), but a multi-centred struggle in which democratic pluralism was one possible outcome. This was the immanent context for the 18th-century French Enlightenment, with its elevated ontological claims to *nation*, *humanity* and its use of the Platonic metaphor of the cave. The elite lead the prisoners from darkness to the radiance of outside light in a radically dualistic imagining of secular social knowledge as transcendental. This futuristic temporality, conceived within the political context of nation-state formation and the bourgeois public sphere, as a variant on *foundation*, claimed a-temporal status beyond those conditions of everydayness (i.e. immanence) which were the declared site of false consciousness.

Similarly, modernity did not have a single point of origin (i.e. in Europe). This is the projection of a religious-philosophical imaginary. Metaphorically speaking, it was less a unilinear process conforming to a single logic than a multi-centred and interactive game where the rules changed continuously across altering temporal-geographic conditions.[68] Within this game, the politics of hegemony were played out, despite strategic claims by some to have accessed the single hidden logic behind the screen of appearances once and for all.

Thirdly, the 17th-century English Revolution is compared to the 18th-century French Revolution in terms of discursive formations linking Enlightenment and violence. This comparison, firstly, subverts the dominant dualistic conception of transcendent

---

[68] "Games" is used in the pluralistic and open sense articulated by Wittgenstein in the *Philosophical Investigations*.

modernity engendered by the French Revolutionary paradigm (the actors' views of themselves). Modernity and religion were not opposed in any clear inside-out pattern in the English experience (i.e. a Christian discursive universe was employed to achieve secular ends, notably the reduction of the priesthood to a merely natural or political status). The result is a more nuanced and multi-centred conception of immanent modernity where meanings (i.e. of *religion*) are not set in advance upon a transcendental plane. Upon the immanent plane, meanings change in relation to power configurations.[69]

In the French Revolution, secondly, the explicit encasing imaginary of Providence was removed but reinstalled tacitly with similar ideological dimensions as a total claim on historical change. New names and imagined ontological references were supplied. In both the English and the French Revolutions we see a radical new imagining of time. Both contained the underlying imaginative notions of *revenge* and *final assimilation*. These functioned in tension with the aspiration to construct democratic institutional bases for open-ended conflict resolution.

A similarity exists in the tension between the politics of the *everyday* and the politics of *absolute ends*. Mundane institutional guarantees of everyday justice were in tension with empyrean visions of Justice. The latter were to be realized through ontologically sanctified direct action (i.e. violence). The longstanding tradition of European republicanism was in tension with bids for the highest truth. A tacit clash persisted between the pragmatic *openness* of unresolved civil society—permitting a sense of the tragic—and the final resolution of *closure* grounded in ontological postulates. The category of the *secular* did not, with the shift to the French Revolution, deliver modern politics from the temptations of the second variety of political thought. The secular was equally capable of adopting the tacit structure of totality.

It follows that both experiences were divided between two conflicting discursive formations: consensus as a point of departure, based on ontological certitude and defended by sanctified violence; and consensus as a provisional goal to be reached intermittently through discussion among diverse viewpoints. The

---

[69] This seems to be an unspoken but significant assertion in Foucault's work.

interaction of the immanent plane of lifeworlds and the transcendental plane of dogmatic worldviews produced these conflicting temporal horizons. Both revolutionary states, in related fashion, had to compete for the loyalty of the population while also trying to coercively master them. The problem of population and hegemony provided the context for the centralizing state in its adoption of discursive–practical formations.

Both countries experienced the related "ontological" or cultural problem. *Community*, hit by institutional, material and social trauma, and exploring new *modes of imagining*, was heavily mediated by status and never pure. The *ontological* problem sees attempts in modern politics to treat the crisis of the *soul*. The Weberian tradition of conceiving *community* has greater affinity to historical reality than *community* conceived in terms of a Heideggerian romanticism (which dodges the power problem in traditional societies). The ontological crisis produced a rich debate over the meaning of the secular, which produced multiple new discursive formations and practical lessons.

The lesson of the English Revolution was: institutionalized secularism is required to protect the rights of the person, in a way that a traditional discursive universe cannot. Locke's contribution to non-violence was the breaking of the violence–sacred–truth triangle following the English Civil War.[70] Locke's secularism imagined a politics of non-violence breaking with the epistemic paradigm of Plato's cave, envisioning degrees of certainty over absolute certitude (the immanent aspect). At the same time, he conceived Laws of Nature governing History that became a new ontology of violence (against the propertyless, slaves, native inhabitants of the New World) in a variant on the inside-out imagining of modernity (the transcendent). This confirms the assemblage as a tacit and socially immanent process.

The debate between Locke and his pupil Shaftsbury shows that violence, however tacitly buried in a historicist and national dynamic, was a consciously emergent question, as well as the credibility of metaphysical foundations in the inside-out language of the universal. Shaftsbury provided an alternative and

---

[70] The concept of violence–sacred–truth triangle is articulated in Mohammed Arkoun, *The Unthought in Contemporary Islamic Thought* (London: Saqi, 2002).

comparatively immanent secular framework for coping with experiences of early modern nation-making, i.e. in his defining of the *secular community* as unbounded by fixed identity.

Voltaire, inspired by the English experience, articulated political violence as *Nature*, i.e. natural means to a new world against unjust rulers, within the epistemic and elitist framework of Plato's cave dividing light from dark. Voltaire, with Diderot, followed a logical *substantialist* tendency towards *enlightened despotism*. It contrasted with Montesquieu's conception of multi-sided causality (the ancestor of Weber, Durkheim and the Annales School) and institutional rudiments (i.e. division of power) as the basis for democratic and non-violent conflict resolution.

The lesson of the French Revolution in this aspect (for we should examine it through multiple aspects) concerned the violent seizure of state power as a Final End. It posited the intention of transforming society from above through a *rationally necessary* conceptual programme or value-independent universal (the transcendent). It simultaneously devalued existing meanings and customs as merely the *contingent* rubbish thrown up by history (the immanent). This discursive–practical formation undermined democracy, learning and self-reliance—and thereby, paradoxically, the very precepts of Enlightenment in a fatal political self-contradiction.

Chapter 3 discusses the 19th-century Bengal Renaissance and the early Indian national movement, showing how the Enlightenment discourse can and has been used for multiple and sometimes contradictory purposes. It does not harbour an essence, destined for either good or ill, but is composed of *constitutive elements*. In different variants as a discourse of improvement, it was used by the colonial state to justify domination and by Indian activists in early efforts to demand political justice and ultimately independence. A discursive universe is ambiguous: human beings give it meaning in time through action (in Weber's sense of "ethics of conviction" and "ethics of responsibility").

From the late 19th century, the Enlightenment was visible as a tacit background of thought, or mode of imagining constituted of specific temporal horizons—and not necessarily as a self-consciously held doctrine (i.e. the historicist horizon of "origins," the republican conception of politics as risks in time). Emergent discursive–practical formations, sometimes linked explicitly to the historical heritage of Akbar, and sometimes to the French Revolution, were articulated by agents through the precedent-setting trials of practice.

This period sees the emergence of political activism and an Indian civil society—yet within the semi-hegemonic and coercive secular permutations of Empire. The policy of divide and rule saw a campaign to construct an Indian history suited to colonial needs. We see discursive–practical formations embodying the legacy of the French Revolution-nationalism interacting with Indian influences in the multi-poled construction of this legacy in myriad new practical forms and conventions. These early Indian experiences of political struggle suggest that democracy is a mode of life, uniting people through dreams, with an ambiguity and sliding range of possibilities exceeding the "rules" of a given discourse. That is, it is an ongoing practical experience of learnings.

Their struggle was rendered ambiguous by the necessity of the English language in its gamut of limitations and possibilities, the institutional carriers of administration, print industry, factories and schools. This provided the context for the Anglicist and Orientalist debate (1820–30s) with its modes of imagining from future total assimilation to origins and pure identities in the past (discursive formations). The European Enlightenment was seminal in Indian intellectual developments, from the radicalized notion of civil society in Thomas Paine to Comte's *infallible* methodology, as were Indian intellectual traditions in the Vedanta College and Brahmo Samaj.

We see the emergence of two distinctive temporal horizons in moderate and radical Enlightenment, both representing an ambiguous exploration of multiple currents in thought and practice. They take us from *multiple worlds* to *rupture*, and from critiquing specific practices to critiquing the social totality, as two modes of temporal imagining. We move from a critically embedded dialogic reason (also articulated in the Akbar period) to a Cartesian-solipsism. The second posits rational subjectivity beyond social relationships where community as such becomes a falsehood in historicist–determinist terms. Both existed in ambiguous relation to Empire and sought the reform of inherited social-cultural systems of hierarchy and subordination. They constitute emergent discursive–practical formations.

The first is embodied in the figure of Rammohun Roy. Despite a cosmopolitan-inspired national project of eliminating hierarchic obstacles to broad public solidarity, we see a decentred pluralism grounded in a many-sided conception of truth. Like Abul Fazl in the Akbar period, all religions are different roads to a single truth. Because unknowable within human epistemic limits, they cannot legitimately be defended with violence. His campaign crossed a wide spectrum of linguistic and religious boundaries while professing Enlightenment values of liberty, equality and humanism inspired by the French Revolution and emergent post-Napoleonic War European nationalisms. Multiple components interact.

Rammohun Roy's action showed a shift from *being* to *praxis* or everydayness. He affirmed the immanent value in political action in the tradition of the French Revolution, and the tendency to analyze an earthquake or mechanical accident in terms of demonstrable causal hypotheses rather than a partisan "Will of God." He turned the traditional sources of Indian meaning-production—from Bhakti to Islamic monotheism—from ontological figures into radical forces of change and interaction with the flux of modern political temporality. His thought transcended the limits of any particular discursive universe of meaning, entering a secular conceptual space of humanist compassion. His transformations demonstrate the plane of immanence (i.e. the creative mutability of meanings in relation to power configurations).

The ambiguity of Rammohun Roy's exploration of practical capacities in relation to a many-sided conception of truth was *dialectical*; but the epistemic limit in encountering the other and embracing the *unknown as unknown* created a trans-dialectical space grounded in openness and non-violence. The dialectic as an absolute must forever transcend difference in favour of absolute unity through *knowledge* of the *other*. Unlike contemporary European heirs to the Enlightenment in Herbert Spencer and Comte with their ahistorical *finalist* discourses, Rammohun Roy did not relegate or marginalize the problem of pluralistic ethical choice to the unthought and obsolescence in the name of a single mechanistic rationality or *scientific law*.

The second temporal horizon, or radical Enlightenment, emerged embodied in ambiguous fashion in Derozio and consolidated subsequently as a convention by others influenced by his example. This generation, unlike Rammohun Roy, was trained initially (rather than subsequently to traditional learning) in Western education. They took French Revolutionary iconoclasm to new lengths in a mode of imagining centring rupture with the *irrational*. They envisioned a single possible road to modernity patterned on the European experience, which they took to be universal. Their notion of political change featured the compression of time into a totalized instant, a rupture that must negate the past in a renovation of the whole of existence. While Rammohun Roy had embraced the irreducible ambiguity of religious meaning, turning the hermeneutical dimension to democratic advantage, they negated it favour of a single mechanical reason envisioning an ontological narrative of absolute future transcendence based on the dogmas of the 18th-century French Enlightenment.

In fact, the conception of India's past held by the radical Enlightenment stream negated its historical reality. By imposing a logical schema similar to Durkheim's notion of purging confused and disorganized vulgar thought to distil a purely factual and scientific purview, they dogmatically overlooked important 18th-century developments such as emerging states showing Enlightenment tendencies and popular movements showing democratic-egalitarian modes of thought.[71]

Towards the end of the 19th century, we see the emergence of strong revivalist responses to colonial rule (as a common temporal horizon and political convention based on fixed and *pure* collective identity). These presented a negation of the earlier multi-religious egalitarian tendency introduced by Rammohun Roy's Brahmo Samaj. The elite intellectual goal was to restore the Hindu tradition to its *pure sources* and regenerate it for the political purposes of the present. Thus, two imagined communities existed as political options for Indian nationalism between a national community sharing common economic interests and a notion of national community as a distinctive religious identity. It reflected a revolt against the cultural Anglicization of English educated Indian intellectuals, and the apparent ineffectiveness of their political methods in relation to colonial state power.

In this chapter we see the emergence and consolidation of a diverse set of discursive–practical formations, or the pluralism of

---

[71] Emile Durkheim, *Les Règles de la Méthode Sociologique* (Paris: Flammarion, 2009) 77–81.

ethical choice and tacit transmission, to be negated or adopted in subsequent expanding movements of political action.

Chapter 4 locates the Gandhian experience of the Indian national movement within the tradition of Enlightenment and the French Revolution as a crucial moment in practical and intellectual history. We see both extensions and important critiques of these traditions, the affirmation of democratic Enlightenment values and a critique of violent means to those ends. Viewed within this wider matrix, Gandhi gives articulation to the precepts and ideals of the early European natural rights movement (moving through Cusa to Dewey) in the concept of an epistemic limit, cementing this insight to the practical technique of non-violence grounded in Indian traditions reconstituted for the purpose of building a broad based Indian civil society and secular democratic modernity.

Emphasizing means, public self-reliance and mass participation, the Indian experience highlights the pitfalls of using *historicism* as a framework rather than *non-violence*. Historicism identifies certain categories of people as appropriate targets for political violence (punishment, revenge, transcendence) in the name of a higher end (Providence, Lockean *development*, revolutionary terrorist determinism, utopian projections of *modernity*). Gandhian non-violence transformed the nationalist convention from a substantive discourse grounded in the inside-out logic of intrinsic and homogeneous identity to a convention of *nationalism without essence*, pluralism and relational identity—a concept of nationalism without enemies. Thus, there is a discursive shift from transcendence to immanence.

This repeats the dilemma of consensus as either an ontological point of departure or a recurring provisional condition within a democratic-dialogic framework. We see a moral rather than epistemic universalism, or an ongoing ethic of reconciliation without closure. This is based on the premise of difference rather than absolute knowledge as the prior necessary condition for harmonious cohabitation in homogeneity.

This mutation in the discursive convention of nationalism addressed core problems of modern national politics inherited from the French Revolutionary experience: the forcible assimilation of minorities; the notion of a violent war of modern ideas on the past; and the tendency to an absolutist statist ideology championing a single truth system targeting a historical *end product* through violent means. The Indian political experience is compared to a Deweyan conception of temporality and deliberative democracy, a reconciliation of being and becoming and fact and value, the everyday world over the absolute, or the principle of growth over final ends. It is contrasted with Heidegger's romantic idealization of community in *being* as a fragment isolated from the processes of modern democratic change and scientific critique of traditional worldviews as rooted, integral and authentic. Following Deweyan logic, tradition and modernity are combined in proportion to their value in consolidating democratic society.

The Gandhian experience is identified within the second human rights wave, concerned with social as well as political rights. It is identified with humanism, explicitly placing the ethical criterion of human conscience beyond all religious discursive universes in secular fashion. This outlook is exemplified in a prolonged and heated debate over a scripturally sanctioned stoning that took place in Afghanistan, but is a consistent line of Gandhian thought.[72]

This humanism is not a substantive secularism, i.e. a historicist state ideology making claims to new secular truth and identifying enemies of this truth (transcendental). It is secularism as a politics of tolerance and the separation of the state from public truth production (immanent). We see a humanist appeal to solidarity in conscience, public view, lived practically through the body, in progress envisioned as self-sacrifice and suffering for others towards a more democratic and non-violent social order.

Where Hegel had remained ambiguous about whether progress as sacrifice had meant of the self or others, Gandhi clarified this directly—thereby showing the so-called "cunning of reason" as basically an unspoken concern with the issue of violence.[73]

---

[72] We can also identify counter-examples, such as the debate with Tagore over the divine status of the earthquake. Such examples undoubtedly show a momentary failing (i.e. of judgement) requiring explanation—they do not, however, negate the broad general tendency constructed in this analysis and its confirmation at the structural level through institution building linked to specific practices and ideas. That is, a structural passage between non-violence and a commitment to a broad participatory democratic politics in Gandhian practice.

[73] Mark Lilla, *The Stillborn God* (New York: Vintage, 2008), 210.

Finally, it is identified with the tradition of Montesquieu in placing priority upon the functioning of democratic institutions rather than visionary or charismatic qualities of leadership, claims to systems of absolute truth, or other overriding tendencies claiming a higher principle and permitting the absolute concentration of political power. We see an explicitly different mode of imagining the issue of political violence, which by reconstructing the tacit and explicit components of the phenomenon shows that it was never *natural* but *thought-laden*, and subject to the pluralism of ethical choice. Discursive–practical components as tacit transferable power mechanisms are made explicit through comparison.

In one way Gandhi, as a leader, expressed the principle of historical contingency in terms of the decisive function of individuality in historical change within a leadership role. But his thought and practice have an acutely dialectical relationship to the existing Indian public sphere as it had evolved through the 19th century with the Moderates, the Extremists, the revolutionary terrorists, and the emerging religious politics of Hindu and Muslim authenticity (ideologies of modern state-power-resource competition) under the changing political logic of the British Raj. These complex dialectical interactions extend and critique existing and emergent Indian political traditions of thought and practice. They show the logical interrelation of Gandhian thought and the multi-threaded cosmopolitan tradition of Enlightenment and the heritage of the French Revolution. In this way, institution building and institutional values—relevant for an understanding of the Nehru period—can be clarified logically within the conceptual pattern of Enlightenment and understood as a unique historical phenomenon.

These multiple discursive–practical interactions upon the field of power during the struggle over Empire and India's political future are analyzed (through invented tradition, modes of belief and imagining, and modes of being and doing including public discourse and the public gaze) in terms of their construction of the issue of political violence. We see competing constructions of loyalty (secular public or communalist constructions of loyalty) with their crucial political implications. The analysis shows the significance of the Gandhian intervention as a mode of mass democratic mobilization and organization, or *means*. It expands the public sphere in relation to and in tension with convention-forming precedents including the Ganesh Festival, religious riots and revolutionary terrorism in the 1890s, the Age of Consent Controversy (1891), and the politics of the Moderates and the Extremists, in their constitutional and extra-constitutional varieties as *means* (discursive–practical formations).

The Gandhian intervention must be understood within the complex of political and intellectual conditions following World War I, where a humanism of pluralism rather than totality began to be articulated by thinkers from Rabindranath Tagore to Simone Weil—a broad intellectual and political detour from teleological imaginings to the everyday in the tradition of Enlightenment. Varied new democratic experiments were simultaneously underway in the new nations created by collapsed Eurasian land empires.

In contrast to some of these experiments, the Gandhian technique shows a long-term *creative* struggle over hegemony at the level of power and *meaning*, constructing the Indian nation as a political force and multi-class and religious movement committed to secular democratic independence. It is without demands for other ideological and identity commitment. This politics—based on public everydayness and the multi-centred creation of parallel power networks—redefined the conceptual limits of state power, from an elite epistemic *instrument* to a broad network of *relations*. It posited widely based consensus and participation over the instantaneous and violent seizure of power. It is the political logic of mass movement over programme from above. This is a mutation in the French Revolutionary paradigm of mass mobilized political change to another temporality and mass movement.

At the discursive level, this Gandhian intervention self-consciously broke the identity–ontology–violence link with its anti-democratic and anti-secular implications. This had been cemented within the emergent Indian public sphere through earlier discursive–practical interventions by figures as Aurobindo or Saraswati. It had been cast in secular variant by revolutionary terrorists in *determinist* bids for power. We see Gandhian thought manifested as political practice notably in the Non-Cooperation (1919–22), Civil Disobedience Movements (1930–32) and the ongoing Constructive Programme.

Between the French Revolution and the Indian national movement we see two conceptions of truth. In the first, truth is a totality exceeding all limits and permitting all means—precisely the philosophical concern Kant expressed over Spinozist–Hegelian modes of imagining action. In the second, the precondition for seeking truth is the limit of non-violent conflict resolution and mutual recognition of difference. These political moments express crucial and dialectically opposed discursive–practical currents in the historical tradition of Enlightenment. They bring to light broader global linkages in the history of Enlightenment thought and practice on the level of discursive–practical formations.

Chapter 5 recounts the experience of the Ottoman–Turkish Enlightenment, dating back as far as pragmatic modernization efforts in the 17th century in response to international pressures (notably military at this early stage). It took on greater intellectual coherence as a broadly conceived nation-making project—within the multi-centred and contested politics of state centralization—by the late 18th century (i.e. 1720s Tulip Era saw secular rationalist discourses articulated, followed by translations of French Enlightenment texts). By the early 19th century, as European imperial economic penetration reordered the power balance on the economic front, migration, urbanization and popular revolt were precipitated. This altered the *de facto* power sharing arrangements among religious *communities*.

Initially instituting a structural rather than ideological secularization (through the creation of bureaucratic and diplomatic organs), the state formation process gradually dismantled the *heaven sent* hierarchic order and reordered and disintegrated old alliances (Janissary–Sultan–bureaucracy–*ulama*). The "people" were posited as the core principle of sovereignty (1826). The creation of new schools (i.e. military, engineering) required for state consolidation served as powerful ideological carriers and shifted the centre of power and knowledge towards modern temporal–political horizons. These included totalizing positivist ideologies promoting *Westernization* as a universal norm, or the *Laws of Nature*—linked to new global configurations of power. There was a radically altered self-consciousness among the divided political elite, and forged linkages with an emergent Ottoman civil society (pacifist and democratic movements, later labour movements).

INTRODUCTION

Initiated from above, the Ottoman–Turkish Enlightenment was divided historically—within a radical crisis of state hegemony inflicted by imperialism—between two main ideological flows. Firstly, there were statist discourses committed to variants of Central European inspired enlightened despotism as *programme* (against democracy but for efficient mobilization of the population). Secondly, there were broad based grassroots *movements* seeking hegemonic transformation through mass political participation–bridge building conceived by marginalized elites in solidarity with other social classes. These embraced multi-religious secular democracy in theory. They undertook the practical creation of public works, job creation, newspapers, credit organizations, mixed schools, national representative bodies—in sum, civil society building based on public self-reliance and activism.

The Enlightened despotist tendency was exemplified by the Mahmud II period (1808–39) and the Tanzimat revolution–subsequent politics (from 1839). The broad democratic tendency was exemplified in the brief but profound Young Ottoman revolution (1876). In these two competing visions of Enlightenment we see the struggle over a constitution, against the centralization of power–concerning state structure, and over the question of national representation within a highly contested constitutional framework.

There were multiple projects of consciousness-building constituting discursive–practical formations upon the immanent terrain of emergent civil society. The Young Ottoman experience saw grass roots projects aimed at broad multi-religious solidarity. The revolution of 1876 saw mass mobilization with troops, ministers and theological students in important organizing roles. The movement included influential intellectuals such as Namik Kemal who held that national development is valid only when combined with public freedom and participation. He urged the creation of public networks linked by traditional ethical values. Namik Kemal and others like him contributed a forceful democratic critique of Enlightenment ideologies linking development to authoritarianism as a mechanist doctrine. They promoted an alternative Enlightenment discourse insisting upon the centrality of political liberty to nation-making and linked it to the world of traditional meanings and identities.

The Young Turks, formed in 1889, contrasted with the openness and ambiguity of the Young Ottoman Enlightenment politics in advancing a rigidly unified ideological outlook. It heralded back intellectually to the *mechanist* strain in the Ottoman–Turkish experience. The multi-religious inclusivity and ideal of broad popular participation in a hegemonic project yielded to a new Enlightenment ideology. It centred ethnic homogeneity and the revolutionizing of cultural life from above based on "laws of nature," rupture, "general will" and assimilationist notions of antecedent identity.

The Young Turk tendency, itself a response to demographic changes resulting from military defeat, new military schools, and the specific political environment created by Abdul Hamid II, culminated in Mustafa Kemal Ataturk with his Comtean historicist vision of a linear, teleological modern *essence*. The state was constructed as an *instrument* where all means are justified in transforming society according to a *universal* blueprint of *modern civilization*. Ataturk was a radical political thinker and adherent of a vision of Enlightenment influenced by the seminal Turkish intellectual Ziya Gokalp.

In practice Ataturk's transcendental ideal of Enlightenment involved the negation of civil society and manifestations of public self-reliance on the grounds of national *immaturity*. Thus, even as traditionally marginalized sections of the population (i.e. women) were given public visibility and new rights, the general population was disempowered as autonomous social activists in being denied the possibility of creating state-independent organizations. Certain sections of the population who did not fit into the conceptually laden state plan of *modernity* were deemed, in historicist terms, to be primitive throwbacks or not to exist (i.e. Kurds). Above all, Ataturk self-consciously cemented a link between violence and truth in a politics of direct seizure of state power where the dialogic is suppressed in the name of epistemic totalization. The impressive if troubled Turkish democracy of today is the product of the long term struggles of the Turkish population partly as a result of, but also in spite of, the Kemalist political legacy. As a self-conscious project of Enlightenment, it envisioned democracy as secondary to the revolutionizing of *culture* according to a *universal* epistemic blueprint.

INTRODUCTION

Chapter 6 demonstrates Nehru's originality as a thinker-statesman within the Enlightenment tradition, through a broad sketch of the post-independence Nehru period. There are important linkages between Nehruism and the Indian national independence movement under Gandhi. Out of competing forms of political loyalty and mobilization strategies, Nehru upheld the secular national-democratic principle following the Gandhian ideal. Pakistan, meanwhile, constructed a new republic based on religious identity.

Nehru followed the lessons of the Gandhian period in crucial ways: the ideal of non-violence as a means, an inclusive moral universalism rather than epistemic totality as the basis for national belonging, a subordination of politics to liberal democratic institutional procedure, and a context-specific groundedness in the everyday as an approach to political change. Thus, the Gandhian modifications of the received Enlightenment tradition were transferred to India's post-independence politics in the Nehru period. This was done through the difficult shift from a mass movement to a political party, via a mode of institutional ethics. These ethics were most visible in the pluralist and non-interventionist solutions to the various centre–state and civil society dilemmas facing the new Indian republic.

Through pluralistic mechanisms power was negotiated through a many-sided politics grounded in the principle of self-reliance and an ethic of reconciliation. The chapter discusses the post-independence language policy, linguistic state reorganization, the accession of Princely states and tribal policy as a pluralistic and many-sided form of politics. It rejects historicist political modes of imagining which construct an often authoritarian single centre of power linked to a linear unfolding of truth (i.e. as a fixed narrative). These experiences make clear that Nehru saw liberty as multiple, conflicting and sometimes mutually subverting freedoms—and that he did not conceive nation-making as a single scientifically determined destiny.

It follows that Nehru attempted to seriously reckon with existential issues of selfhood, loyalty and values, rather than steamrolling such differences under a programme of Utilitarian uniform interest. Nehru followed a middle road between traditional claims to being (values, identity) and modern political–economic becoming through a critical democratic framework based on the humanist ethical principles inherited from the national movement. The precondition for this politics was the non-negotiability of secularism—not as a substantive ideology dictating the truth, but as a public space open to multiple points of view and lines of action based on the principle of non-violence.

The chapter makes the case that the historical prerequisite for these political experiments was the prior popularization of democratic politics on the ground during the struggles of the national movement—or the long-term struggle over hegemony concerning legitimate political authority, ideas, values and meanings.

It follows that Nehru—who clearly saw the link between dogmatic ideological certainty and political violence in the Soviet Union and China—did not envision development based on a discourse of universal laws where science and technology are linked to a specific and whole claim to truth. It is for this reason that Nehru, in contrast to many of his political contemporaries, regularly emphasized the crucial role of the dialogic and insisted upon the irrelevance of forcing any ideas upon the diverse Indian population.

Nehru's outlook is captured in one of his letters, where he speculates about the creation of a classless society through non-violent methods. He denounces coercion and the "language of violence" in favour of "peaceful democratic pressures." He denounces the tendency to think that "a principle can only be stoutly defended by language of violence" in a political imaginary where "there are no shades, [but] only black and white." He identifies this tendency in modern politics with "the old approach of the bigoted aspect of some religions." It contrasts with "the approach of tolerance of feeling that perhaps others might have some share in the truth also." This latter approach he explicitly identifies with his ideal of the scientific approach as an open minded basis for thought and action.[74]

Chapter 7 traces the historical experience of the Iranian Enlightenment through the broad social movement known as the Popular Movement. It was grounded in largely non-violent, mass based and multi-class and ethnic political protests committed to national independence and constitutional democracy. It is

---

[74] Jawaharlal Nehru, *Letters to Chief Ministers, Volume 5* (New Delhi: Oxford University Press, 1989), 83.

traced from the Tobacco Revolt (1890–91) and the Constitutional Revolution (1906–11) through to the National Front period under the leadership of Mohammed Mosaddeq (1941–53). Mosaddeq emphasized public self-reliance, liberty and social rights. He promoted non-violent mass participation in the nation-making process as the long term basis for rooting a secular democratic Iranian political culture. He consistently emphasized independence from foreign domination as the prerequisite for nation-making, and strived to reconcile democratic modernity with Iranian traditions.

The Enlightenment ideals embodied in this grassroots movement coexisted in profound historical tension with alternative visions of authoritarian Enlightenment inspired by the discursive–practical model of Kemal Ataturk. These were to be imposed upon a passive population from above. It was envisioned as a *total regeneration* upon a transcendental *Western* pattern (Reza Khan, Muhammad Reza Shah). This practice derived stability from collusion with the foreign domination which bedevilled 19th- and 20th-century Iran. This was due to its location between an expanding imperial Russia and the British Indian Empire (and from 1900 because of oil). The boundary between these two discursive–practical Enlightenment flows as organized responses to imperial pressures and proliferating internal division — between a pluralist democratic and authoritarian Eurocentric politics — was often ambiguous among early intellectuals and leaders in their exploratory struggle.

A new intellectual and social reformist movement exemplified in Malkom Khan emerged in the mid-19th century, responding to Nasir al-Din's state modernization efforts (1848–96). It self-consciously identified with the philosophy of the European Enlightenment (notably, Comte and Saint Simon) as a championing of secular knowledge. It also developed in dialectical relation to earlier Iranian religious reformist moments including the often anti-clerical and monarchic Isma'ili, Shaikhi and Babi movements, and going back to the immanentist intellectual revolution initiated by Mulla Sadra (d.1640).

At the popular level the movement for democratic modernity was influenced by migration patterns among Iranian workers and merchants, who were exposed to modern political concepts abroad (notably in India) and initiated the Iranian socialist movement at the opening of the 20th century—this later evolved into the initially popular and pluralistic Tudeh Party. This ultimately compromised itself through ideological and political subservience to the Soviet Union.

We see a growing public consciousness within an intermittent constellation of often multi-ethnic civil society organs (newspapers, trade unions, parties, associations) that the state routinely sought to undermine. The experiences of seminal thinkers and activists such as al-Afghani and Malkom Khan are interpreted within this multi-centred international pattern of politics and idea production. The evidence points to these thinkers failing to recognize this multi-centred dynamic of modernity. They largely embraced a Eurocentric theoretical interpretation of modernity as a single unified flow emanating from the West.

Meanwhile, the practical experiences of the multi-class Tobacco Revolt and Constitutional Revolution showed, at the popular level, an impressive degree of non-violent organized resistance. They were grounded in Iranian national traditions of protest while serving modern democratic political ends. Popular activism forced the state to bow to its demands on successive occasions and finally established constitutional rule of law and a National Assembly.

Early national leaders failed to fully appreciate this potential at the theoretical level. The predominant worldview among early intellectuals took a narrow view of Iran's rich past as purely reactionary. Along French Revolutionary discursive–practical lines, the past was suitable only for a total moment of *rupture*. Yet the reality of public participation in these movements did not reflect the dogma that all religious people, ideas and values are *inherently reactionary* by some *law of history*. The idea of any anti-thesis between *Islam* and *democracy* at this historical period appears largely unknown to the popular outlook. The initial lines of division appear to have pitted a multi-class popular movement (containing its own contradictions) against a tentative modernizing state linked to imperialism along self-protective lines of anti-violence—that is, a broad public against the arbitrary and self-serving violence of the authoritarian state. *Islamism* as a discursive–practical formation was later fostered—in innovatively imaginative fashion—in several specific contexts within concrete moments of power struggle. It first manifested itself in historically minor but symbolically important fashion in 1907–08.

Mosaddeq, as the dominant nationalist leader after 1949, provided an organizational alternative to Left individuals following the decline of the Tudeh Party. A courageous anti-imperialist, he and his contemporaries critiqued communist politics for its violence and disrespect of political freedom. They identified Iran's struggle with Nehruvian politics in India and worldwide progressive independence movements linking democratic modernity to local tradition and culture. The National Front coalition movement was based on an ethic of inclusion and reconciliation within a pluralistic public organization—showing a powerful discursive–practical break from earlier intellectual trends borrowing Eurocentric and elitist frameworks of modernity.[75]

Its various organs drew intellectual inspiration from Montesquieu to Bertrand Russell and Marx, as well as indigenous Iranian sources and the political tradition of the Popular Movement generally. Mosaddeq rejected a single voice or completed identity for the nation, including the homogenous ethnic identity constructed and violently perpetrated as a staple of national politics by the Shah. He promoted non-violent political means rooted in the unrestricted growth of a plural civil society within the framework of law as well as direct public action through mass strikes and demonstrations. He affirmed an open ended nationalism without essence, or moral rather than epistemic universalism.

For a wide number of reasons that are addressed in the chapter, this experiment did not finally succeed. It was the successful crushing of this movement by foreign and domestic forces, and the reinstatement of the Shah's foreign-backed authoritarian regime, that paved the way for the eventual popularity of a Shi'i Islamist politics. This was based on ideologically constructed notions of *authenticity* as influenced by thinkers such as the Heideggerian Ahmed Fardid, the Ernst Junger-inspired fiction writer al-e Ahmad, and the sociologist Al-e Shari'ati who combined Marxist revolutionary theory with modern Islamism. These intellectuals

---

[75] We should note that such Eurocentric frameworks have little to do with the *West*, but are often inspired by such supposedly *scientifically* authoritative writers as Comte. Islamism, too, has heavily borrowed from Western self-critical discourses to attack the West—in a vein having a more imaginary than realistic quality.

paved the way for an educated middle class acceptance of the Islamist ideology as an anti-imperialist politics that rejected democracy as a foreign importation. This was a discursive–practical turning harbouring grave consequences for Iran's future, and particularly its long-term democratic aspirations. The multi-class mass movement for democracy in today's Iran provides proof that the nation's population has come to recognize the bankruptcy of this ideological option, and that the Iranian Popular Movement is still alive and growing as a tradition.

CONNECTING THREAD

The connecting thread between these chapters is the project of explicitly articulating the discursive–practical means-ends ensemble in modern nation-making experiences. This entails a project of demystifying violence. If we consider the famous study of violence by Georges Sorel, we see a promotion of the opposite tendency for purposes of increasing the hope of revolutionary success. He wrote:

> men who are participating in great social movements always picture their coming action in the form of images of battle in which their cause is certain to triumph. I proposed to give the name of 'myths' to these constructions, knowledge of which is so important for historians: the general strike of the syndicalists and Marx's catastrophic revolution are such myths. As remarkable examples of myths I have given those which were constructed by primitive Christianity, by the Reformation, by the Revolution, and by the followers of Mazzini. I wanted to show that we should not attempt to analyze such groups of images in the way that we break down a thing into its elements, that they should be taken as a whole, as historical forces, and that we should be especially careful not to make any comparison between the outcomes and the pictures people had formed for themselves before the action.[76]

---

[76] Georges Sorel, *Reflections on Violence* (Cambridge: Cambridge University Press, 2004), 20.

Rather than wilful lapse into self-deluding mental states of *faith* that sublimate ordinary violence to an imagined higher level, the analysis in the following chapters encourages a lucid evaluation of means and ends premised on an ethic of non-violence. Sorel was right to recognize the centrality of collective struggle in creating a just world, but wrong to celebrate messianic violence as harbouring any positive practical quality. It was the modern ideological delirium of such Messianic violence that encouraged nearly an entire generation of the Left to support the criminal acts of Stalin, and convinced the September 11 hijackers that they were liberating the subjugated Muslim world and earning a place in Paradise.

The common idea running across the work is an alternative historical construction of the Enlightenment heritage for nation-making projects. This is best exemplified in the Indian National Movement under Gandhian leadership—but these exemplifying tendencies were present also in Turkish, Iranian and European historical experiences. There are three levels to Gandhi's political contribution to the legacy of Enlightenment: the question of values, the epistemic problem, and finally the issue of practice. The practical aspect points to the problem of violence and the heritage of the French Revolution as a paradigm of political action within the Enlightenment tradition. The point of discussing Gandhi in the context of Enlightenment is not so much to claim him for Enlightenment—as if Enlightenment were some massive block defined by a single identity or essence, and we fall squarely inside or outside of it. One purpose of the discussion should be to reappraise the Enlightenment as a multi-centred, heterogeneous, and non-Eurocentric heritage—a departure from the views of both its conventional admirers and detractors. Enlightenment is a tradition, yet one where ongoing appropriations and interpretations are invariably selective and function in a pluralistic context. Therefore in discussion of the heritage of Enlightenment on the broad scale of the Indian national movement and the other cases it is really difference to be explored rather than sameness.

1

Akbar's "Universal Peace" (*Sulh-i Kul*): Relevance to the Enlightenment

EXPERIMENT IN "UNIVERSAL PEACE"

In the 16th-century Mughal state under Emperor Akbar (reigned 1556–1605)—coterminus with Philip II's (reigned 1556–1598) Inquisitional campaign of Catholic purification in Spain—we find a political experiment defined by ideological precepts significantly comparable to the spirit of the later European Enlightenment. Yet it was derived from local cultural resources in response to new global conditions of early modernity. This political experiment in state-making—with its self-consciously articulated philosophy of cosmopolitan tolerance—presented certain continuities with existing Indo-Islamic political traditions. It also showed surprising intellectual innovations suggesting the emergence of a secular rationalist world view. The rationalist free thinkers who rose to prominence at Akbar's court were known as the "enlightened philosophers," rejecting the "chill blast of inflexible custom."[1]

Akbar, in the same spirit, commended 'obedience to the dictates of reason" and reproved "a slavish following of others."[2] He therefore affirmed rational autonomy—though not the autonomy of pure reason—one central tenet of the Enlightenment as a movement. The kingdom's experiment in Universal Peace (*Sulh-i Kul*) was described by the court historian and philosopher Abul Fazl (1551–1602) as an earnest search for truth and dispelling of

---

[1] Eugenia Vanina, "Describing the Common, Discovering the Individual: A Study in Some Medieval Indian Biographies," in *Mind over Matter. Essays on Mentalities in Medieval India*, eds. D.N. Jha and Eugenia Vanina. (New Delhi: Tulika Books, 2009), 91.

[2] Ibid.

"the darkness of the age by the light of universal toleration."[3] He thus introduced by coincidence the Cartesian metaphor of light in the century prior to the famous *Discourse on the Method* (1637). This movement sought to reconcile multiple religious perspectives with a broad principle of reason, making it comparable to (as well as different from) the European moderate Enlightenment rather than the more radical stream that culminated in the *tabla raza* politics of the French Revolution.[4] They promoted a universal religiosity, meaning that all religions present different paths to a single existential experience of truth. This was based on an epistemic limit characterizing the human condition, where nobody could be certain of possessing absolute truth. It was not an attempt to create a rupture with the past. In seeing all religions as equal, however, universal religiosity implied a form of secularism. It also implied an attitude of change towards the past, a willingness to reform it based on moral norms independent of any specific religion, and this in turn implied a readiness to alter the future. Akbar said: "No one should be allowed to neglect those things that the present time requires."[5] We can talk of the emergence of a new temporal horizon, which lent itself to state patronage in science and technology, translation and secularized forms of the arts, recruiting talent irrespective of religious affiliation.

Universal Peace (*Sulh-i Kul*) confronted the dilemma of violence, finding the cause of silence and fear in "fanatics who lust for blood."[6] Akbar expressed remorse over forced conversions in the early part of his reign: "we by fear and force compelled many believers in the Brahmin religion to adopt the faith of our

---

[3] Syed Athar and Abbas Rizvi, "Dimensions of *Sulh-i Kul* (Universal Peace) in Akbar's Reign and the Sufi Theory of the Perfect Man" (unpublished paper from the Akbar Fourth Centenary Conference, 28–30 October, 2006), 15.

[4] Jonathon I. Israel, *Enlightenment Contested. Philosophy, Modernity, and the Emancipation of Man 1670–1752* (Oxford: Oxford University Press, 2008), 11.

[5] Abraham Eraly, *The Mughal World. Life in India's Last Golden Age* (New Delhi: Penguin, 2007), 341.

[6] Abul-Fazl, *The A-In-I Akbari. Volume I*, Tr. H. Blochmann (New Delhi: Low Price Publications, 2008), 171.

ancestors."[7] He later agreed to turn converted mosques back into Hindu temples.[8] This elite Mughal movement sought to break the truth–violence–monotheism triangle: "Each one regarding his own persuasion alone as true, has set himself to the persecution of other worshippers of God, and the shedding of blood [has become] the symbol of religious orthodoxy."[9] At the root is clinging to an idea, instead of the autonomy of people judging for themselves. For with reflection, people "shake off the prejudices of their education, the threads of the web of religious blindness break."[10] By contrast, Akbar observed, "What constancy might one expect from those converted under duress?"[11] Akbar thus anticipated the Lockean insight concerning the superior quality of faith based on reason rather than coercion.

The *Ibkahat* (house of worship) became an open symposium for members of all religions—Sunnis, Shi'as, Hindus, Jains, Zoroastrians and Christians—to meet and conduct dialogues non-violently in the search for truth. Abul Fazl argued that since persecution thwarts earnest inquiry, the state has an obligation to provide friendly assemblies under the guidance of impartiality where calmness of mind and freedom of expression may discuss and severe truth from error.[12] We see a tacit acknowledgement, albeit at the elite level, of the need for institutional defences of freedom that would later be articulated theoretically by Montesquieu. Although the *Ibkahat* was created from above as a dialogical public sphere within the composite nobility, the pattern of the *Sulh-i Kul* was preceded by a broad Hindu–Muslim unity impulse at the popular level. This was by way of Bhakti and Sufi movements united through the shared habitus of yogic practices and convictions about tolerance. It was these social energies that the Mughal state tapped into during Emperor Akbar's reconstruction of political power along the lines of an early modern

[7] Harbans Mukhia, *The Mughals of India* (New Delhi: Blackwell Publishing, 2004), 37.

[8] Ibid., 23.

[9] Fazl, *A-In-I Akbari, Volume III*, 5–6; On the truth-violence-monotheism triangle see Mohammed Arkoun, *The Unthought in Contemporary Islamic Thought* (London: Saqi, 2002), 70.

[10] Fazl, *A-In-I Akbari, Volume I*, 171.

[11] Mukhia, *Mughals*, 38.

[12] Fazl, *A-In-I Akbari, Volume III*, 5.

new monarchy at the point of state consolidation, on the exceptional basis of multi-religious equality.

AKBAR'S BIOGRAPHICAL DIMENSION: EARLY EXPERIENCES OF A MULTI-RELIGIOUS LIFEWORLD, RELIGIOUS PERSECUTION AND VIOLENCE

The Mughal emperor Akbar started out his life (1542) in a state of exile following the routing of his father Humayun's kingdom, depending upon the good grace of strangers on the long road between Delhi, Qandahar, Kabul and Tehran. His father was a Sunni Turk, his mother a Shi'i Iranian, and he was born in the home of a Hindu raja who had given shelter to Humayun during his flight to Iran.[13] Akbar was raised under the guardianship of Bairam Khan (a Shi'ite) and Mir Abdul Latif, who had been persecuted in Iran for alleged Sunnite beliefs while being taken for a *Shi'ite* in India.[14] The damaging effects of religious persecution, as well as the bare human reality of religious pluralism, were therefore a part of Akbar's lifeworld from the very beginning. This perhaps explains why throughout his life as emperor he grew progressively more open to views from outside of the Sunni orthodox tradition, in spite of the bitter hostility of the conservative *ulama*. His son Jahangir recalled: "My father always associated with the learned of every creed and religion."[15]

The emperor Humayun (reigned 1530–56) had encountered tremendous difficulties in his struggle to retain and expand Babur's conquests in India. He retreated into a year of inactivity under the influence of opium. Later routed by the Afghans in 1540, he was driven into a 15-year period of exile at the Safavid court of Shah Tahmasp (reigned 1525–76) in Persia. There he accepted the Shia faith under duress in order to preserve his life

---

[13] C.M. Naim, "Popular Jokes and Political History: The Case of Akbar, Birbal and Mulla Do-Piyaza," in *Cultural History of Medieval India*, ed. Meenakshi Khanna (New Delhi: Social Science Press, 2007), 28.

[14] Iqbal Husain, "Iranian Ideological Influences at Akbar's Court," in *A Shared Heritage: The Growth of Civilizations in India and Iran*, ed. Irfan Habib (New Delhi: Tulika Books, 2002), 118.

[15] Andre Wink, *Akbar* (Oxford: One World, 2009), 14.

and those of several hundred followers. One day after a long period Shah Tahmasp decided to underwrite Humayun's attempt to regain power in India. In 1555, Humayun entered Delhi and restored Babur's monarchy amid the starvation and disease attending the break-up of the sur administrative system.[16]

Akbar later spoke of his arrival in India (Hind) as if he had arrived at the place of his birth as an outsider. Yet he expressed love for India as his homeland. By Akbar's time, the "concept of India had ... gone much beyond a purely geographical one in the Indo-Muslim tradition with which Akbar obtained familiarity first." In October 1578, 23 years after his return and with a great deal of water and blood under the bridge, we hear of Akbar referring with affection and pride to the people of India (Hind) when he "praised the truth-based nature of the people of India."[17]

We may therefore characterize Akbar's relation to India as one of deep love and terrible violence. From the earliest period of his reign he was haunted by the climate of violence that coloured the mission of imperial conquest that he had inherited from his father, Humayun, and his grandfather, Babur, who founded the Mughal Empire. One year after Akbar's return to India, in 1556, and the year of his father's accidental death on the library steps, he slew a fallen adversary following the battle of Panipat at the age of 13.[18] Decades later, the memory continued to trouble him. Within the aristocratic milieu in which Akbar grew up, a royal refugee between Persia and India, violence was sublimated as a righteous part of power in a nobleman's rise to greatness. Yet we hear that as a child Akbar enjoyed the *masnavis* of such liberal Sufi thinkers as Maulana Rumi and Hafiz, the first of whom urged a universal compassion as the true meaning of religion: "We are all the children of God and His infants ... From mosquito to elephant, all are his family."[19] Later in his royal court the emperor was directly exposed to those philosophies of non-violence which

---

[16] John F. Richards, *The Mughal Empire* (New Delhi: Cambridge University Press, 2008), 6–29.

[17] M. Athar Ali, 'The Perception of India in Akbar and Abu'l Fazl," in *Akbar and His India*, ed. Irfan Habib (New Delhi: Oxford, 1997), 219.

[18] Mukhia, *Mughals*, 30.

[19] Sadia Dehlvi, *Sufism: The Heart of Islam* (New Delhi: Harper Collins, 2009), 23.

have profound roots in Indian tradition, via the representatives of Jainism, and also to the popular Bhakti and Sufi movements that became an important anchor of his political legitimacy. These encounters deeply transformed both Akbar's ethical worldview and the policy of the Mughal Empire through the grand political experiment in tolerance known as *Sulh-i Kul* (Universal Peace).

Akbar was a statesman and pragmatist, and adapted these individual philosophies of spiritual salvation (*fana*, seeking annihilation through the extinction of the passions and desires, becoming a drop of water in the ocean) to a practical public policy of non-violent and dialogic conflict resolution among the composite multi-religious nobility of the heterogeneous Mughal Empire. With the assistance of the court philosophers, he transformed pantheist mysticism into a form of rationality appropriate for building and governing a state. We see the creative blending of Islamic traditions with other deeply rooted Indian traditions. The consequence of this unusual experiment in early modern state formation and empire consolidation was the marginalization of the orthodox Sunni *ulama*, the closest ideological allies of the invading Mughals in the earliest phase of military conquest. It was also the public promotion of a tolerant and open ideal of Islam based on the partial truth of all world religions, and the absolute certainty of none. In accordance with Jain ethics, the policy of compassion extended beyond human to animal life and welfare as well. We see a radical rethinking of boundaries at many points. A climate of enquiry prevailed, such that disapproving court historian Abd-Al-Qader Badauni observed that Muslim radicals

> tempted mankind by suggesting the forgery of the Koran, and by going out of the way to show the impossibility of inspiration, and by throwing doubts on the authority of prophets and Imams, and utterly denying the existence of demons and angels, and mysteries and signs and miracles.[20]

---

[20] Eraly, *Mughal World*, 320.

AKBAR AND EARLY MODERNITY: THE GLOBAL SPACE

India was a "major center in the early modern world economy."[21] The latter part of Akbar's reign coincided with profound economic transformation upon the subcontinent as a market society expanded to monetize lifeworlds. At the close of the 16th century, the Indian subcontinent

> absorbed enormous quantities of New World silver and as a consequence possessed highly monetized economies. This monetization penetrated to the bottom of the social order, as the import of copper, cowries and badams and other low value money materials would suggest.[22]

The "insatiable appetite for Indian cottons in markets around the world [explains] why silver flowed from America, Europe and the Middle East to the Indian subcontinent," as well as from China and Japan.[23] We see the Indian subcontinent enter

> a 200-year commercial boom in which the supply and use of money expanded, markets became a growing feature of daily life for much of the populace, and large merchant fortunes were built. In Bengal and other manufacturing regions, the rising demand for cotton textiles led to the reallocation and more efficient use of resources. Across the subcontinent, the production of cloth for export created a sizable long-distance trade in raw cotton, dyestuffs and the cloth itself.

Further, "standards of living in Europe and India were more comparable than once imagined, which would mean that the economies of the subcontinent were more productive and advanced than has been long believed."

---

[21] Prasannan Parthasarathi, *Why Europe Grew Rich and Asia Did Not: Global Economic Divergence, 1600–1850* (Cambridge: Cambridge University Press, 2011), 22.
[22] Ibid., 60.
[23] Ibid., 26/48.

As a case study in the history of ideas, the Akbar experience expresses merely one moment within a broader pattern of creative intellectual responses to problems posed by these emergent material conditions: "In the period from 1600 to 1800, intellectual life in the Indian subcontinent was far from stagnant and there were intellectual shifts which led to self-conscious searches for new forms of knowledge."[24]

It is significant that Akbar's reign occurred within the newly expanding space opened up at the beginning of the modern age. Columbus arrived in America in 1492 which coincided with the final destruction of the Muslim state of Grenada in Spain. With hindsight, a feeling of foreboding colours the scenes and situations which link human actions—conscious and unconscious—from the dreams of Reconquest in Philip II's Spain to the ships plying the Indian Ocean toward the ports of Gujarat. The intense religious and political court debates that marked Akbar's reign—seeking a way through metaphysical doubt and legitimacy crisis—were linked to unsettling secular circumstances at the global level. Ultimately, a process was underway that "moved the textile manufacturing center of the world from India to Western Europe."[25] But, grounded in temporal horizons, actors faced specific problems within specific situations (i.e. as Britain faced the competitive challenge of Indian cotton).[26] Akbar could know but relatively little of this coming storm from encounters with armed Portuguese traders and Jesuits invited to the royal court: "information about the Europeans was available to Akbar and his contemporaries," who were "aware that the Europeans had discovered the Americas, which [they] called *Alam-i Nau*, or the New World."[27] Akbar was keenly interested in the technologies and scientific discoveries of Europe and sent "craftsmen to Goa to procure European goods and to learn European crafts."[28]

---

[24] Ibid., 4–6.
[25] Ibid., 18.
[26] Ibid., 17.
[27] M. Athar Ali, *Mughal India. Studies in Polity, Ideas, Society and Culture* (New Delhi: Oxford University Press, 2006), 67–69.
[28] Eraly, *Mughal World*, 342.

Such knowledge "could not but engender questioning about the finality of traditional knowledge."[29]

The emperor's self-emancipation from the customary constraints of the orthodox Sunni *ulama*, the gradual conversion of powerful and proud local rulers into a broad service class of dependent officials, new openness to the general population through public dawn meetings, the patronizing of new translation bureaus to create a multi-lingual integrated public and the making secure of roads and transport for military, trade and taxation purposes: these new moments of political organization, in their different geographical and demographic context, strongly suggest early conditions for the emergence of the modern nation that we usually identify with the new monarchies of 16th-century Europe. Akbarian Mughal India experienced economic progress: urbanization, monetization, increased cash crop production, interregional trade and increased demand for luxury goods resulting from the widespread elite adoption of the Mughal lifestyle with political unification.[30] The northern Indian heartland, from Delhi to Lucknow and eastward to Benares, constituted the Mughal Empire's core in the late 16th and 17th centuries. Although it did not export "on the same scale as the maritime regions of India, it was a highly commercialized region and its wealth and dense population created a large concentration of production and consumption."[31] Emergent commercial and political classes—which distinguished emergent modernity in parts of Europe—were lacking.[32] Yet in Mughal India—this chapter documents one pattern—we see important creative tensions in "the diffuse nature of political power translated into a decentralized administrative order [of] great variety, fluidity and contestation."[33]

It is methodologically anachronistic to seek emergent modernity in terms of a *universal* pattern identifiable in Europe, as if a single teleological endpoint were already inscribed in historical existence. In the Mughal experience—and certainly elsewhere on

[29] Ali, *Mughal India*, 67–69.
[30] Eraly, *Mughal World*, 174.
[31] Parthasarathi, *Why Europe Grew Rich*, 14.
[32] Eraly, *Mughal World*, 321/175.
[33] Parthasarathi, *Why Europe Grew Rich* 56.

the subcontinent (Mysore was a site of great innovation, technical progress and scientific interest)—the imperial stereotype of frozen ontological stagnation outside of an expanding European modernity is empirically false.[34] There was a common space of emergent global modernity where, at this stage, an Asia-centred global economy still persisted. The radical geo-political reversal of the Industrial Revolution, in the 19th century, marked the emergence of a transfixing and widely shared unifying horizon in imagining modernity's potential future. What are visible in late 16th-century Mughal experiments are synergetic patterns of diversity in labour and society, mutually dependent power networks, and productive cultural processes suggesting plural paths of development produced through human agency and choice and shaped by social, political and economic context.[35]

The waning feudalism and greater territorial cohesion of early 16th-century European states derived from productivity and expanded trade, necessitating an alliance between new absolute monarchy and the rising burgher class. The logic of these new monarchies often suggested nothing of an emerging democratic order at either national or European levels. There was "more religious freedom in India than contemporary Europe…or in any Muslim state outside India."[36] Portuguese royal domination of burghers and nobles derived from colonial acquisition in the Indies and Brazil, spices, jewels and the slave trade. Spanish royalty used the Inquisition as a unifying tool, crushing religious dissidents and subordinating the nobility, with power derived from colonies and American silver and gold flows from 1501. Henri IV's (1589–1610) short-lived 1598 Edict of Nantes, issued after victory in the bloody religious civil war (1562–98), appealed for tolerance and reconciliation against waves of violence driven by perceptions of "safeguarding and defending a sacred notion of community defined by religion."[37] Hapsburg Charles V, Holy Roman Emperor from 1519, nurtured obsessive if futile dreams of restored Christendom. He saw final Habsburg fragmentation

---

[34] Ibid., 14.
[35] Ibid., 9.
[36] Eraly, *Mughal World*, 226.
[37] Mack P. Holt, *The French Wars of Religion, 1562–1629* (Cambridge: CamMubridge University Press, 2005), 195.

in 1556 as his universal empire disintegrated into early European modernity amidst a climate of violence accelerated through post-Reformation religious wars. Elizabeth I (1558–1603), trying to keep England aloof from the dynastic religious wars engulfing Europe while consolidating Henry VIII's Reformation, attempted a politics of tolerance under perpetual invasion hysteria. Conflicting tendencies abounded, but there was simply no underlying democratic teleology or universal structure pulling early modern Europe towards a politically emancipated future.[38]

The Mughal Empire (1526–1857), meanwhile, existed broadly within the Islamicate world comprised of mobile wealth, long-distance trade, extensive monetization and military slaves. Turko-Persian states emerged far and wide, their military leadership drawn from outside recruits rather than territorially rooted warrior lineages. Decentred since the Abbasid caliph's death in the Mongol siege of Bagdad (1258), succession claims fostered inter-state tensions. The Islamicate was a multi-ethnic and trans-regional world space woven together in shared political norms (the Mirror for Kings, emphasizing wealth, subjects and justice), cultural values and aesthetic tastes (wearing apparel, court etiquette). Within this context, the Mughal Empire was "renowned as the largest, richest and most dynamic Muslim kingdom in the world—the land of opportunity for Muslims everywhere [with] a steady migration of Muslims from Central Asia and Persia into India."[39]

By the 16th century we find a broad cosmopolitan cultural zone where, even in predominantly non-Muslim regions, the political, literary and aesthetic influence of Islam was pervasively infused with the locally dominant religion.[40] This phenomenon existed among East Christian, Hindu and Theravada Buddhist peoples, the Islamicate transregional zone extending from the Hindu Vijayanagara kingdom in southern India to Northern Sicily. The Vijayanagara kingdom shared a similar form of military organization, political economy, royal dress and public comportment

---

[38] Fernand Braudel, *Grammaire des Civilisations* (Paris: Flammarion, 1993), 421.

[39] Eraly, *Mughal World*, 21.

[40] Willem Floor and Edmund Herzig, ed. *Iran and the World in the Safavid Age* (London. New York: I. B. Tauris).

to the neighbouring Islamic Bahmani kingdom, while founding its legitimation upon a geographic focus in enchanted nature, the river goddess cult of the Tungabhadra River.[41]

Within the Islamicate world space, the Mughal, Ottoman (1299–1922) and Safavid (1501–1736) empires were defined by an ideal of universal kingship, where power was equated with the patronage of multiple religious groups.[42] Their practice involved a layered and shared form of sovereignty which "aspired to be the repository of the highest level of sovereignty, leaving room for negotiating the terms of imperial unity with a plethora of regional and local governments."[43] In this personalized (not strictly unitary) practice of sovereignty, rule was vested in subservient yet autocratic local chiefs. They shared an imperial concept designed for accommodating ethnic and religious difference within large heterogeneous empires, making a virtue out of tolerance of religious difference—given the understanding of ultimate Islamic supremacy. Far from the stereotype of Oriental despotism recycled from Francois Bernier to Adam Smith and Montesquieu—and enshrined most vividly in Hegel's Philosophy of History—power presented a multi-centred phenomenon that interacted with global change. For the Mughal, Ottoman and Safavid Empires, the 16th century "signified increasing contact with the outside world, the creation of unified states, new intellectual horizons."[44]

Akbar came to the throne in 1556 but began to rule independently in 1560. By the end of his reign in 1605, the Mughal Empire extended from Kabul to the Deccan and from the Arabian Sea to the Gulf of Bengal, forming the third player in the "triumvirate of giants of South and South-West Asia, the Great Turks [the Ottomans], the Great Sufi [the Safavids] and the Great

---

[41] Richard M. Eaton, "The Articulation of Islamic Space in the Medieval Deccan," in *Cultural History of Medieval India*, ed. Meenakshi Khanna (New Delhi: Esha Béteille Social Science Press, 2007), 126–36.

[42] C.A. Bayly, *The Birth of the Modern World: 1780-1914* (Malden: Blackwell, 2004), 34/220.

[43] Sugata Bose, *A Hundred Horizons. The Indian Ocean in the Age of Global Empire* (Ranikhet Cantt: Permanent Black, 2006), 41.

[44] André Clot, *Suleiman the Magnificent* (London: Saqi, 2005), 6.

Mughals."[45] In the 16th-century Istanbul was an urban monster with 400,000 inhabitants, requiring "every available flock of sheep from the Balkans to support it; rice, beans and corn from Egypt; corn and wood from the Black Sea; and oxen, camels and horses from Asia Minor."[46] Both the Ottoman and the Safavid empires were dwarfed by the Mughal Empire, with an estimate for the population at 108 million during Akbar's time.[47]

The Ottoman and the Safavid empires, both born of the disintegrated Timurid Empire (late 15th century), clashed continuously for control of Bagdad, southwestern Iran and Azerbaijan in a conflict given bitter sectarian dimensions by the Sunni and Shi'i split. From the early 16th century, two centuries of intermittent warfare between these giants ensued with many thousands of lives lost. In the appalling Battle of Chaldiran (1514) we see the use of European cannons and muskets for the first time in Central Asia, following their invention near Calais (1347) and first major use in the 1494 French invasion of Italy.[48] These new forms of violence also suggest the silent impact of new technologies as the moving force of economic histories in expanding unseen but interlinked sociopolitical patterns.

The effect of this technology was to strengthen the power position of large states in relation to local rulers, a significant military touch of the 15th-century revolutions in artillery, printing and ocean navigation. Such new military violence was the antecedent condition for the large state-formation processes that followed, just as the new ocean navigation powers soon created a new asymmetry in the world.[49] It was likewise the new foundation for conquest in artillery that forced Afghanistan into Babur's new India based empire from 1529, ensuring military control of

---

[45] Ebba Koch, "The Intellectual and Artistic Climate of Tolerance at Akbar's Court" (unpublished paper from the Akbar Fourth Centenary Conference, 28–30 October, 2006) (New Delhi: Indian Council of Historical Research), 2–3.

[46] Fernand Braudel, *Capitalism and Material Life: 1400–1800* (London: Weidenfeld and Nicolson, 1973), 21.

[47] Sumit Guha, *Health and Population in South Asia: from earliest times to the present* (Ranikhet Cantt: Permanent Black, 2001), 32.

[48] Satish Chandra, *Medieval India: From Sultanat to the Mughals. Part II* (New Delhi: Har-Anand, 2008), 42.

[49] Braudel, *Capitalism and Material Life*, 285.

the twin northern gates of Kabul and Qandahar for the first time since antiquity. This strengthened Mughal security by fixing access to multiple foreign trade routes from China to West Asia, making India a core player in Central Asian politics and guaranteeing the close diplomatic attentions of Ottoman Turkey and Safavid Persia. Artillery made killing faster and easier, destroying the old noble *lifeworlds* based on slow, ritualized and graceful modes of combat much as we see in 15th-century Europe, Japan after 1543 and most fatally of all in the total massacre of the Incas by Pizarro in 1532.[50]

We see Akbar—amidst this new life of violent machines—constructing the Mughal composite nobility through an experimental policy of non-violent reconciliation grounded in an emergent humanist discourse. Of course the outlands remained targets of imperial military expansion: Bengal (1576), Kabul (1585), Kashmir (1586) and Qandahar (1595). The mass of the population—many barely scraping out a living—remained targets of ruthless exploitation.[51] Yet from 1579 we hear of Hindustan, following Akbar's experiments in Universal Peace, having now become the centre of security and peace, and the land of justice and beneficence as the refuge and new home to floods of Iranian refugees fleeing the religious persecution of the Safavid court.[52] A number of Persian poets also fled to "Akbar's land of religious freedom" where Iranian Shiites were permitted to practice openly.[53] This happened only some years after the Massacre of the Night of St. Bartholomew in France, in 1572, the culmination of the Religious Wars since 1562, where 30,000 people were killed in a single night.[54]

The reigns of Akbar and Philip II of Spain, both beginning in 1556, present contrasting strategies of imperial consolidation. Both inherited large realms which they expanded and

---

[50] Jared Diamond, *Guns, Germs and Steel: A Short History of Everybody for the Last 13,000 Years* (London: Vintage, 1998), 257/68.

[51] Eraly, *Mughal World*, 112.

[52] Chandra, *Medieval India*, 174.

[53] Iqtidar Alam Khan, "The Mughal Empire and the Iranian Diaspora of the Sixteenth Century," in *A Shared Heritage: The Growth of Civilizations in India and Iran*, ed. Irfan Habib (New Delhi: Tulika Books, 2002), 107–8.

[54] Michael Curtis, *The Great Political Theories, Volume I* (New York: Harper perennial, 2008), 263.

consolidated with determination, and both acted within the space of the *modern world* opened up by the discovery of the Americas and the shift to Atlantic trade routes.[55] The silver mined in Philip's American colonies financed his continuous wars and much of it also arrived in India to help monetize the land revenue—the basis of Akbar's expanding power. Following the Spanish seizure of Portugal in 1580, Philip became the head of the Portuguese *Estado do India*. Akbar initially welcomed the Portuguese as traders bringing silver to India and as protectors of Mughal ships taking Muslim pilgrims to Arabia. He declared, regarding new commodities arriving from Europe, that "we must not reject a thing that has been adopted by people of the world, merely because we cannot find it in our own books; or how shall we progress?"[56] This surprising dismissal of the finality of Revelation, and affirmation of the positive value in historical change, was very much in the spirit of the Enlightenment worldview. It was also, with hindsight, a radical underestimation of the dangers to local sovereignty of emerging global merchant capitalism. Akbar gradually came to recognize the Portuguese threat, but opted to avoid confrontation.[57]

Akbar and Philip both faced the problem of organizing an early modern state, depending on expensive artillery and a large standing army which require a reliable tax base and efficient territorial administration. Both, being early modern states, relied on the personal ties of the monarch with the ruling elite of his realm rather than impersonal institutions. This presented the ethical alternative between tolerance and intolerance as two possible strategies of imperial consolidation faced with heterogeneity and recalcitrant local nobles. Akbar undertook a 1582 correspondence with Philip II over political and religious principle, voicing a strongly rationalist outlook: "men most [being] fettered by bonds

[55] Dietmar Rothermund, "Akbar and Philip II of Spain: Contrasting Strategies of Imperial Consolidation" (unpublished paper from the Akbar Fourth Centenary Conference, October 28–30, 2006) (New Delhi: Indian Council of Historical Research), 1.

[56] Amartya Sen, *The Argumentative Indian: Writings on Indian Culture, History and Identity* (London: Penguin, 2005), 291.

[57] K. S. Mathew, "Akbar and Portuguese Maritime Dominance," in *Akbar and His India*, ed. Irfan Habib (Calcutta, Chennai, Mumbai: Oxford University Press, 1997), 256–65.

of tradition, [and] imitating the ways followed by their fathers," and "ignoring arguments and reasons were thus excluding [themselves] from the possibility of ascertaining the truth, which is the noblest aim of the human intellect." He requested that "we associate at convenient seasons with learned men of all religions, thus deriving profit from their exquisite discourses and exalted aspirations." This call for the joint development of an independent reason—as opposed to following "the religion in which [one] was born and educated"—is striking in its secular implications at a time of religious sectarian massacre in Europe.[58] The sectarian Battle of Chaldiran, too, had evoked pining for revenge in Persia's Shah Ismail (1502–24).[59] In contrast to this prevailing sectarian mood coloured by childhood indoctrination, Akbar was stating that human beings are not obliged to think as their ancestors did, and that one should receive one's heritage in a critical and autonomous manner. He also stated that all different points of view have something of value to offer, implying a dialogic rational alternative to the sectarian violence gaining ground in India as surely as it had seized much of Europe.

Such a sectarian worldview, with its tacit violence, was expressed by the Jesuit Father Monserrate while visiting Akbar's court: "the king cared little that in allowing everyone to follow his religion he was in reality violating all."[60] Mulla Badauni, Akbar's severest critic among the orthodox, noted scathingly that participants in the *Ibadat Khana* "only settle things with appeal to man's reason."[61] These critics were attacking a pluralist principle of secularism, intellectually based on a posited limit to human knowledge, without the term being available to them at the time. They attacked in the name of an ontological certitude—quite prevalent then as now—justifying violence. As J.M. Roberts noted in a different context, "the realities came first, before the principles and theory of lawyers and political scientists."[62] In this

---

[58] Emperor Akbar, "A Letter of the Emperor Akbar Asking for the Christian Scriptures," tr. Edward Rehatsek, in *The Indian Antiquary*, 1887, 137.

[59] Clot, *Suleiman the Magnificent*, 32.

[60] Akhtar and Rizvi, *Dimensions of Sulh-i Kul*, 14.

[61] Fazl, *A-In-I Akbari, Volume I*, 206.

[62] John Morris Roberts, *The Penguin History of Europe* (London: Penguin, 1997), 194.

polemical tension over a still unrevealed practical reality, we see where the frontiers between the thinkable and the unthought are tacitly tested and pushed.

Akbar followed a policy of tolerance or *Sulh-i Kul* (Universal Peace) because it was an effective strategy of imperial consolidation while Philip II stressed Catholicism as the leading principle of his realm in a violent and exclusive manner, consigning non-Catholics to the category of non-persons suitable for expulsion or extermination. His organization of the Inquisition not only in Spain, but also in the Netherlands and Latin America, went beyond a matter of faith and functioned as an instrument of political consolidation. Philip II was a practical man, the first Western ruler to build a modern bureaucracy.[63] Yet beyond their practical orientations as statesmen there was a fundamental difference of ethical perspective regarding the relation between religion, the state and personal belief. While Akbar affirmed freedom of belief, Philip dedicated himself to fighting heretics.[64] On the path of reason (*rah-i-aql*), Akbar claimed from the 1570s, anyone being forced to abandon his rites of worship is a violation of *Sulh-i Kul*.[65] Hindus had been second class citizens subjected to political, social and economic disability, but under Akbar "their inferior status virtually disappeared."[66] In the case of Philip the state was used as an instrument for the violent elimination of anything but True Belief; while for Akbar the truth became the end result of a dialogic thought process rather than the immediacy of a given religious revelation. Transcendental and immanent notions of truth confront one another within the silent flicker marking the thinkable and unthought frontier.

Following the opening of the *Ibadat Khana* in 1575, Akbar reached the humanist conclusion that

> there are wise men to be found ready at hand in all religions, and men of asceticism and recipients of Divine revelations

---

[63] Walter Kirchner, *Western Civilization from 1500* (New York: Harper Collins, 1991), 56.

[64] Rothermund, *Akbar and Philip II of Spain*, 1–5.

[65] Iqtidar Alam Khan, "Akbar's Personality Traits and World Outlook—a Critical Reappraisal", in *Akbar and His India*, ed. Irfan Habib (Calcutta, Chennai, Mumbai: Oxford University Press, 1997), 95.

[66] Eraly, *Mughal World*, 25–26.

and workers of miracles among all nations. Truth is the inhabitant of every place; and how could it be right to consider it necessarily confined to one religion or creed.[67]

Sometimes we are told that the post-reformation religious wars transpired because there were no alternative views publically available, and the perpetrators were merely products of the limits of their time. This story, providing proof of a cosmopolitan humanist horizon, also deconstructs the assumption of a homogenous historical overmind in a given period.

Akbar corresponded with Shah Abbas (1587–1629) of the Safavid Empire, suggesting in 1594 that he follow the Mughal example of "making no distinctions among his subjects on the basis of cult or creed." Shah Abbas replied in 1599 denouncing the Mughal doctrine of *Sulh-i Kul* on the grounds that "all prophets have condemned lawless people."[68] In a sense he was right, because Akbar with his dialogic experiment was promoting a principle of rationality outside the sectarian legal framework of then existing states. Today we have a name for such a system of law in modern secularism. The Akbarian experiment constituted historically identifiable ideational and practical components of this institutional potentiality in a particular historical formation (i.e. not a systemic or unified teleological totality). It remained blind to the far larger geo-political process rapidly encompassing it.

The geographic zone of intersection between the Islamicate civilizational space and emerging colonial European interventionism was the Indian Ocean, now linked to the growing Atlantic economy. The Persian Gulf and the Red Sea were "longstanding destinations for both Indian traders and Indian goods," with "Indian cottons ... also exported to Southeast Asia [and] exchanged for spices [and to] East Africa [making possible] the slave armies that were fielded by the Islamic kingdoms of the Deccan in early-modern times." The European penetration into the Indian Ocean opened new markets for Indian cloth

---

[67] Rizvi, *Dimensions of Sulh-I Kul*, 9.
[68] Iqtidar Alam Khan, "The Mughal Empire and the Iranian Diaspora of the Sixteenth Century," in *A Shared Heritage: The Growth of Civilizations in India and Iran*, ed. Irfan Habib (New Delhi: Tulika Books, 1992), 107–8.

via Portugal, from where textiles were distributed to Holland and England that in turn became "the leading trading nations of Europe in the seventeenth and eighteenth centuries."[69] The 16th-century Indian Ocean was a long established and integrated trade system, monopolized by Islamic trade centres along the edges of empty spaces peopled by Arab and Indian merchants, linking Bombay to Aden and Mombasa.[70] India was geographically centred on a linkage network joining the Red and Arabian seas, South East Asia and China, a system excluding interlopers. The Portuguese—on India's western coast, the Malayan peninsula, and Indonesian Spice Islands—forced their way with new Renaissance land war guns, transforming the game rules of war at sea. By the 1480s, Portuguese expeditions along Africa's shores aimed to penetrate and dominate the Indian Ocean trading system. With the 1498 rounding of the Cape of Good Hope, war, discovery and trade became interchangeable terms in the period of armed cargo ships.[71] Northwestern Europe struggled to escape its spatial marginality in relation to the dominant interlocked trade networks centred on the Indian Ocean.[72] That until about 1500 the net flow of technology was overwhelmingly from Islam to a less advanced Europe, with China still more innovative than medieval Islam, suggests the eventual magnitude of this shift in the world's centre linked to the ascendency of the Atlantic economy, new sea based empires and the revolutionary technologies of early capitalism.[73]

The Mughal structural dimension concerned technology, artillery and currency as the basis for consolidating the empire. The system of coinage. "linked to the Spanish discovery of the New World" and the "heavy influx of silver, plundered extracted from the newly discovered continents" ended "the silver famine that had prevailed [in India] since the fourteenth century."[74] There

[69] Parthasarathi, *Why Europe Grew Rich*, 23.

[70] See Bose for detailed elaboration of these many patterns and connections.

[71] Michael Howard, *War in European History* (London: Oxford University Press, 1976), 41.

[72] Jozsef Borocz, *The European Union and Global Social Change: A critical geopolitical-economic analysis* (London: Routledge, 2010), ch. 1.

[73] Diamond, *Guns, Germs and Steel*, 253.

[74] Ali, *Mughal India*, 69.

was greatly expanded money circulation not only in the absolute terms of metal but in transactions or an expansion of trade. Thus, we have "two new sources of strength and stability that 'modern' developments gave to the Mughal polity—the silver influx, a component of the Price Revolution, and the artillery, an early product of modern technology."[75] The towns made possible the manufacture of muskets and guns, providing the new military basis for political and military domination over the countryside and the means to effective revenue collection. Abul-Fazl's detailed studies of patterns of Mughal administration were a contemporary attempt to analyze this in social scientific manner. From the Akbar period onward, all state communication was systematically preserved.[76]

These patterns of transformative tension, within a short time, extended to important new forms of labour organization within an emergent early modern economy impacting the lifeworlds. With the 17th- and 18th-century commercial boom, market expansion extended the division of labour, increasing productivity gains through specialization. Growing European demand for cotton textiles from 17th-century Bengal led to a labour and capital reallocation for the manufacture of high value goods. In numerous Indian regions, growing demand for commercial agricultural products in the 17th and 18th centuries "sparked a shift to higher-yielding, capital-intensive techniques on more specialized and better quality soils."[77]

Within the broader shaping force of technological and economic change, the class idea of the ruling Mughal elite materialized in new practices and an altering state apparatus. The court ideology, to be sure, contained the abstract universal idea of justice. Yet its significance remained limited to the newly emergent composite nobility within the dialogic space of the court. These were the powerful, for there was "no avenue other than imperial service for a man to get ahead in life."[78] This dialogic space produced specific legal reforms, but their impact on the encompassing peasant and popular lifeworlds was minimal as

---

[75] Ibid., 69–79.
[76] Eraly, *Mughal World*, 231.
[77] Parthasarathi, *Why Europe Grew Rich*, 61.
[78] Eraly, *Mughal World*, 181.

the "government did not have the capacity to routinely intrude into [the common people's] lives." People conformed to the customary law of their caste or village (local bodies or guild council) but would "obey the laws of the state only under coercion."[79] The expansion of Enlightenment ideals—in seeking to pattern and structure the emergent economy—collided with the institutional limits of the state apparatus. Akbar ordered secular-oriented reforms in education:

> [E]very boy ought to read morals, arithmetic, the notation peculiar to arithmetic, agriculture, mensuration, geometry, astronomy, physiognomy, household matters, the rules of government, medicine, logic, the *tabi'i* (physical sciences), *riyazi*, (the sciences that treat of quantity, and comprise mathematics, music, astronomy, mechanics) and *ilahi* (theology), sciences, and history ....[80]

Yet there were neither universities nor organized centres of learning. Akbar similarly encouraged agricultural reform, once ordering a provincial governor to "turn his attention to the increase of agriculture and the flourishing condition of the land and earn the gratitude of the people by the faithful discharge of his obligations."[81] Yet the institutional infrastructure for realizing such a vision was limited.

For all this, state-making on the Indian subcontinent showed dynamic new adaptive tendencies during the early modern period:

> The pressure to amass greater military capacities, a prerequisite for political success in the competitive Indian world, gave rise to innovations in administration, including incipient state bureaucracies, fiscal rationalization, standardization of weights and measures, and military reorganizations. All of these required heavy state expenditures. To meet these new financial demands, states also promoted the

---

[79] Ibid., 259–61.
[80] Ibid., 350.
[81] Ibid., 187.

economic development of their realms, including support for the expansion of agriculture.[82]

There were no—and here we are reading backwards anachronistically for clarification purposes—resources for a politics of bio-power where the population becomes the object of a future-oriented political strategy.[83] Thus, the Akbarian experience as a policy experiment neither extended wealth accumulation nor significantly altered the Mughal class structure, i.e. investing in the economy or public works, fostering trade or industry, or in promoting a stable landed aristocracy. The court dialogic revolution could not, of itself, counterbalance the wider field of forces shaped by the Mughal history of violence. Underlying emergent relations of meaning grounded in Enlightenment discourses were embedded relations of power. The growing empire, rooted in a politics of exploitation, was organized to view growth (i.e. increased consumption or merchant activity) as an occasion for extortion. The very climate of emergent industrial violence—the proliferation of new arms, the military-scientific dimension of state-making—made state survival dependent upon patterns of predatory wealth accumulation severely in conflict with the emergent ruling ideology of "Universal Peace." Institutional ensembles have a language of action not necessarily in harmony with the more limited ends of their official discourses. The geographic-spatial arrangement of the empire—as an extractor of surplus and war machine—implied an opposed ideology as it faced the rudimentary limits of conquest. This double personality was manifested at the porous frontiers of the Mughal Empire:

> [T]he humid conditions of Bengal, in combination with its extensive network of waterways hindering the movement of cavalry, contributed to Bengal's relatively independent position throughout its history. The Mughals considered it an area of almost permanent sedition, a *bulghakkhana*, or a 'house of strife', as they called it.[84]

[82] Parthasarathi, *Why Europe Grew Rich*, 57.
[83] Michel Foucault, *Security, Territory, Population. Lectures at the College de France 1977–78*.
[84] Jos Gommans, *Mughal Warfare: Indian Frontiers and High Roads to Empire 1500–1700* (London: Routledge, 2002), 40.

The Mughal world in the Akbar period was like several jigsaw puzzles mixed together: extraordinarily progressive in parts, but the parts did not all fit together. Yet given the Indian subcontinent's 17th- to 18th-century commercial boom, and emerging elite awareness of political stakes in multiple alternative state-making futures, it is difficult to say what might have happened had the British not subordinated (i.e. deindustrialized) India's economy to that of industrializing Britain—thereby dissipating the "reservoir of knowledge and skill that had been amassed in India over many years" and producing a 19th-century "divergence not only in income but also in skill."[85]

INSTITUTIONAL AND IDEATIONAL TEMPLATE BETWEEN COURT POLITICS, PUBLIC POLICY AND EVERYDAY LIFE

In 1562, Akbar was moved by the music of some minstrels to make the pilgrimage to Khwaja Mu'inu'd-Din Chishti's shrine. The shrine of this 13th-century founder of Chishti Sufism, who taught that "if one is very hurt, one should pray to God to guide one's enemy toward the right path," became a frequent pilgrimage site for the Emperor.[86] He sometimes went barefoot to display modesty. The Chishtiyya were consistently non-violent. Shaikh Hamidu'd-Din, from among the founders, urged that no harm be done to any form of life and pleaded that his followers be totally vegetarian. On being asked by a disciple where the harm lay if the meat came from a butcher shop, the Shaikh replied "the butcher would have to kill again in order to replace the meat that was sold."[87] They also valued dialogue to resolve difference rather than force: "Annihilate the enemy by discussion."[88] These attitudes represent moral over coercive power, or the principle of non-violence.

---

[85] Parthasarathi, *Why Europe Grew Rich*, 13.
[86] Saiyid Athar and Abbas Rizvi, *A History of Sufism in India: Volume I* (New Delhi: Munshiram Manoharlal Publishers, 1997), 123.
[87] Ibid., 128.
[88] Ibid., 147.

It is from 1562 that many of Akbar's humanitarian reforms began.[89] The 1562 decree to "abolish the enslavement of the families of captives finally stemmed the tide of forcible conversions to Islam." Akbar's rejection of proselytization formed part of a broader Chishtiyya Sufi outlook.[90] The Chishti treatises of Akbar's time expressed a "plea for the illegitimacy of considering Islam as superior to any other religion." They argued that as the "whole world is a manifestation of love," there is "no precedence of one religion over another."[91] This reflects the predominant influence upon them of Ibn Arabi (1165–1240) since at least the 14th century.[92] By the 1570s Akbar appeared to be an exclusive devotee of the Chishti saints.[93] On this basis we may consider Akbar as belonging in a paradoxical way to the tradition of non-violence in Indian political and intellectual history. Paradoxical because, for example, he laid down humane rules for awarding punishment and from 1582 prohibited the imposition of capital punishment by his officers—yet, as an absolute autocrat, preserved that prerogative for himself.[94]

The politics of Akbar's reign was directly enmeshed in the tensions resulting from the "strife between *shariat* (Muslim Law) and *tariqat* (Sufism) which had started in West Asia with the rise of Sufism."[95] For important Sufi currents, the way to God was through the unique individual path leading to extinction of desire and conscious thought rather than outward obedience to traditional religious authority. Al-Hasan al-Basri (643–728 BC) said: "I have not served God from fear of hell for I should be a wretched hireling if I served him from fear."[96] The long-term struggle of the *ulama* to keep the ambiguous pantheistic tendencies of

[89] Ibid., 126.
[90] Ibid., 425.
[91] Muzaffar Alam, "The Mughals, the Sufi Shaiks and the Formation of the Akbari Dispensation," in *Modern Asian Studies*, ed. Joya Chatterji (Cambridge: Cambridge University Press, 2008), 28.
[92] Neeru Misra, *Sufis and Sufism: Some Reflections* (New Delhi: Manohar, 2004), 129.
[93] Alam, *Asian Studies*, 29.
[94] Eraly, *Mughal World*, 265.
[95] Chandra, *Medieval India*, 431.
[96] Quoted in William Theodore de Bary, "The Mystis," in *Sources of Indian Tradition,* comp. Arthur Llewellyn Basham, Ramchandra Narayan

predominant Chishti Sufism in conformity with received doctrine was transformed into a public sphere of open contestation with *Ibadat Khana* (house of worship). The *Ibadat Khana*, a large rectangular building built around the cell of a Sufi saint, was opened for theological consultations or discussions in 1575. It is possible that, reflecting upon his unbroken line of success in empire building, Akbar initially turned to the Sunni theologians to instruct him in implementing the dictates of God (the *Shari' a*) as a show of gratitude. He was about 30 years old. We hear: "Moved by a feeling of gratitude for his past successes, he would sit many a morning alone in prayer and mediation on a large flat stone from an old ruined building, which lay near the palace in a lonely spot."[97]

The influence of Safavid Iran may also have figured: when Shah Ismail proclaimed Twelver Shi'ism the basis of the Safavid regime founded in 1501, he established his own unlimited sovereignty as religious guide. Akbar may have aspired to such a status within the Sunni framework and hoped to obtain recognition from theologians of his own supreme position. Shah Ismail also imposed an organized class of orthodox Shi'ite clerics assigned to oversee the elimination of all religious dissent. If Akbar was inspired by the first step, seeking his own unlimited sovereignty, he rejected the second step because tolerance was the religious cornerstone of his practical policies.[98]

Whatever the initial motivation, the upshot of the project of *Ibadat Khana* was that the theologians quarrelled fiercely, and Akbar grew disillusioned. Thus, although at first only Muslims were admitted (Sufi shaikhs, *ulama*, learned men and the Emperor's companions) after 1578 Akbar made the unprecedented move of opening the doors of the debate to Hindus, Jains, Christians and Zoroastrians. The ensuing collision of discursive universes undermined the consensus over fundamental issues such as the finality of the Qur'anic revelation.[99] Mulla Badauni described the spirit of enquiry: "Night and day people did

---

Dandekar, Peter Hardy, Venkataraman Raghavan, Royal Weiler (New York: Columbia University Press, 1958), 405.

[97] Husain, *Growth of Civilizations*, 120.

[98] Habib, ed., *A Shared Heritage: The Growth of Civilizations in India and Iran* (New Delhi: Tulika Books, 2002), 29.

[99] Chandra, *Medieval India*, 169–72.

nothing but inquire and investigate ... Profound points of science, the subtleties of revelation, the curiosities of history, the wonders of nature ... were ever spoken of."[100]

This occurred following Akbar's illumination of the same year, when he called to a halt the projected mass slaughter of thousands of hemmed in wild herds in a gigantic military exercise intended to demonstrate the empire's might.[101] The animals were released into the wild and messages sent that "no one should be guilty of even killing a sparrow."[102] In the history of nonviolence, this was perhaps a pinnacle symbolic moment of moral over coercive power. This series of explorative actions, showing an inner spiritual malaise and growing separation from tradition, express a crisis of doubt about the legacies of the past. Akbar's courtier Asad Beg expressed this view: "Things must be judged according to their good or bad qualities, and the decision must be according to the facts of the case ... every custom in the world has been new at one time or another."[103]

Discussions at the *Ibadat Khana* bear testimony to this emergent worldview. Father Monserrate of the Jesuit Mission, a guest at Akbar's court, recorded the emperor saying:

> I perceive that there are varying customs and beliefs of varying religious paths. ... But the followers of each religion regard the institutions of their own religion as better than those of any other.... And this has caused me many serious doubts and scruples.[104]

In this, we have the Enlightenment criticism of the violent practical implications of dogma. Akbar elsewhere described the world as a distressful place of contradictions where "dimness of comprehension, and conceit, are heaped up, layer upon layer, [so] not a single step can be taken without the torch of

---

[100] Eraly, *Mughal World*, 341.
[101] Ali, *Mughal India*, 153.
[102] Shireen Moosvi, *Episodes in the Life of Akbar: Contemporary Records and Reminiscences* (New Delhi: National Book Trust, 2007), 71.
[103] Eraly, *Mughal World*, 341–42.
[104] Rizvi, *Dimensions of Sulh-I Kul*, 13.

proof."[105] Dogma was to be superseded by autonomous intellectual judgement.

Of growing significance in Akbar's experiment in *Sulh-i Kul* was the experience of doubt, or sceptical reason. Mulla Badauni remarked: "The discussions passed beyond the scope of the controversies of the Sunnis and the Shi'as, Hanafis and Shafi'as, and lawyers and philosophers, they attacked the very basis of faith."[106] In the process, lines of reciprocal exclusion between religions were also undone. Akbar's vow "to liberate and dissociate himself (*ibra wa tabarra namuda*) from the traditional and imitative religion (*din-i-majazi wa taqlidi*)" followed naturally from his doubts.[107] Closed in 1582, the experiment had two important consequences. It firstly convinced Akbar "that all religions had elements of truth, and all of them led to the Supreme Reality," and, secondly, publicly demonstrated the narrowness of views, bigotry and arrogance of the court *ulamas*. The basis for religion became the common faith of humanity, not unique truth built on sectarian hostility. It was a great undoing of walls. This experience for Akbar "led to the evolution of the concept of *Sulh-I Kul*" and had—in providing a creative reformist impulse and dialogic basis for conflict resolution—a "crucial role in the emergence of a new liberal, tolerant state."[108]

A major wave of humanitarian measures came after 1579 in the second phase of Akbar's reign following the onset of *Sulh-i Kul* with the abolition of slavery (1582), forced labour (1597), the decree concerning monogamy (1587), forbidding of child marriage (1595) and the outlawing of *sati* or widow immolation as a duty of the wife (1583). Akbar was quoted as saying that "the consent of the bride and the bridegroom and the permission of parents are absolutely necessary in marriage contracts."[109] There were also numerous policies concerning the welfare of animals: the learned Jain saint Hariji Sur persuaded the Emperor "to issue an edict forbidding the slaughter of animals for six months ...

---

[105] Ibid., 9.
[106] Ibid., 8.
[107] Ibid., 20.
[108] Chandra, *Medieval India*, 169–72.
[109] Eraly, *Mughal World*, 149.

and to set free many snared birds and animals."[110] Cow slaughter was prohibited.[111] That these policies were influenced by discussions with Jains is evidence of the multi-religious input shaping Akbar's policy. At the same time these reforms were articulated in a language of rationality based on compassion rather than appeal to any specific religious authority. Thus, we see a departure from a religious discursive universe (however unconscious) and entry into a new secular realm of ethics and policy. In 1580, for example, Akbar announced that "no man or woman, minor or adult was to be enslaved and that no concubine or slave of Indian birth was to be bought or sold, for this concerned priceless life."[112] The value of human life in itself became the criteria for condemning certain previously accepted practices. Elsewhere, Akbar directed judges—in secular terms—to pursue truth through "manifold inquiries, by study of physiognomy and the exercise of foresight."[113]

Akbar's reign covered "perhaps one of the most dynamic periods in Indian history, a time of profound social, intellectual and religious transition."[114] Within this setting Akbar created something new from the resources of the Islamicate universe as multiple cultural reference frames, each constituted of diverse political traditions often unfolding in mutual tension. Among the Indo-Muslim traditions was religious coexistence in the ruling apparatus, going back to the Delhi Sultanate, where we see Hindu officials in Muhammad Tughluq's administration (1324–1351). This pragmatic experiment was at the centre of impassioned cultural adjustments. In reaction we see Ziauddin Barani (1285–1357)—a court philosopher notable for his sober and neutral analysis of the role of violence in political change[115]—condemning the state as un-Islamic (*jahandari*) in its religious

[110] Pushpa Prasad, "Akbar and the Jains," in *Akbar and His India*, ed. Irfan Habib (Calcutta, Chennai, Mumbai: Oxford University Press, 1997), 99.

[111] Eraly, *Mughal World*, 115.

[112] Irfan Habib, "Akbar and Social Inequities: A Study of the Evolution of His Ideas," Proceedings, IHC: 53rd Session, 1992–93, 301.

[113] Eraly, *Mughal World*, 264.

[114] Koch, *Intellectual and Artistic Climate*, 2.

[115] V.R. Mehta, *Foundations of Indian Political Thought: An Interpretation (From Manu to the Present Day)* (New Delhi: Manohar, 2008), 134–57.

freedom and dangerous in recruiting the low born into administration (wine distillers, a cook, a gardener, a weaver's son, a low caste, a slave).[116]

It was also the era of Amir Khusrau (1253–1325) and Nizamuddin Auliya (1238–1325), Chishti Sufi saints revered by Hindus and Muslims alike. Amir Khusrau, a popular court poet, articulated India as a common home to all religions: "If a Khurasani, Greek or Arab comes here. He will not face any problems. For they will treat him kindly, as their own."[117] His father had been uprooted from Central Asia by the Mongol invasions and arrived in India as a refugee.[118] He celebrated love beyond the boundaries of religious difference.[119] His poems advanced an ethical principle of alleviating human suffering, evoking the pain of the mother in losing children to war, asserting the slave to be the child of a man, and appealing for Hindu–Muslim unity through everyday metaphors of non-violence: a "needle is better than a [cutting] sword" because it "binds."[120] These multiple discursive formations embedded in struggles over political power and meaning—rather than concerning merely administrative issues—helped to forge the boundaries defining India's evolving lifeworld.

Akbar was therefore not the first to undertake the experiment of constructing a composite nobility, but he was the first to create an enduring one.[121] During his reign, administrative religious coexistence ceased to be merely pragmatic and intermittent and was consciously raised to the level of ethical principle. It was in defiance of the Islamization project promoted by important sections of the *ulama* within the royal court. In the polem-

---

[116] Vanina, "Describing the Common, Discovering the Individual: A Study in some Medieval Indian Biographies," in *Mind over Matter. Essays on Mentalities in Medieval India,* ed. Dwijendra Narayan Jha and Eugenia Vanina (New Delhi: Tulika Books, 2009), 88.

[117] Sunil Sharma, *Amir Khusrau: The Poet of Sufis and Sultans* (Oxford: Oneworld Publications, 2006), 88.

[118] Rizvi, *History of Sufism,* 168.

[119] Satish Chandra, *Essays on Medieval Indian History* (New Delhi: Oxford, 2007), 297.

[120] Amir Khusrau. *Between Kings and Masses.* Print exhibition at Jawaharlal Nehru Institute of Advanced Study, Jawaharlal Nehru University, New Delhi, 2010.

[121] Ali, *Mughal India,* 64.

ics, a rich reservoir of historical components was available for reconstruction: the Islamicate Turko-Mughal and Afghan traditions, the Timurid traditions influenced by Ibn Arabi's philosophy of *wahdat-al-wajud* (Unity of Being), and the Persian absolutist tradition. These converged with the rich and diverse universe of Indian political traditions going back to the non-violent messages of the *Mahabharata* and Emperor Ashoka (3rd century BC), who promoted a public policy based on an ideal of universal tolerance and rationality: "a man must not do reverence to his own sect or disparage that of another without reason. Depreciation should be for a specific reason only, because the sects of other people all deserve reverence for one reason or another."[122] Ashoka, a proponent of non-violence, converted to Buddhism after being horrified by the carnage of his own victorious battle. He subsequently laid down perhaps "the oldest rules for conducting debates and disputations," demonstrating the historical depth of India's dialogic tradition as a political alternative to violence.[123] Ashoka's reign belonged to the period of early Indian republics from about 600 BC to 200 AD, based on "village councils composed of elected representatives with wide executive and judicial powers" including "distributing land and collecting taxes."[124]

By creatively selecting from this wealth of currents and rejecting others, however tacitly, Akbar affirmed certain contemporary values over others as an institution builder within the specific political horizon of his time. We see the emergence of an institutional ethics. The ideal, if not the reality, of the Islamicate universal empires of the 16th century was heaven sent stasis. Yet with Akbar's reign, whatever his real intentions, we see the liberation of temporal sovereignty and energies from theological dogma grounded in the religious neutrality of the state: "No man should be interfered with on account of his religion, and everyone should be allowed to change his religion, if he liked."[125] This is a surprising declaration from a 16th-century Islamic state, and requires

---

[122] Amartya Sen, *Development as Freedom* (New Delhi: Oxford, 2000), 236.

[123] Sen, *Argumentative Indian*, 37.

[124] Alan Thomas Wood, *Asian Democracy in World History* (London: Routledge, 2003), 33–35.

[125] Fazl, *A-In-I Akbari. I*, 217.

elucidation within a multi-layered context We see many important turning points within the space of roughly three decades, from 1560 to 1590. Although at spatial remove, the broader world of Mughal public policy and the narrower one of royal court politics were not two parallel entities. They were interlocked and developing worlds harbouring fierce tensions over alternate goals and values. While Akbar's public policy increasingly aimed at the rule of multi-religious composite nobility, the Sunni *ulama* continued to dominate the court from the early 1560s to the mid-1570s bent on a programme of Islamization. Finally, beyond the enclosed and limited political drama of the royal court, and the macro-changes instituted by the Mughal policy of centralization, we have the far broader world of everyday life constituted by almost limitless temporal horizons: youth old age, work, pregnancy, prayer, consumption, habit, sickness, hunger, migration, death, renunciation, exile, revolt, dreams, marriage and so on.

Much of the population did not *exist* at least politically from the point of view of the state: peasants were exploitable and nomads were non-persons to be eliminated. An insurmountable barrier separated the emperor from his subjects.[126] Yet these three domains, often conditioned by overlapping religious frames of reference, interacted constantly in multi-centred fashion. The conquest, centralization and urbanization triangle oppressed the peasantry and revolts over taxes spanned the Mughal period.[127] In the artisanal sector, a tradition of *hartel* existed, with the whole multitude shutting up shop.[128] We find that, at the phenomenological level, this was not *necessarily* an Islamic state at all. In Rajasthani literature, we hear that "Akbar's is a Hindu Raj"; the bardic Rajput traditions of the era often equate Akbar with Ram.[129] The ambiguous logic of such pervasive popular attitudes—clearly not based on the Aristotelian metaphysical principle of essential identity (nature, substance, being *qua* being, or what something *really is*)—was hinted at in the writings of

---

[126] Eraly, *Mughal World*, 222.

[127] Irfan Habib, *Essays on Indian History: Towards a Marxist Perception* (New Delhi: Tulika, 2007), 145–55.

[128] Ibid., 256.

[129] Mukhia, *Mughals*, 63; Richards, *Mughal Empire*, 23.

Amir Khusrau, who formed a link between the royal court and the popular Sufi movements.

By contrast, such Aristotelian principles were politically in play where tensions within the royal court were being directly aggravated by upheavals in the surrounding society. The Islamicate world in the later 16th century experienced general anxiety as Islam neared the first millennium of its existence. A yearning for the imagined purity of the Prophet's era erupted into a swarm of millennial protest movements against the decrepitude of the existing order. The most powerful Indian variant, the Mahdawi movement, targeted the *ulama* as the source of corruption and the rulers as their protectors. Although the Mahdawi members were mostly Afghans, vanquished in the Mughal–Rajput–Afghan wars and subsequently excluded from the new order, their struggle was envisioned beyond such political contingency. Their actions were linked to unique contact with the pristine universal.[130] We must differentiate between Islamic millenarianism as essentially radical movements appealing to a higher universal force of mysticism beyond formal legalism, and the orthodox *ulama*, which remained firmly anchored within the existing power arrangement—adhering defensively to conservative politics as the true embodiment of the universal. Both views, however, share the logic of essential identity typical of either official defenders of institutional religion (Muslim or Hindu) invested in power structures—or those employing religion as an axis of politicization for violent and exclusivist purposes. Short of an Archimedean view, glimpsing total reality from outside of the world, there exists no basis for ontological judgement over whether popular or official, or Arabian, Kashmiri or Senegalese, manifestations of religious practice and experience are more or less pure, diluted, authentic, etc., as traditions, except from a purely human and immanent perspective.[131]

Instead, we have to look at the historicity underlying views and identities. Historicity implies temporal horizons and power arrangements. The conservatism of the Sunni *ulama* was based

---

[130] Richards, *Mughal Empire*, 38.
[131] The "Archimedean" is Akeel Bilgrami's concept: see his "Secularism, Nationalism, and Modernity," in *Secularism and its Critics*, ed. Rajeev Bhargava (New Delhi: Oxford University Press, 2009).

ideologically on al-Ghazali's (1058–1111) creed of pristine revival—a legacy of intellectual revolt against the dominance of Greek philosophy, Ibn Sina's inviolable natural law and the Mutazilite philosophical tradition of rational free will, in the name of unquestioning observance of outward form in daily life.[132] Their contemporary anxieties concerned the dual threat of menacing changes in the Emperor's politics and the danger of millennial revolts. They accordingly organized a counterattack targeting anyone who stepped outside the lines of orthodoxy. As Akbar increasingly "made the Mughal Empire into a neutral force as far as the internal controversies of Islam," the orthodox elements, experiencing the loss of their power, "inflated the decline of the *ulama*'s influence into a decline of Islam."[133]

Thus, the orthodox Shaikh Abdun Nabi set about making life impossible for all those who differed with him. He undertook an "orgy of capital punishments in the name of elimination of sinful innovations and of retrieving the prestige of orthodox Sunnism."[134] We notice a link between inflated ontological claims and violence, when something rather more personal was at stake. Mounting tensions between the Emperor and the *ulama* reached a critical level in 1579. When a Mathura Brahmin usurped public funds intended for a mosque to build a Hindu temple, he was executed on the *ulama*'s orders despite Akbar's misgivings.[135]

Victims of this persecution wave included those enlightened philosophers who would later dominate the politics and intellectual life of Akbar's court: Shaikh Mubarak and his sons Abul Fazl and Faizi. Mubarak's public discourses in Agra in 1543 earned him the suspicion of the *ulama*, and in 1569 he was banished on charges of spreading heresy. The Mubarak family experienced social exile and extremes of privation because of the persecution.[136] To their good fortune, Faizi—admitted to the court in 1567—pleaded on their behalf. In 1569–70 the family was saved

---

[132] Imam Abu Hamid al-Ghazzali, *Revival of the Religious Sciences*, trans. Muhammad Mahdi al-Sharif (Beirut, Lebanon: Dar al-Kotob Al Haditha), 392.

[133] Ali, *Mughal India*, 166.

[134] Rizvi, *Dimensions of Sulh-I Kul*, 10.

[135] Chandra, *Medieval India: Part II*, 172–173.

[136] Harbans Mukhia, *Exploring India's Medieval Centuries: Essays in History, Society, Culture and Technology* (New Delhi: Aakar, 2010), 10–11.

from its fugitive status by "the Emperor's compassion."[137] Under Mubarak's influence, from 1571, Akbar grew interested in the Sufi pantheistic doctrines of Ibn Arabi's radical non-dualism: from God as the cause of everything, to God manifested in infinite forms. The dualism of Islam versus *Kufr* (infidel) was also thereby rejected. His religion of love openly embraced tolerance where the heart becomes the "receptacle of every form."[138] *Wahdat al-wajud* (unity of being) presented the main intellectual challenge to orthodoxy in the post-Ghazali world. Ibn Arabi's replacement of the "finite God of religion" with the "infinite God of mysticism" accommodated all religious experiences and proclaimed a common human faith.[139] Ibn Arabi's ideas came under attack from groups targeting Shiites and Buddhists, who saw in the popularity of his thought an obstacle to their violent plans. In Bukhara his books were burned by a hostile sect.[140] Ibn-Arabi's infinite God of mysticism corresponded to Akbar's universal religiosity and his finite God of religion to the sectarian religion of the orthodox *ulama*. We see with Akbar the official sanctioning of the view that all religions are lived and used by people to reach a source of inner truth, and it is narrow mindedness to insist that only one is right or impose this judgement by use of violence.

Abul Fazl was raised by his father on Ibn Arabi's pantheism[141] and the Persian Illuminationist philosophy linked to Mulla Sadra (1571–1641). He was also versed in Aristotle and Ptolemy, Avicenna and Alberuni. His writings showed a consistent interest in rational philosophy and scientific reasoning.[142] His worldview impacted the emerging Mughal political arena as a public sphere. Abul Fazl and his brother won the Emperor's favour by

---

[137] Irfan Habib, "Two Indian Theories of the State: Barani and Abu'l Fazl," in *Mind over Matter*, 30.

[138] Rizvi, *History of Sufism*, 108–9.

[139] Rom Landau, *The Philosophy of Ibn Arabi* (London: Routledge, 2008), 27.

[140] Rizvi, *History of Sufism*, 250–54.

[141] Technically, his doctrine holds that God is transcendent and is never contained in the universe.

[142] Shireen Moosvi, "Abu'l Fazl: A Sixteenth Century Spokesman for Science and Reason," unpublished paper from the Akbar Fourth Centenary Conference, 28–30, October 2006 (New Delhi: Indian Council of Historical Research).

successfully contesting the theologians in open debate upon entering the royal court.[143] From 1572, Akbar's disgust over the *ulama*'s recent spree of violence engendered a change of political alliances and reconfigured the power arrangement. Shaikh Mubarak, Faizi and Abul Fazl therefore gained ascendancy at the Mughal Court. Abd al-Nabi and a companion, the main clerical opposition, were exiled to Mecca.

The enlightened philosophers introduced a rationalist approach to "fight against sectarian and communal biases in the society."[144] Abul Fazl pantheistically placed all religions in equality upon a secular plane: "... what is religion, what is World? There is one heart ensnaring beauty which casts splendour through many thousand veils. They have spread an expansive carpet, and it sheds forth many colours."[145] Widespread and innovative intellectual changes took place in the court. Abul Fazl's historical writing broke with the traditional *hijra* framework based on the *jahiliya*-Islam rupture, where only ignorance preceded Islam. The spectacular modern rupture of the French Revolution had an intellectual ancestor in this powerful Qur'anic ideal.[146] Following Ibn Arabi, Abul Fazl conceived an alternative time flow based on the birth of humanity where thousands of Adams existed before Adam, and considered the birth of the universe against the evidence of astronomy.[147] His works, with their concern for accuracy in temporal calculation, show a newly emergent humanist temporal horizon in history writing and the articulation of human autonomy. He advocates the notion of a social contract over a theocratic regime.[148] These scientific elements were in tension with the teleological mysticism invested in the person of Emperor Akbar—i.e. "light shedding ray from this Sun of the Absolute"—in the mode of early modern state-forming ideology that unconditionally preserved the sacred-violence link

---

[143] Habib, *Mind over Matter*, 30.

[144] S.M. Azizuddin. Dept. of History, Jamia Millia Islamia, New Delhi. "Legacy of Ibn-i-Sina (980–1037)." *Proceedings of Avicenna International Colloquium*, 10.

[145] Habib, *Mind over Matter*, 32.

[146] Its significance, however, has been exaggerated for literary effect, as by V.S. Naipaul in *Beyond Belief*.

[147] Mukhia, *Medieval Centuries*, 7.

[148] Habib, *Mind over Matter*, 29.

for absolute power.[149] The immanent and the transcendental coexisted in tension, with the institution of empire always fundamentally embedded in a sacred violence restricted to the agency of the emperor. Just as Elizabeth I had a man's hand cut off for writing a pamphlet, Akbar once had a man's feet hacked off for stealing slippers.[150]

Abu'l Fazl's writings showed an interest in secularized knowledge, including such advancing Mughal patronized technology as gun-making, prefab and moveable structures, textiles, air cooling and refrigeration devices, water lifts and ships.[151] This was part of a more general pattern of "growing Indian interest in scientific and technical knowledge from the late 16th to the late 18th century."[152] In all such technology, we see a reshaping of boundaries and a transformation of the future underway. There was an interest in scientific advance: Abu'l Fazl pointed out that zinc as a separate metal was unknown to the ancients, and so charged that "al-Ghazali spoke nonsense when he condemned sciences that were not manifestly based on the Qur'an."[153] Thus, the post-Ghazali animosity to secular science shared by the Sufis—that nature was an unforeseeable succession of unique divine interventions and not a predictable systemic order—is openly rejected by Abu'l Fazl. He declared the possibility of secular epistemic advance beyond Qur'anic revelation. His declaration of advance over the ancients is a heralding of modern knowledge. Abu'l Fazl was "more conscious of the geography of India than any previous writer."[154] He made unprecedented use of statistical information. His survey of the Hindi language and the Indian philosophical tradition showed an "essentially secular or non-sectarian perception of Indian culture."[155]

From 1571–80, a large influx of Persian refugees arrived and many entered the Mughal nobility. Hakim Abul Fat'h, whose

[149] Eraly, *Mughal World*, 48.
[150] Simon Jenkins, *A Short History of England* (London: Profile, 2012), 126; Eraly, *Mughal World*, 265.
[151] Habib, *Akbar and His India*, ch. 11.
[152] Parthasarathi, *Why Europe Grew Rich*, 185. See Chapter 7 "Science and Technology in India, 1600–1800."
[153] Ali, *Mughal India*, 70.
[154] Ali, *Akbar and His India*, 220.
[155] Ibid., 222.

father had been tortured to death by Shah Tahmasp on heresy allegations, became close to Abul Fazl. Mulla Badauni alleged that their influence turned the Emperor away from conventional Islam. In the Mughal court climate of "learned discussions" and "enquiries into subtleties of philosophy and *fiqh*," these newcomers brought some radical and unsettling ideas. Members of the Nuqtavi order taught that "particles of the body do not disintegrate on earth but are absorbed as a single mass into the soil and then re-emerge in vegetation or solid form possibly to be consumed by living things."[156] Fathullah Shirazi (d.1588), another Persian immigrant, gained favour at the court owing to his knowledge of mathematics and astronomy, and was asked to create a solar calendar later proclaimed by Imperial Decree.[157] We thus see, in the 1570s, the state try to intervene into the narrow parameter of public life (i.e. excluding the majority of the population) through permutations in the collective experience of time.

Abu'l Fazl characterized the transformation in Akbar's worldview from 1578– to 1582 as "the elevation of intellect (*Khirad*) to a higher pedestal (*buland paigi*)."[158] It could be that not only the new ideas, but also the personal experiences of these refugees pushed the Emperor to extend the humanitarian policies he had initiated more hesitantly, and mixed up with some markedly intolerant impulses, in 1560s (i.e. *Fathnama-i Chittor* in 1568).[159] Akbar's early reign had been more politically conventional. It was characterized by warfare and conquest against Afghan and Rajput kingdoms over northern India, with massacres, revolts and ritual suicides among the survivors of fallen cities.[160] Although Akbar condemned a massacre at Malwa, in 1561, he was by all accounts an enthusiastic adherent of the Islamic imperial cause in his youth. There is evidence that from 1562 (also the year of the Chishti shrine enchantment) Akbar's attitude changed towards Hinduism with his marriage to the daughters and nieces of a number of Rajput chieftains. He allowed his Hindu wives to

[156] Husain, *Growth of Civilizations*, 120–21.
[157] Irfan Habib, *Medieval India: The Study of a Civilization* (New Delhi: National Book Trust, 2007), 199.
[158] Khan, *Akbar and His India*, 87.
[159] Ali, *Mughal India*, 159.
[160] See Richards for a detailed account of this period.

keep their religion and even performed a form of fire worship in their company.

This story began when Akbar, at about 17, was marching near Jaipur and a Rajput chief offered the emperor one of his daughters, Bai Harkha, in marriage. Such Rajput–Mughal marriages became the basis for a diffuse political system based on the obligations of patrilineal kinship—an integument in the broader state centralization process. Rajput princes were admitted to high political and administrative office, while being permitted to retain their beliefs, customs and honour as Hindu chiefs. A mixed stratum of Rajput, Jat and other dominant castes became intermediaries between imperial power and the producing peasantry, while streams of wealth from the empire were diverted to their homelands.[161] No single group could occupy a position of dominance.

According to the testimony of the orthodox Badauni, the Hindu princesses had a role in influencing Akbar to "forswear beef."[162] By his own account, Akbar came to believe in the necessity of protecting animals and tried to refrain from animal food.[163] He said: "It is not right that a man should make his stomach the grave of animals."[164] Elsewhere we hear that Akbar's forbidding of the slave trade was in response to the pleas of a Brahmin girl who he kept as a mistress.[165] Thus, Akbar's illumination in liberating the wild animals and his opening of the *Ibadat Khana* to all religions in 1578, in sum his existential confusion, had for its partial precondition cultural difference mixed with the troubled experience of ordinary human love. As a 16th-century Indian Sufi wrote, metaphorically explaining the Unity of Being: "love appears easy. But in reality it reduces the lover to ashes."[166]

By the mid-1560s, a new pattern of emperor–noble relationship had evolved which fulfilled the expanding Mughal State's defence requirements in terms of a nobility of diverse ethnic and

[161] Richards, *Mughal Empire*, 14–20.
[162] Fazl, *A-In-I Akbari. I*, 202.
[163] Fazl, *A-In-I Akbari. III*, 446.
[164] Ibid., 443.
[165] Shireen Moosvi, "The Road to Sulh-i Kul: Akbar's Alienation from Theological Islam," in *Religion in Indian History*, ed. Irfan Habib (New Delhi: Tulika, 2007), 170.
[166] Misra, *Sufis and Sufism*, 133.

religious groups "amongst whom the Hindus and the Shi'as came to occupy a dominant position." This was incompatible with Sunni *ulama* Shaikh Abdu'l-Haqq's articulation of legitimate Kingship as "narrowed down to the exclusive benefit of Islam."[167] The state policy of multi-religious recruitment expressed deeper tensions between a new politics of individual merit and the persistence of the aristocratic hierarchic principle. Abul Fazl wrote that Akbar "respected merit, not recommendation" and "knows the value of talent, honours people of various classes with appointments in the ranks of the army, and raises them from the position of a common soldier to the ranks of a grandee."[168] To dispel any notions of impending democratization, we must note that the pool for selecting such talent was highly narrow, reserved mostly to upper castes.

However, at the level of popular attitudes, the historical interaction of Bhakti and Sufi movements climaxed in the 16th century.[169] This was the underlying popular wave giving Akbar's reign its vitality from below. There was Dadu (1544–1603), a cotton carder in the Kabir tradition, who became a popular preacher in Rajasthani, Punjabi, Gujarati and Persian, teaching the unity of political authority and denouncing the divisions of caste. We therefore see a democratic tendency in ideas from below. It was linked to a notion of unified political power. Dadu preached that there "would be peace only if there is unity of political authority."[170] In this example, we see a correspondence between a broad and anterior popular worldview as expressed through the spokesmen of the Bhakti-Sufi movement and the emergent *Suhl-i kul* philosophy as an adjunct of state centralization.

The rise of the Delhi Sultanate (1206–1527) had seen the Brahman nobility demilitarized and sent into rural exile, entailing the extinction of certain doctrines and practices of the Brahmin lifeworld. This permitted the flourishing of heterodox, anti-caste Bhakti monotheist movements.[171] Growing from the popular

---

[167] Rizvi, *History of Sufism*. II, 363.

[168] Mukhia, *Mughals*, 59.

[169] Satish Chandra, *State, Pluralism, and the Indian Historical Tradition* (New Delhi: Oxford, 2009), 149.

[170] Mukhia, *Mediæval Centuries*, 96–99.

[171] Chandra, *Medieval Indian History*, 300.

classes in expanding urban centres, the Bhakti both challenged the Brahmins and provided new social energies to be harnessed in renewed state-making efforts: the forces of civil society always having ambiguous reversible functions upon the multi-centred field of power. The Bhakti was historically linked to the spread of agriculture and the state based on it. In claiming that the pathway to God is a matter of individual choice, Bhakti literature contributed to a new valuing of individual autonomy. Akbar revered Bhakti saints to the point that, by one account, he stopped hurting living beings after meeting Dadu.[172] Dadu, in the tradition of Kabir, refused the Hindu–Muslim dualism: "Fierce and terrible have they become, when they saw I was of neither faction."[173]

Dadu's influence on Akbar represented a link between the royal court and the general population, for Bhakti popular psalms in many languages were widely revered across India among both Hindus and Muslims. Hailing from every social stratum including the untouchables, and with several important woman saints (Mirabai, Lalla), these saints reveal the prevailing popular valuation of sincere character over nobility or high birth.[174] Rooted in Shankara's (788–820 BC) monistic (*Advaita*) overcoming of all duality (agent and action, self and other) and placing self-knowledge above sacrificial rituals, the Bhakti tended to have a humanist worldview oriented to the life of this world.[175] The tradition contained a legacy of pluralism and tolerance.[176]

Kapila, founder of *Sankhya* (reasoning), asserted in an influential *Purana* that the "path of devotion is conceived in various ways" because "the minds of men differ," and hence condemned "intolerance."[177] Kabir (1440–1518), a low caste weaver in

---

[172] Vanina, "*Mind over Matter,* 85.

[173] *Sources of Indian Tradition,* 532.

[174] *Sources of Indian Tradition,* 351.

[175] R. Champakalakshmi, "*Patikam Patuvar*: Ritual Singing as a Means of Communication in Early Medieval South India," in *Cultural History of Medieval India,* 65; Shankara, "Commentary on the Vedanta Sutras," in *Sources of Indian Tradition,* 315–27.

[176] We should emphatically not assume that any religion is "inherently" tolerant, as if corresponding to an "essence." This "ontological" claim, sometimes made for Hinduism, is undermined by other experiences of violence and exclusion within the same religious tradition.

[177] Kapila, *Sources of Indian Tradition,* 336.

Varanasi, pioneered devotional verse in the vernacular to draw from both Hindu and Muslim traditions: "It is needless to ask to a saint the caste to which he belongs...The barber has sought God, the washerwoman, and the carpenter...Hindus and Muslims alike have achieved that End, where remains no mark of distinction... he who has seen the radiance of love, he is saved."[178] He declared the lord of the Hindus and the Turks to be one and the same, and urged the renunciation of all family, caste and clan.[179] Kabir also articulated concerns over the injustice of social inequality: "You've stacked up wealth and material things—all of which are someone else's."[180]

The Sufi Chishtiyya order, India's most widespread, arrived in the 13th century from Central Asia with an exodus of scholars and holy men fleeing the Mongol invasions.[181] Central Asian Sufis had experienced earlier formative exchanges with Buddhism in the 11th century.[182] With the 1258 sacking of Baghdad, North India (Hindustan) became widely seen as Islam's refuge and final hope. From its earliest days, this order adapted Hindu practices including devotional music, yogic breathing and concentration exercises.[183] The avowed principle of the order centred "universal love, malice toward none, simplicity and generosity."[184] This order, rather than Mughal state might, contributed predominantly to the spread of Islam among the Indian popular masses—as evidenced by the largest distribution of Muslim populations being remote from political centres in the 16th century.[185]

Chishtiyya's popular presence was widespread prior to organized Mughal power, and opposed the practice of conversion

---

[178] Kabir, *Sources of Indian Tradition*, 360–61.
[179] Kabir, *The Weaver's Songs* (New Delhi: Penguin, 2003), 120–21.
[180] Ibid., 118.
[181] Rizvi, *History of Sufism.II*,133–34.
[182] Thierry Zarcone, "Central Asian Influence on the Early Development of the Chishtiyya Sufi Order in India," in *The Making of Indo-Persian Culture*, ed. Muzaffar Alam, Francoise 'Nalini' Delvoye, and Marc Gaborieau (New Delhi: Manohar, 2000), 103.
[183] Chandra, *Historical Tradition*, 150.
[184] Phyllis G. Jestice. *Holy People of the World: A Cross Cultural Encyclopedia* (ABC-CLIO 2004), 178.
[185] Chandra, *Medieval Indian History*, 300.

in favour of spreading the faith merely by virtuous example.[186] We are thus required to think about social change in terms of non-violence as the alternative to coercive power, or the popular precedence of everyday ethics (character, habit, aiming for the good life) over official morality (norm, set of rules). Finally, the interaction between these popular forces and the state in this early modern context indicates the emerging political problem of hegemony. This is especially so because the Sufi shaikhs of the Chishti order, despite deliberate avoidance of contact with the state, became the preeminent patrons of the Delhi Sultanate. Though often living in seclusion and intense hardship—Baba Farid's children died of starvation in infancy—they played a paradoxically powerful role in politics.[187] For this the *ulama*, who never the less presided over important life functions (marriage, birth, death), was often jealous of their greater popularity *and* power.[188]

The relation of Sufis to state builders was fundamental: it was believed that spiritually powerful Sufi shaikhs were the valid sovereigns over this world. With the end of the caliph in 1258, Sufi shaikhs lent judicial and religious legitimacy to Indo-Muslim states. The Chishti belief that the state should strive for the wellbeing of the whole empire without privileging certain religious communities had acute significance.[189] It provides the ethical context, perhaps, for Akbar's 1564 banning of the *jizya* pilgrim tax which had done most to hurt the popular classes, or his 1575 pledge to pay anyone's pilgrimage to Mecca at state expense.[190] Emperors consulted Sufi saints as oracles. The Sufi, it was thought, had merely leased out political sovereignty to kings in order to avoid the squalor of administration, taxation and warfare, and to focus purely on spiritual affairs. Shah Ni'mat Allah Kirmani, the most eminent Persian shaikh of his time, spoke condescendingly to Timur, who had just conquered half of the known world in the late 14th century, saying, "My state is a

---

[186] Rizvi, *History of Sufism. II,* 166/226.
[187] Ibid., 148.
[188] Ibid., 161.
[189] Ibid., 225.
[190] Eraly, *Mughal World,* 227/317.

world without end."[191] The territorial sovereignty of Sufi shaikhs was theoretically unlimited, for their "home was eternity."[192]

At the beginning of the 16th century, inspired by the Sufi-bhakti alliance, the Indian subcontinent was deeply influenced by pantheistic philosophical views. Akbar's *Sulh-i Kul*, within this broader context, was derived conceptually from the pluralistic Chishtiyya order. This displaced the Naqshbandi order, who were 16th-century newcomers riding upon Babur's 1526 conquest. They were committed to promoting total conformity and obedience to the traditions of the Prophet and discouraging the customs of strangers.[193] A Naqshbandi sect undertook political intervention to this end, functioning as an active link between nobles opposing Akbar's political and religious innovations. The lead was taken by Baqi Billah of the orthodox Naqshbandi sect in a movement against the liberal, eclectic policies of Akbar. The Chishti sect, meanwhile, led a trend favouring "liberal elements under the slogan of *wahdat-al-wajud*" (unity of being).[194] This illustrates the depth to which abstract or philosophical ideas lent themselves to contestation among opposing political forces in relation to class, status and power. These ideas were anchored in tacitly democratic and open or totalizing and violent values and visions. They constituted discursive–practical formations, which the historian may interpret like many small smooth blue hills of mounting energy upon the historical ocean surface.

The visible convergence of Sufi and Bhakti movements merely expressed the deeper everyday world as "a force of social energy greater than the state."[195] It is false to exaggerate the unity of 16th-century Hindu and Muslim lifeworlds. Yet cross fertilization existed.[196] Hindu–Muslim marriages at the level of popular Indian culture were plentifully recorded, with a fluidity of conversion to accommodate family demands. In Varanasi 20 Muslims converted to Hinduism upon falling in love with Hindu women. When challenged by the Muslim witness visiting from

---

[191] Eaton, *History of Medieval India*, 134.
[192] Rizvi, *History of Sufism. II*, 172.
[193] Alam, *Asian Studies*, 24.
[194] Chandra, *Medieval India*, 431/265.
[195] Mukhia, *Mughals*, 33.
[196] Eraly, *Mughal World*, 314.

Central Asia, "they pointed towards the sky and put their fingers at their foreheads" to infer the role of Providence. Reconversion from both sides was frequent. It was common for Muslim girls to marry Hindu boys and convert to Hinduism. There is at least one case of a Hindu widow converting to Islam to avoid the *sati* obligation. A Hindu saint Kalyan Bhati travelled to Iran, converted to Islam for a period, and subsequently returned home to Hinduism without batting an eye.[197] In Kashmir, Muslims were known to worship at Buddhist shrines, and in western India Muslim cultivators offered vows to Hindu gods.[198] A Hindu sage in Bundelkhand wrote *Mahitaryal* which combined Qur'anic verses with the Vedas to demonstrate their shared underlying message.[199]

In sum, much of the population did not conform to the set rules of morality upheld by the official authorities of either major religion, spurning the strict closure upon identity. Identities were amorphous and barriers permeable, with the absence of sharp we and they distinctions.[200] And yet this was not a sign of decadence: the population was also deeply ethical. They identified with the values and ideals embodied in the Bhakti and Sufi popular heroes, who affirmed religious traditions while negating their exclusivity, hierarchy, essential identity and avowed political violence. This explains why the violent *ulama* efforts to restore order through capital punishment as a public spectacle paled with comparison to the non-violent demonstrations of self-constancy and ascetic self-mastery shown by Sufi and Bhakti saints in everyday life.

The Sufi and Bhakti popular saints met intellectually on the plane of immanence, where Advaita and the unity of being constitute a commonly inclusive worldview. It is without the ontological, stratified hierarchy of either the caste system or the notion of the infidel. This has tacit democratic implications. But their primary concern was self-mastery in the continuous spiritual struggle opposing inner peace and inner violence: "Keep your internal self better than the external one"; "One should not curse

---

[197] Mukhia, *Mughals*, 35–40.
[198] *Sources of Indian Tradition*, 384.
[199] Eraly, *Mughal World*, 315.
[200] Ibid., 22.

anyone."[201] Their values affirmed being over knowing (including ontological claims), habitus in the everyday over the best argument: "Fasting was half of the way along the Sufi path."[202] The underlying temporality was confined to the unique holy moment of the al-Ghazali-Ibn Arabi tradition. They viewed experience from minute to minute, as metaphor and fatalistic destiny. The two thinkers, while diverging on the issue of tolerance, shared a conception of time that greatly truncated the application of reason. The ground for the unity of being was prepared by al-Ghazali's conviction that the world continued to be created anew by God with every new moment. Consequently, to a Sufi "a new day ushered in a new hope of God, and a concern for future needs was seen as totally opposed to a complete trust in Him."[203]

For Akbar, as a state builder, such an understanding and experience of time was impossible. New temporal horizons were required for the conditions of early modern politics. He was forced to define a secular and historical time where the state may act in addition to the Sufi notion of present time: "engaged in worldly pursuits (a man) should pass his days in righteousness and well-doing, and in garnering the needs of his time; and if of a retired habit, he should live in warfare with himself and peace with others."[204] Akbar split worldly and retired time. The Sufi must carry on the inner struggle within his legitimate temporal sphere, while the duty of the statesman is to take action with respect to the needs of his time according to a secular rationality: "A man is the disciple of his own reason." Akbar defined the nature of being human in terms of reason: "The superiority of man rests on the jewel of reason." Finally, religion within this secular sphere is a misuse of its true purpose: "Most worshippers of God are intent on the advancement of their own desires and not on His worship."[205] There was a tacit claim to a superior sovereignty of political, secular and historical time over the eternal time of the Sufi saints in these remarks on reason.

---

[201] Rizvi, *History of Sufism. II,* 147/123.
[202] Ibid., 156.
[203] Ibid., 142.
[204] Fazl, *A-In-I Akbari III,* 439–40.
[205] Ibid., 425–26.

But unlike the post-scientific revolution thinkers in 17th-century Europe, Akbar's notion of reason did not regard morality as originating in a mechanistic and demystified world. It required no basis in objectified science. He persisted in viewing morality through the Sufi terms of inner struggle: "The first step in this long road is not to give the rein to desire and anger, but to take a measured rule and align one's actions thereon." In this non-violent spirit where self and other are one, one should "overlook the intervening enemy and view the Deity beyond."[206] Akbar remained attached to the Sufi tradition: it permitted him, in his struggle with the *ulama*, to bypass the Shari'a and establish a direct relationship to God as absolute ruler. This was the secular significance of the 1579 *mahzar* that permitted Akbar to rule on religious issues above the *ulama*'s authority.[207] Yet non-religious moral laws were prescribed within a universal secular space whose constraints extend to the state itself: "Tyranny is unlawful in everyone, especially in a sovereign who is the guardian of the world."[208] Akbar's concept of time evokes Dante's concept of temporal monarchy: "Temporal monarchy, or empire, is a single government extending over all people in time, that is, over all things that are measured by time."[209] All of this served practically in the construction of a multi-religious composite nobility and state centralization. It explains the tolerance of criticism in the time of Akbar's court.[210] It also explains the lethal capacity to respond to formidable challenge: Akbar undid the prevailing Islamic violence-sacred linkage, but reconstructed it to empower the early modern centralizing state. An early modern monarch in the Louis XIV mould, he reportedly never spent a moment idly or uselessly.[211]

---

[206] Ibid., 430/437.

[207] Moosvi, "The Road to Sulh-i Kul: Akbar's Alienation from Theological Islam," in *Religion in Indian History*, ed. Irfan Habib (New Delhi: Tulika Books, 2010), 173.

[208] Fazl, *A-In-I Akbari. III*, 451.

[209] Dante, "On World Government (De Monarchia)," in *The Great Political Theories (Vol. 1)*, ed. Michael Curtis (New York: HarperCollins, 2008), 180.

[210] Eraly, *Mughal World*, 343.

[211] Ibid., 41.

With Akbar, therefore, we see the articulation of a new secular temporal horizon in the Indian politics of the day. This was part of a larger secular trend that was structural rather than ideological. In the 16th century, a change transpired in the noble attitude toward commerce, with the traditional aristocratic disdain being replaced by a strong interest in trade activities.[212] Akbar once described the labour of a craftsman in his workshop as a form of piety, emphasising the desacralization of transcendental time and the new value in everyday experience. Abul Fazl urged a practical direction over Divine sanction from the past. He declared, within a clearly secular framework, the "duty of the ruler to work for the welfare of the common people."[213] In this spirit, around 1576, Akbar sought to curb "oppression of peasants by middle men."[214] Court painting during Akbar's reign was also released from traditional religious connotations.[215] Yet these changes coexisted with the ideal of universal religiosity. In 1587, Akbar founded a translation bureau or *maktab khana* to reach the "transcendent truth of religions" and Abu'l Fazl declared that "the pillars of blind following were demolished and a new era of research and enquiry to religious matters commenced."[216]

The year 1579 presented an open revolt. It was the culmination of a power struggle between Akbar and the dominant section of the *ulama* wedded to elements of the Naqshbandi movement. In 1580, rebellions erupted among a section of the nobles resisting centralization measures in Bihar and Bengal, and elements of the *ulama* took a leading role. Mulla Yazdi from Persia issued a *fatwa* insisting on the duty of taking the field and rebelling against the Emperor in a Divine vengeance. It concerned the *ulama*'s loss of their *madad-i mash* grants due to the alteration of the political power balance.[217] After 12 months the Emperor crushed the

---

[212] Chandra, *Medieval Indian History*, 239.

[213] Iqtidar Alam Khan, *Akbar and His India*, 90.

[214] Eraly, *Mughal World*, 276.

[215] Som Prakash Verma, "Akbar's School of Painting Mughal Vision and Approach," in *Akbar and His India*, ed. Irfan Habib (Calcutta, Chennai, Mumbai: Oxford University Press, 1997).

[216] Rizvi, *Dimensions of Sulh-I Kul*, 14–15.

[217] Chandra, *Medieval India*, 175.

rebellion and was "free to implement his policy of *Sulh-i Kul* which by now had crystallized."[218] With the 1580–81 rebellion, the alienation of Akbar from Islamic Orthodoxy was sealed.[219] The onset of *Sulh-i Kul* "put an end to the domination of orthodox *ulama* on the politics of government and administration."[220]

Akbar died in 1605. Shaikh Abdu'l-Haqq used his alliance with powerful dignitaries in seeking to replace "Akbar's policy of 'peace with all' by strict Sunni rule as envisaged by Ghazali."[221] We see the emergence of political contentions staked in open ideological difference, most notably in the War of Succession (1657–59). Akbar's great grandson, Dara Shikoh (1615–59), employed the Qur'anic injunction that no land is left without the guidance of a Prophet to assert the divinity of the Vedas and the Upanishads. He argued for the essential unity of Islam and Hinduism in his *The Mingling of Two Oceans* (*Majma-ul-Bahrain*). The work declared religions "separate in name, but in essence one with God" using the metaphor of an "ocean' which transforms "itself into drops, waves and bubbles."[222] Dara Shikoh translated the Upanishads into Persian to make them accessible to Muslims. He went to war against his brother Aurangzeb who was firmly identified with orthodox piety, the legacy of al-Ghazali and the Naqshbandi order. Aurangzeb won the war while Dara Shikoh was condemned as a heretic and executed in a campaign pledging to "uproot the bramble of idolatry and infidelity from the realm of Islam."[223] Had Dara Shikoh won the war, it is likely that broader appeal would have attended his reign and almost certain that an alternative political course would have unfolded. It was a horizon of meaningful differences, with values and possible futures at stake.

---

[218] Rizvi, *Dimensions of Sulh-I Kul*, 12.
[219] Ali, *Mughal India*, 160.
[220] Rizvi, *Dimensions of Sulh-I Kul*, 20.
[221] Rizvi, *History of Sufism*. II, 87.
[222] de Bary, "The Mystics," 438.
[223] Richards, *Mughal Empire*, 164.

CONCLUSION

In Western classical authors, we find selected components of the comprehensive notion that makes up the contemporary idea of political liberty, and support for such components can be found in writings in many Asian traditions as well. Just as Aristotle wrote on the *value of personal freedom* for a certain class, while rejecting the *equality of freedom* where women and slaves were concerned, we find many affirmations of the value of freedom in writings within Asian intellectual traditions. Yet the championing of the compound of the value of personal freedom and the equality of freedom for all human beings is of recent origin all over the world. The same logic applies to esteeming the *value of toleration* and *equality of tolerance*. Thus, Amartya Sen has argued that the "roots of modern liberal and democratic ideas can be sought in terms of constitutive elements, rather than as a whole."[224] We need not think in terms of a transcendent universal structure, with its tacit belonging to a specific geographic region and implication of being already completed outside of ordinary human time and space. In Indian traditions, we find a variety of views on freedom, tolerance and equality, and these currents informed political and social change in the modern Indian historical context. Sen's concept of constitutive elements implies the interaction of geographically or culturally diverse ideas as ambiguously colliding particles, avoiding the sterile debates on the clashing of monolithically conceived civilizational worldviews anchored in an abstract and tensionless Platonic essence.

Sen has also noted that the Mughal state under Akbar not only self-consciously projected a universal message of tolerance and dialogue but was also a forerunner of secular and democratic aspects of modern Indian state policy since independence. Because Sen evokes components, we do not need to suppose a long term 'Indian' structure of monolithic dimensions (as Ramachandra Guha has suggested)—Sen's theory suggests precisely the breaking down of elevated teleological abstractions linked to a single identity.[225] The Akbar experience, in this sense,

---

[224] Sen, *Development*, 234.
[225] Ramachandra Guha, "Arguments with Sen," (book review). *Economic and Political Weekly*, 8 October, 2005.

points to an alternative source of Enlightenment ideology in the context of organizing the early modern state, as well as a particular heritage of Enlightenment indigenous to India but which has also been influential elsewhere.

Akbar posed the question at the time of the religious debates, "Why assert one thing and deny another, and claim pre-eminence for things which are not essentially pre-eminent?" This expressed a denial of the kind of religious ontology that espouses a narrowly mono-religious view of any civilization, identifying one real heritage at the expense of all others. These thoughts expressed a step into a secular rationality—the value of a person, idea or culture transcends confessional identification and is to be judged based on its own distinctive merits.[226]

The following are the central ideas: *(a)* an *epistemic conception of God* as opposed to an immediacy of religious experience. This is to say that "God is to be grasped and worshipped by different men according to the limitations of their knowledge."[227] *(b)* The first is linked directly to the *distinction between blind following (taqlid) and reason (aql)*, for "blind following" is an immediate form of experience unmediated by reflection or rationality and at worst leads to the violence of mob conformism. Akbar came to consider organized religion as mere reflex.[228]

The essence of religion, Akbar argued, was "not in reciting the article of faith or getting circumcised, but in one's readiness to fight against overpowering worldly desires or urges."[229] The meaning of worldly desires as what comes unbidden, such as hunger, lust, mood, illness, fear, impulses to conformity, etc., are the key to the meaning of rationality in *Sulh-i Kul*. This is close to the pre-Hobbesian notion of rationality as the generally spiritual part of us which is capable of making decisions based on the reflective consideration of existing alternatives. This view corresponds to the *Ibadat Khana* practice as an informed choice made among multiple points of view. The new conception of religion developed through *Sulh-i Kul* centred the individual

---

[226] Rizvi, *Dimensions of Sulh-I Kul*, 9.
[227] Ali, *Mughal India*, 161.
[228] Ibid., 162.
[229] Iqtidar Alam Khan, *Akbar and His India*, 86.

consciousness, as "Divine Reality (is) to be reached not through formal prayers, but only by cultivation of the self."[230]

This public reasoning, polyvocal and consequential rather than metaphysical, avoided some of the trappings that have dogged Western Enlightenment reason in terms of solipsism, subjectivity and the peril of categories in political totality. These intellectual trappings were made visible with the French Revolutionary leadership as the opening of the Enlightenment as a mass political experience—the truly democratic historical moment on the level of popular practice. What is distinctive about the Akbar experiment, for all of its limits, is that it attempted seriously to undertake a politics of reconciliation. Such an ethic of reconciliation has sometimes been lacking in dominant frameworks of modernity as an avowed war on the past: we see examples of this in Western and non-Western nation-making experiences. The Indian National Independence Movement, also grounded in an ethic of reconciliation, introduced an alternative model of mass politics based on overlapping but distinctive Enlightenment principles. The comparison points to the ethico-political problem of means-ends in social change and the structure of the state in its interactive relation to civil society. This was one of the major political lessons of the 20th century, learned at excruciating cost.

[230] Ibid., 89.

2

The European Enlightenment: Between Revenge and Reconciliation

EUROPEAN ENLIGHTENMENT AS TWO COMPETING TEMPORAL HORIZONS

The 18th-century French Enlightenment notion of a "general will"—as a new theory of power—was indirectly enmeshed in newly crystalizing cosmological vistas. Underlying the choice of "light" as central imagery was the 17th-century revolution in cosmology produced by the discoveries of Copernicus (1473–1543) and Galileo (1564–1642). It established the sun at the centre of the universe, and undid the Ptolemaic system. Thus collapsed a mental horizon cherished since antiquity of man as the centre of a small cosmos where the Biblical drama of sin and redemption unfolded, i.e. Christendom. The political order based on the pre-Copernican imaginary institution of society was thereby forced onto the defensive. Members of the ascending bourgeois class between 1620 and 1650, enabled by new commercial profits and the centralizing state, conducted scientific research and initiated a "critical mass revolution" in the order of thought.[1] We see, in the foundation of Greenwich (1675) and Paris (1671) observatories, a growing government investment in science intended (in this instance) to assist navigation in the interest of overseas trade.[2] Fontenelle (1657–1757), a member of the French Academy of Sciences, expressed the haunting existential dimension of these

---

[1] Pierre Chaunu, *La Civilization de L'Europe des Lumieres* (Paris: Flammarion, 1982), 8.
[2] Colin A. Ronan, *Science: Its History and Development Among the World's Cultures* (New York: Hamlyn, 1982), 373.

changes: "Behold a world so immense that I am lost in it. ... I am just nothing at all. Our world is terrifying in its insignificance."³

The ethical implications of this insignificance were already recognized in the 15th century by the German cardinal, mathematician and astronomer, Nicholas of Cusa (1401–64). In denying the finiteness of the universe and the earth's exceptional position he promoted "learned ignorance" as the "recognition of this necessarily partial—and relative—character of our knowledge, of the impossibility of building a univocal and objective representation of the universe."⁴ He extended this insight in *On the Peace of Faith* (1453), the year that Constantinople fell to the Ottomans. It imagined a meeting of all nations and religions dedicated to a single faith in tolerance manifested in different rites. Politically, "learned ignorance" prioritized provisional consent among diverse perspectives: "Since all men are by nature free, every government ... is derived solely from the common agreement and consent among the subjects."⁵ Insisting that "all spiritual power is properly founded in liberty, not in coercion," he valued flexibility and adaptation in a process of learning, and suggested an ethic of reconciliation with its tacit non-violence.⁶

Hegel later articulated the powerful nostalgia fuelled by feelings of cosmic inadequacy: "Virtue in the ancient world had its own definite sure meaning, for it had in the *spiritual substance* of the nation a foundation full of meaning."⁷ The political implication is an established consensus preceding the construction of the nation, or "general will" as the unifying soul of a people. But having lost this primordial innocence of the ancient world, Hegel envisioned the perfected and harmonious community restored through the full objective self-realization of universal knowledge. The ultimate unity of thought and being implies the

---

³ Bernard le Bovier de Fontenelle, *Conversations on the Plurality of Worlds* (1686) (San Francisco: University of California Press, 1990), 32.

⁴ Alexandre Koyre, *From the Closed to the Infinite Universe*. (John Hopkins University Press, 1968), 8.

⁵ Nicholas of Cusa, "De Concordantia Catholica," in *The Great Political Theories. From the Greeks to the Enlightenment*, ed. Michael Curtis (New York: Harper Perennial, 2008), 179.

⁶ Ibid., 213.

⁷ G. W. F. Hegel, *Phenomenology of Spirit* (Oxford: Oxford University Press, 1977), 234.

retrieval of a cosmic horizon in the human situation on the level of public meaning.

In the 20th century, John Dewey was closer to Cusa in articulating an ethic of reconciliation grounded in intellectual modesty. He urged a "chastened sense of our own importance."[8] Dewey similarly evoked a many-sided conception of existentiality, rejecting a fixed and completed conception of public meaning demanding final assimilation (i.e. Comte's "laws" of society or history). He wrote: "Poetic meanings, moral meanings, a large part of the goods of life are matters of richness and freedom of meanings, rather than of truth."[9] This denied total understanding as the prerequisite for peaceable cohabitation among different individuals or peoples—on the contrary, respect is in *acknowledging* rather than *assimilating* the other within a plurality of meanings and practices. Dewey shared Cusa's modest temporal horizon rather than the Hegelian temporal horizon of universal unity in absolute knowledge as a mode of imagining public conflict resolution. The logical consequence was an ethic of reconciliation: " faith in the possibilities of continued and rigorous inquiry does not limit access to truth to any channel or scheme of things (or insist) that truth is universal (with) but one road to it".[10] It is an everyday horizon: "experience means primarily not knowledge, but ways of doing and suffering".[11]

The line of continuity traceable between Cusa and Dewey illustrates the compound of intellectual pluralism, an ethic of reconciliation and a tacit practice of non-violence in Western Enlightenment thought. The more famous French Revolutionary discourse of "rupture" within the same tradition, however, has manifested epistemic totalization and political violence. It negated, notably during the Terror of Year II, the spirit of toleration and pluralism at the origin of 17th-century natural rights discourses. Two conflicting temporal horizons therefore compete in the modern Enlightenment tradition: consensus as a provisional

---

[8] John Dewey, *The Philosophy of John Dewey* (Chicago: University of Chicago Press, 1973), 336.

[9] Ibid., 337.

[10] John Dewey, *A Common Faith* (New Haven: Yale University Press, 1960), 26.

[11] Dewey, *Philosophy*, 78.

end realized in multi-centred and nonviolent fashion through civil society, and consensus posited as the point of departure based on claims to ontological certainty (i.e. in "Nature," "History") and upheld through violence wielded by the will of the modernizing state. Often tacit ontological constructions of violence have been integral to the differing currents of the Enlightenment heritage.

The first temporal horizon concedes that all representational regimes must accept the inevitable pluralism of party politics. The second is expressed vividly in Rousseau's general will:

> [I]t is always right and tends to the public advantage; but it does not always follow that the deliberations of the people are always equally correct. Our will is always for our own good, but we do not always see what it is [12]

Ordinary human blindness is ranked below a transcendent public will, known only by the state elite on the road to a liberated future. The Enlightenment thereby negates its own premise in personal autonomy or self-reliance. This totalizing idea lent itself to the 18th-century policy struggle over primitive accumulation, or bringing populations and notably "peasants more directly under the state's control" in order to "enhance their productive capacity," ability "to pay taxes" and "produce more surviving children."[13] The second temporal horizon in totalizing Enlightenment has an authoritarian historical pedigree.

Combined with universal mechanism, one mid-17th-century "natural philosopher" advocated experimentation as the unique road to "the management of this great machine of the world."[14] There was a confusion of levels in this metaphoric mode of imagining, between law-governed inanimate matter and living beings. This had anti-democratic practical implications. Underlying this all-unifying temporal horizon was the successful Scientific

---

[12] Jean-Jacques Rousseau, "The Social Contract," in *The Great Political Theories. From the French Revolution to Modern Times*, ed. Michael Curtis (New York: Harper Perennial, 2008), 22.

[13] Isser Woloch, *Eighteenth-Century Europe Tradition and Progress, 1715-1789* (New York: W.W. Norton, 1982), 74.

[14] John Morris Roberts, *The Penguin History of Europe* (London: Penguin, 1997), 266.

Revolution, where Newton's universal gravitation replaced the double laws of celestial and terrestrial bodies with one basic law under a universal physics.[15] The Newtonian universe functions in a causally self-contained way with neither meaning nor subjectivity, in tension with the endless plurality of human imaginative lifeworlds. The totalizing Enlightenment has its doppelganger or ghostly double—but not "other"—in Romanticism. If "other" is being apart, Enlightenment is dialectically related to Romanticism. Each continuously recreates the limits of the other. Romanticism is the door that never closes despite imagined closures. The modern Gothic (i.e. Mathew Lewis' 1796 *The Monk*) celebrates the ephemerality of human lives and the longer—but equally doomed—ephemerality of power and states. At stake are different temporalities: inanimate matter is unerring, while living beings exist in achievement or failure. Social progress is the parallel development of capabilities and liabilities.[16] Continuously created new problems imply eternally varying fallibilities. The ethic of reconciliation recognizes the unfinished universe or the tacit dimension as the existential condition of problematic meaning upon everyday life horizons.

Between Descartes (1596–1650) and Vico (1668–1744), two temporal horizons compete between exorcism and reconciliation of the lifeworld. Cartesianism lent "ideological support to the linkage between science and state power," affirming Colbert's (1619–83) ideal of the scientist as a "disinterested servant of the state."[17] Cartesianism belonged to the new "adversaries of history" which opposed historical to "perfect knowledge."[18] For Vico, in the *New Science* (1725), the power of reason is generated imaginatively through a socially embedded historical process. He promoted an art of "middle terms" in political science, or the probable explanation from studying both sides of a question.[19] We see that

---

[15] Ronan, *Science*, 348.

[16] Michael Polanyi, *The Tacit Dimension* (New Delhi: Penguin, 2009), 50.

[17] Margaret C. Jacob, *Scientific Culture and the Making of the Industrial West* (New York: Oxford University Press, 1997), 48–49.

[18] Paul Hazard, *Crise de la Conscience Europeene. 1680–1715* (Paris: Fayard, 1961), 53.

[19] J. J. Chambliss, *Imagination and Reason in Plato, Aristotle, Vico, Rousseau and Keats* (The Hague: Martinus Nijhoff, 1974), 30.

"reason" was openly contested between the mono-vocal state and many-sided civil society on the issue of social progress.

Of the two temporal horizons, modernization as a purely "objective" process—excluding "subjective" values and ideas—emerged as the dominant mode of imagining Enlightenment and nation-making in European modernity. Hobbes (1588–1679), terrorized by 17th-century state collapse and seeking enduring political institutions, asserted: "between true Science, and erroneous Doctrines, Ignorance is in the middle. (...) Nature it selfe cannot erre."[20] This tendency reached its apogee in the French Revolution (in its "general will" dimension), where Robespierre (1758–94) said: "Everything has changed in the physical order; and must also change in the moral and political order."[21] In these two early modern examples of men confronted with the terror of state collapse, the conceptual construction of a unified Nature became ontologically primary. Its other was identified in the centrifugal ghost time of past ages. It is a dichotomous monotheism for the modern period, its historicist faith touched by the ghostliness of historical ephemerality.

The second temporal horizon—grounded in an ethic of reconciliation—suggests that there are multiple paths to Enlightenment. Between the two, the practical choice is between a ruling party and its *programme* of expectations based on "scientific" certainty, or the mass *movement* grounded in an open ethical norm in a consciousness-building and modernization process involving multiple subjectivities, i.e. mass participation. These alternative Enlightenments oppose an authoritarian metaphysic of historicism (total time) and a democratic ethic of non-violence (every day time). Interventionism opposes self-reliance as two possible conventions in response to the challenge of hegemony, i.e. the modernizing state's dependence on the solidarity and support of the mass of the population. Hegemony involves the tripartite interaction of multi-centred everyday life, the nuts and bolts of nation-making practice, and the irreducible depths of the social imaginary dimensions shaping the lifeworld.

---

[20] Thomas Hobbes, *Leviathan* (1651) (London , Penguin, 1985), 106.
[21] Hannah Arendt. *On Revolution* (New York, Penguin Books, 1990), 46.

EUROPEAN ENLIGHTENMENT AND EVERYDAY LIFE

The wider and often analytically invisible everyday lifeworlds were early European modernity's primary sites of struggle: the democratic ideal expanded under the pressures of emergent state formations, linked to the consolidating trade-war matrix. The individual body subjected to recurring scarcity and rising prices was drawn into regular revolt.[22] The everyday lifeworlds, state modernization bids and revolutions form a triangle: revolutions require popular movements, and "state modernization ... is a necessary prerequisite for revolution."[23] This triangle was the crucible for discursive–practical formations. The English rural illiterate masses, four-fifths of the population, reduced by steady price rise from the early 16th century to the subsistence level, were excluded from the emerging national politics of the 17th century.[24] Yet after James II's 1688 flight an angry crowd of thousands, including men and women of all social categories, intervened to force the nobles' hands when they tried to unilaterally decide the succession issue.[25] This new politics of the crowd was articulated by the Levellers, where "before the [English] Civil War no-one was heard asking for liberty in a 'general sense'."[26] They advanced a secular moral universalism: "regardless of religious differences, [men] are all equal and alike in power, dignity, authority and majesty."[27] In the Putney debates (1647) national enfranchisement and citizenship were conceptually democratized when the Levellers advanced the birthright argument. This rejected the hierarchic Roman republican and Machiavellian traditions based on education and reason. And so it was across Europe. In the summer of 1672, responding to French military

[22] Michel Foucault, *Security, Territory, Population: Lectures at the College de France 1977–78* (New York: Picador, 2007), 30.

[23] Steven Pincus, *1688: The First Modern Revolution* (New Haven: Yale University Press, 2009), 33.

[24] Maurice Ashley, *England in the Seventeenth Century* (London: Penguin Books, 1961), 23/81.

[25] Pincus, *Modern Revolution*, 7.

[26] Christopher Hill, *The Century of Revolution. 1603–1714* (London : Sphere Books, 1969), 49.

[27] Micheline R. Ishay, *The History of Human Rights. From Ancient Times to the Globalization Era* (New Delhi: Orient Longman, 2004), 77.

victory, a wave of popular protests and riots also swept across the Netherlands to transform the republic into a quasi-monarchical regime.[28] From the 1620s to the 1640s "whole [French] provinces [were] in bloody clashes with tax collectors" in protective countermovements against the exploitation of French absolutism under Richelieu's coercive politics (1585–1642).[29] England's 1786 "Free Trade" treaty with France inflicted French unemployment resulting in the wrecking of cotton machinery by Normandy workers.[30]

European states had historically been created "through a process of bottom-up, organic formation" where "rulers had to rely on the corporate bodies they inherited from the past, the local governance they enabled, and the resources they could provide."[31] New institutionalized modes of political participation were often

> unintended outcomes of the efforts of European statemakers to build their armies, keep taxes coming in, form effective coalitions against their rivals, hold their nominal subordinates and allies in line, and fend off the threat of rebellion on the part of ordinary people.[32]

This many-sided material struggle was the context for producing Enlightenment discursive–practical formations. With nascent capitalism and the new science, a border divided "cultural universes of the poor and the prosperous" just as the gap between rich and poor was widening.[33] Yet the struggles of ordinary people generated new democratic discursive–practical formations, suggesting that the components of liberty and equality might be extended beyond a single class or group to human beings as such.

Everyday life formation was multi-centred and long term rather than a teleological design stemming from a founding

---

[28] Pincus, *Modern Revolution*, 35.

[29] Jacob, *Scientific Culture*, 19–20.

[30] George Rude. *The Crowd in History* (London: Serif, 2005), 125.

[31] Avner Greif. *Institutions and the Path to the Modern Economy: Lessons from Medieval Trade* (Cambridge: Cambridge University Press, 2006), 397.

[32] Charles Tilly, "Europe and the International State System," in *Nationalism*, eds. John Hutchinson and Anthony D. Smith. (Oxford, Oxford University Press), 251.

[33] Jacob, *Scientific Culture*, 19–20.

moment of departure. It is the intersubjective world preceding individual existence and the world of work, where the "environment refers always to a horizon of potential social environments [and] a transcendent infinity of the social world."[34] Modernity, without point of origin, was globally created in widely spanning relations of interdependence via nation states and capitalism through the multiple struggles of everyday life—a multi-verse of interlinking conditions. The Industrial Revolution of the 1780s taken as a causal trigger—without temporally wider consideration of the coal industry, the post-Reformation land market, enclosures and overseas adventures—is a "capricious starting-point."[35] Everything was happening in socio-structural simultaneity through hidden interconnected factors and effects; yet within the dynamic phenomenological openness of labour processes embedding productive-material conditions linked to state modernization horizons (i.e. centralized bureaucracies, tax collectors, police). Viewed thus, modernity could hardly have originated in Europe or any particular country. The formative phenomenological particulars did not systematically conform to the logic of a single universal principle at the higher social physical level. Modernity was not created, as with the miraculous designer of the monotheist imagination, but emerged independently at a number of points within multiple provisionally stabilized hierarchic formations.

Theoretical objectivity attempted to identify a universal core in collective human interaction. Nation-making practice, analyzed pioneeringly by Machiavelli (1469–1527), promoted secular maintenance from above as a discursive–practical formation. The nation should "avail itself of the population in important undertakings" and build the institutional "ways and means" to do so.[36] Machiavelli centred the problem of foundation, where the republic confronts early modern centrifugal temporality. It

[34] Alfred Schutz, *On Phenomenology and Social Relations* (Chicago: University of Chicago Press, 1970), 246.
[35] Eric Hobsbawm, *The Age of Revolution: 1789–1848* (New York: Vintage, 1996), 27–28.
[36] Nicolo Machiavelli, "The Discourses." in *The Portable Machiavelli*, eds. Peter Bondanella and Mark Musa (New York: Penguin Books, 1979), 184.

THE EUROPEAN ENLIGHTENMENT 61

seeks stability within a "stream of irrational events conceived as essentially destructive of all systems of secular stability."³⁷ His concept of *foundation* was inherently linked to violence, referring to the "difficulties of preserving a newly acquired state" where the total "effacement of memory" among the population remains impossible.³⁸ He evoked the problem of hegemony within the inherently violent context of state building among a population united through outside conquest and subjected to the introduction of "a new order of things." Only effective violence can prevent the acts of "revenge."³⁹ The reference to violence and memory indicates the brutal stakes in nation-making from above, i.e. totalizing Enlightenment. It is as if Europe colonized itself.

The European social-imaginary of nation-making and violence were crystallized in the 16th-century religious wars—"the last medieval crusade [combined with] the first modern war between nation-states."⁴⁰ By 1564 the ideological contestation was exhausted and "each side sought to convert the other by brute force."⁴¹ Simultaneously, a principle of imminent value in political action was established: from 1560 Western European rulers were unable to blunt the revolutionary force of the religious crisis in a wave of civil wars and rebellions against constituted authority. These experiences constituted discursive–practical formations: "sixteenth-century Calvinists organized themselves into the first modern radical political party, analogous to the Jacobins."⁴² In time, the ideological content of such formations underwent profound mutation while retaining the exoskeleton structurally suited for political violence.

Top–down pressures interacted with new global linkages in collisions between placeless and accelerating market forces (futuristic horizons) and the cyclical embeddedness of localized

---

³⁷ J. G. A. Pocock, "*The Machiavellian Moment. Florentine Political Thought and the Atlantic Republican Tradition* (New Jersey: Princeton University Press, 1975), 8.

³⁸ Niccolo Machiavelli, *The Prince* (Hertfordshire: Wordsworth, 1997), 15/19.

³⁹ Ibid., 9/18.

⁴⁰ Richard S. Dunn, *The Age of Religious Wars* (New York: W.W. Norton and Company, 1979), 11–12.

⁴¹ Ibid., 13.

⁴² Ibid., 14–15.

traditional habitation rooted in geographical space.⁴³ In rural France, authority *was* the village, not something erected over and against it, and life consisted in repeating the same chores, the same festivals, the same loves, the same hates, the same stories listened to and learned by heart.⁴⁴ The new concept of civil society, meanwhile, was used by European urban intellectual elites in the battle against centralizing regimes, not for democracy.⁴⁵ Thomas Paine later adopted and radically transformed the term civil society to give it a popular and global democratic meaning. He transformed this discursive–practical formation to new ends. In 1774, Paine learned of atrocities committed by British soldiers and fortune seekers in Bengal and Bihar—mass shootings, plunder, famine—and relayed these images to American colonists on the western margins of British rule.⁴⁶ This act suggested the slow but meaningful viral power of popular movements emerging through the interlinked lifeworlds.

SEVENTEENTH-CENTURY NATURAL RIGHTS AND THE 18TH-CENTURY FRENCH ENLIGHTENMENT

The 18th-century French Enlightenment, an intellectual movement reflecting unprecedented educational advance, enters political and intellectual focus against this multi-centred background.⁴⁷ It viewed itself as an elite intellectual movement standing in principle for the cause of light, conceiving itself as the party of humanity representing the general will of the nation. It affirmed

⁴³ Karl Polanyi, *The Great Transformation* (Boston: Beacon Press, 2001), 35–42.

⁴⁴ Emmet Kennedy, *A Cultural History of the French Revolution* (New Haven: Yale University Press,1989), 32.

⁴⁵ Frank Trentmann, "The Problem with civil society: Putting modern European history back into contemporary debate," in *Exploring Civil Society: Political and Cultural Contexts*, eds. Marlies Glasius, David Lewis and Hakan Seckinelgin (New York: Routledge, 2004), 27.

⁴⁶ J. M. Opal, "*Common Sense* and Imperial Atrocity: How Thomas Paine Saw South Asia in North America," 9, no. 4 (July 2009), www.commonplace.org (accessed 24 December 2013).

⁴⁷ William Doyle, *The Oxford History of the French Revolution* (Oxford: Oxford University Press, 1989), 399.

the dynamic new horizontal plane over the vertical patchwork world of particular interests, estates, or castes of the declining feudal order and Papal jurisdiction. This critical moment combined science and economic development in a futuristic temporality. Throughout the 18th century, Western Europe literate publics came to believe in science and its power within the new civil societies and forms of associational life created with urbanization.[48] Here we find revolutionaries and civil engineers in the cafes, new scientific associations, the emerging public sphere and the expanding urban populations of brutal early state modernization drives who participated in the food riots of Britain and France out of hunger.[49]

The 18th-century French Enlightenment conceived human nature as an unvarying substratum underlying historical changes, and thus an Aristotelian substance beyond the temporality of conditioned relations. This substance was mired in a past of superstition and darkness lacking rational or necessary development. Through the "advance in the science of human nature ... to the discovery of the laws governing its manifestations," the philosophers anticipated "a Utopia in which all of the problems of human life should have been solved."[50] It is not hard to see that the substantive conception of human nature was comparable to Machiavelli's project of foundation with a similar tacit violence targeting those human vestiges of the past unwilling to cooperate with the single design anchored in the certainty only mechanism can provide. This was a shared discursive formation lending itself to authoritarianism.

These closed discursive structures of European Enlightenment are traceable, paradoxically inverted, to the 17th-century natural rights movement that valued intellectual humility and an ethic of non-violence anchored in a new secular worldview. Europe was divided ideologically between the national models of Louis XIV's Catholic Absolutism in France—hunting down his feudal enemies

---

[48] Jacob, *Scientific Culture*, 6.

[49] Jurgen Habermas, *The Structural Transformation of the Public Sphere: An Inquiry into a Category of Bourgeois Society* (Cambridge: MIT Press, 1991), 57–73.

[50] R. G. Collingwood, *The Idea of History* (1946) (New Delhi: Oxford University Press, 2000), 82/80/85.

like wild game to secure the unity of the nation—and the experiment in constitutional government of the Dutch Republic.[51] Very rarely did the early natural rights thinkers take an anti-religious stance: they sought to rescue religion from instrumentalization by violent and narrow sectarianism, by insisting on the ethical limits posited by imperfect human knowledge. They envisioned its transformation upon a public plane of immanence, not its destruction in an eternal battle structured by transcendental laws.

The individuals who conceived these early natural rights discourses were often political refugees, exiles of the long religious wars. Their doctrines promoted tolerance as openness to multiple ways in rejection of traditional Providence as a closed single way. The dangerous political stakes were newly centralizing nation states under powerful monarchs. The Providence discourse had traditionally decreed that "no diversity can be tolerated within Christendom" with "just one interpretation of God's commands, one road to salvation."[52] Early modernity introduced a dynamic discursive element: "God's knowledge made apparent to us as foreknowledge" with "no way of knowing it from within time."[53] This paradoxical claim to eternity provided a means to substantiating power claims within conditions of political disorder and multiple claims to sovereignty. It sublimated violence on transcendental grounds. The Revocation of the Edict of Nantes in 1684 and the Inquisition of Philip II provide practical demonstrations of the imaginative narrative of Providence as a national program of religious homogenization through state violence. Philip II's Inquisition provoked a Moorish revolt followed by forcible resettlement of "80,000 survivors in other provinces of Spain," the obliteration of their silk industry and the "last remnants of Arabic scholarship for which Spain had once been famous ... destroyed."[54]

Hugo Grotius (1583–1645), the founder of modern natural right theory, was a Dutch refugee in Paris in 1625 during the

[51] Walther Kirchner, *Western Civilization from 1500* (New York: HarperCollins, 1991), 58.
[52] Dunn, *The Age*, 11–12.
[53] Pocock, *The Machiavellian Moment*, 39–40.
[54] Dietmar Rothermund, *Empires in Indian History and Other Essays* (New Delhi: Manohar Publishers, 2013).

religious wars. He urged that the supernatural and divine be substituted with the imminent order of nature (a disenchanted nature) as an ethical mode of non-violent conflict resolution. The secret designs of God, routinely used to justify atrocities in the name of Providence, could thereby yield to an accessible and neutral natural law through which such violence might be overcome by autonomous human agency.[55] Recognizing the dangerous tendency of power to overextend itself, Grotius rejected the notion that might makes right and aspired to control more effectively our violent impulses and restrain them within proper limits. Conceiving public reasoning as polyvocal and dependent on self-reliance, he emphasized the "power of discrimination which enables [human beings] to decide what things are agreeable or harmful."[56] Pierre Bayle (1647–1706), a French Protestant refugee in Holland, argued in 1686 that concord in a state with 10 religions would follow if each religion adopted the spirit of tolerance on the grounds that it is "impossible in our present condition to know with certainty whether or not what appears to us to be the truth [of religions] is absolute truth."[57] Bayle made the link explicit between epistemic modesty and non-violence, while indicating the need for a secular and disenchanted space for public understanding and law within a functioning multi-religious society. He openly condemned Saint Augustine's (354–430) doctrine on the permissibility of compulsion in religious matters, which had been used abundantly by Catholics to justify violence against the Protestants.[58] These discourses of intellectual modesty, pluralism and toleration, often articulated by survivors of religious violence, attempted to create an alternative to the prevailing consensus on political violence as a solution to problems of religious pluralism in early modern state-making. They challenged the core notion of Providence that nature, society and war are ordered on behalf of a chosen side by a singular eternal will

[55] Hazard, *Crise de la Conscience*, 256.

[56] Hugo Grotius, "The Rights of War and Peace," in *The Great Political Theories from the Greeks to the Enlightenment*, ed. Michael Curtis (New York: HarperCollins, 2008), 321–22.

[57] Pierre Bayle, "Philosophical Commentary on the Words of Jesus Christ, "Compel Them to Come In"(1686–1687)," in *The Portable Enlightenment Reader*, ed. Isaac Kramnick (New York: Penguin Books, 1995), 79.

[58] Hazard, *Crise de la Conscience*, 128.

to the inevitable detriment of the non-believers. It was a demand for accountability in practice, against the necessary blindness inherent in action itself claimed by Providence discourse.[59] They were discursive–practical formations based tacitly on the ideal of non-violence.

Arguments for Providence-based divine right theory were themselves early modern, despite claims to a deep historical lineage. In their immanence, they tried to claim a transcendental root. They served centralizing states countering multiplying waves of rebellion and assassination.[60] This discursive–practical formation was inverted. Divine sanction was employed across the political spectrum: by aristocratic and bourgeois Calvinists to justify rebellion, constitutionalism and limited government, by Jesuits to justify the deposition of heretical rulers and by radicals to justify republicanism, democracy and communism.[61] All of them had God on their side. Providence was used to seal the hermeneutical-political vacuum produced by the Reformation and religious wars. It linked political violence to the sacred, inscribing the horror and pain of ordinary people in wartime with a mythic aura of beautiful fatality. The Thirty Years war (1618–48) saw civilians, in order to survive, turning mercenary as "their homes [were] burned and their families butchered."[62] In some places the German population was reduced by a third or more, with famine, disease, roaming packs of wolves, witch trials and mass migrations to America.[63] This was the immanent plane of ordinary violent death, later occluded by discursively reconstructed public memory claiming transcendental gears behind the violence.

The same natural right spirit of rejecting religiously sanctified violence moved Benedict Spinoza (1632–77) to argue that he "who loves God cannot strive that God should love him in return."[64]

[59] Collingwood, *The Idea*, 46.
[60] Dunn, *The Age*, 18.
[61] Ibid., 18.
[62] Michael Howard, *War in European History* (London: Oxford University Press, 1976), 37.
[63] Ernst Hans and Josef Gombrich, *A Little History of the World* (New Haven: Yale University Press, 1985), 194–96.
[64] Spinoza, "Ethics," in *The European Philosophers from Descartes to Nietszche*, ed. Monroe C. Beardsley, (New York: The Modern Library, 2002), 19.

A radical religious thinker of the Dutch Jewish community whose family survived the Spanish Inquisition, his writings caused his expulsion from the Jewish community in 1656 and later exile from Amsterdam by the civil authorities. Rejecting Providence, he argued that citing the will of God to explain events was the refuge for ignorance.[65] On these grounds he distinguished the political order from the prophetic order, arguing that "the true aim of government is liberty" while "complete unanimity of feeling and speech is out of the question."[66] This goes to the core of the difference between the two Enlightenments. Spinoza articulated a secular politics where "laws dealing with religion and seeking to settle its controversies are more calculated to irritate than reform" and "laws dealing with speculative problems are entirely useless." It is a usurpation of the rights of subjects to seek to prescribe what shall be accepted as true.[67] Through a political principle of offices, based on the Dutch Estates General, Spinoza urged a society where "men may live together in harmony, however diverse, or even openly contradictory their opinions may be."[68]

Spinoza's thought was a theory of conflict resolution for early modernity centring an ethic of reconciliation. He redefined God as limitless singularities unfastened to any metaphysical or teleological end, arguing that "there is nothing which necessarily exists except things finite."[69] Yet Spinoza, through philosophical Rationalism, envisioned a substantialist "programme for a science of mind [based] on the analogy of the established sciences of nature."[70] From this confusion of levels he held 'real existence' to exist eternally, from its own non-relational inner necessity, and that therefore "Evil and error are impotences; futile gestures against omnipotence; against Being."[71] This widespread tacit assumption, in time, provided a harvest of justifications for secular or scientific violence against error through epistemic

---

[65] Spinoza, *Theologico-Political Treatise*, ed. Monroe Beardsley (New York: Modern Library, 2002), 233.
[66] Spinoza, *Theologico-Political Treatise*, 228–29.
[67] Ibid., 233/227.
[68] Ibid., 232.
[69] Spinoza, *Ethics*, 146.
[70] Collingwood, *The Idea*, 84.
[71] (See *Ethics* definition 8/Quoted in) Dewey, *Philosophy*, 340.

totalization. This irony is grim when considering Spinoza's commitment to toleration, pacifist outlook and persecuted life of modesty and simplicity.

Historically and practically, then, the European Enlightenment was internally contradictory. The 17th-century natural rights tradition significantly differed from the universal logic of Enlightenment identified with the French Revolution: sometimes it inverted the modernity–tradition paradigm in its inside–outside configuration. These large inversions suggest the immanent interaction of multiple ideational components, not the universal as a supreme being independent of all that exists.[72]

ENGLISH CIVIL WAR: LOCKE AND THE BRITISH MORALISTS ON VIOLENCE

The case of the British Isles and the Wars of the Three Kingdoms—within the intertwined Dutch Revolt and the Fronde (1648–53) constituting a broader European crisis of absolutism—presented a curious inversion of the logic of the French Enlightenment. The discursive universe of Christian prophecy was used by the Puritan underground in England to deny divine law and traditional Episcopal claims, and assert an exclusively political or natural origin for the orders of the Christian priesthood. Radical Puritanism, as a phenomena of pre-Enlightenment, was an ambiguous mix of the deeply secular and deeply spiritual, with an anticlerical/hierarchical belief in the "priesthood of all believers."[73] This wresting of power from the priesthood by a large, able and noisy minority within the Church was coupled with a politically dangerous soteriological enthusiasm committed to public salvation at all costs.[74] Merchants, weavers and squires, organized into networks or synods, were hostile to the whole machinery of

---

[72] This is a reference to Hegel's 'absolute'. Otherwise, Hegel's dialectic went impressively far in explaining such inversions.

[73] J. G. A. Pocock, "Post-Puritan England and the Problem of Enlightenment," in *Culture and Politics from Puritanism to the Enlightenment*, ed. Perez Zagorin (Los Angeles: University of California Press, 1980), 96.

[74] Ashley, *England in the Seventeenth Century*, 26.

church discipline, their revolt grounded hermeneutically in the "right of the individual Christian to interpret the Scriptures."[75]

The clergy itself, following the Protectorate (1653–59), expounded a rational rather than prophetic conception of religion to defend their interests or appropriate civil power. Denials of their legitimate role in civil power were equally secularized calls for liberty over enthusiasm reflecting 1690s English deism — a response to grim memories of revolutionary Puritan excess.[76] It is unclear where modernity opposed religion in any inherent pattern within these seminal experiences in the early formation of Enlightenment thought and politics. Rather, the "Glorious Revolution ... pitted two groups of modernizers against each other."[77] The conflicting temporal horizons — consensus as a provisional end to be achieved in nonviolent fashion, and consensus posited as an original ontological certainty (in Providence) to be upheld through state violence — are a visible discursive–practical pattern in this early modern nation-making experiment.

The English Puritan movement originated in a mission of violence: the vocal platform of waging war for the Protestant cause in the Thirty Years war. Targeting the Arminians ostensibly over the predestination-free will debate from Saint Augustine's *Confessions*, the direct concern was the Arminian-James I (1566–1625) pattern of alliance followed to a fatally bloody end by Charles I (1600–49).[78] The secular ideological source of their ideas was Francis Bacon (1561–1626), who catalyzed the scientific revolution and argued that virtue was a social rather than natural creation. The plasticity of social and political forms, the shifted line of intellectual ancestry from Aristotle to Machiavelli, and the empirical centring of experience over authority were his intellectual legacy when "after 1640, all Baconians were parliamentarians."[79] These holy avengers, steeped in the early discourse of European Enlightenment, embodied colliding components and dispel delusions of pure identity.

---

[75] Ibid., 31–32.

[76] Pocock, *The Machiavellian Moment*, 105.

[77] Pincus, *Modern Revolution*, 8.

[78] Irene Carrier, *James VI and I, King of Great Britain*, (Cambridge: Cambridge University Press, 1998), ch. 3.

[79] Hill, *The Century of Revolution*, 89.

Although valuing the ideal of tolerance, the English Revolution was often conceived along political lines that subverted the pluralist premise of secular politics. This was notably in Cromwell's (1599–1658) belief that God's will was actively directing worldly affairs through the elect. In political practice we see "a minority's imposition of doctrinal and moral Puritanism by law not only on conservative and royalist Anglicans, but on dissenting religious minorities."[80] From the tension between the politics of the everyday and those of absolute ends, following the experiences of civil war and Godly rule, we see the campaign against enthusiasm that characterizes post-Puritan England.[81] This was one instance of a learning concerning the tendency of power to overextend itself from behind any ideological disguise. It was experienced a second time more than a century later in neighbouring France.

The English Revolution confronted the central Machiavellian problem of hegemony, or consent among an often resistant population within a centralizing regime newly established through a traumatic experience of political violence. The nationwide and professional New Model Army, created by Parliament to replace mercenary forces in 1645, played a revolutionary role in national centralization. It served as an enabling framework in mass political participation with its principle of merit over birth. The Levellers emerged from its lower ranks. Cromwell referred to "the people dissatisfied in every corner of the nation" and appealed for unity to "strangers ... coming from all parts."[82] The struggle for hegemony raged between the poles of consensus as an ontological *point of departure* to be maintained through state violence and efforts to organize the division of political power in an *effort to reach* consensus from multiple points of view. Ultimately unsuccessful experiments veered between "healing and settling" political orders (1653–54) based on the mechanisms of mutual promise, reciprocity and legitimacy implicit in (highly restricted) parliamentary politics, and exercises in the Godly rule which sought through military dictatorship to speed the religious reformation of the national population and so create the basis for

[80] Roberts, *The Penguin History of Europe*, 284.
[81] Pocock, *The Machiavellian Moment*, 101.
[82] Oliver Cromwell, *Speeches of Oliver Cromwell*, ed. Ivan Roots (London: Everyman History, 1989), 24/13.

a saintly social and political order (the Barebones Parliament of 1653 and the Major-Generals of 1655–56).

A dominant discourse arose linking the representative principles of republican politics centring justice and tolerance to a higher ideal of religious truth as the means to attaining the political closure of the Promised Land, or the "many signs and wonders towards a place of rest."[83] The dominant Cromwellian political discourse was a fusion of violence and the sacred in an intellectual climate where the idea of the union of Church and State had not yet been seriously challenged.[84] Cromwell consistently made the case that Providence was at work behind the curtain of history, linking violence and the sacred to a national destiny. In seeking to dispel doubt around the prospects for a successful invasion of Ireland in 1649, he admonished those who interpreted events as a "thing of chance" and thereby "rob God of all the glory."[85] In justifying the subsequent massacre at Drogheda to the Parliament he asserted that "this was a righteous judgement of God upon these barbarous wretches who have imbrued their hands in so much innocent blood."[86]

The question of violence, however, was not uncontested. Gerrard Winstanley (1609–76) of the Diggers said "We abhor fighting for freedom. Freedom gotten by the sword is an established bondage to some part or other of the creation."[87] Cromwell reflected on the question of violence in musing over the "strange windings and turnings of Providence, those very great appearances of God in crossing and thwarting the designs of men," and marvelled that God might "raise up a poor and contemptible company of men" to obtaining power over the nation. He linked violence to the sacred in asserting that "God blessed them and all undertakings by the rising of that most improbable, despicable, contemptible means," or violence. The "act of violence" finds its "justification" in our "hearts and consciences," and conscience is based not on "vain imaginings ... but things that fell within the

---

[83] Cromwell, *Speeches of Oliver*, 29.
[84] Ashley, *England in the Seventeenth Century*, 34.
[85] Cromwell, *Speeches of Oliver*, 6.
[86] Ashley, *England in the Seventeenth Century*, 94.
[87] Mark Kurlansky, *Non-Violence: The History of a Dangerous Idea* (London: Vintage, 2007), 73.

compass of certain knowledge" (i.e. Providential knowledge).[88] Violence and knowledge were cemented in a discursive–practical formation.

The uncertainty in applying the notion of Providence to a movement for change rather than preserving a static hierarchy was resolved hermeneutically by reference to the concept of progressive revelation by which "in every dispensation" including "the pulling down of the Bishops ... change of government, whatever it was—not any of those things but hath a remarkable point of Providence set upon it, that he that runs may read".[89] The image of running affirms the moment of pure action or experiential immediacy as deciding a transcendental meaning. From this precept a Divine Will was to produce law based on the interpretation of signs among the elect, and the sheer process itself became law in an ontologically conceived voluntarist idea of the historical dynamic.

Cromwell simultaneously embraced early Enlightenment ideals. He held dear liberty of conscience, asserting that "the judgement of truth will teach you to be as just towards an unbeliever as towards a believer."[90] He permitted the return of the Jews to England in 1655 after their expulsion at the end of the 13th century.[91] This outlook existed in inherent if unthought tension with his ideal of the nation as a vehicle of public salvation, as a "door to usher in things that God had promised and prophesied of."[92] Milton (1608–74), certainly a true believer in the Puritan cause, would champion natural rights doctrine in insisting that men "should be free ... openly to give opinions of any doctrine, and even to write about it, according to what each believes."[93] He argued that "all men naturally were born free."[94] He denied that either the church or the magistrate has a right to "impose

[88] Cromwell, *Speeches of Oliver*, 14.
[89] Ibid., 10–11.
[90] Ibid., 21.
[91] David S. Katz, *The Jews in the History of England, 1485–1850* (Oxford: Oxford University Press, 1994), ch. 3.
[92] Cromwell, *Speeches of Oliver*, 25.
[93] Christopher Hill, *Milton and the English Revolution* (London: Penguin Books, 1977), 154.
[94] Milton, *Political Writings* (Cambridge: Cambridge University Press, 1991), 8.

their own interpretations on us as laws, or as binding on the conscience."⁹⁵ But Milton also failed to differentiate between soteriological concerns of salvation and secular political liberty. He finally confused freedom and authenticity in a significant discursive formation. Following the disappointments of the revolution he came to "believe that a convergence of the human with the divine would be necessary before a good society could be built."⁹⁶

We see profound ambiguity in the practical and unconscious struggle between a modern and secular notion of knowledge. It is epitomized in Cromwell's 1654 aphorism that the magistrate "is to look to the outward man, but not to meddle with the inward"—implicitly based on a public ethic of trust and shared accountability—and his probably equally modern authoritarian observation in 1653 that "God hath in the military way (...) acted with (the chosen) and for them; and now he will act with them in the civil power and authority."⁹⁷ In this context, "opponents of the aims of the elect, as men well affected to religion and the interest of the nation, are not legitimate dissenting voices but merely interested and biased men of corrupted conscience and noisome opinions."⁹⁸ Hence, the historically recurrent discursive–practical dilemma—between public consensus as a unified ontological point of departure and a possible outcome of dialogic practice—rematerializes anew. This pattern later tragically haunted the French Revolution in its radical new secular language. We therefore see that secularism as such does not provide a solution to the risks of politics based on totalizing conceptions of truth.

The English Puritans were colourful and creative in their hermeneutical re-rendering of received religious tradition, "with a literary backing ... strengthened by a whole battery of pamphlets."⁹⁹ The central Reformation injunction, of basing authority on the Divine Word itself instead of received tradition, inevitably opened up a labyrinth of formlessness concerning religious interpretation through the minimalist framework they adopted.

---

⁹⁵ Milton, "*A Treatise on Christian Doctrine,*" in *Prose Writings* (London: J.M. Dent and Sons Ltd, 1958), 126.
⁹⁶ Hill, *Milton and the English Revolution*, 336.
⁹⁷ Cromwell, *Speeches of Oliver*, 32/25.
⁹⁸ Ibid, 18/17/32.
⁹⁹ Ashley, *England in the Seventeenth Century*, 41.

If they looked back, it was to a past so creatively conceived that it could only be of the future or at least the moment. That is why we find Milton in the Puritan tradition defending Galileo against the Inquisition, speculating about an infinite universe in the intellectual company of Giordano Bruno (1548–1600), and articulating an early discourse of natural right. Then, just as surely, we find Puritan and Parliamentarian Robert Harley (1579–1656) smashing the stained glass windows of Westminster Abbey and St Margaret's Church and setting alight the embroidered alter cloth of Canterbury Cathedral driven by an inquisitorial morality.[100] The Puritan opposition to the monarchy was itself based on hermeneutics. They rejected "Divine Right because they saw little in the Scriptures to support, and much to contradict it."[101] In sum, though the wide latitude of possible interpretation testifies to the human imaginative power in engaging a given text, hermeneutics based on any single discursive universe provides no secure foundation for the respect and freedom of the person.

The dominant and enduring discourse to emerge from the experiences of the two English revolutions—and which shaped 18th-century French Enlightenment thought—was John Locke's (1632–1704) formula by which the opposite of force is reason. Opposing points of view in the Royalist–Puritan debate—the first univocal, the second pluralistic—had both remained grounded within the hermeneutical space of the Christian discursive universe. Milton had argued that "we have no warrant to regard conscience which is not grounded in scripture."[102] Locke, taking the Puritan side in this debate, argued that the religious duty consisted in arguing, thinking and acting upon the problems of the world. To this extent Locke shared Milton's fundamental concern over correctly interpreting one's duty to God in a changing world—in an age where, cut off, the Book of knowledge presents a universal blank.[103]

---

[100] Ashley, *England in the Seventeenth Century*, 19. For Milton's defense of Galileo, see *Areopagitica,* 170. For his ideas on astronomy see the introduction to *Paradise Lost* (London: Pengiun, 2000) by John Leonard.

[101] C. V. Wedgwood, *The Trial of Charles I* (London, Penguin Books, 1983), 12.

[102] Milton, "Areopagitica" in *Prose Writings*, 182.

[103] Milton, *Paradise Lost*, 54.

Yet the breaking of the truth–violence–sacred triangle, an epistemological–ethical revolution tacit in natural rights discourse, was specifically Locke's contribution. He transcended this core Puritan tradition in a rupture with its hermeneutical grounding and entered a secular and material conceptual realm. While far from hostile to religion, Locke rejected the political discourse of Providence linked to Divine Right. He modified the epistemic demand for perfect certainty to degrees of assent. This was a critique of violence as theologically legitimized and a descent of reason from the unitary heights of the Platonic Idea. It entered the world of human temporality and dialogue. The rejection of the innate constituted a new temporal horizon.[104] By centring the "conception of human knowledge as falling necessarily short of absolute truth and certainty," the Lockean "moment of clarity" reoriented "philosophy in the direction of history."[105] It lent itself to an ethic of reconciliation over claims to totality.

Having lived through the Civil War, Locke was concerned with non-violent conflict resolution. His father, a Parliamentarian cavalry captain, being hostile to the Loyalists, had applauded the abolition of the royalty and the proclamation of a republic.[106] Shaken by doubt and political unrest, Locke by 1660 resembled his fellow country-men in being deeply fearful of political disorder. Locke was for a time a political refugee, escaping into Dutch exile in 1683 with the *Two Treatises on Government* (considered a seditious manuscript) and two years later managed to elude the British government's efforts at extradition. Locke's concern with non-violence was expressed in his "Letter Concerning Toleration" (1689), which declared it "necessary to distinguish *exactly* the business of civil government from that of religion," and "to settle the just bounds that lie between one and the other." The alternative, he maintained, would be "no end to the controversies that will be always arising."[107] Questions of an otherworldly or

[104] John Locke, *An Essay Concerning Human Understanding* (London: Penguin, 1997), Book 1, pp. 55–109.

[105] Collingwood, *The Idea*, 73.

[106] See biographical account by Simone Goyard-Fabre in John Locke, *Traité du Gouvernement Civil* (Paris: GF Flammarian, 1984), 1–15.

[107] Locke, "A Letter Concerning Toleration," in *The Selected Political Writings of John Locke*, ed. Paul E. Sigmud (New York: Norton and Co., 2005), 129.

metaphysical nature can never be exhausted by rational public debate, and must remain confined to the private sphere, or the "inward persuasion of the mind."[108] Locke identified as *above reason* questions over matters such as bodily resurrection after death. It is because they are *above reason*, and concern personal faith, that such inherently open questions are publically answerable (i.e. closed) only through political violence. People are forced to appear to agree.

Locke, at the same time, believed with conviction in religious phenomena. Indeed, he envisioned an unbreakable link between religion and civil society.[109] Whatever the limits of Locke's notion of the public, he never said religious *beliefs or values* should have no participatory role in the formation of democratic modernity; he only rejected a monopoly of religious meaning over public life by a particular religious *institution*. Locke implied that only specific secular questions of public policy (sanitation, health, education, employment, taxation) concerning the objective, if not necessarily always harmonious, interests of all citizens permit of tangible final answers reached non-violently in forums of open public debate (the public sphere). Where Hobbes had seen only uniformity of religion as the key to a functioning civil society (echoing, after all, Philip II, and foreshadowing Rousseau's civic religion), Locke saw the danger not in religious diversity but in violent state intervention in the private sphere of pluralistic belief.

There was no need, for Locke, to fit the incompatible pieces of diverse religious perspectives together into a seamless and final public whole as an epistemic project. Locke's secular political outlook was grounded in a temporal epistemology, demanding a halt to all quests for "final knowledge" and a forsaking of futile intellectual plunges "into the vast Ocean of *Being*."[110] This broke with an absolutist epistemic tradition going back to Plato (424–348) in the Western tradition.

Locke followed the earlier natural rights discourses in arguing that epistemic uncertainty cannot permit of religious violence: "in this great variety of ways that men follow, it is still doubted which

---

[108] Locke, *A Letter*, 130.

[109] Trentmann, *The Problem with civil society*, 26–35.

[110] Locke, *An Essay Concerning Human Understanding* (London: Penguin, 1997), 58.

is the right one," but "does it therefore belong unto the magistrate to prescribe me a remedy, because there is but one, and because it is unknown?"[111] Locke therefore denied the right to punish.[112] Political claims to absolute knowledge, he argued, are driven only by the desire for temporal dominion.[113] He thus rejected sheer force as the highest principle driving human affairs. Locke ripped the democratic discourses of the first English Revolution out of their religious moorings in the discourse of Providence. A relative—rather than absolute—epistemology substituted hermeneutics. This empiricist outlook, affirming the reality of God, asserted the independent existence of an autonomous system of natural law and thereby denied any reality to Providence except as a naturalized form of Deism or natural theology.[114]

The departure from the Providence framework drew from early modern historical and material developments to construct a new imaginary. The human is not a natural term in the social sciences: it was historically constructed. Unlike Milton's vision of an American Eden, Locke invented a moving machine of successive historicist grades beyond the enclosed world of anxiety that is the Garden. This discursive formation affirmed modern historical energies and emerging patterns of domination. The primary focus was the 17th-century English market that created a social situation where "estatelessness undermined the very foundations of judgement about the self and the world."[115] There was also anxiety provoked by the discovery of worldly diversity with expanding global capitalism. Locke questioned "that vast store which the busy and boundless fancy of man has painted [upon] with an almost endless variety."[116]

The discursive formation had practical correlates in Locke's real life. He participated in emerging colonial institutions, as he

[111] Locke, *A Letter*, 141.

[112] Ibid., 135.

[113] Ibid., 139.

[114] Locke's views are rather complex, accepting miracle and revelation within the limits of reason. His epistemology, however, undercuts the traditional political function of Providence.

[115] Jean-Christophe Agnew, *Worlds Apart: The Market and Theatre in Anglo-American Thought, 1550-1750* (Cambridge: Cambridge University Press, 1986), 62.

[116] Locke, *An Essay Concerning Human Understanding*, 189.

"worked closely with the private and state bodies which were responsible for formulating the colonial policies of European countries during the period."[117] His philosophical historicism is almost certainly linked to his professional life as a man implicated in a globally expanding machinery of violence, domination and coercion. Locke was also one of those "revolutionaries [who] created a new kind of English state after 1689 [and] rejected the modern, bureaucratic absolutist state model developed by Louis XIV in France."[118] Locke's discourse of progress shifted the Puritan transcendental category of the "chosen" from religious qualities to secular powers of development in a new inside/out framework. He promoted England's state transformation "from an agrarian into a manufacturing society [and] the massive military buildup ... necessary to fight a war against the greatest military power that Europe had ever seen".[119] In spite of attempting to formulate an argument "completely independent of historical example" and based on "universal principle" in *The Second Treatise on Government*, "most of the crucial steps in Locke's argument actually depend on references to America."[120] It was "under the influence of the prosperous conditions of the colonies of the New World"—America as the imaginary of worldly prosperity—that Locke interpreted labour as the source of all wealth rather than the appanage of poverty.[121]

Locke's intellectual worldview, then, was at once emancipatory and coercive. He promoted a modernizing interventionist state capable of extending its "tendrils ... deeper and more extensively into society than they had ever gone before."[122] The point of exclusion targeted those who defy God's law by leaving the land in waste, who fail to demonstrate rationality, as illustrated by the wild Indian in the "wild woods and uncultivated waste of America, left to nature, without any improvement."[123] He prescribed a colonial logic for the as yet undeveloped expanse

[117] Peter Hulme and Ludmilla Jordanova, *The Enlightenment and its Shadows* (London: Routledge, 1990), 17.
[118] Pincus, *Modern Revolution*, 8.
[119] Ibid.
[120] Hulme and Jordanova, *Enlightenment and its Shadows*, 26.
[121] Arendt, *On Revolution*, 23.
[122] Pincus, *Modern Revolution*, 9.
[123] Locke, *The Second Treatise on Government*, 33.

of the Americas, and implicitly anywhere else where European colonial power may militarily gain the upper hand. His criteria for reason targeted the unproductive landowning aristocracy of 17th-century England, defending the enclosure of common land into private property for the accumulation of capital, notably in the draining of the Great Fens (1630s) which "provoked protests from the local population who were accustomed to extracting a meagre living from keeping geese, hunting wild fowl, and catching pike."[124] The same logic applied to the nomadic and uncontrolled element in the British population produced by policies of improvement. The most extreme form of such exploitation was slave labour, where Locke worked as "a counsellor and secretary on colonial boards setting slave policy" and "as a merchant adventurer and profiteer in the Royal African Company."[125] Locke's secular-transcendental development paradigm—as a tacit discursive formation—was subsequently redeployed. At the onset of the French Revolution, Sieyes (1748–1836), in *What is the Third Estate?*, used the same inside/out logic to exclude the aristocracy from the nation, writing that the class "is assuredly estranged from the nation by its idleness."[126]

The issue of violence was broached subsequently in a new way by the Earl of Shaftesbury (1671–1713), who had been Locke's pupil in childhood. This demonstrates how deeply contested the lifeworld of the secular was, and the imaginative lengths in trying to articulate its dimensions objectively. The secular was a discursive–practical problem, not an unveiled reality. His "Inquiry Concerning Virtue, or Merit" (1699), a response to Locke's *Essay Concerning Human Understanding* (1690), argued that prior to reason, interest or education is a moral sense grounded in nature, and common to human beings everywhere.[127] We see an alternative and more open approach in the natural rights tradition to

[124] Ashley, *England in the Seventeenth Century*, 16.

[125] James Farr, "So Vile and Miserable an Estate": The Problem of Slavery in John Locke's Political Thought," in the *Selected Political Writings of John Locke*, 377.

[126] Albert Soboul, *Understanding the French Revolution* (New Delhi: People's Publishing House, 1989), 21.

[127] Shaftesbury, *Inquiry Concerning Virtue or Merit* in *British Moralists: Selections from Writers principally of the Eighteenth Century* (Oxford: Clarendon Press, 1897), 47.

either Hobbes or Locke in articulating a coherent premise for secular values.

Shaftesbury believed that Locke's concept of human nature as a blank slate had "struck at all fundamentals, threw all order and virtue out of the world" and reduced them to fashion and custom. He intended, by contrast, to demonstrate that a feeling for others was *"naturally imprinted* on human minds."[128] We see the continued ambition to define Nature for the purpose of undergirding civil society in the wake of the separation of history from the encompassing ethical framework of Providence. Adam Smith (1723–90) wrote, along these lines, that "We endeavour to examine our own conduct as we imagine any other fair and impartial spectator would examine it," and society is our mirror grounded in original passions of human nature.[129]

Shaftesbury based secularism on a public moral sense independent of religious affiliation while rejecting the historicism tacitly grounding Locke's system as a universal claim to the nature of historical truth. The natural Affection is prior to all speculative Opinion, and no belief can *"immediately* or *directly* ... exclude or destroy it."[130] The main danger to the public moral sense is moral passion or enthusiasm, because by its excessive character it tends to destroy its own End.[131] Shaftesbury saw dogmatic convictions of an inflexible nature leading to acts of violent fanaticism against others, and so he called for "a more easy and pleasant way of thought."[132] He called for tolerance, variance of opinion and focus upon means in a deepened articulation of the ethic of reconciliation. He endeavoured to keep the public space open. Shaftesbury rejected the notion of a prior ontological premise as the basis for public consent, as "never can such a Phantom as this be reduc'd to any certain Form."[133] Refusing a single definition of Truth, he

---

[128] Quoted in Gertrude Himmelfarb, *The Roads to Modernity. The British, French and American Enlightenments* (New York: Alfred A. Knopf, 2004), 29.

[129] Adam Smith, *The Theory of Moral Sentiments* (New York: Penguin, 2009), 133–34/13.

[130] Shaftesbury, *Inquiry*, 20.

[131] Ibid., 30.

[132] Shaftesbury, "On Enthusiasm," in *The Portable Enlightenment Reader*, ed. Isaac Kramnick (New York: Penguin Books, 1995), 92.

[133] Shaftesbury, *Inquiry*, 48.

dismissed metaphysical problems, arguing that it is of no concern to his argument whether experiences "are Realitys, or mere Illusions; whether we wake or dream."[134] The means to a just order of society requires no supreme truth or foundation, making the 18th-century French Enlightenment ideal of war against error meaningless. Far more strongly than Locke, Shaftesbury presented a critique of violence in the call for a world beyond "bloodshed, wars, persecutions and devastation." He called for public diversity over negation of the past, encouraging the return of "the whole train of heathen gods (in order to) set our cold northern island burning (with alters)."[135] In an important discursive evaluation, Shaftesbury esteemed tolerance and humility as the highest virtues over the "perfectibility of human societies."[136]

We thus see to what extent the British Enlightenment, from its 17th-century Puritan political roots to the 18th-century moral philosophers, differed from the French experience. Yet both struggled between the two poles of an ethic of reconciliation and claims to ontological totality as a basis for modern politics.

EIGHTEENTH-CENTURY PHILOSOPHIES AND THE CONSTRUCTION OF VIOLENCE

The tension between an ethic of reconciliation and a claim to totality was also at the core of the 18th-century French Enlightenment, which adopted Locke's philosophy while transforming him into a materialist.[137] Voltaire (1694–1778) praised Catherine II of Russia for her tolerance of all religions.[138] His *Lettres Philosophiques* (1734) established its argument in obsessive reference to post-Reformation memories of religious violence, persecution and civil war. The dominant French Enlightenment belief that all truths could be reconciled was attractive in a world where prior religious wars had been fought over conflicting claims to truth. Rousseau (1712–78) maintained that "Everything that destroys social unity

---

[134] Ibid., 63.
[135] Shaftesbury, "On Enthusiasm," 96.
[136] Soboul, *Understanding the French Revolution*, 1.
[137] Hazard, *Crise de la Conscience*, 235.
[138] Soboul, *Understanding the French Revolution*, 6.

is worthless".[139] Fontenelle argued that "A work of politics, or morality, of criticism, perhaps even of literature, will be finer, all things considered, if made by the hands of a geometer."[140]

The dominant stream in the 18th-century French Enlightenment was the mechanist notion that nature (and therefore life) is as a jigsaw puzzle. The pieces can be assembled into one coherent pattern like a well-made machine. The wide consensus was that Newton's achievement in physics could be applied with "equally splendid and lasting results in the world of morals, politics, aesthetics, and in the rest of the chaotic world of human opinion." This was combined with a classical search for perfection in "the network of logical relationships of which the universe consisted and which reason could grasp and live by."[141] Within the completed sphere of positive knowledge, it was believed, all values must be compatible with one another. In the universe as a rational whole, conflict over truth could only result from logical error. This formula—implying totality over an ethic of reconciliation—ultimately negated the natural rights premise of autonomy. The Enlightenment therefore finished by negating itself in political practice through the wedding of violence to certitude.

In the final decades of the *Ancien Regime* "public opinion was defined as the precise contrary of the opinion of the greatest number." Both Condorcet (1743–94) and d'Alembert (1717–83) opposed the opinions of literate people to those of the "multitude."[142] Constructed upon reason, public opinion was therefore the "opposite of a popular opinion that was multiple, versatile, and shaped in its habits by prejudices and passions".[143] The *Encyclopedie* (1751–72) took for "incompatible the hard demands of the popular condition and the participation of reasoned conduct in the government."[144] Rousseau argued concerning the General Will, the common good can have no incompatible or conflicting interests for it is always unchanging, incorruptible

---

[139] Jean-Jacques Rousseau., *The Social Contract* (London: Penguin, 1968), 160.

[140] Isaiah Berlin, *The Roots of Romanticism* (London: Pimlico, 2000), 26.

[141] Ibid., 24/32.

[142] Roger Chartier, *Les origines culturelles de la Revolution francaise* (Paris: Editions du Seuil, 1990), 47.

[143] Ibid., 48.

[144] Ibid., 50.

THE EUROPEAN ENLIGHTENMENT   83

and pure.¹⁴⁵ Montesquieu (1689–1755)—who contributed deeply to a pragmatic and context-specific recognition of the political value in democratic institutional structures—evoked for a point of departure a single principle of truth underlying the "infinite diversity of laws and mores," and claimed to have identified it in drawing his "principles not from prejudices, but from the nature of things."¹⁴⁶ These various visions shared a tacit historicist substratum defined by successive grades, a combination of substantialism and the goal of progress.

The first model of political practice to grow out of the French Enlightenment was therefore the ideal of nation-making from above. "Enlightened monarchs," such as Fredrick the Great of Prussia (1740–86) and Joseph II of Austria (1765–90), also "compared the state to a machine," insisting that any "flaw in the machine's operation could be attributed to a lack of skill." Therefore, "to learn how to work the machine, future officials would have to study its principles, just as a physician studied the fundaments of anatomy." They considered their method to have "provided the best road to modern nationhood." Yet there was no debate over power or sovereignty, it being "taken for granted that this lay entirely with the monarch" as the state "loomed above the constituent elements of society, drawing them together and harnessing their energy."¹⁴⁷

It is therefore ironic that Voltaire embodied autonomy, activism, struggle, and the public sphere—the very opposite of the machine. He had been beaten, imprisoned in the Bastille and exiled to England before finally becoming highly influential as the prototype for the intellectual-activist, providing an alternative standard of progress and modernity in his criticisms of the French absolute monarchy under Louis XV (ruled 1715–73). Seeing his works publicly burned on several occasions, he published anonymously and his correspondence constituted a network throughout Europe's intellectual circles. This signalled the rise of an alternative and rival source of civil power—largely composed of barons, marquis, counts and other noblemen—among

¹⁴⁵ Rousseau, *The Social Contract.*, 122/124.
¹⁴⁶ Montesquieu. *De l'esprit des lois : I* (Paris: G. F. Flammarion, 1979), 115.
¹⁴⁷ Woloch. *Eighteenth-Century Europe*, 249–51.

the educated strata of the public and centred in the salons.[148] Voltaire based his ideal of progress and modernity on the English experience, lauding what he saw as political and intellectual freedom, religious pluralism and a commercial policy conducive to national prosperity. There was a call for development in this assertion that the energies and aims of the newly rising French middle class could find no outlet under the existing status quo — or a discursive-formation establishing the political changeability of the future.

Despite taking the model of the 17th-century English revolutions, Voltaire did not consider direct adoption of a constitutional regime to the French context. Like most Paris Encyclopaedists, he hoped to transform the monarch, once submitted to natural law, into the first servant of the national community with the people as the object of his care. Following the logic of the machine philosophy, no active role was envisioned for the general population. Diderot argued that the world was no longer of God, but "a machine which has its wheels its ropes, its pulleys, its springs and weights."[149] He argued that the "general mass of men are not so made that they can either promote or understand this forward march of the human spirit."[150] The multitude was described by him in terms of "wickedness, stupidity, inhumanity, unreason and prejudice."[151] This came to constitute an anti-democratic discursive–practical formation.

To both Voltaire and Diderot, the central obstacle to the free development of the machine of the French nation — and indeed humanity — was religion. Just as the *Encyclopedie* sought to represent the totality of human knowledge, Voltaire's writing tended to attribute a total nature to Christianity and beyond that to religion as such.[152] He extended the substantialist tradition that considered a single definition to be truly representative in a totalizing principle of identity. That is, he thought in ontological

[148] Berlin, *The Roots*, 39. Berlin gives an account of the social background of the French *philosophes*, all of whom were of noble origins with the exception of Diderot and Rousseau who were commoners.

[149] Diderot, *Pensées philosophiques* (Paris : G.F. Flammarion, 2007), 67.

[150] Diderot, "Encyclopedia," quoted in Himmelfarb, *The Roads to Modernity* (New York: Knopf, 2004), 304.

[151] Diderot, "Multitude," in *Encyclopedie*, X, 860.

[152] Hulme and Jordanova, *Enlightenment and its Shadows*, 1.

terms of "Nature" as the primary reality grounded in universal necessity, prior to the false consciousness of all particular sects and subjectivities. Both Voltaire and Diderot saw the Christian history of Europe as a corrupting and often criminal period of decline, one that had destroyed the Greek and Roman civilizations which had aspired to live by reason.[153] The particular scientific narrative they introduced as a concurrent to religious narratives was derived from the ancient Platonic construct revived since the Renaissance. It was a vision of perfection in which certain axiomatic and unbreakable truths can be obtained by a mathematical method leading to an absolute knowledge and correct organization of human life.[154] Voltaire asserted the "unchanging and eternal certainty of mathematics" and the certainty that "I exist. I think, I feel pain" based on the principle that "a thing cannot exist and not exist at the same time." This is an essentially ontological premise for certitude (i.e. based on a single definition of existence) by which he claimed an "equal value" to mathematics.[155] This reproduced a confusion of immanent and transcendental levels.

The second concept of practice to grow from the 18th-century French Enlightenment was public activism from civil society. It concerned the problem of how the legitimate enlightened representative was to gain ascendancy over illegitimate powers mired in the stasis of the past. Voltaire replied to this practical question of the means to emancipation in his *Lettres Philosophiques*: The "English nation is the only one on earth which managed to regulate the power of kings through resistance." Though "it had doubtlessly cost dearly to establish liberty in England," requiring "seas of blood" to "drown the idol of despotic power," the English did not "believe themselves to have paid too dearly to obtain just laws."[156] This division of means and ends at the ethical level was an unreflecting echo of Machiavelli's earlier maxim on nation-making: "one should reproach a man who is violent in order to

---

[153] Woloch, *Eighteenth-Century Europe*, 233.
[154] Berlin, *The Roots*, 2.
[155] Voltaire, *Dictionnaire Philosophique* (Paris: G. F. Flammarion, 1964), 106.
[156] Voltaire, *Lettres Philosophiques* (Paris: G.F. Flammarion, 1964), 55–6.

destroy, not one who is violent in order to mend things."[157] Both projected a unilinear nation-making process where violence was instrumental in an accumulating discursive–practical formation.

The imagined historical identification of legitimate political violence to authentic national origins was expressed in the central debate between Montesquieu and Voltaire. Voltaire viewed the nobility as the source of tyranny in France, and the monarch as the legitimate heir of French national authority. Montesquieu viewed, conversely, the nobility as the true heir to the French nation and the monarch an impostor and the cause of tyranny.[158] Following the pattern of the Norman Yoke construction from the English Civil War, these narrative modes of political imagining have been identified as a discursive-formation envisioning history as a war between two enemies with opposed interests and identities.[159]

The multiple roads in emergent historical consciousness—or imagined time-schemas—competed for the plateau of the absolute. The absolute road in nation-making, pervasive in the French Enlightenment, ultimately compromised Montesquieu's secular ideal of institutionalized non-violence based on legal separation of power. It yielded to higher truth. Montesquieu had, foreseeing abuse of power, written that virtue itself requires limits.[160] Empirical evidence and institutional justice succumbed to genius/pure consciousness most vividly during the French Revolutionary Terror. Robespierre, proclaiming sheer vision over institutional law, would argue that "a regenerator must see big, he must mow down everything in his path."[161]

The discourse of genius had been articulated previously by Rousseau. Following Locke, Rousseau rejected Providence or Divine Intervention in the founding of nations. He substituted it—thereby lifting the category above merely arbitrary violence—with genius.[162] Another variant on the foundation discourse, it

---

[157] Machiavelli, *The Portable Machiavelli*, 201.

[158] Woloch, *Eighteenth-Century Europe*, 248.

[159] Michel Foucault, *Ethics: Subjectivity and Truth 1954–1984* (London: Penguin, 1997), 63.

[160] Montesquieu, *De l'esprit des lois*, 293.

[161] Francois Furet and Mona Ozouf. *Dictionnaire Critique de la Revolution Francaise. Idees* (Paris : G. F. Flammarion, 2006), 160.

[162] Rousseau, *The Social Contract*, 48.

provided a sublimation of political violence. The norm in modern society should be the rule of law; but the founding moment in law giving, the work of genius, is a work of pure creativity necessarily unfettered by any ordinary limits of morality or convention. For Rousseau, true genius is creative and makes everything from nothing.[163] It is this genius which lies behind all lasting things.[164] This genius or lawgiver is the engineer who invents the machine.[165]

Rousseau's secular discourse involved a civil religion to supplant existing religions on pain of death, paradoxically liquefying those beliefs constituting a threat to tolerance by force from above.[166] The violent memories of the religious wars, which made "men breathe only murder and massacre, and believe they are doing a holy deed in killing those who do not accept their Gods," convinced Rousseau that it is "impossible to live in peace with people one believes to be damned."[167] The creation of the nation, he was convinced, was incompatible with the survival of divisive beliefs. His vision thus tended to transcendence of difference in a grand project over the everyday ethic of reconciliation, remaining anchored in a tacit eschatological metaphysics.

Rousseau's stance, never the less, is grounded in a deeper critique of the link between violence and sacred truth (inherited from Locke) in the concept of Providence. Rousseau argued that violence has no moral content, as it is merely "a physical power; I do not see how its effects could produce morality." Taking the line further, he writes that "(a)ll power comes from God" but "(a)fter all, the pistol in the robber's hand is undoubtedly a power."[168] Power (i.e. violence) is not something to be accepted fatalistically, because it comes from God, but to be negotiated and controlled through the modern rule of law.

Rousseau thus reversed the Aristotelian claim that slavery is founded in immutable nature and human nature, and insisted that human nature is universally conditioned by arbitrary social

---

[163] Ibid., 50.
[164] Ibid., 48.
[165] Ibid., 44.
[166] Ibid., 166.
[167] Ibid., 161/167.
[168] Ibid., 5/6.

conditions and conventions.[169] In this aspect, a genealogical or unmasking undertow exists in Rousseau's writing—lost to his contemporaries who sought Necessity in new terms—that foresees the Nietzschean intellectual revolution.[170] The implied view of politics as historical convention had the revolutionary effect of unleashing "doubt that poverty is inherent in the human condition" or that the "distinction between the few, who through circumstances or strength or fraud had succeeded in liberating themselves from the shackles of poverty, and the labouring poverty-stricken multitude was inevitable or eternal."[171] This was a subversive critique of necessary violence.

This was a departure from the universal absolute and into the flow of temporality. Yet a lingering substantive Nature grounded Rousseau's coercive conviction that deliberate political planning could mould this malleable human nature in pursuit of perfection. Those involved in "the enterprise of setting up a people must be ready, shall we say, to change human nature, to transform each individual ... into a part of a much greater whole."[172] Hence, a discursive prototype of nation-making from above was established where any resisting the General Will "shall be forced to be free."[173] This political ontology, dichotomizing collective belonging and the enemy, endorsed organized violence for purposes of national unity. In putting the guilty to death, we slay not so much the citizen as an enemy.[174]

This foreshadowed the two French Revolutions between representation and regeneration. Montesquieu, following the English political tradition, was concerned above all with the institutional *form* of political power and saw the guarantee of liberty in the separation of powers. This implies a continuous negotiation of difference, and so an ethic of reconciliation. The issue was at the heart of his disagreement with Voltaire, who saw the guarantee of liberty rather more metaphysically in the *intention* of the ruler.

---

[169] Ibid., 4.

[170] Of course we know that Nietzsche hated Rousseau, and dismissed him as a resentful romantic.

[171] Arendt, *On Revolution*, 22.

[172] Rousseau, *The Social Contract*, 44.

[173] Ibid., 19.

[174] Ibid., 38.

Both shared a negative definition of freedom, i.e. the absence of outside restriction. Within this debate, Rousseau introduced a radically alternative discourse of freedom into the Enlightenment heritage in positive freedom, or a philosophical key to a better and transformed future.[175]

In this, the 18th century, French Enlightenment answered the existential dilemma of habitation and belonging, as well as pluralism, which racked early modern centralizing states. The state for Rousseau was a citadel driven dynamically according to some higher form of existential knowledge. He argued that the function of a just state is not merely to govern but to educate, to introduce an ethical imperative and create a context for a moral life. He promoted a "civil religion in which these values would be evoked ritualistically."[176] This totalizing ideal, though grounded in a worldly basis, threatened the link between secularism and freedom of thought.

Rousseau substituted a narrative of historical origins for the traditional Biblical narrative which lent itself to multiple future accounts of a lost national golden age. The simple virtue of original and natural man had been atrophied by the corruption of civilization itself as an enfeebling and degenerate force. He evoked—in still another imaginative twist upon the nature discourse—an original equality. Secularized national origin was extended to a deeper ontological level beyond the competing claims of multiple political agents, with the legitimate sovereign uniquely embodied in the people themselves as a primal unity. His *Discourse on the Origins of Inequality* (1754) combined images of the native inhabitants of America and historical memories of Spartan civilization, producing a vision of nature as innocence and virtue.[177] This discursive formation lent itself to authenticity as a mobilizing ideal.

---

[175] Isaiah Berlin, *Liberty. Incorporating Four Essays on Liberty* (Oxford: Oxford University Press, 2002), 166–217.

[176] Woloch, *Eighteenth-Century Europe*, 258.

[177] Rousseau. *Discours sur l'origine et les fondements de l'inegalite parmi les hommes/Discours sur les sciences et les arts* (Paris: GF Flammarian, 1971), 36.

FRENCH REVOLUTION BETWEEN DEMOCRACY AND THE ABSOLUTE

The French Revolution, a historically specific interval of national modernization, introduced radical new conventions of popular political action (i.e. the arming of all citizens in a people's war) and formative new discourses.[178] It has often been conceptualized as a universal paradigm. That it deeply reset human history in a more democratic direction seems beyond doubt. We must recall, however, that France's own violent struggle among competing political forms endured until at least the 1871 massacre of the Communards at Pere-Lachaise.[179] Its often conflicting discourses centred on historical origins/historicism and national identity/ political ontology. These were combined with an appeal to universal human emancipation possibly embedded in older religious ideals of toleration.[180]

The practical experience of the French Revolution profoundly unsettled the confident 18th-century belief in modern knowledge as necessarily constituting a single and final universal pattern joining social life to positive knowledge. This disillusionment, the soil of Romanticism, was embodied in the debate between Thomas Paine (1737–1809) and Edmund Burke (1729–97) as distinctly opposed temporal horizons. Beyond its dialectical tensions, the French Revolutionary experience presented a paradigm of modern politics in which action as a value in itself "exhausts the world of values, and so the very meaning of existence."[181] Paine's rejection of governing beyond the grave and urging that "the living, and not the dead ... be accommodated" suggests the new temporal horizon: limitless human imagination emancipated

---

[178] Doyle, *The Oxford History*, 188.

[179] Norman Rich, *The Age of Nationalism and Reform, 1850-1890* (New York: W.W. Norton, 1977), 188.

[180] Dale K. Van Kley, *The Religious Origins of the French Revolution: From Calvin to the Civil Constitution* (New Haven: Yale University Press, 1996), 1–14.

[181] Francois Furet, *Penser la Revolution Francaise* (Paris: Gallimard, 1978), 90.

from tradition with the lightness of an atomized lifeworld.[182] Burke contrastingly urged that human survival required the lifeworld restrictively patterned by the temporal density of "analogical precedent, authority, and example."[183]

From the tumultuous French Revolutionary years, two discursive–practical paradigms subsequently shaped movements claiming democracy as a national ideology: firstly, Constitutionalism or representation (civil equality centring institutional formations) and, secondly, politics of the general will (equality based on the attainment of a transcendent human order).[184] From 1789 to 1791 the conciliatory period saw "a quest for unity amid centrifugal forces generated by the Great Fear of 1789."[185] Protestants and Jews were given civic rights in this early experiment tending towards an ethic of reconciliation.[186] Press freedom was declared, although censorship persisted sometimes more strictly than during the old regime.[187] Manichean dualism was already visible, with the "targets of denunciation [including] priests, aristocrats, army officers" and others.[188] There were early warnings of things to come. For educational reform, Mirabeau (1749–91) explained that "In order to reconstruct everything, it was necessary to destroy everything."[189] This totalizing temporal horizon negatively impacted literacy and poor relief.[190] The revolutionary mentality grounded in fear, defensive reaction and punitive will, constituted an important key in the unfolding narrative of the French Revolution.[191] We see a discursive–practical

[182] Thomas Paine, "The Rights of Man," in *The Great Political Theories: From the French Revolution to Modern Times*, ed. Michael Curtis (New York: Harper Perennial, 2008), 65.

[183] Edmund Burke, "Reflections on the Revolution in France," *The Great Political Theories: From the French Revolution to Modern Times*, ed. Michael Curtis (New York: Harper Perennial, 2008), 53.

[184] Arendt, *On Revolution*, 76–79.

[185] Kennedy, *Cultural History of the French Revolution*, 238.

[186] Georges Lefebvre, *The French Revolution* (London: Routledge, 2001), 145.

[187] Kennedy, *Cultural History of the French Revolution*, 321.

[188] Ibid., 308.

[189] Ibid., 157.

[190] Doyle, *The Oxford History*, 399.

[191] Lefebvre, *The French Revolution*, 118.

pattern of retribution at the origins of justice. Yet serious efforts at a politics of compromise persisted until Lafayette's (1757–1834) efforts to reconcile monarchy and constitutionalism were violently undone in 1790.[192] Subsequently, 1791 to 1793 saw politically organized ascendance towards an imagined absolute, until the demise of the Jacobin movement with the 1794 Thermidorean Reaction.

It was a global event, showing the growing political importance of public opinion or hegemony in shaping national events as a key democratic element in self-protection. Genevan banker Jacques Necker (1732–1804) published statements on royal accounts in 1781, encouraging the public to view social problems in the secular terms of failed public office and government tax policy.[193] The Necker conflict unveiled global linkages: the American War of Independence and dominance of the sources and supply of those tropical luxuries for which Europe was developing an insatiable need. The Enlightenment as a symbol figured perversely in these international developments. As the slave trade in the 18th century expanded to an average of 55,000 slaves per year one of the ship owners christened his ships with the names *Voltaire*, *Rousseau* and *Social Contract*.[194] The international context saw rising English capitalism linked to the weakening of Holland and the continuing struggle against rural French stagnation.

It was a modernization crisis, where the French regime sought self-empowerment and European supremacy at the cost of its poor.[195] From 1733 to 1770 the French economy was on the upswing. It was "through the exploitation of the rural worker, paid less and exempt from corporative control, that scattered manufacturing and commercial capitalism were developed."[196] Agricultural and industrial productivity as well as colonial and domestic commerce were expanding. After 1770 contraction set in, with falling agrarian income, languishing industry and rising

---

[192] Ibid., 136.

[193] Robert D. Harris, *Necker and the Revolution of 1789* (United States: University of America Press, 1986), 146–58.

[194] Michel Beaud, *A History of Capitalism. 1500–2000* (New Delhi: Aakar Books, 2004), 45.

[195] This confirms central tenets of Samuel Huntington's *Political Order in Changing Societies*.

[196] Soboul, *Understanding the French Revolution*, 9.

THE EUROPEAN ENLIGHTENMENT   93

unemployment.[197] France lost footholds to England in India, China, and Canada, and fought three worldwide wars resulting in colossal debt. It was also a cultural crisis. French public literacy had risen due to Reformation and Counter-Reformation propaganda campaigns, with formal schooling playing a lesser role in grounding an expanding urban civil society.[198] At the national level, in 1792, perhaps 50 per cent of the population did not speak or understand French.[199]

The key totalizing shift in the discursive–practical region of density was in 1793 when "[parliamentary] speakers and listeners were presumed to have identical knowledge and convictions." We see the centring of a unifying political ontology with "consensus as [a] goal ... superseded by a discourse in which consensus was the premise and its celebration the end."[200] It is partly explained by the 1792 French war offensive against Europe with its dichotomous purpose of obliging "compatriots to come out clearly for or against the Revolution." The Revolution adopted the Manichean figure of being with or being enemy, and set about the revolutionizing of all Europe "if necessary by force of arms."[201] At the Continental level, the Church of Rome completed the rupture between Rome and Paris by opposing its doctrine to the Declaration of the Rights of Man and Citizen.[202]

The French Revolutionary ideologues claimed their origins and legitimacy in the tradition of the "century of Enlightenment."[203] Their notion of natural right was "based on philosophic, non-temporal values, which required expression in universal terms."[204] They condemned the estates system for its labyrinthine legal

---

[197] Theda Skocpol, *States and Social Revolutions. A Comparative Analysis of France, Russia and China* (Cambridge: Cambridge University Press, 1979), 121.

[198] See Furet and J.Ozouf, *Lire et ecrire: l'alphabetisation des francais de Calvin a Jules Ferry* (Paris: Les Editions de Minuit, Paris), ch. 3.

[199] Eugen Weber, *Peasants into Frenchmen. The Modernization of Rural France* (Stanford: Stanford University Press, 1976) Chapter 6 "A wealth of Tongues."

[200] Kennedy, *Cultural History of the French Revolution*, 303.

[201] Doyle, *The Oxford History*, 218.

[202] Lefebvre, *The French Revolution*, 170.

[203] Furet/Ozouf, *Dictionnaire Critique. Idees*, 276

[204] Lefebvre, *The French Revolution*, 142.

complexities left without codification since the 1670s and urged that it be harmonized with Nature.[205] Enlightenment discourses identified the church at the root of existing social evils, condemning superstition and disproportionate wealth for its members. They viewed their task in finding "a new absolute to replace the absolute of divine power."[206] Moved by the "pathos of novelty," where nothing of comparable "grandeur and significance had ever happened," they believed in a "new beginning" linked inextricably to violence as the means to creating a "new body politic."[207] The Revolution, Robespierre argued, with neither intellectual nor political precedent, had its modus operandi in a war for eternal truth pitting two global forces (reason and tyranny).[208] Sieyes proclaimed the need to be open in showing our hatred of internal enemies of the nation as an expression of patriotic feeling and the first, initial act of public justice.[209] Although exclusion and violence was sown into the French revolutionary nationalist discourse from the outset, it was only with the Second Revolution that the premise of a legal framework for resolving conflicts was jettisoned in favour of an open ideology of war. There was "faith in the regenerative power of war."[210] Saint Just (1767–94) expressed this violence-virtue linkage: "A republican government has virtue for its principle; if not terror. What do those want who want neither virtue nor terror?"[211]

Economic failure impacted the broader French public, inflicting famine and triggering the violent 1789 popular mass intervention into the political process. Mass intervention made possible the National Assembly's bending of the King's will.[212] This collective practical formation radically expanded the category of the public in a key democratic moment. The urban French Revolutionary

[205] For discussion of estates system, see Michael Fitzsimmons, *The Night the Old Regime Ended: August 4, 1789, and the French Revolution* (Pennsylvania State University Press, 2003), 1–47.

[206] Arendt, *On Revolution*, 39.

[207] Ibid., 34/35.

[208] Robespierre, *Robespierre: Entre Vertu et Terreur*, 209/226/255.

[209] Emmanuel Joseph Sieyes, *Political Writings* (Indianapolis: Hacket, 2003), 41.

[210] Doyle, *The Oxford History*, 179.

[211] Kennedy, *Cultural History of the French Revolution*, 139.

[212] Doyle, *The Oxford History*, 122.

unfolding transpired through *journees*, sans-culottes and Jacobin club linkages. A spreading agrarian revolt against the seigneurial system meanwhile forced the abolition of feudalism.[213] These intervening new forces of the multitude, linking elements of popular will to a party, took the Revolution to radically unexpected places. It reconfigured, undoubtedly forever, the political and social landscape of European and global modernity. If the 1789 Declaration of the Rights of Man held precedent in the 1776 new American Republic's states' rights documents, it expanded the political scope beyond contemporary imagining.[214] The Haitian Revolution followed, inspired by the discourse on the Rights of Man, with the country achieving independence in spite of colonial assaults in 1804.[215]

June 1789 saw sovereignty transferred from the King to the nation. This dismantled the first major obstacle on a revolutionary path that declared absolute monarchy (as opposed to constitutional) on the wrong side of the rupture in the order of historical time implemented by the revolutionaries of 1789. Only in 1792 did monarchy *as such* become perceived as an opponent to national progress, upon the wave of a popular movement spearheaded by the sans-culottes. They embodied a specifically constructed historical consciousness. Plans for school history programmes now described ancient monarchies as "shaped in a time of barbarism ... offering little of interest to republicans."[216] This emerged in tandem with an increasing rejection of religious tradition. Many clergy had initially greeted the Revolution positively, and by first breaking the ranks of the privileged orders in 1789 they contributed to the transformation of the Estates General into the National Assembly.[217] If the 1789 revolution embodied an alternative modernization bid, the leaders now discursively reconstructed the revolutionary history as an eternal war of

---

[213] Skocpol, *States and Social Revolutions*, 127.

[214] Frederic Rouvillois, *Les Déclarations des droits de l'homme* (Paris: Flammarion, 2009) for discussions of the cumulative historical roots of these legal documents, and the longstanding myth that the 1789 declaration emerged pure "from the brain of God," 26.

[215] Carolyn E. Fick, *The Making of Haiti: The Saint Domingue Revolution from Below* (University of Tennessee Press, 1990),183–204.

[216] Kennedy, *Cultural History of the French Revolution*, 165.

[217] Doyle, *The Oxford History*, 136.

modernity against tradition grounded in an ontological truth of Nature. The initial democratic impulse was stifled under a discursively redressed religious fervour.

The revolutionary years experienced a crisis and struggle over the meaning of the emerging modern French nation. This led to show trials, rigged elections, death sentences for one's future potential and denial of citizenship on the grounds of identity — in rejection of the politics of reconciliation in favour of unified national totality.[218] Inspired by Rousseauian philosophy, they found the idea of political parties abhorrent.[219] The progressive national defining of "enemies" corresponded to rising efforts to stifle a multi-centred civil society for purposes of "unity" (i.e. the National Assembly prohibited all worker organization, industrial action, and political clubs).[220] It is ironic that an important initial popular impulse for the Revolution had been against centralization.[221] This national discursive–practical assemblage came to represent the ideal meaning of modernity for a long time accepted almost as universal, in which the past and the future are divided with the imaginative calibre of the parting of the Red Sea.

How did a historical fissure come to be conceived in terms so absolute as to crack human history into a binary between the old and new world which expanded with the violence of a black hole in the minds of the revolutionary actors? The King's 1791 flight to Varennes instigated the Second Revolution embodied in the Jacobin club. The 1789 Constituent Assembly had aimed to create a national market and give France a uniform, decentralized and representative system of government. The 1789 Jacobin club initially functioned as a parliamentary adjunct for discussing texts destined for Assembly debate. It followed in the 'English' Lockean representative tradition of 1688 celebrated by Montesquieu and Voltaire in aiming for a legal closure to the revolutionary process. The concept of equality' was transformed in a discursive shift from institutional *legal* guarantees of political justice to a quest to establish transcendental or *ontological* foundations in Reason (i.e. nature). It entered the realm of transcendental truth.

---

[218] See Ibid., chapters 10–12 and 14.
[219] Ibid., 235.
[220] Ibid., 149.
[221] Ibid., 241.

The Jacobin club became the symbolic centre of the urban masses for controlling the Constituent Assembly and so embodied a principle of direct democracy. When the Constituent Assembly prepared to compromise with the King over the 1789 August 4 decrees (the abolition of feudalism, privileges and venality), the Jacobin club linked to the popular masses—inspired by Marat's invocation of an aristocratic conspiracy—forced total surrender. It removed the royal family from Versailles to imprisonment at the Tuileries. By 1790, the Jacobin club constituted a political network extending throughout the nation and financing local political organizations. It had created for itself a *de facto* political and national legitimacy in the struggle over hegemony. Hence, the democratic mass movement was wedded to a secular leadership that took its authoritarian design for the sole road to a "free state."[222]

The French Revolution leads us down a path to which the nation becomes the universal limit to human possibility in a bid to transcend the problem of difference. Hidden and dangerous thoughts, potentially linked to the great conspiracy, are declared a threat to social harmony and public virtue embodied in the popular will. Marat (1743–93) denounced "traitors from every quarter" and "perfidious enemies" who "assail" him from "every side."[223] It was a politics profoundly linked to violence, with Marat insisting in 1792 that "at least 70,000 more heads are necessary in order to re-establish the republic."[224] Saint Just, in his 1794 declaration for the Committee of Public Safety, defined the Revolution as a "heroic endeavour leading between peril and immortality, the latter being secured through complete immolation of enemy factions."[225] Here was the basis for a uniform social order or eventual conflict free society. Robespierre, in his 1794 speech on political morality, argued that the end of the Revolution was to "fulfil the wishes of Nature, realize human destiny [and] uphold the promises of philosophy."[226]

---

[222] Saint Just, *Œuvres Completes* (Paris: Gallimard, 2004), 675.
[223] Kennedy, *Cultural History of the French Revolution*, 300.
[224] Ibid., 311.
[225] Saint Just, *Œuvres Completes* (Paris: Gallimard, 2004), 708.
[226] Robespierre, *Robespierre: Entre Vertu et Terreur*, 225.

The leaders aspired to reach and master the population, creating strong regional resistance over forced military conscription and heavy taxation that equalled the feudal burden.[227] In this discursive transformation we see a fundamental reorientation of the role of the nation state. Its arbitration between the private and the public spheres undertakes a mission of creating mono-vocal public meaning whose culmination was the eclipse of civil society by state ideology. This was expressed in the Festival of the Supreme Being in June 1794. The political art and political doctrine that British public life had evolved during the 17th and 18th centuries embodied the exercise of public liberties unspecifiable because embodied in action [rather than] expressed in rules of action.[228] Those nuances of immanent practical habitus, where temporal depth or tacit aspect complicated transmission, were replaced by a seamless philosophical metaphysics of freedom in Nature.

With the power-transfer from the Triumvirat to the Left, the Jacobin club transformed from a talking club into a political machine focused on the conquest and exercise of power. The power-seizure as the defining moment in a new dawn, or foundation, was the core practical formation transmitted to future generations by the French Revolution. Saint Just argued that "insurrection is the guarantee of peoples, which can be neither forbidden nor changed." Grounded in a totalizing metaphysic of the enemy and violence, it opposes "artificial men" with a "sacred love of nation." It is "so exclusive as to burn all without either pity, fear or human respect."[229] The democratic ideal was wedded to an incompatible ontological criterion of exclusion.

The Jacobin club created a counter-Assembly, culminating in the August 10 overthrow of the monarchy and the creation of the National Convention in 1792.[230] The legalist line was definitively abandoned in a reversal of the original principles of 1789. By 1793 the Vendee Rebellion (itself a popular anti-centralization movement, yet artificial men) set the conditions for dictatorship by the

---

[227] Doyle, *The Oxford History*, ch. 10.

[228] Michael Polanyi, *Personal Knowledge: Towards a Post-Critical Philosophy* (Chicago: University of Chicago Press, 1962), 54.

[229] Saint Just, 675/706.

[230] Doyle, *The Oxford History*, 189.

Committee of Public Safety and the creation of the machinery of the Terror. The Terror expressed a historicist principle of total rejection of the past, as the bodies of France's kings were exhumed and their corpses thrown into a pit of lime with the victims of the guillotine. Their tombs were "saved to illustrate the centuries of art from the middle ages to modern times."[231]

We see France purged of error based on the index of reason as libraries were emptied of all books connected to the rejected past: "books about theology, mysticism, royalism, feudalism and oppressive legislation."[232] There was "nothing worthwhile to expect from the national past, the very richness of which was perceived as a misfortune and even a curse."[233] The city of Lyons, for presenting resistance, was decreed in 1794 by the Committee of Public Safety to be destroyed. Its "very name" was to "disappear" except upon a monument proclaiming that it had "made war on Liberty."[234] Thus, the Jacobin Club transformed into a political machine for the production of social unanimity under an ideology of public virtue dedicated to fighting a hidden conspiracy. Liberty was radically redefined as a war on hypocrisy conducted through both inner and outer (i.e. émigrés) purging of vestiges of the old order among the population and the creation of a new man.[235] They reproduced Milton's error of a century before in confusing liberty with authenticity—this time on secular grounds.

The Second Revolution therefore saw ideological hegemony transferred from the legal-constitutional framework to the ideal of total regeneration beyond the law in a shadowy realm of perpetual emergency. By 1794, Robespierre and Saint Just had opposed the rest of the Committee of Public Safety, in the name of purity of intentions and a declaration of war.[236] In a negation of the modesty of thought as conceived by 17th-century natural rights thinkers, we see the Jacobin dictatorship being conceived

---

[231] Kennedy, *Cultural History of the French Revolution*, 208.
[232] Ibid., 214.
[233] Furet/Ozouf, *Dictionnaire Critique. Idées*, 375.
[234] Doyle, *The Oxford History*, 254.
[235] Furet and Ozouf, *Dictionnaire Critique. Idées.*, See "regeneration."
[236] Doyle, *The Oxford History*, 277–79.

as perfectly compatible with popular sovereignty.[237] Saint-Just called such a totalizing politics the perfection of happiness.[238]

The politics of the Terror comprised three factors: the war of mass mobilization unleashed against France by its European neighbours following the King's 1791 flight to Varennes, the mass counter-Revolutionary basis created inside of France with the Civil Constitution of the Clergy (forcing citizens for the first time to publically choose for or against the Revolution),[239] and the discursive formation of equality mutating into the Second Revolution. The Second Revolution attempted to impose a politics tacitly based on a Platonic essence involving a radical cut with the inherited corruption of the traditional past and the creation of a new order and pure foundation. It tried to exit the very flow of historical time in the corruption of its impurity or conditioned genesis. This ideology of national regeneration presented a tangle of problems concerning the issue of matching means to ends and political violence in the process of nation-making.

With the shift from legal to revolutionary legitimacy in 1792, we see the emergence of an ideology centred on the razor's edge of the guillotine that aimed to organize, systematize and accelerate the repression of internal adversaries of the Republic. It featured a Manichean inside/out politics wedded to an ethic of revenge (as late as 1795 embodied in an obligatory "oath of hatred" for the enemy), and a substantialist rather than pluralist notion of secularism (expressed in the state attempt to single-handedly regenerate national religious life and organization).[240] The Jacobins decided to choose "terror, with its suppression of civil liberties, to master [an] uncertain future."[241] Saint Just envisioned the guillotine in this context as "the fatal instrument which decapitates in a single sweep both the conspiracies and the lives of their authors."[242] The guillotine gave embodiment to the philosophically inspired ideology of revolution as a radical and permanent cut with a past resisting its annihilation through

---

[237] Kennedy, *Cultural History of the French Revolution*, 299.
[238] Quoted Furet/Ozouf, *Dictionnaire Critique. Idees*, 428.
[239] Doyle, *The Oxford History*, 144.
[240] Ibid., 334/384.
[241] Kennedy, *Cultural History of the French Revolution*, 303.
[242] Saint Just, 675.

the persistence of an aristocratic conspiracy. In this setting terror and unanimity were blurred as a discursive–practical formation concerning public control.[243]

The imagined conspiracy had a central role in the discursive-practical history of the French Revolution. Paranoia became a public ceremony and exercise of personal survival. Conspiracy as a discursive formation conceives a global narrative which attributes uniform motivation to countless people based on one external facet. It explains, in transcendental colours, what is happening in the world. Its underlying romantic logic significantly undermined the original legalist orientation, and pushed practical efforts in exiting the 1791 national crisis to flower into political carnage.

The war launched by France's neighbours in 1791 significantly destroyed the opposition-treason divide. The Terror, however, also originated from the discursive–practical formations adopted collectively by the revolutionary leaders. The germ of the Terror had been contained, though never predetermined, within the early 1789 discourses in the discourse of an aristocratic conspiracy. This state of mind was expressed in the violence of July 14, 1789 and given theoretical articulation the following September in Marat's *Friend of the People*. This serialized newspaper evoked in paranoid terms the hidden other nation, the deadly abstract shadow inflated to the level of invisible totality and set in Manichean opposition to the purity of the public will.[244]

In his *Report on the Police* (1794), Saint Just evoked the new politics in the vocabulary of regeneration as the passage from evil to good, from corruption to integrity.[245] The regeneration is thus an interval of time or a means toward the highest end, which can never be won at too high a price. As Marat argued, drops of blood are to be poured to avoid floods.[246] The term regeneration, visible in pamphlets as early as the first meeting of the Estates General, gained ascendancy and radical ideological redefinition with this new political wave.[247] With the aim of creating a new people, the

---

[243] Kennedy, *Cultural History of the French Revolution*, 308.
[244] Furet and Ozouf. *Dictionnaire Critique Acteur*, on Marat.
[245] Saint Just., 747.
[246] Furet and Ozouf, *Dictionnaire Critique. Acteurs*, 188.
[247] Furet and Ozouf, *Dictionnaire Critique. Idees*, on regeneration.

ideology of regeneration had its roots in the 18th-century obsession with a second birth or innocence regained. These images in part derived from experiences of the newly conquered Americas, in which the Huron presented the icon of a pure man untouched by the advance of civilization.[248]

Hence Saint Just described the Revolution in terms of a struggle of truth against hypocrisy, in which the aim was to make nature and innocence the passion of all hearts in the formation of the nation as inspired by the wisdom of children.[249] This idea of innocence or purity borrowed religious discourse in which a true regeneration must first and foremost transform the heart. Robespierre, distinguishing constitutional from revolutionary government, defined the latter's mission in 1793 as "directing the moral and physical forces of the nation."[250] It was a utopian vision of total change, after which "everything would be peaceful."[251] The concept of regeneration, by its logic of total transformation, rejected both legalism and the Constitution in a campaign to purify a corrupted past requiring elimination in its entirety. As early as 1789 Clermont Tonnerre articulated this tension: regeneration could never be "the mere reform of abuses and the reestablishment of a Constitution." He debased the French Constitutional tradition in the name of a higher order of politics.[252] The Montagnard Society expressed this historicist vision: "Each day reason makes new progress among us ... Imposture, fanaticism, superstition are overthrown and confounded ... truth alone triumphs."[253] The diverse criticism of the 1789 cahiers was replaced from 1793 by adulation for the "Holy Mountain."[254] The internal conflict harboured within the French Revolutionary discourse from the beginning resulted in a clouding of practical ethics. It ultimately subverted the institutional rudiments of secularism. The question of means and ends perished against the

---

[248] Ibid., 374.
[249] Saint Just, 1089.
[250] Robespierre, *Robespierre: Entre Vertu et Terreur*, 209.
[251] Kennedy, *Cultural History of the French Revolution*, 312.
[252] Furet and Ozouf. *Dictionnaire Critique. Idees*, 375.
[253] Kennedy, *Cultural History of the French Revolution*, 304/305.
[254] Ibid., 304/305.

brilliant vision of regeneration as Saint Just argued that for its sake "everything must be permitted."²⁵⁵

Saint Just's view of a morally limitless party machine was linked to the heart of the ideology of regeneration. The *regeneration* as a total ideology automatically implied the absence of limits. As Arendt has observed, the poison of Robespierre's virtue "was that it did not accept any limitations."²⁵⁶ It was the premonition of this trauma that engendered Immanuel Kant's (1724–1804) conviction that the state is the most difficult problem, one for which a complete solution is impossible.²⁵⁷ After the Revolution in 1794, Kant affirmed the ethical need for epistemic limitation in politics, calling for a term *"more modest* than the expression *providence*, especially a providence understandable to us."²⁵⁸ The liberal tradition may have been morally hypocritical and bankrupt concerning slavery, colonialism and the rights of working people—but in this philosophical principle of non-violence it had already deeply grasped an elementary feature of modern politics.

In the refusal to recognize limits to the Revolutionary path, the only possible explanation for inevitable difficulties remained the persistence of enemies in a boundless hunt for hypocrites. Robespierre's war on hypocrisy "carried the conflicts of the soul ... into politics," where they became murderous because they were insoluble.²⁵⁹ Locke's idea in secularism had been precisely to preserve the public sphere from such insoluble conflicts which must lead to violence. The institutional construction of secularism therefore yielded to a philosophical ambition with the Second French Revolution. Robespierre was hunting for truth.²⁶⁰

By 1793, the dualism of the people and their representation in the Assembly finally yielded to the purity of a unified sovereign will as the Girondins were purged and the Committee of Safety under Robespierre assumed dictatorial powers. At this time Robespierre articulated the progress of the regeneration in terms

---

²⁵⁵ Furet and Ozouf, *Dictionnaire Critique. Idees*, 427.

²⁵⁶ Arendt, *On Revolution*, 90.

²⁵⁷ Immanuel Kant, "Idea for a Universal History with Cosmopolitan Intent (1784)," in *Basic Writings of Kant*, ed. Allen W. Wood (New York: Modern Library, 2001), 125.

²⁵⁸ Kant, *Basic Writings of Kant*, 451.

²⁵⁹ Arendt, *On Revolution*, 97.

²⁶⁰ Ibid., 101.

of a perpetual struggle against "the intransigents who sought to replace other intransigents."[261] With 18 floreal (June 8), the Cult of the Supreme Being was introduced in a celebration of the end of factions. It was accompanied by calls to punish the surviving hidden networks of agents and conspirators. Robespierre proclaimed this "God of nature" in terms of the eternal principles on which human weakness finds the support for launching itself on the path of virtue. The Cult of the Supreme Being, according to Robespierre, announced the dominance of one truth in dealing a blow to fanaticism by which "all fictions disappear before the truth and all nonsense succumbs to reason."[262] Invoking Providence, he described a supreme being who essentially influences the destiny of nations and watches with peculiar love over the French Revolution surrounded by vile intrigues and so many enemies.[263] At the 1794 speech on the Festival of the Supreme Being, he praised the inspiration of Rousseau's idea of a civil religion.[264] These visions derived from older and half buried discursive structures of a religious nature, which Rousseau himself had slipped into as he confused life for literature.

On 10 June, 1794, the Law of Prairal (increasing the vagueness of the 1793 Law of Suspects) defined enemies of the people in terms of "those who have sought to mislead opinion... to deprave customs and to corrupt public conscience." With acquittal or death as the only possible verdicts, revolutionary justice dispensed with any pretence of law. Legitimacy was grounded in an intangible and transcendental quality of the mind: "the conscience of the jurors, enlightened by love of the nation."[265] In this way, as Saint Just put it, the Revolution was frozen, yet done so in the tape loop of a paranoid replay where the secret conspiracy was unveiled and exterminated only to be uncovered again. It was an eternally recurring step towards an imagined new dawn that was never to materialize.

---

[261] Furet and Ozouf. *Dictionnaire Critique. Acteurs*, 263.

[262] Ibid., 266–268.

[263] Henry Lewes. *The Life of Maximilien Robespierre* (Boston: Adamant Media Corporation, 2001), 240.

[264] Doyle, *The Oxford History*, 276.

[265] Duncan Townson. *The New Penguin Dictionary of Modern History. 1789-1945* (London : Penguin, 1994), 334.

The political logic followed the monotony and futility of the insatiable appetite for sexual violence found in the Marquis de Sade's (1740–1814) *Justine, or the Misfortunes of Virtue* (1794). This left only an arbitrary politics of state and popular violence (i.e. the state made use of armed gangs)[266] grounding a national identity discourse of integration and exclusion, where in 1792 half of the prison population of Paris was killed. Although labelled as enemies, the victims were often neither from the clerical nor noble orders but were largely common criminals—ordinary people like the tradesmen and artisans who carried out the ideologically veiled mass murders.[267]

As the legal framework of justice disintegrated entirely, and a state of perpetual war advanced against the ubiquitous mask shielding the conspiracy, Saint Just argued that "the detentions do not have their source in judicial relations." Rather, they found their justification as a means to "establish an order of things in which a single universal tendency to good will prevail."[268] In a praise of equality as virtue or a pure and unified public identity which may distinguish truth from hypocrisy, Saint Just defined the function of the state: "If there were morals, everything would be fine; we require institutions to purify them."[269] Institutions, then, ceased to instrumentalize non-violent conflict resolution over issues of public discord in Montesquieu's sense (i.e. the function of democracy and basis for an ethic of reconciliation). Instead, swarming across the never-broken frontier, they became the totalizing tools for refashioning the ever intangible soul.

---

[266] Doyle, *The Oxford History*, 143/182.
[267] Ibid., 192.
[268] Furet and Ozouf. *Dictionnaire Critique. Acteurs*, 263–288.
[269] Ibid., 9.

3

Early Indian Nationalism: Between Liberty and Authenticity

The Enlightenment discourse regularly functioned as the tacit coefficient in defining experiences of modernity for Indian thinkers from the late 18th century. Consider Abu Taleb (b. 1752), visitor to London. He came of age in the seminal conjunction between 1757 and 1765, the battle of Plassey and the British attainment of control over Bengal. Embittered by experiences of working for both the Bengal government and the British East Indian Company, he took to sea for Europe with a Scottish friend. He secretly longed for an accident to be "delivered from the anxieties of the world."[1] Upon arrival in London, he met with popularity among the English aristocracy, being celebrated as the Persian prince. This reflected the late 18th-century Orientalist discursive expansion beyond the limits of the Greco-Latin heritage, embracing a new universe in writing containing infinity of literatures and innumerable civilizations.[2]

This period, upon examination, does not conform to the classical dualism of growth-stagnation dividing Europe and Asia—the metaphysical story told by Empire to justify its power and its deeds. India's advanced regions were "dynamic commercial economies ... engaged in substantial local, regional and long-distance trade [which] gave rise to economic specialization ... and witnessed economic growth and high levels of prosperity." Indeed, Indian competition "propelled British innovation in textiles in the 18th-century" and thereby had an instrumental

---

[1] Abu Taleb, "The Travels of Mirza Abu Taleb Khan," in *Sources of Indian Tradition*, eds. William Theodore de Bary, Stephen Hay, Royal Weiler, Andrew Yarrow (New Delhi: Motilal Banarsidass, 1992), 560.

[2] Edward W. Said, *Orientalism: Western Perceptions of the Orient* (New Delhi: Penguin, 2001), 77.

role in triggering the Industrial Revolution.³ Historical and economic development was "a complex parallelogram of forces," rather than the impact–response paradigm where a dynamic and expanding centre acts upon a stagnant encompassing periphery.⁴

Abu Taleb reflected in wonder that future "philosophers will look with as much contempt on the acquirements of Newton as we now do on the rude state of the arts among the savages." This expressed a radical new temporal horizon that he called the English notion of "perfection." He also voiced anxieties over new forms of violence in neighbouring France, observing that the King "took no step to oppose the Revolution till it was too late."⁵ This suggests political mutability as a game played well or badly. It confirms Paul Hazard's ground breaking thesis on the Enlightenment as a discourse appealing to societies being forced from the spatial political mode of traditional empire into the turbulent zone of modern temporality — a mode of thinking suited to uncontrolled change.⁶ Both reflections expressed discursive formations of the emerging European Enlightenment: the historicist horizon and the republican preoccupation with the risks of action in time. The situation overall suggests the increasingly unequal power relations underlying these encounters: Anquetil-Duperron and William Jones were collecting new information on the Orient to reveal its texts, languages and civilizations to Europe, while the British East India Company had laid the foundations for a new colonial order on the road to the 1803 occupation of Delhi. At the start of the 19th century, with the Industrial Revolution already underway, the standards of living between Western Europe and the rest of the world became significantly marked. With retrospect, that moment of historical divergence was discursively elevated to fixed inflationary ontology fit to be recycled imaginatively without rational scrutiny.

---

³ Prasannan Parthasarathi, *Why Europe Grew Rich and Asia Did Not: Global Economic Divergence, 1600–1850* (Cambridge: Cambridge University Press, 2011), 84/115.

⁴ Christopher Alan Bayly, *The Birth of the Modern World: 1780–1914* (Malden: Blackwell, 2004), 7.

⁵ Taleb, *The Travels of Mirza Abu Taleb Khan*, 563–565.

⁶ Hazard, Paul, *La Crise de la conscience européenne 1680–1715* (Paris: Boivin & Cie, 1935), 9–40.

Nationalist assemblages, of temporally conditioned genesis, are highly variable on practical and discursive levels. We see a rising self-consciousness for British imperialism, which had fumbled experimentally and sometimes unsuccessfully through the wars and crises with France and many Indian states during the 18th century. It reflected the aggressive new imperial nationalism to emerge in Europe with the Austrian succession (1740–48) and the Seven Years War (1756–63).[7] There was a rising self-consciousness of all-India nationalism as a possibility. It is not tangible like an inanimate stone, but with the existential depth of a problem that reveals itself in unexpected ways through exercise and conduct. In this way, it is a comprehensive entity. Without homogenous essence, it is the practical consciousness of a growing political existence that changes in function of new learnings within the sharpening conflict situation of foreign domination. A reflexive process creates new moral, social and political problems. In this period distinctive temporal horizons, political conventions and discursive–practical formations emerged through this many-sided passage of struggle. The tacit dimension or unthought implies a principle of marginality where the future remains ultimately open despite varying accumulated regions of density—some of which harbour lethal ethical implications.

The 19th-century intersection between the British colonial empire and the Bengal Renaissance/early nationalist movement opens a prism permitting us to assess in what measure the onset of modernity in the Indian historical experience constituted a rupture with the past. The Mughal period suggested that modernity did not begin with the ascendancy of British colonialism: neither markets, reason nor even property protection were lacking in the emergent early modern Indian lifeworld. Regarding property protection, we know that

> Indian merchants operated vast empires [spanning] the subcontinent as well as the Middle East, Central Asia, East Africa and Southeast Asia, which is indicative of the security of mercantile property. By the 18th century, the advanced areas of India possessed highly productive

[7] Charles Breunig, *The Age of Revolution and Reaction, 1789–1850* (New York: W. W. Norton, 1977).

agricultural orders based on generations of investment, which is evidence that agrarian property rights were also well defined.[8]

It therefore goes against the evidence to say that "the British provided this ancient civilization with the external stimulus it needed in order to catalyse its evolution into a modern nation."[9] The evidence supports, rather, an explanation linking the compound of technology and power: the "divergence between Europe and Asia from the late eighteenth century was not a matter of markets but of technology."[10] By the mid-19th century,

> the scale of production in Europe was staggering. The decline in prices for cotton yarn and cloth, iron and other manufactures had no precedent in human history and the export of these goods led to deindustrialization in India, China and elsewhere. By 1850, Western Europe was the undisputed center of a new global manufacturing order.[11]

This fact has profound significance for a history of ideas, in terms of bending the heterogeneous quality of historical time into a universal imagining of a single historical future:

> With hindsight one can conclude that industrialization produced the divergence between Europe and Asia, but neither Europeans nor Asians in the seventeenth or eighteenth centuries were attempting to develop an industrial society. Only from the nineteenth century did men and women make economic and political choices with that goal.[12]

In sum, the so-called Industrial Revolution—upon closer examination linked to multiple globally dispersed industrious revolutions—constituted a profound region of density in ideas and imagining of nation-making enshrining:

---

[8] Parthasarathi, *Why Europe Grew Rich and Asia Did Not*, 5.

[9] Abraham Eraly, *The Mughal World. Life in India's Last Golden Age* (New Delhi: Penguin, 2007), 387.

[10] Parthasarathi, *Why Europe Grew Rich and Asia Did Not*, 62.

[11] Ibid., 1.

[12] Ibid., 9.

mechanical and physico-chemical powers of literally transhuman dimensions [which] enormously magnify muscular strength ... refine powers of control ... embody intelligence [and] endow men and women with endurance and resilience far beyond those of flesh and bone.[13]

From this perspective, India was rendered backward in the 19th century with forced de-industrialization; it is a-historical and essentialist to argue that India was somehow backward in-itself against ample evidence of dynamism, growth and experimentation throughout the 17th- and 18th-century experiences of early modernity.

Identities were transformed with 19th-century de-industrialization, impacting their imaginative and intellectual formations as political entities. With the colonial transformation of Indian society, "caste became a more rigid institution in the nineteenth century." Despite the caste-occupation correspondence, "in the commercially and politically dynamic world of the eighteenth century individuals and groups moved not only between occupations but also up and down the economic and political hierarchy." There had existed "a great deal of fluidity and mobility," as in 18th-century South India where "some of the most highly skilled weavers belonged to untouchable communities while members of so-called weaving castes worked as agriculturalists, traders and soldiers."[14]

For much of the 19th century, we see the Indian intellectual elite (from Dayananda Saraswati, indigenous educated, to English educated Keshub Chunder Sen) transfixed by British rule and calling it Providence (It "is Providence that rules India through England").[15] Indian intellectuals articulated such technical achievements as something supernatural. The historical juxtaposition of Empire and Renaissance reveals the concrete

---

[13] Robert L. Heilbroner and William Milberg, *The Making of Economic Society* (Boston: Pearson, 2012), 66.

[14] Parthasarathi, *Why Europe Grew Rich and Asia Did Not*, 59.

[15] Keshub Chunder Sen, "Philosophy and Madness in Religion," in *Sources of Indian Tradition*, eds. William Theodore de Bary, Stephen Hay, Royal Weiler, Andrew Yarrow (New Delhi: Motilal Banarsidass, 1992), 618; K. N. Panikkar, *Culture, Ideology, Hegemony: Intellectuals and Social Consciousness in Colonial India* (New Delhi: Tulika, 1995), 69.

meaning of Enlightenment: a discourse capable of reversible and contradictory effects in conjunction with specific power configurations from emerging civil organs to state modernization (or deindustrialization) projects and ultimately popular democratic uprisings. Like any discourse, it is plural, without essence and can be instrumentalized in multiple ways. It has never existed, in practice, in pure form, having no holistic identity prior to discursive and power effects that shape it within a specific social and historical moment of human action. It is human thought and action interacting with the involuntary[16] that gives any discourse substance in time as an evolving and selectively constructed heritage. In 19th-century India, the context was colonialism. Colonialism, a violent and humiliating infliction of power, is a form of extortion and violation of human dignity whose material and spiritual effects are enduring. A fancifully constructed theodicy is required to canonize the victors, the shock or impulse from without as Genesis narrative. There is a need to open up and discover the value systems of the defeated in order to grasp the multiple meanings—and hidden faces—of the Enlightenment heritage in its often finer hours.[17]

With the Industrial Revolution, change was imposed as the norm, at such a quickened pace that the problem of means was frequently eclipsed as we rushed towards the ghost of the future. It was at great cost that we have learned to consider the means (or difference) when we talk about improvement, and not remain focused on the sameness of absolute ends. Nineteenth-century Indian intellectuals and activists were preoccupied with beginnings and origins and finally divided over the question of means in political transformation. Despite this, from Saraswati to Surendranath Banerjea, they all looked at the future in terms of *some* vision of transformation identified with certain values; sometimes taking models for action from as far away as Russia or drawing from India's own legacy of political techniques and

---

[16] The "involuntary" is Paul Ricoeur's term for the existential conditions of being in the world and being who we are (i.e. from geography to community).

[17] Refers to lecture by Aditya Mukherjee at Caen University, France. "What Human and Social Sciences for the 21st Century?" 7 December, 2012, Caen, France.

practices.[18] Each assemblage or worldview represented variously interacting components, received piecemeal in unique moments and reconstructed under the context-specific pressures of collective life.

In Rammohun Roy, Henry Derozio, Dedrenath Tagore, Keshub Chunder Sen, and the entire movement of Brahmo Samaj with its array of social reforms and civil society organs, tracing sharply contradictory discourses and attitudes, there is a flowering of radical human hopes with the inner turmoil of alien state-driven transformations; these gradually recognized on economic grounds as a negation of the hopes promoted by the state's own Enlightenment-infused elite English educational programme. These elite true believers nurtured, until as late as Dadabhai Naoroji's unprecedented theoretical intervention around 1870 (the "drain theory"[19]), a profound if troubled confidence in the agentative and transformative powers of what they viewed as a modern progressive state. Its appeal was its power of radical change via science and technology, its propaganda of prophetic idealism and the example of faraway Britain itself that they took for the "original" under the influence of such propaganda: "England was a mirror of their own future."[20] To the popular peasantry, by contrast, it meant a progressively harder life of exploitation, dislocation and periodic famine while state revenues soared.[21] Naoroji's intervention deconstructed the aura of Providence that had gathered around reigning colonial power. He revealed it as merely the product of a human historical process grounded in mechanically increased productivity and the power of denying others access to the goods that constitute wealth.

---

[18] For a study of the historical depth of the civil disobedience tradition in India, see Dharampal, *Civil Disobedience and Indian Tradition* (Varanasi: Sarva Seva Sangh Prakashan, 1971), 9–18.

[19] Dadabhai Naoroji argued that Britain was extracting wealth from India "as the price of her rule in India" and short of "self government the Indians can never get rid of their present drain." See Bipan Chandra, *The Rise and Growth of Economic Nationalism in India: Economic Policies of Indian National Leadership* (New Delhi: People's Publishing House, 1969).

[20] Panikkar, *Culture, Ideology, Hegemony*, 22.

[21] Bipan Chandra, *Essays on Colonialism* (New Delhi: Orient BlackSwan, 2009), 139–146.

The English-educated intelligentsia, a creation of the colonial order for purposes of cheaper British administration and trade, had come into existence in Bengal by the first decades of the 19th century. Muslims, considered the defeated ruling order from the medieval *dark age* within the historicist grammar of origins, participated less in the emergent colonial order. Although Delhi College figured significantly for elite Muslims in the 1830s, it suffered a setback after the 1857 Revolt when Muslims were branded untrustworthy. We see an elite group of upper caste Hindus, tied in various ways to the order of power, seizing the new opportunities of the colonial state.[22] These liminal souls, with their intermediary role between occupying state and the popular masses, often proved themselves to be exceptionally capable men in both the spheres of thinking and acting. They aspired to be rulers of a new Indian nation within the politics of Empire, but were denied even an advisory role to the foreigners in power. If one's speech has no effect it can hardly be said to be in the public sphere.

Yet in Indian civil society they used both propaganda and organization to undertake regionally limited but highly influential reform projects, proving that by taking sustained action human beings start processes with consequences that cannot be reversed. They created an Indian public sphere in spite of prevailing political conditions. While the basic violence and intellectual hegemony of the colonial order was a powerful agency shaping their horizons, they also struggled passionately to shape and think their own futures. They were far from merely imprisoned in determinate structures of thought.[23] Modernity was, indeed, profoundly connected for them to political subjection and epistemic-ontological crisis. Precisely for this reason the process of thinking involved a radical struggle for redefinition, moving across multiple boundaries and searching, and was essentially plural and hence ambiguous.

---

[22] These developments are detailed in Yogendra Singh, *Modernization of Indian Tradition* (Jaipur: Rawat, 2009).

[23] Partha Chatterjee, *Nationalist Thought and the Colonial World: A Derivative Discourse* (New Delhi: Oxford University Press, 1986), 79–81, for the case that they were, and that Indian political thought continues to be to this day.

This radical ambiguity in modernity has deeply emancipatory potential, just as it can usher in backlash in the form of hierarchical and militarized forms of mobilization along multiple ideological axes of politicization. The article of faith that the modernization of humankind *must* mean its democratization is without evidence: colonialism as a modernization process was one proof of this. Modernity is not a pure epistemic object permitting teleological access to a higher world: say, the unified world of science, democracy and nationalism.[24] The very notion of history as an unfolding of self-consciousness overlooks much of the ambiguity and contingency in the frequent blindness of experience, the distinctive temporal rhythms and differences, and the corresponding element of ceaseless risk in practice that must be mediated methodologically through learnings. Learning for them, to be sure, was as insidious as a game of chess. The emerging Indian intellectual elite under the Raj confronted complications in relation to English as the world imperial language. If Latin or Arabic had been languages of universal land-based empires, implying ontological *belonging* within global religious communities, the sea based empire of the British Raj restructured the politics of language with secular dimensions. It was English that permitted the emerging Indian middle class their elite position of mediation.

In 1823, Rammohun Roy recognized that English, the world imperial language, constituted a wall to science and technology for the Indian population. Knowledge of the English language constituted not belonging but access to the secularized realm of *knowledge and power* for civil engineering purposes as well as military purposes of violence. It was the language permitting nationalists from different Indian regions to communicate and organize at the national level—a bitter and insoluble paradox that had to be lived with and turned to the service of emancipation. Finally, as Bankimchandra Chattopadhyay recognized vividly in 1870, the English language constituted a wall separating the new elite

---

[24] This perspective is sometimes suggested by Meera Nanda, *Prophets Facing Backward: Postmodernism, Science, and Hindu Nationalism* (New Delhi: Permanent Black, 2004) in an otherwise interesting study of the linkage between postmodernist theoretical stances and Hindu nationalist politics.

from the many regional languages of the popular masses: "they are deaf to our eloquence."²⁵ He articulated the possibility of mass mobilization following the Saraswati line of mono-religious democratic thinking.

In 1835, we see the seminal debate between the Orientalists and the Anglicists (1781–1843) culminate in the introduction of English education for the Indian civil service. Thomas Macaulay (served on the Supreme Council of India 1834–38) famously promised in the name of Enlightenment that a "new class" would be "Indian in blood and colour, but English in taste, in opinions, and in morals."²⁶ This reflected a new politics of cultural assimilation that, different from older religious conversion, represented both social power and the difficult becoming of a particular subject with morally dislocating consequences: language, manners, habits and travel abroad across the forbidden *black waters*. Education, moreover, had a teleological function—science, engineering, and medicine imparted skills to realize the goal of building a new India like England. There was a worldview and set of values tacit in this mode of existence. It undermined Brahmanism and the entire Aristotelian tradition of pure contemplation as ontologically superior to hands-on technical labour. Negating the category of the slave, it favoured the value of production and change within an ideologically disguised coercive political and economic set up.

The literary content of the new education, focused on the European Renaissance, Reformation and Enlightenment, was far from European history *as such*. It constructed European history in privileged moments: the ascendant middle classes and their vision of the world. It was part of a general historical-discursive reconstruction of nations.²⁷ Through the concrete and institutional process of learning—within a racically unequal relation of power—the copy-historicist-Eurocentrist and analogical

---

[25] Bankimchandra Chatterjee, "A Popular Literature for Young Bengal" (1870), in *The Picador Book of Modern Indian Literature*, ed. Amit Chaudhuri (London: Picador, 2001), 14.

[26] Thomas Babington Macaulay, "Minute on Education," in *Sources of Indian Tradition*, eds. William Theodore de Bary, Stephen Hay, Royal Weiler, Andrew Yarrow (New Delhi: Motilal Banarsidass, 1992), 601.

[27] The education programme is detailed in Yogendra Singh, *Indian Tradition*, 101–7.

Enlightenment[28] was materially transmitted to the Indian elite class of intellectuals, who struggled with it to reckon with the oppressive ambiguity of the colonial reality. The Indian thought on European Enlightenment was an interactive, creative and syncretic selection process without closed identity—despite certain self-conscious and dogmatic efforts to break with the Indian past in the name of *pure* modernity.

Emergent regions of density varied in pluralistic fashion between anarchic and authoritarian impulses. In the 1840s, the first generation of English-educated Bengalis read Thomas Paine's *Rights of Man* with its democratized reconstruction of civil society against the dominant elitist grain of European thought;[29] or Bengal was for a while enchanted with Comte and his infallible positivist method of discovering new truths about social and political change.[30] The appeal of the Enlightenment tradition was powerful if ambiguous: among independence leaders Mahadev Govind Ranade (1842–1901) advocated Bacon's message, Gopal Krishna Gokhale (1866–1915) thought J.S. Mill's method of empiricism alone was reliable, and Sri Aurobindo (1872–1950) combined Darwin and Einstein.[31] Calcutta, like Bombay and Madras before it, was a doorway to India from the sea. India was a main centre of world trade and industry at the start of the 18th century. Peter the Great (1682–1725) of Russia had said: "the commerce of India is the commerce of the world ... he who can exclusively command it is the dictator of Europe."[32] The Calcutta of the 1820s in which Rammohun Roy (1772–1833) and Henry Derozio (1809–31) were active was at the centre of emerging dimensions within the "empire of nature" and the "empire of

---

[28] See Robin George Collingwood, *The Idea of History* (New Delhi: Oxford University Press, 2000), 84, for an analysis of this moment in European Enlightenment thought.

[29] Bayly, *The Birth of the Modern World*, 87; On Paine, see Marlies Glasius, David Lewis and Hakan Seckinelgin, eds. *Exploring Civil Society: Political and Cultural Contexts* (Oxon: Routledge, 2004), 28.

[30] David Gosling, *Science and the Indian Tradition: When Einstein met Tagore* (London: Routledge, 2008), 15.

[31] Ibid.

[32] Bipan Chandra, *History of Modern India* (New Delhi: Orient Blackswan, 2009), 44.

force."³³ From having been three neighbouring villages along the Hooghly River, it emerged as the first colonial city and the second city of the Empire.

It was a key point in a worldwide trade network and, from Britain's perspective, a source of boundless wealth. A struggling band of merchants and missionaries had become a state perceiving itself, and often perceived with a mix of hostility and awe by its educated subjects, as a divine instrument. There were the armed colonial fortifications, indigo fields, the planters, and emerging leaders of Indian social and intellectual life—notably the Tagores who were themselves planters and capitalist entrepreneurs. Sometimes the new money, as with the Tagore family, permitted experiments in new ways of living. Such fortunes were themselves complicit in colonialism. By the 1870–80s Jute factories lined the banks of the Hooghly River. A printing–publishing industry had emerged in Calcutta with standardized prose, providing the technical basis for new forms of wealth and new experiences of community based on simultaneity.³⁴

Rammohun Roy, from a devout Brahmin family in rural Bengal, was a doorway between India's richest traditions and the new dynamism of emerging modernity. He achieved this on the deceptively simple premise of restructuring Hindu belief as a pure monotheism derived from Shankara's Advaita Vedanta and *dharma* as a rationalist and egalitarian ideal. He remained anchored in living Indian traditions in a multi-centred way, resisting the force of the storm-blast of early modernity that drove distant contemporaries such as Wordsworth (1770–1850) to explorations of irrationalism, fantasy and nightmare. He absorbed, with remarkable spiritual strength, new traditions from Europe and new energies from a specific modernity framed by the obscurities of colonial domination. His ideas and practices proved that "[j]ust as western influences did not automatically lead to 'progressive' social and political consciousness, traditional influences did not invariably create conservative attitudes."³⁵

---

³³ Simone Weil, "The Iliad or the Poem of Force", in *An Anthology*, ed. Sian Miles (London: Penguin, 2005), 190.

³⁴ Benedict Anderson, *Imagined Communities: Reflections on the Origins and Spread of Nationalism* (New York: Verso, 1991), 37–47.

³⁵ Panikkar, *Culture, Ideology, Hegemony*, 69.

He set an enduring pattern for the 19th-century Indian intellectual and political movement through the Vedanta College (1825) that became Brahmo Samaj (1829), the vehicle for new ideas and reforms.

From the age of 15 to 20 years Rammohun Roy simply wandered India in search of knowledge. Thus, prior to his engagement with Western philosophies and religion, he had studied Sanskrit literature and Hindu philosophy at Varanasi and the *Mutazilite* tradition in Islamic philosophy in Patna (including Aristotle and Euclid). This is how he had knowledge of Arabic and Sanskrit, and read the Qur'an in Arabic. He had also spent several years studying Buddhism in Tibet, as well as acquiring knowledge of Jainism.[36] Having mastered the Persian language in order to follow his forefathers in Mughal government service, he ended up being an employee of the British, where he gained fluency first in English and later in French. In his studies of the Bible he learned Greek, Latin and Hebrew. We can say he lived in a world of decentred pluralism. His thought and practice, as a unique reckoning with modernity, were grounded in the ethic of reconciliation. In his journalistic work, Rammohun Roy published newspapers in Bengali, Persian, Hindi and English, promoting scientific ideas and discussing social issues: he thus assisted with the creation of a literate, self-imagining and simultaneous community within several logospheres.[37] We may identify him with the later muckraking tradition of Stephen Crane (1871–1900) in the United States. He opened several schools and colleges: the English school in Calcutta (1817) which taught mechanics and the philosophy of Voltaire, and the Vedanta College (1825) that taught Indian traditions and Western social science as well as physics.[38]

Rammohun Roy was also an activist who initiated important lines of social reform. Arriving in Calcutta in 1814, he organized a campaign against the popular worship of idols and the rigidity of the caste system. He condemned the priestly class. In these actions targeting oppressive social legacies and heterotopic

---

[36] Panikkar, *Culture, Ideology, Hegemony*, 66–69; Chandra, *History of Modern India*, 128–33; Chandra, *Sources of Indian Tradition*, 571.

[37] Term coined by Mohammed Arkoun.

[38] Chandra, *History of Modern India*, 131.

belief we see an underlying nationalist conception and a will to a public realm built upon the terrain of immanence. His principle motivations were political, idols and caste being in his view obstacles to the process of nation-making. He clearly differentiated a secular political realm and assigned it priority in relation to the traditional hierarchic-dynastic religious universe: "the present system of religion (is) not calculated to promote political interests." Clearly, secularism concerned a response to changes in the order and relations of power, and not an unveiling of the true world beyond a prior world of enchantment. Idols represented the mediation of religious experience to illiterate masses by way of visual creations that are local and particular, and far from a broadly shared literate religious community based on standardized conventions. Again evoking society as a unified secular realm, he wrote that idolatry "destroys the texture of society."[39]

Rejecting the mediation of the priestly class, Rammohun Roy argued on the basis of egalitarian religious ethics that every individual consciousness can have access to God. To this end, he produced and freely distributed translations from Sanskrit to several vernaculars, claiming that Vedanta is "little known to the public" and "concealed within the dark curtain of the Sungscrit language."[40] Similarly, he condemned the caste system as being "the source of want of unity among us."[41] In Rammohun Roy, we have the paradox of a man building the foundations of a nation in numerous languages and for a variety of different religious cultures, and combining elements of the French Revolutionary legacy with a religious universalism. The poly-linguistic and multi-cultural discursive–practical formation in Indian nation-making was likely initiated through his efforts.

Rammohun Roy was a man of the Enlightenment and its core values in liberty and equality. He fought tirelessly against censorship by the colonial state, demanding "unrestrained liberty of publication", and on behalf of "civil rights."[42] In sum, he

---

[39] Rammohun Roy, "To the Believers of the Only True God," in *Sources of Indian Tradition*, eds. William Theodore de Bary, Stephen Hay, Royal Weiler, Andrew Yarrow (New Delhi: Motilal Banarsidass, 1992), 572–75.
[40] Roy, *To the Believers of the Only True God*, 574.
[41] Quoted in Chandra, *History of Modern India*, 132.
[42] Rammohun Roy, *For Freedom of the Press*, 586.

took the colonial state to task in the name of the principles of Enlightenment, accusing it of violating them: thus we see the discourse was employed not merely by the state to justify its domination in the name of improvement, but by those it dominated to fight for a change in the order of power in the name of specific values. Discursive–practical formations have multiple-reversible functions.

Rammohun Roy rejected the aggressive proselytising of Christian missionaries, even as he affirmed the value of Christianity as part of a wider and deeper human heritage. Thus, he embraced components of the Christian heritage while rejecting others. He energetically fought a campaign against the Christian missionaries in their efforts to convert Hindus and Muslims by threat, pressure and fear, arguing that every man should live "according to the dictates of his own conscience," and religion spread by "force of argument" rather than "abuse and insult."[43] Thus, he opposed an Enlightenment discourse to the least tolerant component of the monotheist heritage. His campaign against the subjugation of women—concerned with polygamy, widow remarriage, equal inheritance rights and the historic agitation against *Sati* initiated in 1818—also involved the effort to form a national consciousness through the spread of propaganda, organization of action groups (to keep watch and prevent violence to women). He organized a countermovement against those orthodox Hindus petitioning Parliament to withhold the ban on *Sati*. Thus, he initiated practical formations for transforming the public realm. Rammohun Roy's notion of humanism rejected essentialism and affirmed the power of education to change people: "as you keep women generally void of education and acquirements, you cannot therefore in justice pronounce on their inferiority."[44] By the same humanist logic, he extended his attentions to the welfare of India's peasantry.

Rammohun Roy was attacked by orthodox Hindus—according to one critic—"in the same light as Christians do Hume, Voltaire, Gibbon and other sceptics."[45] The thought and struggle

---

[43] Rammohun Roy, *A Counterattack against the Missionaries*, 578–79.
[44] Rammohun Roy, *In Defense of Hindu Women*, 582.
[45] Lynn Zastoupil, *Rammohun Roy and the Making of Victorian Britain* (New York: Pelgrave, 2010), 136.

of Rammohun Roy embodied a transition in values from being to praxis. He recognized the immense power in everydayness. Contrary to the Law book of Manu, nobody, in reality, possesses force: power relations can change at any moment. This is the insight of the Machiavellian republican tradition, voiced memorably by Rousseau in his quest for an "immovable" foundation: "all human institutions seem at first glance to be founded merely on banks of shifting sand."[46] Rammohun Roy interpreted the concept of dharma through this political plane of immanence. An admirer of the French Revolution (Metternich's "revolutionary virus"[47]), he drew on the historical energies that emerged from this formative experience. It is clear, from the sum of his actions, that Rammohun Roy was a visionary with a consistent idea but who was also very much at home in the realm of public action. His basic idea was drawn from the multiple sources that had shaped his life: both the Bhakti milieu of his village and the Islamic *madrasa* deepened his conviction of monotheism, one of the main premises for his purification and restoration of the Hindu tradition as the monotheistic "basis of Indian unity."[48]

Rammohun Roy's personal mission in nation-making was therefore an ambiguous response not only to the presence of British colonial domination in Bengal, but to the global French Revolutionary aftermath of which he was profoundly aware. That is to say, post-1815 Europe where territories were shifted from one state to another without consideration for the German, Italian or Polish inhabitants, and the rise of popular nationalisms embedded in Enlightenment philosophy and the French Revolutionary politics of popular sovereignty. Such territorial transfers from above had been practiced for centuries according to the traditions of European diplomacy, but in the years following the Napoleonic wars feelings were remoulded: states and nations should coincide in self-determination free from foreign control, and should control their own history.[49] This development points to the power of something invisible, a history of

---

[46] Rousseau, *The Social Contract and Discourses* (Gurgaon: Everyman, 1993), 48.
[47] Breunig, *The Age of Revolution*, 181.
[48] Gosling, *When Einstein met Tagore*, 15.
[49] Breunig, *The Age of Revolution*, chapter 3.

consciousness as the discovery of problems with immense material force for good or ill.

The 1821 failed revolution in Naples caused Rammohun Roy considerable grief, while he was overjoyed at the 1823 revolution in Spanish America.[50] This cosmopolitanism deserves close analysis. Rammohun Roy's conception of immanence in political change and consciousness of a simultaneous globalized struggle for change indicate a new temporal horizon that is ephemeral and not ontological. Yet he employed the energies of various traditions to navigate through these unprecedented changes, rather than rejecting them. He sometimes used the authority of Hindu sacred books to show that certain practices (idolatry, sati) were in contradiction with the spirit of the religion, and at other times employed a secularized humanist logic that separated moral precepts from religious discourse. Unless we accept a clear binary dividing tradition from modernity or Enlightenment as a pure object (i.e. being "governed by rules of the language of post-Enlightenment rational thought"[51]), these ambiguities — or explorations of practical capacities rather than mere contemplation — are scarcely contradictions in our real lives.

Rammohun Roy accepted the metaphysical and self-serving Raj historical construct of the Indian past, a narrative of *origins* combining the William Jones Orientalist and James Mill liberal schools. This error had long-term harmful political effects as a divisive discourse.[52] A historical past within a standardized frame is not naturally given: it is a nation in the secularized space of modern politics that constructs a history. It is a problem of agency, and clearly within the contexts of Empire and war history is constructed through a Manichean logic of exclusion. As Orwell observed in his distopic vision of modern power, "Who controls the past controls the future."[53] The Raj employed James Mill's narrative to construct the Indian past in the historicist terms of a Hindu period, a lost golden age, and the Muslim period, a time

---

[50] Chandra, *History of Modern India*, 133.

[51] Chatterjee. *Nationalism. A Derivative Discourse*, 39.

[52] Sekhar Bandyopadhyay, *From Plassey to Partition: A History of Modern India* (New Delhi: Orient BlackSwan, 2009), 245.

[53] George Orwell, *1984* (London: Penguin, 1989), 260.

of stasis and decline ("the dark age"). A transcendental schema simplified everything.

Partly on this basis Rammohun Roy sought *pure* Hinduism in the ancient scriptures and denounced contemporary practices (idolatry, sati) as illegitimate accretions produced during the *decline*. He seems to have glided into the Rousseauian concern with distinguishing "between what is original and what is artificial in the actual nature of man," the project of "origins" and "foundations."[54] He argued that Baconian philosophy might one day do for India what it had done for the West using a tacit analogical or historicist logic. An 1823 letter asserted that the introduction of "real knowledge" through Baconian philosophy in Britain had displaced the ignorance perpetuated by the scholastics, and urged that the same measure might be taken regarding the "darkness" of Sanskrit education. His advocacy of "mathematics, natural philosophy, chemistry (and) anatomy" is reasonable in view of his practical ends, but the tacit structure of his argument reveals a complicity with Empire's historical construction of India's past.[55] Rammohun Roy failed to recognize that the conquering colonial power tried to remake the Indian past in order to remake its future, and that a general battle for men's minds among Indians on the subject of India's past was soon to be underway with the onset of the struggle over national politics.

Orientalist scholar William Jones (1746–94) considered the pure source of Hindu and Muslim texts corrupted by historical accretions and set about restoring distinct and separate codes of law for Hindus and Muslims. The great variety of overlapping sectarian Hindu–Muslim communities in the everyday lifeworld were negated by the consequent jurisprudence under Warren Hastings based on two distinct definitions of religious identity derived from *purified* textual traditions.[56] It was Bankimchandra who later recognized how the colonial state constituted the identity of the population through its discourse of "history,"

---

[54] Rousseau, *The Social Contract and Discourses*. 44.
[55] Roy, *Letter on Education*, 592–95.
[56] Barbara D. Metcalf and Thomas R. Metcalf, *A Concise History of Modern India* (Cambridge: Cambridge University Press, 2008), 58; Said, *Orientalism*, 78.

and appropriated this potentially lethal tool for his own political purposes through the powerful vehicle of his Hindu nationalist novels. On the level of modernity as information war, there is a struggle over what the modern mass can be made to accept as natural in a fundamentally uprooted world.

Given the measure that Rammohun Roy accepted the Raj's vision of the past, he accepted its corresponding vision of the future in India's eventual improvement through the logic of free trade as a utopian horizon.[57] Indeed, despite the increasing misgivings throughout his life he held an idealized view of the Raj as a state through which developmental ends might be achieved as "enlightened sovereign legislature" to "improve the inhabitants"—creating a 19th-century legacy among Indian activists and intellectuals fraught with bitter contradiction. He was a *true believer* in the state, and his view suggests radical mutations in the temporal horizon in terms of teleological assumptions and the promise of the future as a domain of improvement—itself a term loaded with ambiguity in terms of what qualities constitute such improvement and for who at the broad level of state transformations. Yet what is certain is that Rammohun fought for the world he envisioned on the ground among the people he hoped to improve, upon the plural and uncertain terrain of community and immanence, visiting the burning ghats of Calcutta, and never as a utopian visionary imposing a *scientific* (or other) agenda from above.

Rammohun Roy's core insight regarding colonial power was the knowledge and power construct at the centre of the Raj's modernity that he identified with the thought of Francis Bacon— this was a matter confronting the immediate social significance for India of new forms of science and technology; of struggling for the right to exist in a world where peoples without these advantages perished as *nations*. Setting a pattern for 19th-century Indian thought, he described the "mechanical arts" as a "ray of intelligence" from Europe while asserting that in "science, literature and religion" India could hold its own in terms of a heritage.[58] Yet in reckoning with new technological and scientific forms of power Rammohun Roy retained the profound ethical

---

[57] For his views on free trade, see Zastoupil.
[58] Roy, *Hinduism is Not Inferior to Christianity*, 580.

notion, embedded powerfully in Indian intellectual tradition, of a many sided concept of truth.

Rammohun Roy argued, therefore, following the Akbarian tradition of religiosity and the Bhakti and Sufi movements of the same period, that all world religions are different roads leading to a single truth[59]—and he rearticulated this traditional secular concept in more radically democratic terms for the challenging modern circumstances he faced. He said that "the reasoning faculty that leads men to certainty in things within its reach produces no effect on questions beyond its comprehension." Because religions "transcend the human understanding, one cannot be preferred to the other." Thus, he opposed "prejudice and partiality to opinions" and the ignoring of "opposite sentiments," placing him within the dialogic tradition of Enlightenment centred on a many-sided ideal of truth based on posited epistemic limits.[60] Yet truth required defence. He wrote: "nothing can more surely impede the progress of truth, than prejudice instilled into minds blank to receive impressions."[61]

The many-sidedness of truth, an Indian tradition rooted in the popular Sufi–Bhakti heritage and not the preserve of any specific religion, has important *ethical* consequences in terms of the openness and non-violence related to fundamental premises of multi-cultural democracy. This central aspect of Rammohun Roy's thinking was significantly different to the closed and ahistorical discourses of *improvement* from Voltaire or Condorcet, or the dogmatic late 19th-century "finalist" claims of the leading thinkers Herbert Spencer (1820–1903) and Auguste Comte (1798–1857).[62] These individuals claimed to have the *secret* of universal progress on *epistemic* grounds—very far from the concept of many-sided truth comparable in some ways to John Dewey's conceptual pluralism. It is because there is no such final *secret* that collective ethical frameworks are required as the ongoing basis for non-violent extra-scientific structures of motivation to avoid destructive instrumentalization of scientific knowledge. This

---

[59] Panikkar, *Culture Ideology, Hegemony*, 31.

[60] Roy, *To the Believers of the Only True God*, 574.

[61] Zastoupil, *Rammohun Roy*, 44.

[62] Eric Hobsbawm, *The Age of Capital: 1848–1875* (London: Abacus, 1975), 295.

pluralist dilemma of existential public meaning was understood better by Rammohun Roy than by these 19th-century European heirs to the Enlightenment—obsessed with imposing mono-vocal truth—despite his admiration for them.

Among the younger generation in the intellectual world of Calcutta another leading figure appeared in the person of Henry Derozio (1809–31) who led the influential Young Bengal movement. Of mixed Portuguese and Indian descent, and raised in the Protestant faith, he received the best English education to be had in Calcutta. We see the beginning of a line of reformers, unlike Rammohun Roy, trained initially in Western education. Trapped in the *abject* space between European and Indian identity, he endured the injustice of being disqualified from a responsible government post.[63] At seventeen, he left Calcutta to work in his uncle's rural indigo factory on the banks of the Ganges. The Romantically inspired poems he wrote there and published in Calcutta brought him fame and he was appointed headmaster of the new Hindu College: "... when your torch [of the youth] shall dissipate the gloom ... That long has made your country but a tomb or worse than tomb, the priest's, the tyrant's den."[64] This language evokes the French Revolutionary experience, and transplants it to India in a celebration of youthful vitality and the ideal of the nation based on the metaphor of light.

Derozio became an impassioned mentor to young Bengalis at this centre of new Western learning. At this point we see an important line of ideological tension streak across the emerging Bengali civil society among its reformist elements. Derozio, like Rammohun Roy, was deeply inspired by the French Revolution: but he took its iconoclastic dimension more closely to heart and so repudiated Rammohun Roy's moderation in religious reform. Derozio attacked the orthodox society, his followers throwing away the sacred thread, publicly eating beef and drinking whiskey as symbols of *rupture* with the *irrational* past.[65] Calling Rammohun Roy a "half liberal," they transferred categories from

---

[63] The term "abject" coined by Julia Kristeva refers to a liminal condition existing between two states but belonging to neither.
[64] Derozio, "India's Youth—The Hope of Her Future" in *Sources*, 570.
[65] Metcalf and Metcalf, *History of Modern India*, 83.

European politics to India and implied a single road to modernity that was all or nothing.[66]

The new group thus steered away from the ethic of reconciliation in favour of modernity as a mission to establish reason through the destruction of outmoded historical forms. The outlook echoed Robespierre's urging that "nothing has been accomplished so long as anything remains to be accomplished," a complete compression of time into a totalized instant.[67] We see the dialogic concept of reason tacit in Rammohun Roy's thought and practice yield to a solipsist Cartesian logic of the sceptical individual. Rammohun Roy had been somehow at ease standing in multiple worlds at one time. The tendency among a strain of the new English educated elite initiated by Derozio was the affirmation of a new temporal horizon in complete rupture with India's past.

With Derozio we see the tendency to individualism in which rational subjectivity inheres irrespective of social relationships, as the community is objectified as the embodiment of historical falsehood. This expresses a power of negation: the sceptical individual as sovereign over the network of obligations that constitutes community. Rammohun Roy had rationally critiqued specific practices within the community while enlisting the participation of its members in securing these transformations (i.e. dialogically), but he had mostly not condemned or derided community as such in the name of a superior principle of higher reason.[68] Derozio's categorical rejection of community, by contrast, was based on a historicist conception of Reason as a superior stage, and he thus saw fit to mock and insult religious communities for their *backwardness*. It is therefore unsurprising that neither he, nor his followers, succeeded in the manner of

[66] A.L. Basham, *A Cultural History of India* (New Delhi: Oxford, 1975), 368.

[67] Maximilien Robespierre, *Robespierre : Entre Vertu et Terreur*, ed. Slavoj Zizek (Paris : Stock, 2008), 61.

[68] In an 1828 letter he wrote that "with few exceptions, (the masses are) immersed in gross idolatry, and in belief of the most extravagant description respecting futurity, antiquity, and the miracles of their deities and saints" (Rammohun Roy, *Appeal to the Christian Public* (New York: B. Bates, 1826), 123. Like other pioneers in thought and practice of this time his view was ambiguous and not fixed.

Rammohun Roy to connect with the population or enter the terrain of nation-making. Historicism as a basis for social reform has tended to be either ineffective or violent, but rarely hegemonic in its consigning of the everyday world to an inferior past.

Derozio's adherence to radical Enlightenment as a consistent line, and departure from Rammohun Roy's moderate Enlightenment was his own undoing as far as a practical legacy. The logical practical conclusion of Derozio's worldview would have been a politics of cultural reform implemented by the state. Yet Derozio in fact showed this tendency as only one among others. In defending himself following his expulsion from Hindu College on charges of atheism, he argued passionately that "humility becomes the highest wisdom" (in the absence of certain knowledge).[69] In this famous 1831 letter his thought is closer to Rammohun Roy's many-sided idea of truth. In sum, Derozio was also an explorer of new ideas and was ambiguous in expressing a plurality of viewpoints. We see several simultaneous emerging currents of political thought that remained partly tacit in the minds of social activists.

It is among Derozio's later followers that we see forms of behaviour offensive to the ordinary Indian population: the students of the Hindu college in Calcutta "adopted an aggressive attitude to everything Hindu and openly defied the canons of their inherited religion ... such as drinking to excess, flinging beef-bones into the houses of the orthodox, and parading the streets shouting 'we have eaten Mussalman bread'."[70] Thus, an emergent region of discursive density became consolidated through practice. Narayan Ganesh Chandavarkar (1855–1923) spoke of the "narcotic influence of custom" and declared that the "whole existence must be renovated." He considered the Indian past a "death in life that we have been living for two thousand years."[71] At this stage the French Revolutionary conception of rupture had been adopted as a discursive fixation. And so we have the second distinctive temporal horizon of reform to emerge

---

[69] Henry Derozio, "Letter Protesting His Dismissal," in *Sources of Indian Tradition*, 568.

[70] Charles Heimsath, *Indian Nationalism and Hindu Social Reform* (Princeton: Princeton University Press, 1964), 17.

[71] Heimsath, *Indian Nationalism*, 17.

from the new civil society space of Empire on the road to the Bengal Renaissance.

This rationalist tendency also marked, in some measure, Rammohun Roy's exclusively English educated followers in the Brahmo Samaj during the first half of the 19th century. Akshay Kumar Datta (1820–86) viewed all "natural and social phenomena" in terms of "purely mechanical processes" and altogether rejected the concern over religious sanction based on hermeneutics in his argument.[72] Underlying this attitude was a tacit temporal horizon. They staked their political activities on the certainty of a future world where religions had either perished under scientific advance, or ceased to exist in terms of any role within the public space. This imaginary expectation conformed to an ontological historicist narrative taken for a certainty, or a distinctive temporal horizon grounded in the wishes of the political imagination.

In this *modernist* vision of total progressive rupture with the static past, the empirical terrain of Indian history yielded to the colonial imagination. Post-Aurangzeb Mughal collapse showed not total disintegration of power, the formless vortex of imperial mythology, but rather the fragmentation of power into various emerging states. These combined Indian traditions and European experimental political dynamisms. Such military-strategic and other experiments were present in the civil unrest of 18th-century India: Haidar Ali (1761–82) of Mysore introduced a modern arsenal and Western military training based on French expertise in 1755, and used them to repeatedly defeat British forces in 1769. His successor, Tipu (1782–99), introduced a new calendar and system of coinage, collected books on military science, medicine and mathematics, and identified enough with the French Revolution to plant a liberty tree and join a Jacobin club. He manufactured weapons in European fashion and, to the astonishment of the British who killed him in 1799, maintained the peasantry at a more prosperous level than in British occupied Madras.

In Kerala, King Martanda Varma (1729–58) introduced a Western army and modern arsenal, undertook irrigation works,

---

[72] Bipan Chandra, Mridula Mukherjee, Aditya Mukherjee, Sucheta Mahajan and K.N. Panikkar, *India's Struggle for Independence* (New Delhi: Penguin, 1989), 86.

roads and canals for communication, and encouraged foreign trade. Martanda's successor, Rama Varma (1758–98), was involved in a revival of Malayalam literature, spoke fluent English and took an interest in foreign affairs, regularly reading newspapers published in London, Calcutta and Madras.[73] The Rajput ruler Raja Sawai Jai Singh (1681–1743) was a lawmaker and reformer as well as man of science, founding the city of Jaipur on strictly scientific principles with broad streets intersected at right angles. The astronomical observatory he built still stands.[74] From the 17th century, moreover, we see

> growing state competition in India [leading] states and elites to seek out scientific knowledge and technical experts for their political usefulness and the contribution they could make to economic and military improvement. Indian rulers ... took a keen interest in attracting skilled and knowledgeable workers to their territories, exploiting foreign sources of knowledge, whether embodied in individuals or texts, and codifying information for study and dissemination.[75]

Evidence thus exists of numerous emergent political formations, with their techno-scientific adjuncts, which contradict the image of an ontologically frozen world foisted upon Indians by the 19th-century colonial education system.

There were also historically anterior practical and discursive formations at the mass level. Nineteenth-century Indian intellectual tendencies were preceded by popular 18th-century movements. Eighteenth-century India was a "highly monetized world" with individuals "embedded in complex networks of exchange that linked local, regional and global economies, and most inhabitants of the advanced, commercial regions were reliant upon trade to meet their daily needs."[76] In 18th-century civil society important movements of protest and dissent, preceding British imperial intervention, impacted the structure and organization of caste and gender. We see the challenging of idolatry, polythe-

---

[73] Chandra, *History of Modern India*, 29.
[74] Metcalf and Metcalf, *History of Modern India*, 40.
[75] Parthasarathi, *Why Europe Grew Rich and Asia Did Not*, 187.
[76] Ibid., 60.

ism and superstition by a large number of such heterodox sects which emerged in nearly all areas of India. They ate together, addressed one another as brother and sister, and translated Vedic texts into simple Hindi for the common man: a practical and democratic affirmation of the plane of immanence. With each sect having a following of 20,000–30,000, we see a developing trend of social protest and religious dissent in 18th-century Indian public life.[77] Precisely because these movements preceded the British, the notion of "impact response" or "rupture"—the Eurocentric construction of modernity—is inadequate for explaining the complexity of events in this period.[78]

Among Indian Muslims, we see a slightly different road. The Muslim elite lost its preeminence with the ascendance of the British regime and much of its confidence and vitality. The military establishments of the Nawab of Bengal ejected large numbers of those who had served in the army. The Muslim judges of criminal courts were removed as an organized group. The Muslim higher classes began to sink into poverty and merge with the underclass, and Muslim education contracted.[79] The 1792 Permanent Settlement empowered Hindu landlords in relation to the Muslim peasantry.

At the same time the railways, steamers and post and telegraph networks drew Muslims together and helped Islam to gain solidarity: technological modernity brought awareness of difference already there and could therefore assist with the politics of standardization. The 18th-century revivalist movement started by Shah Wali-Allah (1703–62), responding to the crisis and decline of Indian Muslim power, sought to reconsolidate the *umma* through a radical purging and return to the basics of Islamic identity. This boded ill for India's popular composite culture: Shah Wali-Allah expressly rejected customs and beliefs shared with popular Hinduism (syncretic shrines, ceremonial dances, planting banana trees around the house with the first menstruation of a girl).[80] Yet unlike his central Arabian contemporary, Abd al-Wahhab (1703–92), Shah Wali-Allah called for women's education in

---

[77] Panikkar, *Culture, Ideology, Hegemony*, 5.
[78] "Impact response" is used by Panikkar, 3.
[79] Singh, *Indian Tradition*, 70.
[80] Basham, *History of India*, 383–85.

his vision of regeneration.[81] His revivalist reformism based on the *Naqshbandi* tradition persisted until the aftermath of the 1857 Revolt, when we see a new *modernist* stream of revolt under Enlightenment-inspired reformer Sayyid Ahmed Khan (1817–98).[82]

Khan believed that interpretations of the Qur'an should conform to the observed truths of science. He distinguished divine and immanent knowledge. It is ironic that his uncritical acceptance of the European paradigm of democratic modernity led to his rejection of democracy as a viable possibility for multi-religious India: "I studied John Stuart Mill's views in support of representative government ... I reached the conclusion that the first requisite of a representative government is that the voters should possess the highest degree of homogeneity."[83] Muhammad Iqbal (1875–1938)—who inspired the divisive Pakistan movement—subsequently inserted a modern romanticism into Indian Islam. He derived his poetic and philosophical vision from Henri Bergson and Friedrich Nietzsche: action is the key to existence and our destiny is to remake the universe. These examples show the futility of invoking some metaphysically bounded Islamic essence in analyzing modern political and cultural developments in the Indian Islamic lifeworlds. Iqbal's revivalism was saturated in European counter-Enlightenment discourses espousing *life affirmation* over scientific knowledge.

Revivalist responses to colonial rule (as a common temporal horizon and political convention based on fixed and *pure* collective identity) also existed among Hindus, notably outside of Bengal. These presented a negation of the earlier multi-religious egalitarian tendency introduced by Rammohun Roy's Brahmo Samaj. The Arya Samaj, led by Dayananda Saraswati (1824–83) was an effective practical response to colonial domination. Its goal was to restore the Hindu tradition to its pure sources and regenerate it for the purposes of the present. Arya Samaj had a broader public appeal than Brahmo Samaj, which appealed mainly to urban educated groups. Saraswati had never received

---

[81] Bayly, *The Birth of the Modern World*, 77.

[82] Basham, *History of India*, 386.

[83] Syed Ahmad Khan, "The Indian National Congress," in *Sources of Indian Tradition*, 746.

Western education after traditional schooling his education was in the rigorous school of moral virtue. The Empire had not yet encompassed the north Indian region where his wealthy Brahmin family lived, and from whom he ran away to become a mendicant. Saraswati did not create an imagined community through mind or subjectivity: his appeal was centred on self-disciplined modes of being and doing rooted in yogic breathing. He learned to respect the Vedas through the hard discipline of his old master in the remote woods. When Saraswati arrived, half naked, in Calcutta to meet the Brahmo Samaj they tried to *civilize* his conduct: but inside they were probably awed by his unpretentious *authenticity*.

Keshub Chunder Sen (1838–84) seemed sometimes in the grip of a contradictory tangle of unconscious thorns produced by serving and becoming the image of the colonial master. Saraswati promoted the same reforms as the Brahmo Samaj: to end child marriage, to permit widow remarriage, girls' education, and to minimize caste status.[84] He admired aspects of Britain as he saw it through the Empire: "Whatever they do, they do after discussing it thoroughly among themselves and referring it to their representative assembly"; "They sacrifice everything ... for the good of their nation."[85] Interested in scientific knowledge, he dissected a corpse to verify descriptions of human anatomy contained in a religious text. He threw both in the river upon finding the account false.[86] He maintained, however, that all modern scientific discoveries were contained in the Vedas. His belief in their infallibility distinguished him from Rammohun Roy's legacy and the Brahmo Samaj: "God's knowledge is infallible and therefore, the teachings of God's book should also be equally infallible."[87]

Saraswati embodied a romantic counter-Enlightenment ideal privileging authenticity. His political vision was anchored in a historicist framework centring the Vedas as absolute

---

[84] Metcalf and Metcalf, *History of Modern India*, 141.

[85] Dayananda Saraswati, "The Light of Truth," in *Sources of Indian Tradition*, 634.

[86] Panikkar, *Culture, Ideology, Hegemony*, 68.

[87] Saraswati, "The Light of Truth" in *Hindu Nationalism: A Reader*, ed. Christophe Jaffrelot (New Delhi: Permanent Black, 2007), 32.

knowledge, which were the fountainhead of an advancing universal civilization

> ... had not God taught the sages the Vedas, and they to others, there would have been no educated men today.... Similarly so long as Europeans like Columbus had not gone to America, the Americans too were devoid of education for hundreds of thousands of years.[88]

This epistemic totalization went with a commitment to guns as a means of political change.[89] Saraswati demanded that social life conform to the limits of the Vedic discursive universe: "... the Vedas are the books of God. All persons should act according to their injunctions. If anybody asks what religion they belong to they should say their religion is Vedic."[90] While Saraswati rejected alternative interpretations of the Vedas, he actively promoted scientific education.[91] The Arya Samaj criticisms of Anglicized Indians concerned practice than rather ideas, evoking "man without dharma ... wading his way to liberalism through tumblers of beer."[92] This was a seminal discursive–practical formation.

Saraswati's vision was modern. Quite probably the exported Napoleonic state of strictly codified law, permitting free reign to Christian missionaries after 1813 within a broader politics of top-down transformation, incited Saraswati's declaration of war on all other religions and his attempted modern codification. He held that "Hindus would disappear in the face of Muslim and Christian conversion."[93] Seeking to be rid of *debilitating* difference, Saraswati declared the Vedic religion the only authentic religion: "It is extremely difficult to do away with differences in language, religion, education, customs and manners, but without doing that the people can never effect mutual good and accomplish their object"; it is "extremely difficult to make any progress

[88] Ibid., 33.
[89] Gosling, *When Einstein met Tagore*, 17.
[90] Saraswati, *Hindu Nationalism*, 34.
[91] Jyotirma Sharma, *Hindutva: Exploring the Idea of Hindu Nationalism* (New Delhi: Penguin, 2003), 14–45; Panikkar, *Culture, Ideology, Hegemony*, 11.
[92] Gosling, *When Einstein met Tagore*, 24.
[93] Metcalf and Metcalf, *History of Modern India*, 141–42.

as long as their religion and their interests are not the same."[94] The distinction between secular public interest and religious affiliation thereby collapsed in this affirmation—partaking of a broader tacit structure—of homogeneity as the precondition for nationhood.

Historicism must ontologize its elements of decline. In Saraswati's historical scheme of *purity* not only were Buddhism and Jainism signs of decline but so were Bhakti movements. Muslims were simply invaders. Note that his conception of the nation was based on his understanding of European experiences as the modern ideal—not modernity *as such* (as if there were such a thing). It is a specific discursive formation traceable to the French Revolutionary ideal of universal assimilation. Such an exclusive national ontology for a multi-religious land must inevitably sublimate the political violence which is its precondition. Components are relational, not essential, and construct each other through patterns of juxtaposition.[95]

Saraswati's vision of the modern nation sought to legally encode the violence already inherent in his means to the pure end. He called for "Shastric based" forms of corporal punishment in which with "whatever limb a man commits an offense, even that limb shall the king remove." Thus the realm of sacred discourse burst into that of public law.[96] Saraswati inspired the late 19th-century Extremists who employed religious symbols to mobilize popular action.[97] Lokmanya Tilak (1856–1920) and Sri Aurobindo (1872–1950), although Western educated, tried to appropriate Saraswati's aura of popular authenticity. The revolutionary terrorists were moved by his example of iron commitment. His influence was divisive; he promoted a mono-religious form of national democracy.

Founding member of the Indian National Congress Mahadev Govind Ranade (1842–1901), by contrast, recognized that revivalism—despite claims to ontological authenticity—was inherently a choice: they are "at sea as to what it is they seem to revive."

---

[94] Sharma, *Hindutva*, 14–45.
[95] This follows Saussure's theory on identity.
[96] Sharma, *Hindutva*, 14–45.
[97] Bidyut Chakrabarty and Rajendra Kumar Pandey, *Modern Indian Political Thought* (New Delhi: SAGE, 2009), 14.

This marks a profoundly different temporal horizon and discursive formation. It is rooted in pluralism and choice over fixed claims to collective truth, and at least tacitly embraces an ethic of non-violence. He urged a humanist ethic based on the "recognition of essential quality between man and man" and rejected the "fictitious differences between men and men." He focused on intellectual virtue: it is "the thought and idea which determines," "inward conscience" and not outward form.[98]

While being critical of aspects of the Indian tradition, Ranade also saw value in the Akbarian moment in India's traditional past: "If the lessons of the past have any value ... in this vast country no progress is possible unless both Hindus and Mahomedans join hands together, and ... follow the lead of the men who flourished in Akbar's time." He warned of the "great danger of the work of Akbar being undone by losing sight of this great lesson which the history of his reign [had taught]." At the same time, Ranade interpreted Indian history through a critical lens in rejecting the "mistakes" of "Aurangzib."[99] Clearly he sought to construct the Indian past in a more democratically empowering way than the ideology of the colonial state, and in a more pluralistic way than the Saraswati *authenticity* discourse. This critical sense of a multiple potentiality in the Indian past was frequent among founders of the Congress; it constituted the dominant temporal horizon. Naoroji too spoke of Akbar as a precedent in multi-religious toleration.[100] Banerjea evoked Nanak, who in the 15th century introduced humanist values into religion while criticizing both Hindu and Muslim orthodoxy,[101] as introducing "the great principle of Indian unity [that] endeavoured to knit together Hindus and Musulmans under the banner of a common faith."[102]

We thus see two emerging streams of nationalist thought among the Hindu religious majority: identity (the essentialist reconstruction of Hindu tradition *itself* as a substantive object)

[98] Mahadev Govind Renade, "Revivalism versus Reform," in *Sources*, 682–88.

[99] Renade, "Hindu-Muslim Cooperation," in *Sources*, 688–89.

[100] Dadabhai Naoroji, "The Blessings of British Rule," in *Sources*, 670–71.

[101] Singh, *Indian Tradition*, 42.

[102] Surendranath Banerjea, "The Need for Indian Unity," in *Sources*, 676.

and pluralism (a synthesis between reconstructed Hindu tradition and the heterogenetic: Islam, the West and other Indian traditions). [103] We may note that those leaders upholding a principle of *identity* tended to put less emphasis on inner consciousness as a scientific ideal, and more on the details of public and private ethical conduct in everyday life—while still promoting scientific and technological advance. Both streams belong within the category of future-oriented modern political thought concerned with power and the state, and their possible roles in structuring or organizing everyday lifeworlds. This temporal horizon is a structural precondition of political participation—the state apparatus thus implants itself through entanglement in human lives whether in alliance or opposition. The nationalist streams differ concerning public conflict resolution between organized violence and an ethic of reconciliation, or authoritarian and democratic political ideals. The differing constructions of violence/nonviolence as means are the central issue, which in turn are linked to distinctive historical reconstructions of India's heritage and identity.

The tradition of the Brahmo Samaj and its reform efforts was resuscitated by Debendranath Tagore (1817–1905) in 1843. He argued that "the message of the Brahmo Samaj does not materially differ from the doctrines of the pure theistic bodies all the world over," thus extending the principle of religiosity or many sided truth initiated by Rammohun Roy. Calcutta's educated elite—the mostly upper caste clerks, merchants, state officials, rentiers—expressed their outrage by establishing the Dharma Sabha, thereby thickening the texture of this emerging and conflicting civil society. The movement was split in 1866 when Keshub Chunder Sen proposed more radical measures than Tagore was prepared to accept in dispensing with the Brahmin holy thread. He too was of the cultural and commercial class intertwined with the colonial order. Keshub Chunder Sen argued that "truths are to be found in all religions."[104] He integrated the Bible, the Qur'an and the Zend-Avesta as the basis for the religious organization of "abstract cosmopolitanism." The 1872 Native Marriage Act contained a clause declaring: "I am not a

---

[103] Singh, *Indian Tradition*, 43.
[104] Panikkar, *Culture, Ideology, Hegemony*, 29.

Hindu, not a Mussalman, not a Christian." He assigned his four disciples a life-long study of the four world religions: Hinduism, Buddhism, Islam and Christianity. Proclaiming "unity in multiplicity", he said "all religions now have become one."[105]

These emergent discursive–practical formations expressed deeper Indian traditions of pluralism. We cannot reduce to an essence their multiple potential applications (i.e. *pluralism* may be used negatively to relativize the findings of modern science and uphold coercive elements in traditional scripture). We may observe, however, that among founders of the Congress the pluralist traditions lent themselves to a political ethic of democratic openness to diverse and conflicting views. Keshub Chunder Sen consistently upheld a line of tolerance:

> [S]ome among us ... denounce Mahomedanism as wholly false, while others contend that Hinduism is altogether false. Such opinions ... only indicate the spirit of sectarian antipathy. Do you think that millions of men and women would to this day attach themselves so devotedly to these systems of faith unless there was something really valuable and true in them?

Notice the emphasis is on religion as an everyday existential experience rather than a truthful or untruthful doctrine. He accordingly retained a critical attitude to religion, noting that "superstition, prejudice and even corruption" required "elimination" despite "a residue of truth and purity." His religious criticism contained a democratic and multi-religious national agenda: in an "age of free inquiry and bold criticism" a "process of purification and development" would create the "future creed of India [as] a composite faith."[106] It is the composite faith of secularity, anticipating Nehru's ideal of equally honouring all faiths and extending them all equal opportunity. The value of differing faiths as a framework for embeddedness in community

---

[105] Arabinda Poddar, *Renaissance in Bengal: Search for Identity* (Simla: Indian Institute of Advanced Study, 1977), 42–49.

[106] Keshub Chunder Sen, "An Indian National Church," in *Sources of Indian Tradition*, 621–22.

lifeworlds is acknowledged, but religion deployed to suppress free enquiry or individual liberty is condemned.

Sen's critical attitude, it follows, entailed his affirmation of the "supremacy of individual reason," "individual conscience" and the "principle of democracy."[107] His recommendations were practical rather than ontological, aiming to create conditions for non-violent conflict resolution in the emerging multi-cultural Indian nation. In moments, he placed the highest value on modern science: "science will be your religion ... above the Vedas, above the Bible. Astronomy, geology, botany and chemistry are the living scriptures of God and *Nature*."[108] Here he flirted with the 18th-century *social* and ontological primacy of "Nature" — inevitably as a human imaginary construct—over sects (assuming there is no metaphysics which corresponds necessarily to scientific method as a total system).

Despite the oft-noted erratic transitions in his ideas, Sen combined the many-sidedness of truth with a liberal democratic politics. Here the Montesquieu tradition of prioritizing democratic institutions over total ideological solutions, the grounds for Durkheimian and neo-Kantian Weberian sociology, gained important ground. The democratic principles of Enlightenment as an institutional project became the basis for extending a tradition of composite faith with deep roots in Indian history. This exemplifies the meaning of the Enlightenment as a multi-centred and non-Eurocentric phenomenon. Components interconnect with varying roots in multiple formations, across a heterogeneous span of times and spaces. There is no inside/out dichotomy. To be sure, there is an element of power in these formations: but power that can be marshalled and turned to collective emancipation. The unfolding of the Brahmo Samaj at this stage shows the linkage between multi-cultural democracy and deeper traditions of non-violence as an Indian tradition with strong syncretic dimensions.

These liberal Indian intellectuals, despite their Anglicization and social location estranging them from the general population, never the less retained a considerable resource of traditional Indian political and intellectual thought in their worldviews.

[107] Poddar, *Renaissance in Bengal*, 42–49.
[108] Gosling, *When Einstein met Tagore*, 17.

Their failure to successfully reach the masses, linked to their appearance as 'collaborators', does not prove the contrary. The fusion of Indian and European composite elements in their thought (confirming Amartya Sen's conception of democratic change) informed their economies of political action. They attempted to maintain a politics of openness to difference based on the many-sidedness of truth as an Indian intellectual tradition. However, their professed identification with the Raj as a historicist instrument of divine transformation made them vulnerable to charges of 'inauthenticity' from the rising Hindu nationalist wave of around 1880. They found themselves torn between loyalty to the state and their own community, to say nothing of the general population who they too often derided as *backward* through a European Enlightenment historicist lens. Their plight surely embodied a false dichotomy, but such dichotomies are regularly manipulated politically.

By 1870, we can already point to a very different outlook articulated in the public sphere by way of the new form of the novel, in Bankimchandra's (1838–94) seminal contribution to a national literature. A brilliant graduate of Calcutta University, this deputy magistrate spent a lifetime in the same position without a promotion—exemplifying the limits to professional possibilities for educated Indians even when fortunate in finding a job. He wrote novels and other literary works in his spare time as a hobby, and ultimately revolutionized the Bengali language with his combination of the vernacular and new literary forms. His work was considerably influenced by German philosophy: particularly Schelling, Fichte and Herder.[109]

For Fichte, the self is the creation of shock or impulse from the outside. He articulated a seminally influential discourse of the modern nation:

> Those who speak the same language are joined to each other by a multitude of invisible bonds by nature herself, long before any human art begins ... they belong together and are by nature one and an inseparable whole. Such a whole, if it wishes to absorb and mingle with itself any other people of different descent and language, cannot do so without

---

[109] Chakrabarty and Pandey, *Indian Political Thought*, 8.

itself becoming confused ... and violently disturbing the even progress of its culture.

Fichte presents authenticity as the basis for nation-making and public belonging. The implications for India as a multicultural nation-in-the-making were grave, implying the ontological impossibility of cohabitation:

> Only when each people, left to itself, develops and forms itself in accordance with its own peculiar quality, and only when in every people each individual develops himself in accordance with that common quality, as well as in accordance with his own peculiar quality then, and then only, does the manifestation of divinity appear in its true mirror as it ought to be.[110]

Bankimchandra's aesthetic triumph was coloured by European counter-Enlightenment ideals.

Bankim was a penetrating critic of modernity. He recognized bitterly that the *modern* lifeworld was not simply the natural condition of reality unveiled (the static 18th-century Enlightenment notion), but in many ways a "change of faith" connected to distinctive modes of everyday life. He saw a new Eurocentric *becoming* where one must "Anglicize one's taste, manners and fashion" within the shortest time possible in a "tearing" of "bonds of social union." Even though the "enlightened human being" and "sound logic" insist that "Hinduism must be destroyed," the "spiritual nature of man abhors a vacuum."[111] *Anandamath* (The Abbey of Bliss), a story of Hindu ascetics overthrowing Muslim power, evokes a Yukio Mishima-like celebration of modern violence linked to the beatific moment of supernatural unity with the earth and nature. It depicts a process of self-creation through modernized traditional habitus: the martial qualities required for national insurrection do not come "like ripe fruit from trees; they

---

[110] Johann Gottlieb Fichte, *Addresses to the German Nation* (1806). Internet Modern History Sourcebook. http://www.fordham.edu/halsall/mod/modsbook.asp

[111] Bankimchandra Chatterjee, "The Confession of a Young Bengal," in *The Picador Book of Modern Indian Literature*, 23.

come by practice." We note an emphasis on moral rather than intellectual virtue.

In the final scene, we learn that "the people of India" are determined by supernatural fate to acquire "knowledge of the physical world from the English" and only then will they "comprehend the nature of the spiritual."[112] The British Empire being merely a pawn in the larger sovereignty of Hindu providence, the immense powers of modern technology are to be wedded to a regenerated Hindu spirituality. In this novel we see how technology interacted with Indian civil society in complex ways beyond merely representing an overpowering force of military domination and displacement of traditional modes of labour. In quite similar manner Ernst Junger (1895–1998) later argued in the 1920s that Enlightenment universalism, or humanist rationalism, as an intellectual proposition was "alien to the German genius." He rejected "empty concepts like humanity." Instead he urged that the "machine … be incorporated into a will to higher and deeper goals" anchored in a uniquely German experience of modern national self-realization.[113]

The point is not to identify these Indian authors with a later fascist movement they would probably have rejected, and that Junger himself rejected. The point, rather, is in their urging that technology be reconciled with the larger communitarian spirit and rules of pre-modern traditions of identity and belonging—a transcendental concept that contains elements incompatible with the multicultural democracy implied as a potential by other living Indian traditions at this time. Here we see the fundamental conflict opposing emerging temporal horizons and discursive formations at the close of the 19th-century in Indian civil society. National consciousness as an emerging phenomenon in India, as elsewhere, was plural: the national discourses of Bankimchandra and Ranade had very different political and ethical implications and did not tend toward a single harmonized end. The notion of a widely conceived uniform purpose, uniting disparate ideologies and violent and non-violent modes of practice, is an oversimplification of some nationalist historical narratives (unless that

---

[112] Bankimchandra Chatterjee, "Anandamath," in *Sources*, 716.

[113] Ali Mirsepassi, *Intellectual Discourse and the Politics of Modernization* (Cambridge: Cambridge, 2000), 141–45.

purpose be the bare removal of the British from India, but that leaves a dangerous amount unsaid).

We see multi-cultural and conversely ethnically homogeneous visions of democracy; both celebrations of the principle of humanism and reductions of a part of the Indian (Muslim) population to a *thing* on the basis of national *difference*. Both are modern, illustrating the alternative between totalizing historicism and a non-violent ethic of reconciliation. For the literary and intellectual elite of the new middle class, within their circumscribed world of debased privilege, there was alienation from the popular Indian lifeworld. Caught between the new principles they evolved and the orders of common sense linked to everyday living, family, community and orthodoxy, they were often excommunicated, rejected by relatives and even threatened with violence.

Rammohun Roy, for his assertions of religious equality between Hindus, Muslims and Christians, endured a social boycott organized by orthodox Hindus in which his own mother participated.[114] Keshub Chunder Sen, for taking his wife to a Brahmo ceremony, was excommunicated by his own family.[115] The cost of rejecting inherited networks is high. The psychological toll is an inner conflict between *honour* (existential acceptance and belonging within the kin-community network) and *principle* (the abstract ethical conviction that practices of the kin-community network are intrinsically wrong). We see a retreat from staunchly rationalist attitudes among important Indian reformers in the later 19th century. Under social pressure, Ranade abandoned his plan to marry a widow.[116] Keshub Chunder Sen, despite having led a prolonged and courageous campaign for a minimum age for Brahmo marriages, inflicted a fatal fission on the Brahmo Samaj movement when he was persuaded to marry his 13-year-old daughter to a Hindu prince.[117]

[114] Chandra, *History of Modern India*, 131.
[115] William Theodore de Bary, Stephen Hay, Royal Weiler, Andrew Yarrow, eds., *Sources of Indian Tradition* (New Delhi: Motilal Banarsidass, 1992), 615.
[116] Panikkar, *Culture, Ideology, Hegemony*, 28.
[117] William Theodore de Bary, Stephen Hay, Royal Weiler, Andrew Yarrow, eds., *Sources of Indian Tradition* (New Delhi: Motilal Banarsidass, 1992), 616.

These are all aspects of a crisis of existence and value, or the "problem of restoring integration and cooperation between man's beliefs about the world in which he lives and values and purposes that should direct his conduct [as] the deepest problem of modern life."[118] Cutting through this dilemma was an acute problem of power: to embrace the reforms of the colonial state, and to instigate them as a method of practice in nation-making, was to be a collaborator with foreign domination. Although these reform efforts sometimes had a prior and even widespread basis in the pre-colonial Indian lifeworlds, they became the target of anger particularly following the 1880 backlash (by people who sometimes agreed in principle, i.e. Tilak) because perpetrated by the colonial state. The notion of an India and other dichotomy was imposed over reformist practices that already had roots in struggles internal to India's early modern history.

This highly sensitive problem, articulated in the dichotomy between social reform and political reform, effected the weakening of the Brahmo in the late 19th century.[119] It paved the way to the political dual between Moderates and Extremists over questions of means to reform and ultimately independence. This became a violent affair with the late 19th-century rise of revolutionary terrorism; it could have become far more so, were it not for the persistence of non-violent Indian political and intellectual traditions into the era of Gandhian mass political mobilization. These non-violent tendencies ultimately predominated and significantly shaped India's political future.

We can distinguish *state-making* as a colonial enterprise involving several radical experiments to transform agriculture from pre-colonial to capitalist, the devastation of the social fabric, and the economic integration with the world system to British advantage, from *nation-making* as a gradual, cumulative and plural movement of Indian civil society from below culminating in the different and sometimes contradictory threads comprising the Indian national independence movement. The frontier sometimes overlapped between these two aspects of modernization. The combination of authoritarian colonial modernization (i.e. to master the population while extracting the maximum of

---

[118] Dewey, *Philosophy*, 577.
[119] Heimsath, *Indian Nationalism*.

resources to empower a foreign nation) and Indian civil society formation constituted a nearly schizophrenic historical ensemble. Some used the divisive social logic of colonialism and the European political ideal of the homogeneous nation for mobilization purposes, while others upheld older Indian traditions of multi-religious unity. These older traditions of tolerance, too, were conditioned by new European and American intellectual formations. Like any experience of political modernity, it was characterized by a radical ambiguity as well as involving efforts to view reality through a set of new scientific lenses. But the significance of the communal issue as a modern tactical construction is put into perspective when we read—even by historical experts sympathetic to colonial empire—that "there were no major communal conflicts in Mughal India."[120]

To understand the profound ambiguity in the Bengal Renaissance and early nationalist period we may look at the surreal meditation on identity in Sukumar Ray's (1887–1923) *A Topsy-Turvy Tale*. We see one identity transformed abruptly into another, or two cancelling each other, in a world where people and animals and mere objects obtain ontological equivalence. He evokes a chaotic whirlpool of corrupted clerks and solicitors, mad barristers talking emptily about rights, monsters muddling through logical conundrums, feathered accountants, and finally the trial of a random innocent condemned to "three months imprisonment and seven days' hanging."[121] Thus, he implies the force of violence underlying these experiences. His writing is a portrait of the disturbing subterranean life (the political unconscious, the episteme, the tacit component, the dream) of an emerging national consciousness though the Kafka-esque experience of colonial modernity.

Upon a more empirical level, where evidence may be marshaled to reconstruct how the National Movement coalesced from myriad factors, we see two imagined communities existing as political options for Indian nationalism. There was firstly a notion of national community as common economic interests: this included such liberal thinkers as Naoroji, Banerjea, Ranade

---

[120] Eraly, *The Mughal World*, 25.
[121] Sukumar Ray, "A Topsy-Turvy Tale," in *The Picador Book of Modern Indian Literature*, ed. Amit Chaudhri (London: Picador, 2001), 65.

and Gokhale. There was secondly, from about 1867, a notion of national community as distinctive civilizational or religious identity in Bankimchandra, Tilak, and Aurobindo Ghose. It was in part a revolt against the cultural Anglicization of English educated Indian intellectuals, and the apparent ineffectiveness of their methods in relation to colonial state power. It was fueled as well by Naoroji's analytical perception of the underlying mechanisms of colonial rule and the radical disillusionment confronting prior 'true believers': "all of these high promises have been pure romance, reality being quite different."[122] This late 19th-century political horizon—what came to be viewed as the irreconcilable contradiction between the Indian nation and British colonialism—forced the radical reconsideration of means that set the context for the explosive events of the early 20th century.

---

[122] Dadabhai Naoroji, "The Moral Impoverishment of India," in *Sources*, 673.

4

The Indian National Movement and Gandhi: The Ethic of Reconciliation as Mass Movement

NATIONALISM WITHOUT ESSENCE AS A DEMOCRATIC ENLIGHTENMENT DISCOURSE

It was in South Africa (1893–1915), not in India, that Gandhi first evolved his vision of Indian nationalism. His idea of "nationalism does not start with locality and then gradually extend itself to province and finally to nation."[1] Gandhi evolved his conception of Indian nationalism from the viewpoint of an outsider, an exile, of being not at home. In South Africa both Hindus and Muslims were persecuted immigrant minorities. In struggling together against experiences of injustice, they came to see themselves in secular fashion as Indians. Imprisoned and severely beaten, Gandhi also remained crucially committed to the humanity of his adversaries. He argued in 1921 that "Our non-co-operation is neither with the English nor with the West. [It] is with the system the English have established in India."[2] When delivering an independence pledge in 1930, he declared his "ambition" as no less than "to convert the British people through non-violence."[3] The experience of South Africa had shaped Gandhi's view of Indian nationalism: a unique vision of nationalism without enemies, or without essence. He rejected Rudyard Kipling's essentialist aphorism on the fundamental divide of *East* and *West*, claiming

---

[1] M.K. Gandhi, *Hind Swaraj and Other Writings* (Cambridge: Cambridge University Press, 1997), 21.

[2] D.G. Tendulkar, *Mahatma*, Volume 2 (New Delhi: Publications Division, 1992), 64.

[3] Tendulkar, *Mahatma* 3, 17.

"no inherent barrier between Indians and Europeans."[4] Like Nagarjuna, he rejected *intrinsic* in favour of *relational* identity.[5]

Gandhi's nationalism focused on the practical *technique* of non-violence and not an intellectual *definition* of identity. The Truth for Gandhi was not ontological, an identity already fixed outside the flow of time, waiting to be discovered. He said: "the real definition [of *Swaraj*] will be determined by our action, the means we adopt to achieve the goal." In this sense it is a temporal choice, a heritage reconstructed by our actions and values today. He continued: "If we would but concentrate upon the means, *Swaraj* will surely take care of itself. Our explorations should take place in the direction of determining not the definition of an undefinable term like *Swaraj* but in discovering the ways and means."[6] Nation-making was grounded on the *moral virtue* of practice rather than *intellectual virtue* (absolute primacy for truth systems i.e. utilitarianism, positivism, Marxism or social Darwinism) as the basis for freedom, happiness, etc, as a historical *end product*.[7] That is to say, it concerned the ethical importance of means in relation to any end to be achieved, and rejected the rupture of Final Ends/Foundation as making all means equivalent.[8] It focused on the immanence of time in a specific context, or the everyday temporality of ordinary people—not the subject matter of metaphysics, which is the absolute.

Gandhi shared Thoreau's view of how change occurs: "it matters not how small the beginning may seem to be."[9] This resembles Dewey's notion of plural temporality as "a thing of histories, each with its own plot, its own inception and movement towards its close, each having its own particular rhythmic

[4] M. K. Gandhi, *The Collected Works of Mahatma Gandhi*, Vol. 9 (New Delhi: Government of India, Ministry of Information and Broadcasting, Publication Division,1984).

[5] Nagarjuna, *The Fundamental Wisdom of the Middle Way*, tr. Jay L. Garfield (New York: Oxford University Press), 138.

[6] Tendulkar, *Mahatma 2*, 240.

[7] Aristotle, *The Nicomachean Ethics*, Book 2 (Hertfordshire: Wordsworth, 1996) for concepts on "moral virtue" and "intellectual virtue."

[8] This was also Emma Goldman's critique of the Russian Revolution.

[9] Henry David Thoreau, "Resistance to Civil Government" (1849) in *The American Transcendentalists: Essential Writings*, ed. Lawrence Buell (New York: Modern Library, 2006), 266.

movement; each with its own unrepeated quality pervading it throughout."[10] It is therefore amazing that Gandhi fought, with so powerful a connection, for something as large as a nation in the act of struggling for independence. Yet even adopting the political grammar of nationalism, Gandhi saw the nation neither as a monolithic whole nor its people as raw material for new creations from nothing.

Nor, however, like the Heideggerian prototype, did he wish to simply "let being be."[11] Gandhi's ideal of *moral virtue* included a core critical component. To those who would shelter religion from public criticism, he replied that "intolerance of criticism is inconducive to the growth of national life."[12] Like Dewey, reason for him had "a practical rather than an epistemological function" as an "organ of modification in traditions and institutions."[13] He made "general humanity the basis of all true religions," linking this with the modern moment in nation-making as a democratic potential.[14]

In his struggle for the equal rights of untouchables in 1925, Gandhi urged upper caste Brahmins to "march with the times, to recognize the time spirit."[15] Gandhi's affirmation of this "age of universal knowledge" embraced Enlightenment as a critical attitude towards tradition.[16] Via moral virtue he embraced the modern critical attitude without the absolute epistemic claims about humanity, history, etc. stemming from late 19th-century confidence that scientific knowledge was now *final*.[17] Gandhi argued that "human society is a ceaseless growth," and that "there is no such thing as perfect rest or repose in this visible universe of

[10] Dewey, *The Philosophy of John Dewey*, ed. John J. McDermont (Chicago: University of Chicago Press, 1973), 555.

[11] Heidegger, "On the Essence of Truth," in *Basic Writings*, ed. David Ferrell Krell (San Francisco: Harper-Collins, 1993), 127–28.

[12] Gandhi, CW 26, 227.

[13] Dewey, *Philosophy*, 56–57.

[14] Gandhi, CW 26, 415.

[15] Gandhi, CW 26, 268.

[16] Gandhi, CW 26, 265. Note this is how Foucault defines modernity in "What is Enlightenment?"

[17] Eric Hobsbawm, *The Age of Capital: 1848-1875* (London: Abacus, 1975), 295.

ours."[18] The instant that we "slavishly copy the past," he insisted, we "cease to grow."[19] Emphasizing continuous growth over Final Ends, Gandhi's point of departure was the humility of thought: "It is impertinence for any man or any body of men to begin or to contemplate reform of the whole world."[20]

Gandhi was a passionate reformer, but rejected historicist teleologies in favour of the multiple patterns of specific and changing conditions. This concerned degrees rather than absolutes.[21] With emphasis on the dialogic, Gandhi stressed that civil disobedience "can never be directed toward a general cause" and the "issue must be definite and capable of being clearly understood and within the power of the opponent to yield."[22] Reform was sought through persuasion and not coercion, through a sometimes slow transformation in consciousness: "Time is on the side of those who will wait it out. Prejudices die hard."[23] He embraced a form of democratic civil society as non-violent conflict resolution.

Gandhian nationalism elevated a moral and humanist, and not epistemic, universalism above any concept of national or religious interest.[24] Yet while rejecting historicism, he embraced historicity, refusing "to admit that any book, however sacred, could be limited to a single interpretation irrespective of time and place; the meanings of great writings were subject to a process of evolution."[25] This was similar to Tolstoy, whose vision of religion was evolutionary and hermeneutical. Tolstoy argued that the

---

[18] Tendulkar, *Mahatma 2*, 225.

[19] Tendulkar, *Mahatma 2*, 51. This point of view makes the claim that Gandhi adhered to belief in a "golden age" untenable.

[20] Tendulkar, *Mahatma 1*, 107.

[21] Gandhi *CW 9*, 479.

[22] Gandhi, *Hind Swaraj*, 179.

[23] Gandhi, *CW 21*, 268. This is grounded in an ethic of reconciliation. It entailed an unwillingness to force people: including high-caste Brahmins over untouchability. This unwillingness to dismantle the caste system is often cited as a weakness in politics based on the ethic of reconciliation. This stance contributed to Gandhi's conflict with Dr. Ambedkar. Also see Jaffrelot, *Dr. Ambedkar and Untouchability: Analysing and Fighting Caste* (New Delhi: Permanent Black, 2005), 52–62.

[24] Gandhi, *CW 32*, 587.

[25] B.R. Nanda, *Mahatma Gandhi: A Biography* (New Delhi: Oxford University Press, 1958), 70.

essence underlying all historically accumulated religious doctrines was a vision of universal human equality.[26] It is therefore unsurprising that Tolstoy wrote to Gandhi condemning Hindu revivalism and urging instead a practice of non-violence.

Gandhi gave clear articulation to those tacit premises of the early natural rights movement subverted by the 18th-century French Enlightenment and the Revolution. He adopted the view that "all knowledge was partial or corrigible," that different people "saw the world differently," and that "violence denied these fundamental facts."[27] Affirming the "courage of limitations and errors," he maintained that "Man need not know all."[28] This conviction was founded in the Jaina doctrine of the "many-sidedness" of religious truth (*anekantavada*) which argues that it is "presumption for any human group to claim to have possession of absolute truth."[29] Gandhi was influenced particularly through his mother and Rajchandra, by Jain ideas and practices, and particularly by the doctrine of *syadvad*.[30]

This doctrine teaches that "reality, whatever it is, expresses itself in multiple forms, with the result that no absolute predication is possible," and is opposed to the "doctrine that reality has but one true nature."[31] This view rejects uniform ontological claims, but not by implication the findings of natural science. It is, rather, a critique of the tacit premises of violence in totalizing certitude. Rajchandra, who assisted Gandhi through a spiritual crisis in 1894, explained dharma as not meaning "any particular creed or dogma," and nor "learning by rote books known as *shastras* (sacred texts) or even believing all that they say." Rajchandra presented a humanistic and pluralistic view of dharma as "the means (*sadhana*) by which we can know ourselves," and we "may

---

[26] Leo Tolstoy, *A Confession and Other Religious Writings* (London: Penguin Books, 1987), 44–70.

[27] Bhikhu Parekh, *Colonialism, Tradition and Reform: An Analysis of Gandhi's Political Discourse* (New Delhi: SAGE, 1989), 156.

[28] Gandhi, CW 26, 407.

[29] Gandhi, *Hind Swaraj*, 48.

[30] Susanne Hoeber Rudolph and Loyd I. Rudolph, *Gandhi: The Traditional Roots of Charisma* (New Delhi: Orient Longman, 1987), 17.

[31] Sarvepalli Radhakrishnan and Charles A. Moore, *A Sourcebook in Indian Philosophy* (Princeton: Princeton University Press, 1957), 261.

accept this means (*sadhana*) from wherever we get it, whether from India or Europe or Arabia."[32]

For Gandhi "man is not capable of knowing the absolute truth and therefore is not competent to punish." This epistemic claim provided the limit of non-violence designed to preserve a condition of dialogic openness. It was the "inability to know this absolute truth that required he maintain an unceasingly open approach to those who would differ from him."[33] He said: "Everyone cannot be of the same mind, and none is perfect. People holding different views on the same question can all be right each from his own point of view. It is necessary for progress that people understand this."[34]

It is a mode of non-violent conflict resolution and political practice based on three levels of persuasion: "through reason," "through suffering" which dramatises the issues at stake to draw the opponent back into discussion, and finally "non-violent coercion characterized by such tools as non-cooperation and civil disobedience."[35] He said: "mere appeal to reason does not answer where prejudices are age-long and based on supposed religious authority."[36] The Gandhian concept was thus invested through the body: dharma is "concerned with practical life."[37] One is confident enough in their belief to suffer publically and even ultimately die for it, but can never have the certainty in it to kill another. John Stuart Mill (1806–73) also argued, "To refuse a hearing to an opinion, because they assume it is false, is to assume that *their* certainty is the same thing as *absolute* certainty."[38] But basing this on a "science of morals" in the "Greatest Happiness Principle" not non-violence, he could also say: "Despotism is a legitimate mode of government in dealing with barbarians, provided the end be their improvement, and the means justified

---

[32] Gandhi, *Hind Swaraj*, 48.
[33] Joan V. Bondurant, *Conquest of Violence: The Gandhian Philosophy of Conflict* (Berkeley: University of California Press, 1965), 16.
[34] Gandhi, *CW 26*, 499.
[35] Bondurant, *Conquest of Violence*, 11.
[36] Gandhi, *CW 26*, 272
[37] Gandhi, *CW 32*, 152.
[38] John Stuart Mill, "On Liberty" in *The Basic Writings of John Stuart Mill* (New York: Modern Library, 2002), 19.

by actually effecting the end."[39] Thus, certitude again becomes a license to inflict violence upon those conceptually deemed within a certain human category.

Gandhi called himself "humanitarian first and to the end."[40] He did not metaphysically define the human. His appeal to human solidarity was predicated on conscience, public view, witness, remembrance, ultimately martyrdom—these are the non-doctrinaire common terms of the moral person. It is the very thing that Nazism, via the secrecy of concentration camps towards the end of the same period, sought to erase in attempting anonymous extermination of the European Jews. The secular universal category of the moral person fulfilled the role of Aristotle's highest good, rejecting the Hobbesian–Lockean tradition which posited the good (interest) as relative to the desires of the agent.[41] This notion of the moral person was dependent, in Gandhi's usage of it, on the power of democratically organized civil society: "public opinion is a far more potent force than a thousand swords."[42] Public view and remembrance implied an expanded public sphere intended to encompass "the whole spectrum of Indian society."[43]

Nationalism without essence founded Gandhi's conviction that Indian "national life is dependent on multi-religious existence" and his passionate struggle for a multi-cultural democratic and cosmopolitan India.[44] His universalism, like the Bhakti–Sufi and early European natural rights traditions, entailed that "all religions are more or less true. All proceed from the same God but all are imperfect because they have come down to us through imperfect human instrumentality."[45] There were, for Gandhi, as "many definitions of God as there are men and women." There were also "conscientious atheists" of higher moral standing than "corrupt religious people."[46] It follows that human conscience—rather

[39] Ibid., "Utilitarianism," 235/239; "On Liberty," 12.
[40] Gandhi, CW 26, 241.
[41] Thomas Hobbes, *Leviathan* (London : Penguin, 1985), 120.
[42] Gandhi, CW 90, 43.
[43] Dennis Dalton, *Gandhi's Power: Non-Violence in Action* (New Delhi: Oxford University Press, 1993), 32.
[44] Gandhi, CW 26, 241.
[45] Tendulkar, *Mahatma* 2, 132.
[46] Gandhi, CW 26, 222–23.

than a fixed ontological concept of nature—precedes all scriptures: "Every religion has in this age of reason to submit to the acid test of reason and universal justice."[47] This humanist priority entailed cosmopolitanism: Gandhi retained Hinduism "so long as it does not cramp my growth and does not debar me from assimilating all that is good anywhere else."[48] He argued that "[n]o nation can find its salvation by breaking away from others."[49] Gandhi therefore acknowledged a cosmopolitan condition, and rejected the romantic ideals of nativism or authenticity.

Gandhi's South African experience of seeing himself as a national outsider placed him at the heart of modernity as a moment of glimpsing the full network of international linkages with globalization. This in turn raised the newly complex problems for universal justice that figure in the Enlightenment. Gandhi worked within the discursive traditions of modernity and Enlightenment in an ambiguous way that critiqued and transformed the intellectual and practical legacy of both. He evoked the authority of this discourse in calling untouchability a "denial of the rights of man."[50] The existential status of outsider in the modern world also underlies the temptation to restore safely fixed boundaries of identity. This has often driven counter-Enlightenment or nativism—the white hot fire of revivalism seeking fantasies of an unbroken past. It was such a vision of 'restored' mono-religious purity and total domination of the other that cost Gandhi his life when he was assassinated by a Hindu nationalist in 1948.

Nationalism is not a *doctrine* per se, but comes out of an *experience* traceable to the French Revolution, which says that a nation can be freed from foreign control by the collective efforts of its population constituted as the people. Where nationalism has been articulated as a doctrine of democratic emancipation, liberal thinkers such as John Stuart Mill or Giuseppe Mazzini (1805–1872) identified the boundaries of the state with a single national culture as the strict condition for free institutions. The British colonial claim that Indians could not be united or free because

---

[47] Ibid., 202.
[48] Tendulkar, *Mahatma 2*, 230.
[49] Tendulkar, *Mahatma 2*, 44.
[50] Gandhi, *CW 26*, 330.

they were a geographic abstraction composed of hundreds of races and creeds, and neither a nation nor a people, was therefore the central line of tension with the emergence of the nationalist movement in the late 19th century. Many earlier nationalists had responded to the discourse of empire on nationalism by attempting to reproduce its mono-ethnic logic in a bid for emancipation. Gandhi directly challenged this mono-ethnic basis as the sole possibility.

The highest value in Gandhi's vision of nationalism without essence, very likely, was in overcoming this dominant paradigm and the shortcomings that have haunted so many national projects: the forcible assimilation of minorities, a war of modern ideas on the traditional past, and a dogmatic epistemic ideal striving for absolute dimensions as a state project. Gandhi argued that "the spirit of democracy is not a mechanical thing to be adjusted by the abolition of forms."[51] These issues are linked specifically to the totalizing potential of state power, and generally to the problem of political violence as ideologically sanctified, two overlapping phenomena. Violence and war in the late 18th century were accepted as a legitimate means of last resort in implementing national republican ideals. Goya's 1821 painting of Saturn eating his children evoked the crisis of European political consciousness in the wake of revolutionary excess, and the *learning* which asks: Which means are justified to promote human rights?

There were, however, distinctive elements in Gandhi's world view which preserved the core of the French Revolutionary inheritance: *(a)* a new concept of legitimacy based on the provisional nature of political institutions, and rejecting the transcendental value linked to the sanction of antiquity; *(b)* The logical consequence in the recognition of the immanent values in political action. A population has the right to take a course of action "to compel justice from" the ruler.[52] Thus, Gandhi regularly reiterated the right "of the subject to refuse to assist a ruler who misrules."[53] He argued that "no state however despotic has the right to enact laws which are repugnant to the whole body of the people."[54]

---

[51] Dalton, *Gandhi's Power*, 50.
[52] Tendulkar, *Mahatma 1*, 300.
[53] Ibid., 297.
[54] Gandhi, *CW 19*, 207.

(c) The third consequence of this line of thought is the legitimization of conscience as a force of political judgement and eventual action, or the principle of human autonomy in relation to tradition and history. *(d)* Finally, Gandhi shared in common with the French Revolutionary tradition the conviction that "political emancipation means the rise of mass consciousness."[55] Where he differed was over the issue of means, which, on closer examination, seems to be a different perception of the problem of time.

The modern tradition of political liberty in India linking the Enlightenment and the public sphere preceded the founding of the Congress (1885), and experienced a metamorphosis with Gandhi from variations on the absolute to a "sea of forms."[56] Gandhi, though sceptical about the political principle of representation, did not reject civil society.[57] His entire political life was invested in building the multiple independent organs of a new Indian civil society. Along with much of the 19th-century post-Industrial Revolution second wave in the human rights movement, he aspired to a civil society embracing social (as well as merely political) rights for the broad mass of the population. Like them, he was critical of capitalism, or fixation on "profit and loss ... regardless of moral considerations," "wealth [as] power over other men," and "conditions of scarcity, unjustly created."[58] He shared many premises of this international movement, affirming free communication of ideas and opinions, free political association, introduction of women into the public space, inclusion of the illiterate and the equal rights of workers and peasants.[59]

Gandhi's scepticism about representation was not grounded in Kantian or Hegelian historicism—the doctrine of exaggerated hopes in a future rational humanity and reign of peace superseding a wholly irrational past (i.e. the differences of civil

[55] Tendulkar, *Mahatma 2*, 227.

[56] Ralph Waldo Emerson, "Nature," in *The American Transcendentalists: Essential Writings* (1836), 42.

[57] Partha Chatterjee's thesis that Gandhi's entire enterprise centred a critique of civil society is slightly off target; Gandhi critiqued representation somewhat in the tradition of Rousseau or Marx while actively building an alternative civil society.

[58] Gandhi, *CW 8*, 258/290.

[59] Micheline R. Ishay, *The History of Human Rights. From Ancient Times to the Globalization Era* (New Delhi: Orient Longman, 2004), 12.

society)—but linked to the value of self-reliance in the tradition of Emersonian American Transcendentalism.[60] Gandhi was not, as historicist knowledge systems necessarily are, utopian (i.e. the end product): "an ideal Swaraj [i.e. a world beyond power] can never be attained."[61] A person oriented deeply to the principle of non-attachment is unlikely to be fixated upon a specific utopia. Gandhi was consistently grounded in practical immanence, a temporal sensitivity to conditions, and even the moment: "... it is wrong to speculate about the future, still more so to anticipate failure. If we take care of the present, the future will take care of itself."[62]

Although giving democratic priority to an active civil society over representative institutions, he consistently put the national democratic principle embodied in the Congress Party above his personal views.[63] He said in 1924, being presently in a position of unrivalled power, that "I cannot impose my personal faith on others, never on a national organization."[64] Upon learning of the new Turkish Parliament in 1908, he expressed great joy: "the world over, we hear the cry of swarajya."[65] He also recognized how the politics of constitutional right, notably in the Indian colonial context, could be misused to foster power seeking and domination over others. This was the basis for his emphasis on self-transformation as a prolonged popular process in Indian civil society (i.e. duties, public obligation and dharma) as the condition for using modern rights democratically and ethically in a free India. Thus, he affirmed human mutability over stasis: "there is no human being in the world who is beyond all hope of change."[66] He argued that "Man is the maker of his own destiny."[67] Indeed,

---

[60] These American reformists, who struggled against slavery and for the rights of women, represent a different Enlightenment tradition to the various European threads based on historicist systemic social change.

[61] Gandhi, CW 32, 528.

[62] Gandhi, CW 85, 9.

[63] Making his various opinions of less consequence than is sometimes maintained by scholars fixated on his ideal projections (of village systems, sexual mores, his dislike of cinema, etc.).

[64] Tendulkar, Mahatma 2, 167. See also Gandhi, CW 32, 450.

[65] Gandhi, CW 8, 421.

[66] Gandhi, CW 32, 187.

[67] Gandhi, CW 26, 294.

he affirmed—without rupture—a new moment in history: "The whole world is shivering from the pains of labour, the indications of a new life are manifest everywhere, and a regenerated India must find its place among the new-born nations of the world."[68]

At the core, Gandhi's activism embraced *democratic* Enlightenment values—political liberty, social equality, reason, or a reformist attitude to tradition seeking to dismantle inherited coercive systems—on the different basis of nationalism without essence (the many sidedness of truth; that all religions are equal; the humility of thought; the common terms of the moral person; all reconstituted aspects of the Indian tradition of *ahimsa*).[69] Gandhi, in the tradition of Enlightenment and the French Revolution, identified conscience with "standing up for truth and reason" and opposing "bigotry, lethargy, intolerance, ignorance [and] inertia."[70] Nationalism without essence has no place for cultural authenticity. Accused of being westernized, Gandhi replied: "My opinions should be considered as they are, irrespective of whether they are derived from the West or the East."[71] It follows that in his view neither India nor the West were constituted of a fixed essence. We notice that Gandhi thought, again like Nagarjuna, in terms of relational rather than inherent existence.[72]

PRE-GANDHIAN INDIAN PUBLIC SPHERE

The universal laws of logic transcend every lifeworld of meaning, but it does not follow that we may effectively understand each other through them.[73] Traditions and histories, through their traces, invest the modern secular realm with meanings of which it is otherwise devoid. The multi-centred construction of such a

[68] Ishay, *The History of Human Rights*, 192.

[69] Partha Chatterjee's placing of Gandhi categorically outside of "post-Enlightenment thought" is based on a concept of Enlightenment so abstractly and narrowly concocted as to be untenable when looking at most concrete social struggles for democratic change. (*Nationalism*, 97)

[70] Tendulkar, *Mahatma 2*, 62.

[71] Gandhi, *CW 32*, 43.

[72] Nagarjuna, *Fundamental*, 154.

[73] Hannah Arendt, *The Portable Hannah Arendt* (London: Penguin, 2003), 466.

modern lifeworld of meanings within the Indian public sphere preceded Gandhi's arrival upon the political scene. He fought to transform the dimensions of the Indian public sphere, or emergent lifeworld, as it had hitherto evolved through multiple state–civil society interactions. His struggle was to engender an ethic of reconciliation against certain accumulated existential textures of intolerance.

The essentialist politics of the *definition* marked the emerging fractured Indian public sphere under the colonial autocracy doubling with liberal political spaces. Although the Raj routinely crushed civil rights and institutions, and quite regularly from 1897, it created a body of civil society that it meticulously controlled and preserved on terms suiting its needs. A new Benthamist–Hobbesian authoritarianism came to predominate in Raj politics under Fitzjames Stephen (1869–72): Jeremy Bentham (1748–1832) had taught that liberty is of lesser value than public happiness, "the sole end which the legislator ought to have in view."[74] Stephen therefore rejected the moral obligation of introducing representative institutions in India, favouring the model of enlightened despotism or the Machine State, i.e. the certainties of intellectual virtue as absolute principle. Gandhi's commitment to self-reliance, human resourcefulness and the capacity for ordinary people to grow links him to Ralph Waldo Emerson (1803–82). It is the polar opposite of the assumption that the state alone can make a population happy or free based on higher knowledge.

Thus, Gandhi later led the Indian civil society to explode into multiple new and unexpected forms that the Raj could neither anticipate nor control. His politics, in this sense, was always predicated on local initiative: "Every Indian who desires freedom and strives for it must be their own guide."[75] Similarly, in 1919 he insisted that 40,000 uncultured and illiterate Indians in South Africa had followed his lead in doing Satyagraha only after each

---

[74] Jeremy Bentham, *An Introduction to the Principles of Morals and Legislation* (1789) in *Selected Writings on Utilitarianism* (Hertfordshire: Wordsworth, 2001); Bandyopadhyay, *From Plassey to Partition*, 280. Fitzjames Stephen represented a policy shift from the more liberal Macaulay.

[75] Bipan Chandra, et al., *India's Struggle for Independence, 1857-1947* (New Delhi: Penguin, 1989), 468.

having examined the position individually.[76] This follows the Kantian injunction to think for oneself in "making public use of [one's] reason," but thinks in terms of multiple conditions rather than the Kantian single teleology.[77]

We can point to three interacting aspects of the state–civil society linkage under the early 20th-century Raj. Firstly, the public aspect of *invented tradition* linked to the standardization of law, administration and education.[78] New state defined spaces constituted human lives as subjects and populations, effecting transformations in self-consciousness. Late 19th-century colonial census made religion a fundamental ethnographic category, each community having an official "definition." The key political mode of organizing and constructing the population under the colonial state was *essential definition*.

Invented traditions formed a complex power mosaic. Regionally identified majorities and minorities created new vulnerabilities. Many people polled indicated their sect or caste rather than *Hindu*, illustrating the modernity of the homogeneous Hindu religious identity. Newly constructed identities were selectively linked to hierarchic state-institutional opportunities—educational facilities, public employment, rights and representation in self-governing bodies. These privileges were concessions aimed at expanding hegemony, managing growing unrest and lessening the burdens of political rule for the Raj. It followed a divide and rule pattern in a society conquered and subdued—involving also bribery, concession and collaboration—through overwhelming military violence over a hundred years. *Invented traditions* competed from above and below. The narrow *essentialist* windows of state power consolidated new modern hierarchies of power linked to new coercions, and served to weaken the emerging national movement growing militant through the realization of its own *de facto* political impotence.[79] Ethnic nationalist

---

[76] Gandhi, *CW 19*, 250.

[77] Immanuel Kant, "What is Enlightenment?," in *The Basic Writings of Kant*, ed. Allen W. Wood (New York: Modern Library, 2001), 136.

[78] Eric Hobsbawm, "The Nation as Invented Tradition," in *Nationalism*, eds. John Hutchinson and Anthony D. Smith (Oxford: University Press, 1994), 76–83.

[79] Bandyopadhyay, *Plassey to Partition*, 240/263.

campaigns of political violence were also *invented traditions* mirroring the logic of divide and rule, a double of colonial politics within an emerging Indian civil society twisted by vulnerability, the absence of freedom and the cycle of famine, disease and violence spreading in parts of the countryside.

Secondly, we have the public aspect of *belief* as power linked to emergent nationalisms: the belief in a common descent, internal solidarity and external differentiation from other groups. These discursive consolidations embodied a top–down and bottom–up interactions. Beliefs were often constructed on the divisive basis of teleological and historicist thematics shaped by orientalist discourses: the lost Golden Age of Hinduism requiring restoration, the Islamic Dark Age of decline requiring punishment. These inside-out historicist discourses originated in 17th-century European imaginings of "history as war": the universal subject negated in favour of battle, adversaries, and struggle against millennial occupations (i.e. the Norman Yoke). Truth is constructed as strategic in a world of violence, passion and revenge.[80]

Alternately, there was belief in a Universalist teleological hope linking universal reason to future imaginings. The "single minded insistence on the future"[81] distinguishing Hobbes' philosophy was reproduced by his Utilitarian heirs and embraced ideologically by the Indian Moderates: components of *political modernity* including citizenship, human rights, civil society, etc, were "projected as ideal milestones ... on the road towards progress."[82] Simultaneously, these educated middle classes found "the domain of reason to be oppressive, as it implied the historical necessity of the 'civilizing' colonial rule."[83] They found themselves, like the European Jews, expected by *universal reason* to transcend their being as Indians in an act of shameful capitulation that was in their best interests.[84] Thus, historicism and teleology

---

[80] Michel Foucault, "Society Must be Defended," in *Ethics: Subjectivity and Truth 1954-1984*. ed. Paul Rabinow (London: Penguin, 1997), 61.

[81] Hannah Arendt, "The Concept of History: Ancient and Modern" in *The Portable Hannah Arendt*, ed. Peter Baehr (London: Penguin, 2003), 301; Hobbes, *Leviathan*, 169.

[82] Bandyopadhyay, *Plassey to Partition*, 211.

[83] Ibid., 236.

[84] Hannah Arendt, *The Origins of Totalitarianism* (San Diego: Harcourt Brace, 1976), 54–89.

were rooted in the social experience of colonial politics beyond simply intellectual abstractions.

Thirdly, we have the aspect of *being and doing* between the private and public spheres with the ongoing radical transformations in meaning. The realm of habitus and moral virtue textures everyday life, and links intellectual elite and popular masses. It provided the ground for eventual mass mobilization in the Indian national independence movement under Gandhi. The largely non-violent and local issue based forms of late 19th-century peasant protest, for example, became mobilized within a broader national movement through transformed traditional meanings.[85] Thus, the crucial importance of leadership and the degree of its quality in creating conditions for national independence.[86]

The Indian public sphere, already shaped by varying discursive–practical currents from the late 19th century, interacted with the being and doing modernization process. One example is the Ramakrishna–Vivekananda phenomenon. It offered simple interpretations of Hinduism and gained popularity among Western educated Bengalis exasperated by the tedium of Raj clerical jobs. This superficially apolitical tendency rejected the clocked in Western habitus and expressed nostalgia for a meaningfully embedded existence. It expressed nothing particularly notable on the level of political ideas, i.e. in terms of a criticism of either colonialism or the West, concerning a mode of being within the domain of moral virtue.

Being and doing illuminate two dimensions within the emerging public sphere: *public discourse* based on print capital (debate and dialogue) and the *public gaze* constituted in performance and visibility.[87] Unhindered by language barrier or literacy, the Extremists employed the public gaze in efforts to reach and mobilize the popular masses. In the prior Moderate phase (1885–1907) public discourse predominated—petitions, memo-

---

[85] Mridula Mukherjee, *Peasants in India's Non-Violent Revolution* (New Delhi: SAGE, 2004), 16–19.

[86] This remains unappreciated by Ranajit Guha in his almost dogmatic insistence on the autonomous "fragment" and the "structural dichotomy."

[87] The concept of public gaze is in Alev Cinar, *Modernity, Islam, and Secularism in Turkey: Bodies, Places and Time* (Saint Paul: University of Minnesota Press, 2005), 33–53.

randa, speeches, public meetings and press campaigns with a view to gradual reform—with the many limits this entailed in terms of language and concepts. These reveal the principle sets of means—constitutional and extra-constitutional—shaping the national movement prior to the 1920 political ascendance of Gandhi. The extra-constitutional dimension raised political violence as a possible means (practical formation) to political and social change.

The Ganesh Festival exemplifies the political interaction of the public gaze with being and doing. Tilak urged all Hindus to desist from the Moharram processions that Muslims and Hindus had traditionally participated in jointly. He then reinterpreted the Ganesh Chaturthi, traditionally a celebration in the private sphere, as a public event with the purpose of uniting and mobilizing Hindus. The Ganesh festival was timed to coincide with Moharram, amounting to a boycott, and thus dividing Hindus along new dualistic lines of authenticity. The festival featured young men dressed as Shavaji's soldiers, evoking the 17th-century Maratha ruler who had defied Mughal power by killing a Muslim noble with a concealed weapon.[88] Such divisive uses of the public gaze scarred the Indian public sphere in terms of mutual trust among different groups. They harmed the potential basis for multi-class and multi-religious popular mobilization of being and doing—the strategy Gandhi struggled to employ in building a secular democratic India.

Public discourse and public gaze regularly interacted in being and doing. Consider the cow killing riots of 1893—a vivid orchestrated instance of the public gaze—and the silence of the Congress during this episode. That it was the major moment of Muslim membership decline in the Congress reveals its importance.[89] The prior 1888 rule passed by the Congress—on the level of public discourse—barring resolutions rejected by the majority of Hindu or Muslim delegates had been intended to allay minority fears.[90] Yet the public gaze overpowered public discourse.

---

[88] Christophe Jaffrelot, "The Politics of Processions and Hindu-Muslim Riots," in *Religious Politics and Communal Violence*, ed. Steven I. Wilkinson (New Delhi: Oxford University Press, 2005), 281.

[89] Bandyopadhyay, *Plassey to Partition*, 233.

[90] Chandra, *India's Struggle*, 75.

The Congress aimed, without a doubt, to unite all Indians across religious, caste and class divides according to a secular democratic agenda. But a public discursive gesture such as the 1888 ruling could not easily outweigh the fear and mistrust incurred by the public gaze episode of 1893. Moreover, the Congress often failed to adequately distinguish itself from floating elements of Hindu revivalism, further eroding minority trust.[91] These public gaze elements consolidated Raj politics in maintaining and maximizing social division as the basis for its continued rule. Thus, an analysis of the emerging national movement purely on the level of intellectual ideas is inadequate, and the phenomenological dimension of lifeworlds (i.e. being and doing) is required for comprehending the course that later events took. The most serious outcome of new public gaze practices in being and doing was the modern authoritarian tendency to sacralize the community. It shifted the essence of religion from spirituality to a physical people, entailing the political ideal of the organic state and its negation of multi-cultural democracy.

In the Extremist reconstruction of the Indian public sphere value in political action was often guaranteed by God. They rejected the compromised Enlightenment–Utilitarian Moderate ideology, based on the visible emptiness of the constitutional power sharing arrangement. The future, not unfolding as promised, revealed the hollowness of colonialist discursive horizons. Colonial disdain for Indian efforts at political participation, the famines attending Queen Victoria's assumption of Empress in 1877, the open racism of the Ilbert Bill controversy of 1883, and the famines and epidemics of the 1890s all compounded the force of the "drain theory" in undermining Raj hegemony in too many Indian eyes.[92] By 1895 the Moderate political tendency, thus, predicated on belief in the good will of the Raj (i.e. pure public discourse), met a dead end.

The Extremists employed many non-violent and public gaze-based techniques of extra-constitutional protest: boycott and public burning of foreign cloth, boycott of government schools, courts, titles and services and strikes, in a bid to extend the scale

---

[91] Bipan Chandra, *Nationalism and Colonialism in Modern India* (New Delhi: Orient Longman, 1979), ch. 9.

[92] Bandyopadhyay, *Plassey to Partition*, 213–54.

of the movement to nationwide proportions with quicker results in terms of democratic reform. However, in seeking to define Indian identity in terms of Hinduism to win majority support, they adversely impacted popular composite culture in their ultimately unsuccessful efforts at popular mobilization. The motivation was to win in a political game of power in which the key, they supposed, was a parallel level of organized force to match and overwhelm the British occupying state. We see the tacit conception, prevalent since the 16th century in Europe and spreading outward by example, where no higher ideal than sheer force exists for deciding the fates of human beings.[93] The pinnacle of this was expressed in the Second French Revolution.

The cultural concept of Hindustan, shared by 18th-century Muslims and Hindus, faded as religious riots became a new phenomenon in the 1870s.[94] The limited colonial public sphere had hitherto been grounded upon secular principles of teleologically deferred liberty and the permanence of *scientific certainty*, opposed to the private as religiously subjective and ephemeral. The parameters of the public sphere altered with a new politics of organized religious masculinity committed to violence. This assumption of the *existence* of the community—as a fixed ontological figure with its own fixed interests—reflected back the essential identities created by the secular political modes of the Raj. Secular and religious mutations were thus profoundly intertwined, and cannot be neatly separated between modern and pre-modern.[95]

---

[93] This underwent evolving forms: from 18th-century history as progress toward rationality to late 19th-century history as evolutionary progress. The ideal of progress was linked to this notion of power. See Collingwood 98–99.

[94] Bandyopadhyay, *Plassey to Partition*, 218.

[95] In light of this the central tenet of Ashis Nandy, the dualism of innocence/modernity, appears essentialist and untenable but convenient for attacking a large inflated intellectual target in "modernity." It is the embodiment of all harm. Nandy prefers not to see that the problem of power exists in all societies, modern or pre-modern. Any intellectual strategy proposing a total exit from power is practically suspect. Chatterjee similarly implies such a possibility through "community." On the other hand, neither is there a "pure" modern self.

The sacralization of community as a discursive formation crept in through specific issues. The most radical expression of the private/public tensions in being and doing was the Age of Consent controversy (1891). We see the negation of criticism in the name of non-interventionist cultural nationalism. The background was the Congress policy of splitting political from social reform confronted with the enormously varied caste and religious conditions throughout India. The problem of *political reform* versus social reform falls right across the public and private divide of being and doing.

The *moderates* had declined the task of "working out a national social philosophy acceptable to all those who agreed on a national political philosophy." They believed a solid line of consensus impossible to reach from such multiple cultural perspectives. Naoroji's 1886 Presidential address at the second Congress in Calcutta asked:

> What do any of us know of the internal home life, of the traditions, customs, feelings, prejudices of any class but his own?... Only the members of that class can effectively deal with the reform there-in needed ... a National Congress must confine itself to questions in which the entire nation has a direct participation.[96]

The public management of a wide pluralism of existing social values and beliefs threatened a crisis of unity, provoking an intellectual slide into an innocuous stance of relativism. When Ranade urged social reform within a national agenda based on individual conscience and humanism, Tilak countered by framing the question in terms of national autonomy versus alien domination. He maintained that, while ready to see reform of abusive Hindu customs, it could not be through an alien bureaucracy imposed from above. Ranade in his reforming efforts was thereby cast as a lackey of the British imperial state. We see the emergence of a new discursive formation: some Indians were collaborators and even inauthentic. Identity and belonging became ontologized to

---

[96] Charles H. Heimsath, *Indian Nationalism and Hindu Social Reform* (New Jersey: Princeton University Press, 1964), 188.

constitute a new politics anchored in the discourse of "history as war."

The related debate around child marriage culminated in the Age of Consent crisis. It culminated in threats to riot and burn down the Congress pavilion by a club of militant Poona youths "trained in physical fitness and the use of arms for the ultimate purpose of undermining British rule." This finally eradicated the option of social reform from the national agenda. Such fitness clubs belonged to a widespread physical culture movement dedicated to restoring masculinity to Hindu culture in a further expression of the public gaze and being and doing.[97] Tilak, evoking religious passion and a foreign conspiracy to destroy Hindu culture, met with the approval of these anti-reformist youths. Damodar Hari Chapekar (1868–98), the leader, praised him for adopting "his manners to the opinions of the community" — taken as a static assemblage of practices based on fixed values.[98]

Yielding to these pressures, Naoroji posed the question: "Should the House of Commons discuss metaphysics?"[99] Issues of ethics — previously deemed secular by the elitist Moderate advocates of English education — thus reverted theoretically to the essentially religious sphere of boundless metaphysical reflection, and practically to the dictates of local predilection and custom. Colonial domination and its murky improvement scheme had fostered a frozen and uncritical idealization of "community" in modern reconstructed form. This was now backed by intellectuals and violent force in the name of tradition. The irony is that the pressure for social reform came largely from Indian society itself, where the Raj had long been reluctant to interfere for reasons of safeguarding stability.

The Age of Consent Crisis, therefore, vividly demonstrated the negation of criticism on the basis of a cultural essentialist politics of nationalism. The juncture saw a rising religious atmosphere in politics, as evidenced by Tilak's Ganapati Festival. By the end of the Age of Consent Bill the "secular approaches to the problem were forgotten, and the controversy raged [over] shastric passages

---

[97] Bandyopadhyay, *Plassey to Partition*, 250.
[98] Heimsath, *Indian Nationalism*, 213. The Chapekar brothers were among the early Indian terrorists, assassinating W.C. Rand in 1897.
[99] Ibid., 213/188.

on the characteristic signs of puberty."[100] The Indian national movement was thus pulled into the orbit of a constructed discursive universe and removed from the earlier secular-rationalist if elitist framework (i.e. the assumption of England's civilizational superiority and right to rule on its own terms).

The most ethically telling moment in the Age of Consent controversy was in 1890 when an 11-year-old girl died from sexual abuse by a husband of 29 years elder to her, just as polemics raged on the conceptual level.[101] The suffering of a specific living person was buried under *larger* goal oriented and modern ideological abstractions. In the game of power, ideologues of the Final End *chose* not to *see* violence. This mirrored the colonial ideology in its readiness to bury countless people for an *idea*, to the extent that an 'idea' was really what was at stake. This scenario constituted a negation of humanism in the sense of Emmanuel Levinas' (1906–95) notion of the moral person. Gandhi's campaign broadsided and overwhelmed rival hegemonic claims — not least the Raj — partly because it rejected the politics of transcendental justice abstracted from the person (and thereby justifying violence). Thus, Gandhi called to a halt an entire nationwide civil disobedience movement in 1922 over the deaths of several policemen at the hands of a crowd. It is partly in this ethically immanentist sense — and not merely as a legal abstraction — that Gandhi meant "The individual is the supreme consideration."[102]

Finally, the pre-Gandhian period also saw the rise of individual terrorism — often linked to the Extremist faction — as a new practice intended to grip the public sphere in its collective imagination. The Indian terrorist movement to emerge in the 1870s acknowledged force as the highest principle of social transformation. One newspaper stated: "The thirty crores of people inhabiting India must raise their sixty crores of hands to stop this curse of oppression. Force must be stopped by force."[103] It was an attempt to play the power game set up by the Raj, this time in the extra-constitutional mode of public assassination. A dramatic and masculinized moment in the public gaze, their acts were

---

[100] Ibid., 168.
[101] Bandyopadhyay, *Plassey to Partition*, 238.
[102] Tendulkar, *Mahatma 2*, 162.
[103] Chandra, *India's Struggle*, 143.

never the less described in terms of absolute intellectual virtue in illicit public print media. The terrorist movement saw itself modelled on the "new scientific discipline of sociology" founded by Auguste Comte and popularized by Herbert Spencer. The central vision was of reality as "struggle, violence, national solidarity and subordination of the individual to the needs of the 'national organism'."[104] Many young Indians of the urban, middle class, educated and unemployed strata, finding a lack of legitimate protest channels, and raised on the stories of 1857, began to believe in "violence as the only available mode of action."[105] The ideas of revolutionary terrorists began to appear in printed and widely communicable form after 1857, well before the establishment of all-India nationalism in the 1880s.[106]

By the end of the 19th century nearly 40 government officials had lost their lives to the movement. That the popular masses would rise up in spontaneous insurrection following such *propaganda by deed* proved without basis. The terrorists saw themselves metaphysically as inevitable, instruments or aspects of human history as a process: "Revolution is law, Revolution is Order and Revolution is Truth"; it is the "eternal conflict between the Old and the New." Bhagat Singh (1907–31), a martyr and the deepest thinker among them, wrote that "we are mere products of the necessity of our times." They were committed ideologically to violence and war. *The Philosophy of the Bomb* declared: "Ours is a war to the end—to Victory or Death." Their views were utopian, projecting "a new order of society in which political and economic exploitation will be an impossibility."[107] Bhagat Singh argued that "the sacrifice of individuals at the altar of Revolution ... will bring freedom to all" as a matter of historical "inevitability."[108] They conceived a totalizing break from the past: "Any man who stands for progress has to criticise, disbelieve and challenge every item of the old faith."[109]

---

[104] Parekh, *Colonialism*, 142.
[105] Ibid., 139–40.
[106] Heimsath, *Indian Nationalism*, 135.
[107] Chandra, *Nationalism and Colonialism in India*, 234–36.
[108] Bhagat Singh, *Selected Speeches and Writings* (New Delhi: National Book Trust, 2007), 11.
[109] Ibid., 59.

We also see religiously infused terrorist ideologies, notably from the Extremist Aurobindo Ghose (1872–1950). He had links to revolutionary terrorists and embraced violence as a means. He represented an overlap between commitment to revolutionary violence and Hindu revivalist claims to authenticity in the early national movement. After a childhood abroad immersed in English culture and deliberately isolated from Indian influences, Aurobindo returned to Bengal in 1883 and began constructing a revolutionary network. During this time he argued that "authentic national destiny was possible ... only through the revival of the Vedic institution of the fourfold order." He later wrote that "nationalism is not politics but a religion [and] it is the Sanatan Dharma which for us is nationalism."[110] This echoed similar sentiments by Tilak (at this time) and Lala Lajpat Rai, who proposed a "Nationalist Movement entirely derived from Vedantic thought."[111]

Adopting a romantic line favouring the spiritual elite, Aurobindo insisted that only "heroes, martyrs, criminals, enthusiasts, degenerates, geniuses, men of exaggerated virtue, exaggerated ability and exaggerated ideas were capable of revolutionizing society and making a nation great and free." This Nietzschean evocation was hardly suitable for inspiring the common people. He characterized existence as "a constant self-feeding and devouring of other life." As far as means, he promoted an idealized violence based on spiritual values which he contrasted with ordinary "violence stripped of its ideal and constructive aspects." He castigated modern Indians as inauthentic (*asuric*) in the name of an ideal of Hindu nationalism.[112] This ideal held that "nationalism is immortal" and "comes from God."[113] His contribution undoubtedly undermined early efforts to build a broad horizontal solidarity network across religious differences within the Indian national movement.

The terrorists, by and large, were not careful planners, failing to research the situation on the ground. They rushed towards

---

[110] Sharma, *Hindutva, Exploring the Idea of Hindu* Nationalism, 46–55.
[111] Heimsath, *Indian Nationalism*, 315.
[112] Sharma, *Hindutva*, 46–55.
[113] Heimsath, *Indian Nationalism*, 313.

a decision.[14] This practical formation as an extreme moment of violence triggering total transformation had roots in the French Revolutionary heritage. Taking inspiration from 19th-century Russian nihilism and Irish nationalism, it developed in more complex ways following the 1917 Russian Revolution and the Bolshevik success in consolidating a new state. Two strands of revolutionary terrorism evolved, in Punjab, UP and Bihar, and the other in Bengal, both influenced by the upsurge of working class trade unionism after the War.[115] The Hindustan Republican Army (1924) worked to organize armed revolution; the year 1925 saw the Kakori Conspiracy Case and in 1928 Bhagat Singh assassinated a policeman to avenge the death of Lala Lajpat Rai. In, 1929 there was the Assembly Bomb Case, and in the year 1931 of Bhagat Singh's hanging two school girls shot dead the District Magistrate.[116] This second wave, again failing to mobilize the popular masses, cast doubt upon the discursive–practical path of violence through guns and insurrection. These terrorists became folk heroes, but this practice remained an individual phenomenon. Although such terrorism continued in spurts, 1907 was already a political dead end for the Extremists. Revolutionary India had reached a grave discursive–practical paradigm crisis.

NATIONAL MOVEMENT AS NON-VIOLENT MASS MOVEMENT

The Indian public sphere had thus taken shape upon Gandhi's 1915 return from South Africa as a respected but still relatively minor figure. Revolution had the negative meaning of ridding India of colonial rule. Gandhi confronted a public sphere shaped by revolutionary terrorism and Hindu revivalism, while expressing affiliation with the now beleaguered secular democratic tradition of the Indian National Congress. He employed established practical formations: city–countryside links forged by the Home Rule Movement under Tilak and Annie Besant in 1916, and the non-violent Extremist practices from the Swadeshi Movement

---

[114] Chandra, *Nationalism*, 228–53.
[115] Chandra, *India's Struggle*, 247–48.
[116] Ibid., 249–53.

of 1903–08 (boycott of foreign goods, government schools, courts, titles, services, passive resistance and strikes). Yet Gandhi rejected the discursive formations dominating the public sphere in Hindu nationalism and Anglicized liberal reformism. He initiated an alternative nationalist vision and direction centring prolonged non-violent struggle with the Raj over hegemony. Giving revolution a positive function in the creation of contestatory public meaning, he wedded public discourse to the public gaze in the first successful Indian mass movement.

Gandhi had previously met Shyamji Krishnavarma, terrorist disciple of Herbert Spencer, in London at the time of Curzon Wylie's assassination in 1909. This encounter inspired *Hind Swaraj*, which omitted to mention the Extremists—knowing of the damage they had done to his projects for nationalism based on Hindu–Muslim unity—and overtly condemned revolutionary terrorism.[117] Gandhi's 1920 assumption of power occurred in the aftermath of World War I, and the heavy political repression inflicted by the Raj during this desperate time. While India was alive with multi-centred forms of political activity, it in no way appeared *fated* to be unified—at least not in a way adequate to the task of mounting a serious challenge to the sovereignty of the British Empire.

The transformation of modern India into a democratic mass society by the Indian National Movement has been described as perhaps "the most colossal experiment in world history";[118] or within the broader historical context as "the third moment in the great democratic experiment launched at the end of eighteenth century by the American and French revolutions."[119] It was a movement of the broad general population "including peasants and workers, artisans, the bourgeoisie, the petty bourgeoisie, the intelligentsia, and sections of the landlords." That the Indian

---

[117] Hind Swaraj is often taken to represent Gandhi's overall philosophy. On a superficial reading it has essentialist qualities—it is a polemic against claims to modern European civilizational superiority—on a careful reading less so. But a balanced reading of the collected works from Gandhi's active political life in India presents a very different worldview which is primarily deeply non-essentialist.

[118] Manfred Steger, *Gandhi's Dilemma. Nonviolent Principles and Nationalist Power* (New York: St.Martin's Press, 2000), 6.

[119] Sunil Khilnani, *The Idea of India* (Farrar: Straus and Giroux, 1998), 4.

national movement was a "popular mass anti-colonial movement," "open ended, without fixed class hegemony or a necessary class character," was significantly linked to the Gandhian strategic departure from the existing revolutionary alternatives linked to the French Revolutionary experience as the total and violent negation of the *errors* of the past.[120]

The Indian national independence struggle, under Gandhi and the Congress, combined elements of tradition and modernity in proportion to their *practical* value in consolidating a new democratic civil society: there was no overriding *metaphysical* inside and out framework. This took place through a largely non-violent struggle for hegemony with the British Raj between 1920 and 1947. This was in the historical blink of an eye between World War I and World War II. Wars are never contained in neat blocks like books on a shelf. They spill out in countless particles of physical and psychological violence that are breathed and transmitted in hundreds of ways over generations. Gandhi's life struggle belonged to this defining interval of the modern world between trenches, gas masks, concentration camps and atom bombs. He conceptualized the invisible spread of hate and war in everyday life as the problem of "inner violence."[121]

Since for Gandhi the impermanence of everyday life was privileged over the valorized actions of the statesmen, these pervading forces of atmosphere within the public Indian lifeworld were of serious consequence. Gandhi made the tremendous power underlying the impermanence of ordinary peoples' everyday lives the new driving force in the Indian public sphere through mass Satyagraha campaigns: the Non-Cooperation and Civil Disobedience Movements displacing the heroic politics of the supreme moment with a multi-centred practice dependent on the combined efforts of thousands. He said: "I disbelieve history so far as details of acts of heroes are concerned. I accept broad facts from history and draw my own lessons for my conduct."[122]

---

[120] Bipan Chandra, *Indian National Movement: The Long-Term Dynamics* (New Delhi:Vikas,1989), 57.

[121] Steger, *Gandhi's Dilemma*, 6.

[122] Gandhi, CW 26, 491. The notion that Gandhi rejected history as such is sometimes exaggerated. He was very interested in the history of crowd politics, for example, the 1819 Peterloo massacre.

Gandhi, accepting Thomas Carlyle's (1795–1881) view that French Revolutionary ideological formulas dehumanized human society, rejected his ideal of the hero. In *Hind Swaraj* he suggested that the power of the state and technology is less great than the power of ordinary people when organized in everyday life.[123] He championed the transient everyday world of ordinary people over symbols of permanent power—in this way it was a radical democratic affirmation of immanence in the modern history of the public sphere.[124]

The Gandhian mobilization strategy requires elucidation of the *conditions* and the transformed mode of imagining the *state structure* as a new temporal horizon. Firstly, the conditions: we see some of the critical factors for a revolution. World War I created the conditions for a mass upsurge in India. Indians experienced dislocation across the class spectrum. Rising defence expenditure, national debt and taxation harmed the common people, creating unprecedented price rise. Severe food shortages observed continued export of food to the army fighting in the Ottoman Empire and Persia, creating conditions of disease and famine. Census of 1921 reported 12 to 13 million people dying in the 1918–19 famine and epidemic.[125] Forced military recruitment created resentment among peasants, while the richer peasantry bore the effects of an export crisis.

These combined conditions produced growing organized peasant resistance, including the 1918 Kisan Sabha. The desperate fiscal situation of World War I had forced the Raj, in conjunction with Bombay commercial class pressure, to undertake a measure of industrialization which was inflicting harsh price rises on the new working class.[126] Such dislocations produced widespread strikes in industry within a broader pattern of mass frustration and popular uprisings. These conditions imply the tremendous potential for increased mass participation in the political activity. We might have imagined any number of revolutionary roads.

---

[123] Gandhi, *Hind Swaraj*, 90–93.

[124] Compare to John Dewey's "transfer of interest from the permanent to the changing" and the "expulsion of fixed first and final causes." Dewey, *Philosophy*, 34/35/36.

[125] Bandyopadhyay, *Plassey to Partition*, 287.

[126] Ibid., 289.

Secondly, the intensification of dissident elite political movements contributed to revolutionary conditions. A wave of disillusionment with the Raj among educated youth was compounded by the practical obsolescence of pre-War Moderate and Extremist wings. World War I, as in many countries, had produced disillusionment with the liberal doctrine of the "constancy of progress" with its linear historicist time based on "ever increasing rapidity."[127] It was a view sustained by a metaphysical vision of "universal history which contains a principle *a priori*."[128] Based on *universal logic*, harnessed to visible scientific and technological advance, this cosmopolitan progress purportedly transcended and delegitimized traditional lifeworlds in the irrefutable argument of history as power (i.e. state top-down). The search for an alternative cosmopolitanism fostered a new temporal horizon in imagining the state structure.

Rabindranath Tagore's (1861–1941) criticisms of the inherent irrationality of power and espousal of an ethic of reconciliation exemplify this changed temporal horizon. With the discrediting of epistemic humanist universalism, the totalizing historical culminations of Comtean terrorists or India's Benthamite rulers, there remained only a practical ethic of "reconciliation" grounded in acknowledgement of "diversity."[129] No new scientific formula, to be implemented as a state program, would deliver humanity to a horizon beyond all power and difference. Nor could traditional religions, within the modern context, fill this gap upon the large multi-ethnic scale of the nation state. Thus, Tagore suggested, a democratic modern politics must focus upon the temporally ceaseless adjustment processes without exit from the differences and risks of an open civil society. He envisioned a world of holes rather than a single unbroken plane.

In Tagore's essay on nationalism, cosmopolitanism is affirmed in political non-violence, creativity in traditional being, and openness to the world's ongoing scientific transformations. Following World War I ("this cruel war that has driven its claws into the vitals of Europe"), he described the horizon of *universal*

---

[127] Arendt, *Portable*, 465–66.
[128] Kant, *Basic Writings*, 132.
[129] Rabindranath Tagore, "Nationalism," in *Rabindranath Tagore Omnibus III* (New Delhi: Penguin, 2006), 32/61.

modernity under the British Raj as a "dead white wall" that "paralyzed" and "suffocated" the diverse Indian population.[130] In deploring the "suffocation of every man, woman and child of a vast population," Tagore articulated the insight that the "progress of power ... outruns the complete humanity."[131] Tagore evoked the tendency that Simone Weil (1909–43) also identified in World War I: "the struggle for power," or that "power contains a sort of fatality [weighing] as pitilessly on those who command as on those who obey"; that "all power is unstable" and so "the race for power enslaves everybody"; that "power is only a means" but "power seeking" becomes a futile but obsessive end.[132]

World War I, initially met with a wild enthusiasm across Europe even among socialist parties, had confirmed the negation of utopia in the above insight about the irrationality of power. Lenin's (1870–1924) historicist declaration that "the state will wither away"[133] in a common human community beyond the violence of power as such was dispelled by the new Soviet Union's intractable entanglement in a global power politics, and the ruthless power struggle within the Soviet Union itself that culminated in Stalin's (1878–1953) murderous dictatorship. Based on such perceptions, highlighting the linkage between 19th-century colonial and 20th-century totalitarian politics, Tagore could condemn "the colourless vagueness of cosmopolitanism" as much as "nation-worship."[134] Yet the ideal uniting Tagore and Weil remained within the Enlightenment project of dismantling inherited institutions of injustice. Weil wrote: "if oppression is a necessity of social life, this necessity has nothing providential about it."[135] Confined within the immanent temporality of power, mundane questions of political forms became paramount as guarantees of non-violence. Intoxicating transcendental dreams

---

[130] Tagore, *Omnibus III*, 45/49.

[131] Ibid., 51–67.

[132] Simone Weil, "Analysis of Oppression," in *Simone Weil: An Anthology*, ed. Sian Miles (London: Penguin, 2005), 149–61.

[133] Lenin, "The State and Revolution," in *The Great Political Theories*, ed. Michael Curtis (New York: Harper Perennial Modern Classics, 2008), 371.

[134] Tagore, 32/61.

[135] Weil, *Simone Weil*, 163.

of utopia at any price yielded to realistic assessments of the existing risks and possibilities of immanent power.

A second post-War global discursive formation was also surfacing, this time of totalizing historical identity metaphors concerned with linking technology to culture. Ernst Junger, in a vein reproduced by Martin Heidegger (1889–1976), wrote: "beneath the regions in which the dialectic of war aims is still meaningful, the German encounters a stronger force: he encounters himself."[136] Also present in the post-War Indian public sphere, such discursive formations were intentionally marginalized by Gandhi: "after [rising] to power ... [he] did not leave the Hindu Sabhaites much room for manoeuvre in Congress, and, more generally, in the Indian public sphere."[137]

Despite the differences between Tagore and Gandhi, they shared this alternative cosmopolitan humanism—based on pluralism rather than substance—and it formed the basis of Gandhi's political ethic of reconciliation and expanded mode of imagining the state structure in the nation-making process. It is a Nagarjunian principle of non-essentialism: "a synthesis out of which a phenomenon not antecedently existent comes to be."[138] It matches Dewey's demand for ending the preoccupation "with ultimate reality, or with reality as a complete (i.e. completed) whole: with *the* real object."[139] We might call it a form of solidarity in human error in which a limit (non-violence) to shared public truth is the only guarantee of liberty. It contrasts with Junger's celebration of the sacralized community as a new axis of political mobilization linked to unbridled power in pursuit of collectively unifying "higher and deeper goals."[140]

Upon accepting the Gandhian ethic, it becomes difficult to believe in some greater destiny than the ordinary life of everyday people—in sum, that the being of the everyday world may be sacrificed to a larger process of teleological becoming. Power,

---

[136] Junger, "Total Mobilization" quoted in Mirsepassi, *Intellectual Discourses and the Politics of Modernization*, 142.

[137] Jaffrelot, *Hindu Nationalism. A Reader* (Princeton: Princeton University Press, 2007) 14.

[138] Nagarjuna, *Fundamental*, 111.

[139] Dewey, *Philosophy*, 88.

[140] Junger, "Fire and Blood" quoted in Herf, *Reactionary Modernism*, 79.

freedom and community are not finished products but continuously lived through ongoing adjustment and contestation. It is a democratic ethic of public self-reliance. Such an insight was the basis for Gandhi's privileging "freedom of conscience, mental independence and independence of action" over "the mechanical right of voting."[141] Rights are given by the state, but what people do with those rights as a form of power depends on their existing mode of being in everyday life (i.e. lifeworlds).[142]

Sensitive to the power of being and doing, Gandhi was concerned that the principle of Benthamite happiness might be "secured at the cost of the minority."[143] He was committed to equality before the law as "a matter of elementary human rights, even as, irrespective of caste, race, creed or colour, we have certain things in common, e.g., hunger, thirst, etc."[144] Yet Gandhi thought that the function of leadership in nation-making was to breathe the moral inspiration of ethical self-reliance into the people rather than depend on ideological formulas to be implemented by the state. Later, as his heir, Nehru coped with the difficulties of reconciling this ethical worldview with the needs of a state undertaking national development on a massive scale.

The simultaneous European context provides counterpoints for these perceptions, implying the multiplying political modes of imagining in the post-War interval. The unexpected post-War collapse of Austro–Hungary produced new democracies seeking to *rationalize* power by eliminating all "inconsistencies and irrational residues of the old feudal order" through utopian juridical perfection—a variant on the French Revolutionary discourse of rupture and foundation. Middle-class lawyers enshrined proportional representation as the legal embodiment of the popular will. The interwar trend towards strong state centralization reflected a tense politics of majoritarian domination—as for the Czech German minority or the Polish Ukrainian one. These new nations claimed a profound democratic precedent—Czechoslovakia

---

[141] Gandhi, *CW 9*, 510.

[142] Consider how ferociously rights were claimed by Southern slave owners in the United States during the struggle of the American Transcendentalists to abolish the institution.

[143] Gandhi, *CW 8*, 240.

[144] Gandhi, *CW 26*, 67.

claimed "modern democracy" as "the ideal of our nation for centuries"—yet with the 1929 Great Depression successive governments shifted to dynamic authoritarian alternatives "to meet the challenge of modernity." Authoritarian top–down discursive–practical formations were no less effective as organizers of society, industry and technology in the quest for order and stability.[145]

The lesson of the Indian National Movement suggests that the state structure requires a broader conceptualization beyond the apex–target of the French Revolutionary political legacy. It is an immanently rather than transcendentally conceived state structure, grounded in the everyday temporality of lifeworlds rather than a totalized horizon. The French Revolution identified the state ideologically with the transcendent substance of the nation in a programme of foundation leading permanently beyond the antagonism and crisis of difference. The Indian National Movement under Gandhi, by contrast, sought to reshape the public sphere through the technique of non-violence: grounded in moral universalism, mass participation and everydayness, as an affirmation of difference based on nationalism without essence. Gandhi presented in vows (i.e. ethical choice) an immanent alternative to absolute foundations or the substantiality of history, i.e. historicism. Vows, taken within a specific context and for specific purposes, do not project a totalizing horizon. Gandhi said in 1929 that a "life without vows is like a ship without an anchor or like an edifice that is built on sand instead of solid rock."[146]

The participatory logic of this alternative state structure was demonstrated in the practical formations that were later redeployed in the American Civil Rights Movement (1955–68) and recently during the Tunisian Jasmine Revolution (2010–11). The Non-Cooperation Movement (1919–22) expanded the Indian nationalist movement beyond the elite bubble of metropolitan cities to workers, peasants and the world of the villages. Moral universalism entailed an appeal to all religions and social classes in the non-violent independence struggle. It was "Muslim participation that gave the movement its truly mass character" and "at

[145] Mark Mazower, *Dark Continent: Europe's Twentieth Century* (New York: Vintage, 1998), 3–9.
[146] Tendulkar, *Mahatma* 2, 364.

some places two thirds of those arrested were Muslims."[147] Calling for the "surrender of all titles of honour and honorary offices, boycott of schools and colleges and law courts and the councils," Gandhi conceived a broader definition of the state apparatus to be transformed including not only the government, the bureaucracy, the police and the military but also the educational system, the media and the judiciary.[148] He compared it to the experience of an earthquake, as a "sort of general upheaval on the political plane [in which] the Government ceases to function ... the police stations, the courts, offices etc. all cease to be Government property and shall be taken charge of by the people."[149]

The entire social environment as the integrated field of state and civil society became involved in the transformation process to a democratic order, and not simply the state as the apex or centre of power to be seized. The state was not an *instrument* under the command of an enlightened subject but a social *relation* among ordinary people, its powers activated by changing sets of agents located in specific areas of the constituting field. In the Indian National Movement, we see the crucial role of parallel power networks, mobilized across the broader state apparatus and struggling to gradually transform relations of power as a practical formation.[150]

This gradualism was grounded in everydayness: in the Civil Disobedience Movement (1930–32) a vastly powerful mass resistance was set off through what appeared an innocuous everyday object of common use, in the salt Satyagraha. Non-violently embodying the power of the public gaze, salt was commonly used by all religions, ethnic and linguistic groups, and social classes. In this instance, over 90,000 people went to jail for civil disobedience and—in the multi-centred constellation of related social protest movements growing from it—boycott of British cloth resulted in imports falling by half. Although Muslim

[147] Chandra, *India's Struggle*, 196.
[148] Tendulkar, *Mahatma 1*, 297.
[149] Nanda, *Mahatma Gandhi*, 229.
[150] For discussion of different views on the state, see Bob Jessop, "The State and State-Building," in *The Oxford Handbook of Political Institutions*, eds. R.A.W. Rhodes, Sarah A. Binder and Bert A. Rockman (Oxford: Oxford University Press, 2006).

participation was less than in the Non-Cooperation Movement, it was still a significant force. We see participation by poor and illiterate people in both the city and the countryside and notable increase in peasant participation.[151]

The varying degrees of autonomy among these multiple public manifestations do not contradict the spirit of self-reliance—or necessarily the public discipline—the Civil Disobedience Movement was intended to engender. These movements did not represent a unified national ideology or aspiration to a single identity, but an increased sense of public obligation and participation committed to an independent and democratic India. It extended its appeal on both the legal level of political liberty and the bread and butter level crucial to the popular masses, combining a concern with social and political rights as the discursive adjunct to the creation of public memories through mass practice and repetition.

This quality of everydayness was most powerfully expressed in the Constructive Programme. The Constructive Programme of 1922 called for national unity between Hindus and Muslims, an end to untouchability, and sought to "foster local industries, improve sanitation, educate all children as well as adults, promote provincial languages as well as Hindi, and emancipate women."[152] It was on this grassroots basis that Gandhi, by way of Constructive Programmes, would launch the national movement afresh from the ground up, employing transformed religious meanings accessible to the popular masses but anchored in a secular and civil rights basis placing among its priorities the achievement of Hindu–Muslim unity at the national level.

Where the Indian National Congress had sought to resolve the reform issue by assigning political reform to the national arena for public discussion, and social reform to the local arena for private action, Gandhi created a national network of Constructive Programmes by which social reforms could be undertaken at the plural, popular and consensual levels. These examples present radical innovations in the practice of Enlightenment politics, centring a public inclusivity and self-reliance over the historicist master plan. The fundamental importance of Constructive Work

---

[151] Chandra, *India's Struggle*, 282–83.
[152] Ronald J. Terchek, *Gandhi Struggling for Autonomy* (New Delhi: Vistaar Publications, 2000), 164.

was articulated when Gandhi wrote that "civil disobedience in terms of independence without the co-operation of the millions by way of constructive effort is mere bravado and worse than useless."[153] This showed the principle of self-reliance and everydayness. Gandhi's experiments from the 1920s created a secular-oriented programme of national reform in which the burden of social reform was placed directly upon the population who stood to benefit from it, rather than imposed from above through the intellectual designs of elites. Emphasizing gradual temporality, Gandhi urged that "as a farmer after tilling the land devotes his entire attention to the growing of crops, so should the Congress workers, after a year of destructive work in the form of civil disobedience, take seriously to constructive side of the Congress programme."[154] Gandhi consistently emphasized the value of time for an inclusive mass movement, arguing that the "pilgrimage to *swaraj* is a painful climb" requiring a "patient, intelligent and constructive effort of tens of thousands of men and women, young and old."[155]

In 1920–21, Gandhi undertook the transformation of the Congress into a mass organization and movement. At the 1920 Nagpur session, the constitution of the Indian National Congress was revised to transform the institution from "an annual pageant and feast of oratory" into "a militant organization in touch with the masses."[156] The smallest unit of the Congress organization became the village Congress committee, a number of which were grouped into a Union Congress Committee, with the All India Congress Committee comprising about 350 members representing the Provinces. The annual fee for membership was radically reduced, and it "ceased to be the preserve of the upper and middle classes" with its doors open to "the masses in the smaller towns and villages whose political consciousness Gandhi was quickening."[157] The creation of a small Working Committee under the direction of the Congress President permitted the organization to function uninterruptedly all year round instead

---

[153] Gandhi, *Hind Swaraj*,180.
[154] Tendulkar, *Mahatma 3*, 64–65.
[155] Parekh, *Colonialism*, 160.
[156] Nanda, *Mahatma Gandhi*, 209.
[157] Ibid., 209.

THE INDIAN NATIONAL MOVEMENT AND GANDHI 183

of merely at annual sessions. The objectives involved fostering Hindu–Muslim unity, the abolition of "untouchability," and the promotion of *Khadi* or local cloth production.

A further expression of the principle of everydayness was in the creation of expanding parallel civil society networks. This tactic replaced continuous obstruction of the government based on the Irish model in favour of the Satyagraha principle of non-violence that seeks to convert through hegemony rather than thwart through power seizure.[158] The Non-Cooperation programme paralyzed the electoral system and involved pulling out of the system at every level, including the legal, tax, educational, industrial and military apparatus, and reconstituting an alternative productive and governing force to the state established as a complex and broadly accessible network throughout the nation. The Congress Volunteer Corps emerged as a parallel police force.[159] What these politics attempted—notably with less success in persuading the military at this stage—was to demonstrate the fading hegemony of the Raj and the hegemonic ascendancy of the Indian popular masses under the leadership of the Congress Party led by Gandhi.

In the substitution of a practical moral universalism (many sidedness of truth; non-violence) for a historicist narrative in struggle and nation-making, we see a tactical shift from public claims to being identity (processions, etc.) to technique (the creation of parallel networks) as the predominant mode of organizing the public gaze-discourse configuration in the Indian public sphere. A historicist scheme requires a starting point, a tacit definition. Consider Hegel's "absolute beginning" and "absolute end."[160] There are infinite patterns in history. In determining one as the ontological substance of national—or universal—history, we necessarily exclude the great majority of people who fall outside the narrative pattern. Consider Vinayak Damodar Savarkar: "in the very dawn of history we found ourselves belonging to the nation of the ... Hindus"; "Nothing makes Self-conscious of itself so much as a conflict with non-self"; in the "prolonged furious

---

[158] Ibid., 208.
[159] Chandra, *India's Struggle*, 189.
[160] G.W.F. Hegel, "Science of Logic," the trajectory from pure being to absolute spirit.

conflict [with Muslims] our people became conscious of ourselves as Hindus"; Christians and Muslims "smack of a foreign origin."[161] The nation, made ontologically in advance, is discovered as an inside and out framework in the moment of battle. It is constituted in Fichtean manner of an essence which excludes the internal other. This view does not merely echo Romanticism. It repeats the founding national principle of the French Revolution. Saint Just insisted that "the nation has only one heart" and "the general will can never harbour any principle alien to itself."[162]

Just as in the Gandhian strategy there were no Final Ends, nor was there a starting point, definition or party doctrine; there was only a practical technique. The Indian National Movement "did not require any particular political or ideological commitment from its activists" and did not "try to limit its following to any social class or group" provided that "the commitment to democratic and secular nationalism was there."[163] In unifying the movement by way of this technique Gandhi demonstrated a radical departure from the French Revolutionary tradition, on the premise of multicultural democratic pluralism rather than a single defining discourse of origin and identity. Philosophically, it is perhaps close to Leonardo Da Vinci's (1452–1519) comment: "Among the great things which are found among us the existence of judgement is the greatest. This dwells in time, and stretches its limbs into the past and future ... It does not, however, extend to the essence of anything ... Nothingness has no centre, and its boundaries are nothingness."[164]

The technique of non-violence centring everydayness permitted wide public inclusion: "The adoption of non-violent forms of struggle enabled the participation of the mass of the people who could not have participated in a similar manner, or whose involvement could not have been so deep, in a movement that adopted violent forms." This was because "Participation in violent activity, whether of a terrorist or a guerrilla nature, or in

---

[161] Sharma, 88–93.
[162] Saint Just, *Œuvres Completes* (Paris: Gallimard, 2004), 529/547.
[163] Chandra, *India's Struggle*, 79.
[164] Leonardo da Vinci, *Notebooks* (Oxford: Oxford University Press, 2008), 260.

an army of liberation, necessarily involves long absences from home, total disruption of normal life, complete abandonment of normal livelihood, and loss of life."[165] For the same reason "in the national movement for Indian Independence, led by the Congress Party, there were many more women in positions of importance than in the Russian and Chinese revolutionary movements put together."[166] Gandhi said: "We were able to enlist as soldiers, millions of men, women and children, because we were pledged to non-violence."[167] Within the inclusive context created by experimentation and non-violence individual people were not perceived as a means to an end but each as an end in themselves, and the focus upon specific problems in everyday life rather than imagined or transcendent horizons. This explains the centrality of *conditions*. Consider Hegel again: the *universal* is the *unconditioned, self-contained* and *self-determining*.[168] Conditions, by contrast, are immanent: "dependence and relational character is incompatible with inherent existence."[169] There is a "nexus between phenomena in virtue of which events depend on other events."[170] A fixed rule of human interest is practically ineffective because "employers take one view of the matter, the workers another," and "attitudes change with circumstances."[171]

Upon release from prison in 1924, Gandhi demonstrated responsiveness to changing context rather than following the pure line. With the Congress split between Swarajists, working within the council against his policy line in his absence, and No-changers adhering strictly to his principle, Gandhi accepted the *settled fact* rather than risking a split in the Congress as in 1907—he remained opposed to council entry, but conceded the value in the Swarajists work in terms of *determination* and *cohesion*. He reasoned that withdrawal would be perceived by the government

---

[165] Bipan Chandra, *Indian National Movement: The Long Term Dynamics* (New Delhi: Vikas, 1989), 46–47.

[166] Ibid., 46–47.

[167] Tendulkar, *Mahatma 3*, 78.

[168] Hegel, *The Essential Writings* (New York: Harper and Row, 1974), 100.

[169] Nagarjuna, *Fundamental*, 118.

[170] Ibid., 1.

[171] Gandhi, *CW 8*, 257.

and the public as weakness or indecision. This expresses the principle of non-beginning in which an existing condition should not be destroyed because this entails violence against people connected to it; it should be transformed to democratic advantage.[172] But upon recognizing its ill effects, we should not continue to uncritically reproduce further institutions of the same kind. Gandhi thus used the modern, as the traditional, pragmatically.[173] However, in the same instant he roundly condemned both Swarajists and No-changers: "Each has claimed the monopoly of truth with an ignorant certainty of conviction."[174] Gandhi, often flexible in practice, was consistently firm in opposing dogmatic ideological attitudes. He rejected the notion of an absolute reality unaffected by conditions, an absolute objective independent of methods of action (historicist teleology) or an absolute evil (the enemy), in favour of the context specific and immanent.

Satyagraha movements during the Indian National Movement were therefore always preceded by careful and extensive periods of research on the ground to ascertain the veracity of the opposing points of view in the dispute. Gandhi's principle involved "never intervening in a situation without first studying it with great care."[175] One example was in Champaran in 1917 when Gandhi was called to investigate a conflict between peasants and European planters. Gandhi and his colleagues "toured the villages from dawn to dusk [and] recorded the statements of peasants, interrogating them to make sure they were giving correct information." Eventually, with "evidence collected from 8,000 peasants, he had little difficulty in convincing the [government] Commission that the *tinkathia* system needed to be abolished and that the peasants should be compensated for the illegal enhancement of their dues."[176]

---

[172] Again, this has relevance in the disagreement with Ambedkar.
[173] Chandra, *India's Struggle*, 238–39.
[174] Ibid., 239.
[175] Ibid., 177.
[176] Ibid., 178–79.

SECULARISM, IMMANENT REASON AND PUBLIC STRUGGLE OVER MEANING

In this lack of ideological fixity and attention to the flux of conditions we have the basic elements of Indian secularism as an alternative to the French Revolutionary war on the traditional past. Most significantly, Gandhi, though deeply religious, explicitly undertook a public struggle to break out of the religious discursive universes that dominated political debate following the Age of Consent controversy. He did so at the risk of losing support among the Indian Muslim population, whose considerable support he had gained through the Khalifat movement in conjunction with the Non Cooperation movement. The most vivid example of Gandhi's uncompromising line in favour of secular humanism as the only viable basis for a democratic Indian public sphere occurred in a debate about a recent episode of stoning in Afghanistan. In response a religiously dogmatic *Young India* reader's claim in 1925 that millions of Muslims who, seeing Gandhi as a guide, philosopher and friend, might be disillusioned by his condemnation of the legitimacy of stoning in the contemporary world, wrote: "I wish that they could say with me that even if it could be established that the practice of stoning to death could be proved [in accordance with holy scripture] they could not defend it as being repugnant to their sense of humanity."[177]

The secularized category of *humanity* demonstrates that Gandhi relativized the religious multi-verse. It does not matter which your religion, or no religion. All religions are equally subject to the rational criticism of human conscience within the framework of non-violence that he saw as the basis of all religions—and the ethics of those non-believers for whom "truth held the same place as God."[178] Gandhi thus struggled to break outside of the limits of a religiously discursive universe in the realm of public debate, affirming an independent secular space. Gandhi affirmed this division between secular and religious in saying:

> There are undoubtedly things in the world which transcend reason. We do not refuse to bring them onto the anvil of

[177] Gandhi, CW 26, 415
[178] Tendulkar, *Mahatma* 1, 32.

reason but they will not come themselves. By their very nature they defy reason. Such is the mystery of the deity. It is not inconsistent with reason, it is beyond it. But stoning to death is no more beyond reason than, say, the practice of honesty or swearing.[179]

Reason is imminent and ethical. The realm of social practices, where violence against the person is a possible concern, cannot be defended against rational criticism on the basis of scriptural sanctity. We thus see Gandhi's reaction and solution to the negation of criticism as it attempted to dominate the Indian public sphere during the Age of Consent controversy. Gandhi's political intervention in shaping the Indian public sphere therefore upheld the modern principle of secularism. His concept of secularism was "philosophically different from the laic, anti-religious secularism that arose in Europe."[180] In practice, it performed the same function in providing a space for multi-religious co-habitation in the modern context. Yet it did not seek to generally and aggressively supersede older forms of traditional belief as a *substantive* ideology. Gandhi insisted that he was ready to

> die for [his religion], but that is my personal affair. The state has nothing to do with it. The state would look after your secular welfare, health, communication, foreign relations, currency and so on, but not your, or my, religion. That is everybody's personal concern.[181]

To be sure, Gandhi accepted a role for religious ideas and values in the Indian public sphere; but he firmly rejected the dominance of any one religion over public meaning through the legal power of the state. And even more so for historically inherited religious rules which violate basic human dignity while claiming a sacred status.

Hannah Arendt has observed that only "in the presence of the enemy can such a thing as *la nation une et indivisible*, the ideal of

---

[179] Gandhi, CW 26, 416.

[180] Anthony J. Parel, *Gandhi's Philosophy and the Quest for Harmony* (Cambridge: Cambridge University Press, 2006), 61.

[181] Gandhi, CW 85, 328.

French and all other nationalism, come to pass."[182] This observation on the supposedly inherent nature of "all nationalism" does not apply to the overall historical experience of Indian nationalism as developed during the independence struggle. Nor, in the Indian experience, is her additional claim that any mass based revolution seeking to tackle the pressing vital issues of material want and hunger necessarily finishing in a totalitarian state borne out.[183] The Indian experience was after all "one of the biggest mass movements modern society has ever seen" but it paved the way to a democracy.[184]

The spread of nationalism within the Indian national movement as conceived by Gandhi was a fight of each individual person against themselves. Gandhi taught his followers to face death and everything short of it fearlessly in the belief that there is no enemy but the one inside which is fear itself. In 1915, he called upon Indian students not to respond to revolutionary terrorist ideology but to "Terrorize yourself; search within; by all means resist tyranny wherever you find it; ... but not by shedding the blood of the tyrant. ... if we are to practise truth, to practise ahimsa, we must immediately see that we also practise fearlessness."[185] The tyrant, the robber, or murderer, etc. is within, even as we attribute these identities to others.[186]

In this way Gandhi was a follower of the Sufi tradition of becoming one's own adversary rather than the Platonic tradition of self-consistency in pursuit of ideal Forms, i.e. "the mind as a whole must be turned away from the world of change [towards] the brightest of all realities."[187] In Sufism one loses oneself to find oneself, a process which goes on without end:

> I am not at all concerned with appearing to be consistent. In my search after Truth I have discarded many ideas and learnt many new things. [I grow] from moment to moment, and therefore, when anybody finds any inconsistency

---

[182] Arendt, *On Revolution*, 77.
[183] See Arendt on the "Social Question" in *On Revolution*.
[184] Chandra, *India's Struggle*, 13.
[185] Tendulkar, *Mahatma 1*, 165.
[186] Ibid., 72.
[187] Plato, *The Republic* (Harmondsworth: Penguin, 1974), 322.

between any two writings of mine, if he has still faith in my sanity, he would do well to choose the later of the two on the same subject.[188]

This viewpoint entails the predominance of a principle of learning over inner certainty: "A moral act must be our own act"; "We must have the liberty to do evil before we can learn to do good."[189] It involves progress, but viewed from the perspective of the humility of thought. It is an immanent reason concerned with how power invests everyday existential conditions—or the inescapable temporality of power. It rejects a transcendental reason assigning ultimate identities—which will inevitably be controversial—linked to future promises.

The absence of historicist ontology (i.e. exit from power) entails the principle of experiment as a temporal horizon. Gandhi believed that "Life is but an endless series of experiments," a point of view similar to that expressed by Dewey when he wrote that "life is itself a sequence of trials."[190] Gandhi considered the idea that one might "lead the nation to its predestined goal" a "hallucination."[191] He conceded that "non-co-operation was a dangerous experiment" in which "there was every possibility of a mistake in its application to large masses."[192] Very much unlike "the Incorruptible" Robespierre of the French Revolution, Gandhi claimed that his was a "struggling, striving, erring, imperfect soul" which could "rise only by experimenting on myself."[193] In this there is a further emphasis on temporality rather than the absolute, and the struggle with the self rather than the claim to omniscience in war against the other.

This mode of thinking implies a form of socialism without enemies, i.e. without the premise of class war as the essential dynamic driving human history. Like other aspects of the ethic of reconciliation, this obstructed a more radical destruction

---

[188] Gandhi, *CW 45*, 61.
[189] Terchek, *Gandhi Struggling*, 24–25.
[190] Tendulkar, *Mahatma 2*, 149; Dewey, *Philosophy*, 353.
[191] Tendulkar, *Mahatma 2*, 136.
[192] Ibid., 149.
[193] Ibid., 149.

of the existing Indian caste system.[194] Yet the Indian National Movement under Gandhi's leadership embraced deeper social egalitarian assumptions identifiable with the socialist tradition, while remaining remote from the Soviet regime's "tone of dogmatic omniscience towards the outside world [while] in fact everything about its colossal new venture remained to be defined, not least in the minds of the leaders."[195] Gandhi insisted that "the claim to infallibility would always be a most dangerous claim to make." As a result, he argued, "no one has a right to coerce others to act according to his own view of truth."[196] Gandhian intervention disclosed a third alternative between social change imagined either in total time as a swift and violent lightning assault upon the state,[197] a supreme moment of revolution, or as within the limits of legal reformism, in the form of a long term mass based transformative project centring direct mass action in civil society—or "the ensemble of organisms commonly called 'private'"—in a struggle over *not merely power* but plural meanings and values largely within the temporal space of everyday life.[198]

In 1924, Gandhi said of the Bolsheviks that while he admired the "motives" he was an "uncompromising opponent of violent methods" and did not "believe in short-violent-cuts to success."[199] Previously, he had criticized Bolshevism in 1919 for its obsession with "materialistic advancement as a goal" at the expense of "liberty."[200] The evolution of the Indian Left in new and original directions in the late 1920s, departing considerably from the prevailing Left paradigm dictated by the Soviet model, was reflected in the election of Jawaharlal Nehru as President in 1936–37. This evolution towards a democratic socialist humanism

---

[194] And thus stands to be criticized by those feeling morally compelled to do so.

[195] Mazower, *Dark Continent*, 116.

[196] Dalton, *Gandhi's Power*, 10–11.

[197] Antonio Gramsci writings pose the problem of the pure instant of "insurrection" versus the longer mediated process of "transformation," calling it a "war of position" and identifying it particularly with "India's political struggle against the English." (Gramsci, *Prison Notebooks*, 229).

[198] Antonio Gramsci, *Selections from the Prison Notebooks* (New York: International Publishers, 1971), 12.

[199] Dalton, *Gandhi's Power*, 10.

[200] Tendulkar, *Mahatma 1*, 248.

reflected a profound and sustained political and intellectual interaction between Indian Left activists and the National Movement influenced by Gandhian Satyagraha technique and philosophy. Each time that Nehru faced a choice "between giving up his Gandhian political practice as the Indian left had done and giving up Stalin–Marxism, he gave up the latter."[201] Among all of the competing and interacting threads giving shape to the National Movement, it was the Satyagraha technique under Gandhi's leadership that pushed elements of the Left in a unique direction in comparison to other national experiences which followed more faithfully on the path of the French Revolutionary model and its supposed unique heir in the Soviet Union.

These two models showed strikingly different ideas of truth: in the French Revolutionary discourse, the absolute absence of limits is the condition for living in Truth, as limits in the public space imply hidden things, shadows veiling conspiracies or doubts, and therefore a compromise of the Truth which is necessarily whole or not the Truth at all. Hegel wrote, very much taking up this line of thought on a philosophical level, that the "True is the whole" and the "whole is nothing other than the essence consummating itself through its development."[202] The essence guarantees the identity of Truth, and in the historical process functions as the Final End in which the Truth already exists as a complete yet unrealized whole or ontological figure. In Gandhi's thought, conversely, the existence of a strict limit (that is, the pledge of non-violence) is the precondition for even the possibility of seeking the Truth. There being no ideal or universal blueprint, social conflicts may only be confronted in the complexity of the everyday world where they are lived. Once violence is introduced, the outcome becomes the random consequence of brute force. He thus argued that "there is no way to find Truth except the way of non-violence."[203]

Non-attachment opposes metaphysics. This in turn implies the contrary to the moral passion of the French Revolution in

---

[201] Bipan Chandra, *Ideology and Politics in Modern India* (New Delhi: Har-Arnand, 1994), 20.

[202] Hegel, *Phenomenology of the Spirit* (Oxford: Oxford University Press, 1977), 11.

[203] Tendulkar, *Mahatma 2*, 236.

the necessity of a "detached state of mind," or the ideal of inner peace at the core of Gandhi's philosophy.[204] He insisted that in "civil disobedience there should be no excitement."[205] In 1925, he argued that it is crucial to conceive nationalism beyond hatred and to struggle for national independence without hating the tyrant.[206] Satyagraha was "a doctrine in which you get rid of that kind of passion and ill will in the quickest manner possible."[207] Gandhi was set apart by his practice from other 20th-century figures—influenced by the French Revolutionary paradigm—who also set upon life paths of fighting oppressive political regimes in the name of radical democratic ends: the tendency to "conflict resolution" rather than "destruction of the enemy," a view to particular situations rather than the uniform political line, open dialogue rather than doctrinal dogma as a basis for social reconstruction, and an ethic of reconciliation rather than revenge. These are the components constituting the Gandhian temporal horizon. There was no "end of history" and nor, as a result, could there be what Dewey has criticized in the dominant Enlightenment tradition as a "call to create a world of 'reality' *de novo*."[208] In sum, Gandhi expressed a more modest but no less critical notion of reason.

Gandhi's axiom, "the non-beginning of a thing is supreme wisdom," suggests a conception of rationality as choosing intelligently among existing alternatives in a given situation to promote certain already existing democratic tendencies and actively oppose others of a socially oppressive nature.[209] This paradigm of rationality within the democratic framework of non-violent conflict resolution conceived existing traditions as organizationally related to "the aspirations and objective needs of the popular social and economic forces."[210] On this basis Gandhi fought against *untouchability* and the oppression of women in Indian society, transforming cultural institutions from within through

[204] Ibid., 181.
[205] Ibid., 82.
[206] Ibid., 199.
[207] Gandhi, *CW 19*, 253.
[208] Dewey, *Philosophy*, 355.
[209] Gandhi, *Hind Swaraj*, 109.
[210] Rudolph and Rudolph, *Gandhi*, 78.

political tactics generating persuasion, and in the overall process of constructive work. The experimental conviction permitted Gandhi to "use the traditional to promote the novel; he reinterpreted tradition in such a way that revolutionary ideas clothed in familiar expressions were readily adopted and employed towards revolutionary ends."[211] This alternative to an inside/out framework is similar to Dewey's concept of "reflective transcendence" where the "choice is not between a moral authority outside custom and one within it [but] between adopting more or less intelligent and significant customs."[212] Dewey viewed reason as "inherently social, embodied, and historically situated" with an emphasis on "practical enquiry" and "beliefs as tendencies to act" over "intellectual abstractions."[213]

In the politics introduced by Gandhi through the Indian National Movement the means became the focus, as a process of growth, over Final Ends, implying an open and communicative (i.e. temporal) rather than teleological and fixed absolute rationality. It evokes Dewey's insight that those "who are less absolutist may be content to think that, morally speaking, growth is a higher value and ideal than is sheer attainment."[214] There was in this outlook a rejection of the premise of ontology that characterized the dominant French Revolutionary paradigm of modernity in its philosophical ambitions. In 1925, Gandhi made this point explicit, stating that "We need not debate whether what we see is unreal, and whether the real behind the unreality is what we do not see. Let both be equally real, if you will."[215] This may be compared to Dewey's concept of "conceptual pluralism," which denies the need for any "assertion about *the* real object or *the* real world or *the* reality," while asserting that "an uncorrupted realism would accept such things (as error, dreams, hallucinations) as real events, and find in them no other problems than those

---

[211] Bondurant, *Conquest of Violence*, 105.
[212] Steven Fesmire, *John Dewey and Moral Imagination. Pragmatism in Ethics* (Bloomington: Indiana University Press, 2003), 12.
[213] Ibid., 28.
[214] Dewey, *Common Faith*, 18.
[215] Tendulkar, *Mahatma 2*, 216.

attending the consideration of any real occurrence—namely, the problems of structure, origin, and operation."[216]

The French Revolutionary paradigm of *rupture* was a quest for atemporal *foundations* in "the goodness of unmasked human nature" or "the infallibility of the people."[217] This had its roots in Rousseau's idea of *l'ame dechiree*. To recover the "foundation" in these "original men" it was necessary only to unmask the artificiality of the socially and politically accumulated institutions to undo the corrupting work of time and lay bare the timelessly pure.[218] This ontology of "man's nature" glistened at the core of the metaphysic of development, justifying change at any cost, with the function of providing certainty or closure where modern social conflicts in fact keep the situation in perpetual unrest. Gandhi, rather, sought to devise tactics for living harmoniously in the continual openness, diversity and uncertainty of a large multi-religious nation state linked to the wider world of globalization. Because of the technique, the masses of India, unlike those in other nations seeking independence and radical social democratic transformation, did not become the victims of the very means they employed to attain liberation under the post-independence regime.

---

[216] Dewey, *Philosophy*, 86, 89. Note the similarity to Shaftesbury's comment (chapter 2).
[217] Arendt, *On Revolution*, 111.
[218] Ibid., 109.

5

The Ottoman–Turkish Experience of the Enlightenment: Mass Movement and Programme

KEMALIST MOMENT IN NATION-MAKING

We find longstanding and internally heterogeneous intellectual and political movements in the Ottoman Empire and, later, the Turkish Republic, centred on myriad Enlightenment concepts. These had an enduring effect on the course of the nation's history, responding to contingent event conjunctures and rearticulating tactical structures. Turkey, including the late Ottoman period, "has the longest parliamentary tradition in the Middle East."[1] The Ottoman–Turkish experience shows several alternative roads to Enlightenment, from the ambiguous force of popular grassroots movements to dogmatic statist programmes implemented from above. The latter were grounded in late 19th-century European doctrines of scientific certainty in social engineering. The 1923 Kemalist revolution represented an extreme variant on this second tendency. While hailing its triumph to the Turkish population and the world through a historicist discursive narrative, the course of actual events reflected entropic and multi-centred human struggle rather than the predestined path of History.

The demise of the Ottoman Empire and the birth of the Turkish Republic were conceived by Ataturk as a historical rupture and founding moment, or the total triumph of modern over traditional modes of thought and being. Ataturk saw teleological inevitability where only one *scientific* road was possible, as he insisted in his famous 1927 speech: "our general behaviour [since 1923] has never deviated from the lines laid down in our

---

[1] Bulent Tanor, "The Place of Parliament in Turkey," in *Turkish State, Turkish Society*, ed. Andrew Finkel and Nukhet Sirman (London: Routledge, 1990), 139.

original resolution."¹ It is a "natural and inevitable" or "fatal course of historical events."² He claimed to have "kept [the outcome] to myself in my own consciousness as a national secret."³ Meanwhile, the Ottoman Empire had, "in each century, each day and each hour ... declined and degenerated more and more, because there were men who permitted themselves to be misled by erroneous [traditional] ideas" which "produce a destructive influence on our nervous system."⁴ Traditional decline was contrasted with the new birth in modernity, as if an ontological fissure divided the Ottoman Empire from the new Turkish nation. Ataturk's vision embodied a specific discursive formation linked to a Eurocentric vision of history, progress and nation-making, which was only one construction of modernity among many in the complex Ottoman–Turkish experience.

It was a vision of transformation anchored in the heritage of the French Revolution, reproducing the categories of the *ancien regime* and the birth of modernity as a single moment to be multiplied around the globe. There were only modernizers and reactionaries in a dichotomous universal battle whose end was predestined. The vision laid claim to a totalized intellectual virtue grounded in the modern subject. The *leader* is to "enlighten and guide the people" with "special qualifications and untiring energy." Sovereignty is to be "confided in the hands of that political party most powerfully representing the general tendency of the nation" (i.e. the general will).⁵

The population was refused political participation until tradition could be overcome by the state in a process of modern self-realization through legislation and education. Ataturk maintained that "historic error" had "for centuries given the nation the appearance of being other than it really was." He aimed to "show the nation's brow pure and luminous, as it is." The Kemalist revolution therefore affirmed the *true being* of Turkish national identity in an ontological politics. It claimed, simultaneously, to dispose of accumulated historical dross by showing "that our

---

² Mustafa Kemal Ataturk, *A Speech Delivered by Mustafa Kemal Ataturk, 1927* (Istanbul: Ministry of Education Printing Plant 1963), 11.
³ Ibid., 12.
⁴ Ibid., 535.
⁵ Ibid., 53–54/183.

people think in neither a fanatical nor a reactionary manner."[6] People's minds would be transformed by unearthing their *true* thoughts hidden beneath the accumulated *illusions*. It was a vision of modern *purity* whose purported scientific truth justified its right to wield unrestricted violence to attain its ends.

EARLY OTTOMAN MODERNIZATION STRUGGLE

Ottoman–Turkish modernity, however, had historically deeper pragmatic–rhizomatic origins. A pragmatic rationality in Ottoman administrative practices—deviating from the Islamic code—developed from the early 16th century.[7] A long centrifugal moment drove the modernization campaign. Peter the Great's (1672–1725) newly modernizing Russia inflicted disastrous late 17th-century military defeats. The Ottomans—initially forced to modernize militarily to compete and survive in the changed global environment—were soon forced by unforeseeable structural consequences to expand modernization to an ever-widening complex of reforms. It followed the logic of Norbert Elias' *monopoly mechanism*.[8] The 18th century saw the emergence of a "new sphere of the political" and "modern tools of dissent" shaped by "different moments in different alliances forging an opposition to the state that saw its goal as reform."[9] These popular tools of dissent preceded the new 19th-century "tools of control," i.e. the shift from "consumption competitions and tax farms to a much larger and professional military and bureaucracy."[10]

These 18th-century experiences responded to "the economic and political exigencies of continued warfare, increased taxation, and poverty." Emergent practical formations transformed the political landscape amidst "manifold rumblings of state-society

[6] Ibid., 739.

[7] Alev Cinar, *Modernity, Islam, and Secularism in Turkey, Bodies, Places and Time* (Minneapolis: University of Minnesota Press, 2005), 4.

[8] Norbert Elias, *The Civilizing Process: The History of Manners and State Formation and Civilization* (Oxford: Blackwell, 1994), 345.

[9] Karen Barkey, *Empire of Difference. The Ottomans in Comparative Perspective* (New York: Cambridge University Press, 2008), 206/225.

[10] Donald Quataert, *The Ottoman Empire, 1700–1922* (Cambridge: Cambridge University Press, 2005), 54.

readjustments."[11] Deep mutations transpired in the social and political surface of the empire as "the traditional system of rule [was] abandoned, and the division between classes ... forsaken for a porous and dangerous movement filling [the military ranks] with undeserving and untrained men." There arose "movements of opposition to the state (or to particular segments of the state) ... developing to connect, unite, and develop common platforms of action; social forces were starting to frame a new state–society compact." The terrain of practice saw "transformations in the associative ability of different social groups and classes in Ottoman society." This signalled a "transformation in the political culture of the empire [as empowerment spread] to the military classes, the ulema, the artisans, and the masses in coalition with a variety of groups." A new basis for emergent popular movements was thus created, representing a shift in power sharing through a "forceful broadening of the base of political power in the empire." It entailed an all-Ottoman transformation of possible political action as "broader political participation" was "spread to the provinces, ignited rebellions, and transformed the nature of factions and alliances in faraway regions of the empire."[12] One probable consequence was that, during the 18th century, "provincial political power seemed to operate more autonomously of control from the capital."[13] Thus, the state-down reform drive, uninterrupted if turbulently contested from the late 18th century, was only the most visible aspect of profound and largely anonymous changes in practical formations at the level of the Ottoman multitude.[14] The overall experience, being pragmatic, was multi-centred rather than unilinear, and tension-laden rather than *pure*.

Until 1856, modernizing the army remained the driving force behind state reform. The core modernizing dilemma was the "immense financial burden [of introducing] a conscript army, the acquisition of modern armaments and the ballooning of the Ottoman bureaucracy."[15] The changing techno-military apparatus

[11] Barkey, *Empire of Difference*, 201.
[12] Ibid., 197–200.
[13] Quataert, *Ottoman Empire*, 46.
[14] Cinar, *Bodies, Places and Time*, 15.
[15] Eric J. Zurcher, *The Young Turk Legacy and Nation Building: From the Ottoman Empire to Ataturk's Turkey* (London: I.B. Tauris, 2010), 45.

and obligatory tax restructuration were linked to gradual centralizing and secularizing effects. This encountered violent contestation from regional or occupational (i.e. Janissary, ulema) vested interests. It was, however, no inherent clash between modernity and tradition. Provided that the clerical establishment retained their government presence, and reform was accommodated under Islam, clerics were prepared to participate in the modernization process.[16] The reform movement had originated among the high-ranking secular educated Ottoman bureaucracy, but some high-ranking ulema collaborated with the reforms of Selim III (1789–1807) and Mahmud II (1808–39).[17]

Modernity is a set of problems, inviting reflection, not a pure object. Among opposing perceptions of the causes of techno-military decline—between neglect of religious duties and deteriorated state machinery—some *Ulama* supported the secular thesis.[18] These very reforms, however, undid their clerical monopoly on education. Their hostility was—in this aspect—structural rather than metaphysical. Their initial intellectual judgement had boomeranged with the onslaught of a brave new world. New technically oriented vocational schools provided trained personnel for the new army and navy, whose number and range constituted a new secular social space throughout the 19th century. Medical, engineering, naval and military schools were staffed by foreign instructors.[19] Status patterns, and soon sovereignty, came to be at stake—as embodied in 731 miles of foreign built railroad track (by 1875) in the European provinces designed to secure foreign financial control.[20] This was no changeless traditional society reproducing old habits, but elite and mass populations entering a modern crisis situation within a capitalist world economic context and seeking multiple ways to quickly adapt. This was

---

[16] Caroline Finkel, *Osman's Dream: The History of the Ottoman Empire 1300–1923* (New York: Basic Books, 2007), 476.

[17] Serif Mardin, *Religion and Social Change in Modern Turkey: The Case of Bediuzzaman Said Nursi* (New York: State University of New York Press, 1989), 106.

[18] Mardin, *Religion and Social Change*, 195.

[19] Finkel, *Osman's Dream*, 476; Peter Mansfield, *A History of the Middle East* (New York: Viking Penguin, 1991), 63.

[20] Quataert, *Ottoman Empire*, 123.

the dynamic context for practical and intellectual mutations in multiple Ottoman lifeworlds of deepening inner contradictions.

The French Revolutionary experience formed a tactical region of density for Ottoman visions of state-making: the "French Revolutionary principles of the rights and obligations of 'Man' instantly had made France into the most powerful nation in continental Europe, with its army recruited from the levee en masse. The lesson was clear: universal conscription meant vastly enhanced military and political strength." This had unforeseeably complex and destabilizing political ramifications, for "to render such conscription palatable, the state had to grant universal rights (to males)."[21] This explains, at the elite level, at least one of the powerful pistons linking this historical experience of struggle to the Enlightenment heritage as a discursive–practical formation.

Post-1683 Ottoman wars became defensive, protecting shrinking borders. The 1699 Karlowitz Treaty—inflicting important European territorial loss—forced adherence to new international law.[22] A panicked European Muslim population mass migrated to Istanbul, creating the deracinated urban underclass of the reformist Tulip Era (1718–30).[23] Diplomacy being privileged over war, the traditional military fell in status below the emergent modern administrative profession.[24] Status groups endangered by modernizing institutions employed tradition as a mobilizing axis of retaliation. A 1703 military-clerical rebellion in Istanbul upheld Muslim honour.[25] A new military engineering school was forced to close by a conservative clerical faction in 1750. To the new urban underclass, Europe was identified with social misery and political corruption. The first major conservative revolt in 1730 undid the Tulip Era, setting a practical formation culminating in the 1859 Kuleli Revolt organized by ulema and military under an anti-Western banner.[26] As the diplomatic network tightened throughout the 18th century, the weightiest strings in the modernization process were clearly pulled from the outside.

---

[21] Quataert, *Ottoman Empire*, 67.
[22] Finkel, *Osman's Dream*, 361/322.
[23] Ibid., 350.
[24] Ibid., 350/368.
[25] Ibid., 319/330.
[26] Mansfield, *Middle East*, 42–43.

Following the 1739 Treaty of Belgrade, unprecedented French power permitted she demand trading privileges previously viewed as a gracious bestowal by the Ottomans.[27]

Islam also manifested new pacifist interpretations in response to the Ottoman crisis of power and meaning. Negation of traditional ideological foundations in ceaseless religious warfare paralleled a new wave of pacifist thought among the developing Ottoman elite and sections of the general public. Among elites, the Tulip Era reformer Damad Ibrahim Pasha expressed commitment to a policy of international peace.[28] In 1781, Ahmed Resmi Efendi (1708–83) rejected Ottoman–Russian warfare in favour of fixed borders and "peace perpetuated through the tools of diplomacy and negotiation." At the popular level, in 1787, the Istanbul population expressed opposition to war with Russia through posters stuck upon public buildings—including the royal palace—or distributed in mosques.[29] Discursive and practical formations claiming Islam were therefore heterogeneous and conflicting. It was perhaps a pragmatic pacifism, responding to the ferocity of new industrial forms of warfare. It may have been an instance of social self-protection in the double-movement of unrestricted market expansion and counter-movements to prevent violence against multiple lifeworlds.[30] Such broader patterns would explain its family links to the French Revolution at the level of underclass manifestations. Global pressures in the Ottoman Empire created a "countermovement of protection" in "institutional reform" from above and "local rebellion" from below.[31]

Emergent modern institutions, meanwhile, were ideological carriers for a "new vision of reality." The "new knowledge" of geography, physics, chemistry and biology was an "expanding body with its own momentum." Emergent status groups had to struggle to keep abreast of changes to be well informed. The *ulama* had traditionally conceived knowledge as a "limited thing ... established once and for all." Increasingly, they were viewed derisively by the emergent foreign-educated bureaucratic elite

---

[27] Finkel, *Osman's Dream*, 363.
[28] Ibid., 349.
[29] Ibid., 377–82.
[30] Karl Polanyi, *The Great Transformation* (Boston: Beacon, 1957), 5–7.
[31] Kasaba, *Rethinking Modernity*, 20.

of the 19th century for having "not kept up with the expansion of the [new] intellectual horizons."[32] By the 1880s, the new bureaucratic elite often imagined the "new knowledge" in totalizing terms. The Ottoman statesman Saffet Pasa (1814–83) urged Turkey to adopt "the civilization of Europe in its entirety."[33] It demonstrates the link between this *new truth* and the emerging global network of European colonial power. Hence, the historically deeper pragmatic and multi-centred effect—unconscious fragments of everyday change requiring technical adaptation—became subsumed under the imaginative ideological projections of a newly dominant intellectual class with their eyes riveted to the West.

The European reality was remote from this imaginary archetype shining down upon the world. We see no military intervention by Western Europe until Napoleon's 1798 Egyptian invasion to sever the British lifeline to India.[34] Yet Ottoman Muslims had already ceased to dominate the empire's commerce during the 18th century, as non-Muslims were integrated into long-distance diplomatic and commercial networks. They wielded this new power against increasingly beleaguered Ottoman Muslim political dominance.[35] Capitalist penetration had produced prosperity among the merchant class and limited commercial companies. The majority of wealth, however, accrued to foreigners benefiting from capitulations. The process eliminated the principle source of state revenues by ending traditional government monopolies.[36] The Ottoman state financed bureaucratic and military expansion partly through rising tax revenues derived from heavier burdens upon the agrarian population and the overall post-1840 economic expansion. When these sums proved inadequate, the state resisted the danger of European loans and concomitant foreign control until mid-century when the Crimean war (1853–56) left no option. By the mid-1870s, the Ottoman state found itself unable to repay its international debts.[37]

---

[32] Mardin, *Religion and Social Change*, 204.
[33] Ibid., 197.
[34] Mansfield, *Middle East*, 42–43.
[35] Finkel, *Osman's Dream*, 470.
[36] Mansfield, *Middle East*, 65–66.
[37] Quataert, *Ottoman Empire*, 71–72.

The mid-19th century balance of economic strength mainly favoured Britain and France. Entering the second industrial revolution, they employed the new political–economic power to forcibly incorporate the Ottoman economy into the 19th-century liberal capitalist system.[38] The years 1820–53 saw foreign trade expanded and handicrafts decline under industrial competition. Agricultural export for the world market grew under British hegemony. The 1838 free trade treaty of Balta Limanı with Great Britain and similar treaties with other powers shortly after removed Ottoman "freedom of action in the sphere of custom duties and tolls."[39] Following the Crimean War—the first great power war to employ railroads—the 1854–76 period saw heavy external borrowing for vital military purchases (i.e. equipment for new armament factories or transport networks).[40] We see the technological stakes in an arms race running the Ottoman state steadily to collapse. A desperate modernization bid produced increased foreign capital inflows and debt correspondingly mushroomed. Direct foreign investment through railroad building followed in the coastal regions controlled almost entirely by foreign financiers. Ottoman financial dependence was hence sealed within a vicious loop.[41]

As the traditional export economy yielded to an influx of cheap European goods, entire lifeworlds disappeared to be replaced by refugees streaming across the empire.[42] Irreversible stagnation plagued the 1880–96 period, following an official government bankruptcy declaration in 1875.[43] Growing European financial

---

[38] Mansfield, *Middle East*, 65.

[39] Zurcher, *Young Turk*, 62.

[40] John Morris Roberts, *The Penguin History of Europe* (London: Penguin, 1997), 406.

[41] Stanford J. Shaw and Ezal Kural Shaw, *Reform, Revolution and Republic: The Rise of Modern Turkey 1808–1975*, Vol. 2, History of the Ottoman Empire and Modern Turkey (Cambridge: Cambridge University Press, 1977), 184.

[42] Donald Quataert, "Workers and the State during the Late Ottoman Empire," in *The State and the Subaltern: Modernization, Society and the State in Turkey and Iran*, ed. Touraj Atabaki (London: I.B. Tauris, 2007), 20.

[43] Mansfield, *Middle East*, 70.

control under inter-imperialist conditions preceded World War I.[44] A 1876 Western study described the empire as "virtually a colony after the old colonial fashion."[45] Ottoman economy and markets were dominated by European markets through networks branching inward through port cities.[46] In Anatolia, the traditional village economy sank. Its communities, remaining inaccessible to development, suffered dire misery. Peasants therefore swarmed into the new towns. With no modern industries to absorb them, they became a rootless and desperate population.[47] A slow incorporation process between European power and emergent modern Ottoman bureaucracy increased capitalist penetration and division of the country into spheres of influence among imperialist powers. World War I imperial occupation culminated in the Turkish War for Independence.[48]

OTTOMAN ENLIGHTENMENT DISCOURSES AND CONTEXT

The Ottoman struggle to reform and survive was often articulated through Enlightenment discourses. At the twilight of the Tulip Era Ibrahim Muteferrika (1674–1745) — who had set up the first printing press in 1726 — presented Mahmud I with his *Rational Basis for the Politics of Nations* in 1731.[49] It distinguished "Divine Prescriptions" from "laws and rules invented by reason" and introduced concepts of sovereignty based on the people

---

[44] Sevket Pamuk, *The Ottoman Empire and European Capitalism, 1820–1913. Trade, Investment, and Production* (Cambridge: Cambridge University Press, 1987), 11–16.

[45] Sir Adolphus Slade, *Turkey and the Crimean War* (London, Smith and Elder, 1867), 31–32; Serif Mardin, *The Genesis of Young Ottoman Thought: A Study in the Modernization of Turkish Political Ideas* (New York: Syracuse University Press, 2000), 166.

[46] Resat Kasaba, "Kemalist Certainties and Modern Ambiguities," in Sibel Bozdogan and Resat Kasaba, ed., *Rethinking Modernity and National Identity in Turkey* (Washington: University of Washington Press, 1997), 20.

[47] Niyazi Berkes, *The Development of Secularism in Turkey* (Montreal: McGill University Press, 1964), 141.

[48] Pamuk, *Ottoman Empire*, 7.

[49] Finkel, *Osman's Dream*, 366.

as one political option.[50] On the eve of the French Revolution in 1788 the French consul noted that the *Encyclopedie* had been translated into Turkish.[51] In 1847, at the height of the Tanzimat era, students at the School of Medicine in Istanbul were reading Baron D'Holbach's manual of atheism *System of Nature* and quoting Diderot's *Jacques the Fatalist*.[52] In 1876, following the creation of the new constitutional government through a series of popular uprisings led by Midhat Pasha (1822–84), discussions of constitutionalism "penetrated the walls of the consultative chambers" to be "disseminated among the common people for the first time."[53]

Despite Ataturk's call for the total adoption of Western civilization, the tradition of Ottoman Enlightenment was never a simple one-directional influence from the West. The Positivist-inspired *pure* modernity of Kemalism—with its exclusive claim to the Enlightenment heritage—embodied amnesia with respect to a diverse and changing historical movement. The Ottoman Enlightenment had selectively adopted European Enlightenment discourses and made use of domestic Ottoman–Turkish–Islamic traditions in articulating the road to a modern nation. There was an "indeterminate richness [to early] Ottoman and Turkish modernization," and the Young Ottomans (1865–76) were defined by an *ambiguity* and *relative inclusiveness*. This contrasted with the later claims to "absolute and complete truth" in the modernization process.[54] The Young Ottoman moment demonstrated that "nation-building is intrinsically tied to the making of the public sphere."[55] They practiced "bridge building" by linking "elite and mass through the recognition of religion as a discourse" and tolerated "social heterogeneity." Both practices were later undermined when the new republican movement embraced the *Jacobin principle* of rejecting popular religion and viewing deviant groups in historicist terms as *feudal remnants*.[56] Two competing discursive–practical elements clashed within the new bureaucratic elite

[50] Berkes, *Secularism in Turkey*, 44.
[51] Ibid., 60.
[52] Ibid., 117–18.
[53] Ibid., 236.
[54] Kasaba, *Rethinking Modernity*, 18/27.
[55] Cinar, *Bodies, Places and Time*, 34.
[56] Mardin, "Projects as Methodology: Thoughts on Modern Turkish Social Science," in *Rethinking Modernity and National Identity in Turkey*,

over the problem of means: modernization from above as a programme was opposed to the involvement of the broad public as a movement in the process of transformation. These two opposed visions of nation-making were embodied in the conflict between the Young Ottomans and the Tanzimat, which culminated in the brief 1876 constitutional period.

An Ottoman state-down politics of Enlightened despotism— comparable to policies in Austria–Hungary and Russia—sought "between 1829 and 1856 ... to strip away the differences among Ottoman subjects and make all male subjects the same in its eyes and in one another's as well."[57] The massacre of the Janissary corps in 1826 by Mahmud II (1808–39) constituted so violent and radical an uprooting—despite deepening corruption and loss of status, they remained the *heart and soul* of the Ottoman *people*— that a comparative docility settled over the Istanbul population in the aftermath of viewing "thousands of Janissary corpses rotting in the Golden Horn."[58] The 1826 massacre constituted one of the two defining moments in the "history of Ottoman labour and state relations in the nineteenth century ... the centralizing Ottoman state destroyed the Janissary Corps and thus violently eliminated its armed source of worker opposition."[59] Central control intensified as a system of local chiefs was abolished (1831) and the Ulema marginalized through control of traditional religious law courts and schools (*medresse*) by new state ministries. New state schools were established to train new elite army officers and civil servants. The Janissary extermination and the newly created conscript army cleared the field for the reforms of Mahmud II, and permitted further reforms throughout the 19th century. The state document abolishing the Janissary order was the first to employ the activist principle—an Enlightenment discursive convention—in an appeal to "all subjeçts."[60] The modern conscript army permitted the masses to pour into the military apparatus and the previously isolated island of Ottoman political

---

eds. Sibel Bozdoğan and Reşat Kasaba (Seattle, Washington: University of Washington Press, 1997), 71.

[57] Quataert, *Ottoman Empire*, 65.
[58] Mardin, *Young Ottoman Thought*, 206. Quote from Namik Kemal.
[59] Quataert, *State and the Subaltern*, 20; Quataert, *Ottoman Empire*, 139.
[60] Mardin, *Young Ottoman Thought*, 173.

power. Soon radical structural changes permitted the common people to enter the administrative and clerical orders, inadvertently creating a new national political culture.

In 1829, Sultan Mahmud II—after a longstanding struggle to control levelling public shows of the new wealth (i.e. ermine fur)—"abolished the old social markers based on wearing apparel."[61] Increasingly, as wealth-based status competed with office-holding status, new groups emerged to challenge the economic, social and political power of the ruling Ottoman dynasty.[62] The divinely ordained strata melted like a tower of wax with new power distributions and market pressures, as "Ottoman Muslims as a major merchant group ... faded in importance during the eighteenth century [as] foreigners and Ottoman non-Muslims became dominant in the mounting foreign trade."[63] French Revolutionary ideals, meanwhile, spread to communities with powerful European trading network links (the Greeks and the Serbs) making possible the fatal interplay of external pressure and separatist nationalism.[64] The modernizing vezir Ali Pasha (1856) urged the undoing of the traditional hierarchy of labour allocation: "Muslims must, like the Christians, devote themselves to [commercial] agriculture, trade, industry and crafts. Labour is the only durable capital."[65] In further evidence of profound social reconfiguration, the level of involvement of women and girls in the workforce—Muslim, Christian and Jewish—mounted strikingly.[66]

The Janissary massacre disintegrated the alliance between the sultan and the bureaucratic elite, as it ended common cause against their powerful anti-reformist foe. If Mahmud II substituted the *people* as the new sovereign principle following the massacre, he saw them as the object rather than the subjective agents of reform. While he had used modern power to implement change in the empire he did not share it, even with the powerful new bureaucratic elite who made such changes possible.

[61] Quataert, *Ottoman Empire*, 148
[62] Ibid.,144.
[63] Ibid., 129.
[64] Zurcher, *Young Turk*, 67.
[65] Finkel, *Osman's Dream*, 471.
[66] Quataert, *Ottoman Empire*, 140.

He underestimated their autonomy in the wake of the 18th-century reform struggles against the Janissaries and the ulema. The Sultan's full control was only imaginary: the human tools he had multiplied were prepared to turn on him for their own ends.[67]

We ultimately see the "Western concepts of constitutional government and the separation of legislative, executive and judicial powers which had penetrated the new Ottoman elite ... turned against the sultan's despotism."[68] Seizing the opportunity of Mahmud II's death in 1839, the new bureaucratic elite set up the semi-constitutional Gulhane Rescript of 1839 and thereby established formal rule of law while tipping the power balance in their favour. The decree embodied an Enlightenment discursive pattern in proclaiming "the need to eliminate inequality and create justice for all subjects, Muslim or non-Muslim, rich or poor."[69] This was a bid to curb the sultan's political power, greatly inflated since the marginalization of traditional counterweights in the Porte, the *ulama*, the Janissaries, workers' guilds, tribes and other intermediating groups. Mahmud II's royal successors were reduced to political bystanders before the expansion and advance of the new Ottoman bureaucracy designed to move and transform the empire in contrast to the previous guiding ideal of administration in *heaven sent* stasis.[70] The year 1839 represented an important discursive–practical shift at the elite political level for the Ottoman Enlightenment as a state-making path.

The traditional Ottoman policy of "tolerance" proved contradictory following the institution of 1839 semi-constitutional charter. The Tanzimat strategy aimed to unite the multiple communities of the empire through the policy of broad Ottoman nationality based on equality before the law—while shunning representation at the national level. Non-Muslim communities within the Ottoman structure received the right of jurisdiction through their respective ecclesiastical authorities, each with particular "traditions as to titles, grades, recruitment, ceremonies, discipline, but [with] absolute loyalty to the supreme ruler."[71]

---

[67] Mardin, *Young Ottoman Thought*, 136.
[68] Mansfield, *Middle East*, 71.
[69] Quataert, *Ottoman Empire*, 66.
[70] Mardin, *Young Ottoman Thought*, 196–252.
[71] Berkes, *Secularism in Turkey*, 12.

These pyramidally constructed autonomies based on unequal religious difference were in practice incompatible with a uniform secular law guaranteeing legal equality under universal Ottoman citizenship. This structural problem penetrated the core of the Ottoman state as a hierarchically structured multiplicity of overlapping communitarian bonds and identities. Yet such equality was the practical prerequisite for the universal conscription that might overcome the two challenges to the Ottoman state's existence: continuous loss of land and population (i.e. tax revenue and labour) through war and the corresponding need to construct a unifying collective Ottoman identity (i.e. hegemony). The need for dismantling of religious, occupational and other traditionally upheld distinctions—and their corresponding military or other exemptions—was the basis for the institutional carrier of a politics of state-down Enlightenment.

The 1839 Gulhane Rescript formalized the breach between temporal and religious domains of power. The bureaucratic elite ascended while pressing downward on "the lower ranking bureaucrats, the majority of the ulema, and the army as a whole."[72] Many came to hate the closed circle with increasing wealth, power and opportunities for social advancement.[73] By the 1850s and 1860s the lower echelons of the Ottoman state service were expressing their frustrated expectations through a "natural progression from anger to alcoholism to loss of health to death."[74] The Young Ottomans, against this social background, remained generally cutoff from the broad mass of the peasant population.

The Young Ottomans founded the Patriotic Alliance during a picnic in 1865, vowing a conspiracy to transform the government from "absolute into constitutional rule."[75] Anything but organic intellectuals, they were the product of the new modernizing state. They were educated in new Western schools and worked in the new administrative machinery—nearly all of them went through the Translation Bureau, "a seedbed of the most progressive minds of the Tanzimat."[76] Pervasive crisis set the context. Several

[72] Mardin, *Young Ottoman Thought*, 121–22.
[73] Ibid., 112.
[74] Ibid., 124–25.
[75] Ibid., 13.
[76] Balazs Trencsenyi and Michal Kopacek, *National Romanticism: The Formation of National Movements* (CEU Press, 2006), 94.

non-Muslim national uprisings linked to European diplomatic intervention occurred firstly in Lebanon in 1861 and soon in the Serbian provinces and Crete. The empire's debt mounted under the extravagant Sultan Abdulaziz (1861–76).[77] The Young Ottomans opposed the tyranny they saw in the new bureaucratic elite running the Tanzimat reform programme. Two visions of Enlightenment therefore stood opposed, between the Young Ottomans and the reigning Tanzimat reformers. The Tanzimat project was based on the "theory of the enlightenment [postulating] the basic similarity of men." It sought to unify the diverse Ottoman population through a policy of "good government framed by an enlightened despotism."[78]

The Young Ottoman critique from the 1360s argued that the "viability of [building the nation state] was dependent upon solidarity and support by the mass of the population." Their demand for "representative government followed from this premise." In their recognition that the "program of modernization of Ottoman institutions could succeed only if it obtained the acquiescence and support of a plurality of the population," the Young Ottomans grasped the fundamental problem of hegemony in movements for social change.[79] They introduced an alternative practical formation, emphasizing grassroots organization, linked to the ideal of popular self-reliance.

The statesman Midhat Pasha (1822–84), the *father* of the 1876 constitution, called for: "making the Assembly truly national, by doing away with all distinctions of classes and religions, and by placing the Christians on a footing of entire equality with the Mussulmans."[80] This discursive formation had an activist practical counterpart. He was involved from 1861 to 1864 in reforming provincial administration in the Serbian province of Nis. He undertook an ambitious public works programme to improve security, start factories and create agricultural credit cooperatives enabling peasants to borrow at low rates of interest. It served

[77] Mansfield, *Middle East*, 72.
[78] Mardin, *Religion and Social Change*, 116.
[79] Ibid.
[80] Ali Haydar Midhat, *The Life of Midhat Pasha: A Record of His Services, Political Reforms, Banishment, and Judicial Murder, Derived from Private Documents and Reminiscences* (London: J. Murray, 1903), 80.

Muslims and non-Muslims equally. He also established local administrative councils representing all religious groups on an electoral basis. His efforts to set up mixed religious schools met fierce resistance. In 1865, he started a provincial newspaper in Nis published in both Ottoman and Bulgarian detailing on-going and intended reforms and speeches from the provincial assembly.

Midhat Pasha later spent five years in Bagdad, where he struggled to introduce similar reforms encouraging public self-reliance. He demonstrated a form of democratic public activism in reshaping civil society from below which scarcely as yet existed in Europe. In 1870, he was appointed as grand vezir but was dismissed after several months due to open criticism of government practices.[81] Midhat Pasha argued in 1873 that "the only way to avoid the imminent destruction of the empire lay in making the sultan's ministers responsible, especially in matters of finances, to a national popular assembly."[82] While opposing the Tanzimat over the issue of national representation, he prioritized institutionalized democratic transformation in the sociological tradition of Montesquieu rather than grand visions of traditional or modern *purity*. The Young Ottomans fought to change meanings and ideas within the public sphere in everydayness. They published newspapers and pamphlets voicing their radical ideas and calling for electoral politics through a National Assembly.[83] When unable to publish inside the empire, they smuggled literature in from abroad. They conflicted with the law and were exiled over staging a nationalist theatre production which met with wild enthusiasm from spectators. While exiled in Paris some of them served with the Republican forces during the 1871 battle of the Paris Commune, cementing a link to the living French Revolutionary tradition of egalitarian politics.[84]

This was a period of profound change in the Ottoman public life. The Ottoman press had previously been "merely a one-way communication channel between government and subjects for the express purpose of disseminating information and positive

---

[81] Finkel, *Osman's Dream*, 464.
[82] Mansfield, *Middle East*, 73.
[83] Mardin, *Young Ottoman Thought*, 26.
[84] Ibid., 56.

commentary on official policies." It had now become the source of a dynamic dialogic space as "new newspapers, such as *Ceride-i Havadis* (1840), and especially *Tercuman-i Afval* (1860) and *Tasvir-i Efk ar* (1862), appeared [and] fostered debate on hitherto unheard of subjects, such as the rights of man, regime types, and economic problems [as well as] information concerning developments abroad." The effect was to remould an "Ottoman public opinion ... hitherto shaped in coffeehouses, salons, and unofficial ulema discussion groups at both popular and elite levels." The circulation figures for some newspapers were "amazingly high, given the low rate of literacy in the empire" and "newspapers were often read aloud in coffeehouses to the illiterate." In response to this fertile emergent civil society, the Tanzimat government issued a series of statutes in 1864 to "regulate journalistic activity and setup the means to punish 'dangerous' publications."[85]

The early 1870s saw flood, drought and famine in rural Anatolia, and the collapsed rural economy produced uprisings against taxation in Bosnia and Herzegovina. Russian and Austria–Hungarian intervention demonstrated the inability of the Ottoman sultan to stand up to outside pressure, eroding the state's public hegemony.[86] In 1876, a clandestinely circulated pamphlet in Istanbul, likely by Midhat Pasha, called for a "representative, consultative assembly." This tract, criticizing the government for subservience to foreign powers, met with powerful public response. Thousands of theological students "massed on the streets of Istanbul" and held "impassioned meetings in the main mosques."[87] Despite government press censorship and suppression of telegraphic communications, the movement won the support of government troops, naval vessels and ministers.[88] Thus, a non-violent battle was waged to wrest power from the state through organized civil society. Popular demonstrations initiated through communication networks effected the deposition of Sultan Abdulaziz and the reinstatement of

[85] M. Şükrü Hanioğlu, *A Brief History of the Late Ottoman Empire* (Princeton: Princeton University Press, 2008), 94–95.
[86] Finkel, *Osman's Dream*, 480.
[87] Ibid., 480.
[88] Mansfield, *Middle East*, 73.

Midhat Pasha to office in the opening days of the constitutional interim of 1876.[89]

The Young Ottomans contributed a revolution in communications which, by opening the terrain of public opinion as a battlefield, radically reshaped the contours of the Ottoman public sphere. Considering literature the "primary vehicle for progress," they introduced the vocabulary of the Western Enlightenment into national political struggle among the Turks.[90] Namik Kemal (1840–88) offered radical new interpretations of the traditional Islamic worldview intended to reconcile it with modern realities and ideas, including the Western Enlightenment. He drew upon the political theology of Qur'anic exegetes, Islamic political philosophers, the "mirrors for Princes," and Turko–Iranian–Mongolian theories of secular legislation.[91] Reconstructing conceptions of time, he introduced a "new historical narrative" through the "textbooks prepared for the new secular institutions of learning" intended to "legitimize the idea of a continuous and progressive Ottoman nationhood in history."[92]

With the 1876 Constitution and the first Ottoman democratic experiment, the Young Ottomans returned from exile to brief positions of power. Namik Kemal played an important role in drafting the Constitution, the first of its kind in any Muslim state. Parliament was opened in 1877 and represented Christians, Jews, Turks and Arabs, not according to religion or nationality but in terms of their proportion within a constituency.[93] A foreign observer noted that "Midhat's ideal of reconciling Turks and Christians was to a certain extent realized. The cleavage in Parliament was not on religious or racial lines."[94] Based on the principle that men of all creeds should be treated as equals, the Parliament annulled Russia's concession-bestowed role as protector of Ottoman Christians. During these same months, however, was the 1876 Bulgarian uprising in the Plovdiv area. It was

---

[89] These 19th-century events demonstrate the falseness of imagining the 2011 Arab Spring as a new awakening after centuries of social inertia in traditional religious habit in the Middle East.

[90] Mardin, *Young Ottoman Thought*, 37.

[91] Ibid., 81.

[92] Trencsenyi and Kopacek, *National Romanticism*, 95.

[93] Berkes, *Secularism in Turkey*, 249.

[94] Harold Temperly, quoted in Berkes, 249.

violently suppressed by irregular Muslim Circassian forces, refugees from the Russian wars and territorial seizures of 1864, causing anger among the British and Russian publics.[95]

Russia seized the moment to declare war, leading to the Russo-Turkish War (1877–78) and the Treaty of San Stefano (1878). This dismembered the empire including Bulgaria, Bosnia-Herzegovina, Romania, Serbia and Montenegro, as well as several eastern provinces ceded to Russia.[96] As Karl Polanyi noted, in

> 1856 the integrity of the Ottoman Empire was declared essential to the equilibrium of Europe, and the Concert of Europe endeavoured to maintain that empire; after 1878, when its disintegration was deemed essential to that equilibrium, its dismemberment was provided for in similarly orderly manner.[97]

Abdulhamid (1876–1909) used this opportunity to dissolve Parliament and suspend the Constitution, thereby restoring the unilateral royal power both the Tanzimat and Young Ottoman movement had sought to disperse—to their significantly differing degrees—more broadly among the population.[98] Autocratic authority—without its traditionally constraining balances—was thereby modernized.

Anticipating suspension of the Constitution, an 1876 self-organizing public movement sought to remove control of the army from the sultan. Midhat and Namik Kemal led clandestine efforts to organize and establish a National Guard or volunteer militia. They sought to win over soldiers with an appeal to "fighting for national independence and political freedom."[99] Citizen's battalions patterned on the French National Guard patrolled Istanbul's streets. However, the grassroots operation was exposed and the leaders exiled. The first Constitutional experiment was terminated and Abdulhamid dominated Ottoman politics for 30 years. Though short lived, the Young Ottoman period introduced

---

[95] Finkel, *Osman's Dream*, 484.
[96] Ibid., 485.
[97] Polanyi, *Great Transformation*, 8.
[98] Mansfield, *Middle East*, 76.
[99] Mardin, *Young Ottoman Thought*, 75–76.

an enduring alternative discourse and practice of modernization into the politics of the empire and later the Turkish Republic. The Young Ottomans critique of the Porte's ideal of modernization from above without freedom argued that freedom and progress are inextricably bound.

The Young Ottoman founder, Mustafa Fazil Pasa (1829–75), articulated the movement's aims in his 1867 *letter* to Sultan Abdulaziz. Introducing a lay ethic, he maintained that religion is a contributing but not predominant factor in social change. He argued that because moral decay results from injustice, liberty of the citizen and not greater state control can guarantee efficiency.[100] This striking argument explicitly linked progress and freedom, or means and ends, in opposition to the official regime ideology. We find the same discursive formation linking development and freedom in building a democratic society as in Gandhi, Nehru or Mosaddeq. This discursive formation, moreover, is always found in opposition to authoritarian ideals of modernization or Enlightenment which envision a politically passive/economically instrumental role for the larger population.

Mustafa Fazil Pasa's *letter* redefined religious experience in secular terms and suited to a modern multi-religious society. Religion, he wrote, "opens for us the perspectives of the future life, but it does not regulate the rights of people." Its place, he continued, is in "the sublime domain of eternal verities." However, "there are no Christian politics nor Moslem politics, for there is only one justice and politics is justice incarnate."[101] This was a secular call for a universal Ottoman citizenship based on constitutional liberty. He articulated a "concept of the equality of all Ottomans as citizens" and developed "this concept to its secular conclusion," arguing that "all Ottomans ought to share feelings of devotion to this territorial entity above all loyalties they might feel to their religious community."[102]

Namik Kemal simplified the Turkish language in a revolutionary way in his writings and poems. This was part of a project of promoting public freedom. During the period, the novel was

---

[100] Ibid., 279.
[101] Ibid., 281.
[102] William L. Cleveland, *History of the Modern Middle East* (Westview, 2004), 85.

"a powerful new tool for highlighting social problems, popular primarily because it was easy to understand." The Tanzimat period, in promoting literature, increased "literary exchanges between the various Ottoman communities." Ottoman communities "read works of authors from other communities on an unprecedented scale" and "local theaters proliferated throughout the empire."[103] Against this creative public background, Namik Kemal wrote that man "always requires freedom. To deprive humanity of it is as if it were to deprive him of food." The material aims of development in stability and order should not outweigh considerations of social justice. He affirmed immanent rationality: "freedom derives from the fact that [man] is endowed with reason," or the capacity to make intelligent choices. He wrote that "sovereignty is present in every man" and even that "everyone is the ruler of his own world." It follows that "the government must choose the road that will least limit the freedom of the individual." He called for an "absolute normative force for the protection of freedom." He accordingly rejected the sacrifice of the individual to larger political ends. Namik Kemal critically engaged the works of Voltaire, Rousseau and Montesquieu.[104] While admiring Rousseau, he rejected the General Will as a threat to liberty. He was disturbed by Voltaire's anti-religious attitude. Namik Kemal's primary influence was Montesquieu, whose concept of the balance of powers as the institutionalization of democratic justice he wrote about at length.

Underlying Namik Kemal's individualism was an Islamic source in the Qur'anic concept of man as "sovereign over things." Though not trained as a religious scholar, he engaged the European Enlightenment through an Islamic religious and philosophical awareness. He saw in Islam a source of values. This remained in unresolved tension with his secular concept of society. He argued that government's function is to protect justice and not to organize the "meaning of life."[105] He maintained that the "mechanics of discussion and the exchange of ideas" lead "to truth," referring clearly to the secular public sphere rather than

---

[103] Hanioğlu, *Ottoman Empire*, 99–100.
[104] Mardin, *Young Ottoman Thought*, see chapter 10.
[105] Ibid., 302.

transcendent religious truth.[106] His writing conceives politics as an independent, autonomous and neutral space outside of particular religious identity. His perspective on the Seriat, then, reveals a critical and deconstructive engagement with religious phenomenon rather than the dogmatic and self-promoting attitude of religious apologetics. His effort was to reconcile modern egalitarianism with Islamic political and cultural identity.

This enterprise was grounded within a largely rural national context—80–90 per cent land-based sustenance—lacking a consolidated public or political Muslim identity, given the "absence of a conception of a unit transcending the village or hamlet." Consciousness building as a political practice—creating a sense of "Muslim," "Ottoman" and indeed other collective identities (i.e. Bulgarian, Serbian, Wahhabi or Arab)—was currently underway through the hard work of dedicated and competing individuals or groups.[107] It is anachronistic and metaphysical to imagine a total or ready-made identity preceding any of these public mobilization efforts. Modern crisis conditions had changed the contours of identity and belonging at the phenomenological level, as well as their stakes. Mostly at the tacit level, these contours and stakes awaited discovery through experiments in practice. Such *identity* experiments often produced entirely unexpected results—as when the 1829 equalizing clothing legislation, designed to impose uniformity and modesty, instead ushered in an era where "wealthy Muslims and non-Muslims ... [dressed] extravagantly in the latest fashions" and thereby reduced the legislation to ridicule.[108]

While liberal arguments favouring constitutionalism, rule of law, electoral procedure, liberty of expression and national independence were the common ideological ground for the Young Ottomans, Namik Kemal's unresolved dilemma suggests the double movement between the violence of unrestricted market expansion and counter-movements laying claim to self-protective ethical doctrines. The Young Ottomans were "critical" of the

---

[106] Ibid., 306.

[107] Serif Mardin, "Religion and Secularism in Turkey," in eds. Ali Kazancigil and Ergun Ozbudun, *Ataturk: Founder of a Modern State* (London: C. Hurst and Co., 1981), 201–2.

[108] Quataert, *Ottoman Empire*, 150.

"secularism" of the "Tanzimat reformers but inspired by the same Western ideas as that group." They attempted to "interpret (and ultimately justify) Ottoman modernization and Westernization in terms of the principles of Islam."[109] Citing the Tanzimat regime's failure to integrate Ottoman traditional cultural resources into the modernization programme, they critiqued an excessively *Western* model which alienated the population for whom the measures were intended.

Western in their sense meant a new imagining of social relations and practices which marginalized codes of conduct for personal relations derived from Islam. The Tanzimat understood "society as an impersonal machine" and the state as "a system of interrelated parts which operate mechanically." It attempted to overhaul military training, education, administration, courts and communications with the aim of gaining a place among the emergent globally powerful.[110] The Tanzimat worldview, then, conceived force as the highest criteria in human affairs, and the "people who lived in Turkey could at most be the objects of their experiments."[111] The Tanzimat rulers were "alienated from both the doctors of Islamic law and the folk, whereas in the past a common idiom and code of conduct [had] linked these elements."[112] There was an authoritarian elitism in the Tanzimat imagining of Enlightenment as a well-run machine.

Industrialization efforts in the 1840–50s had failed under international conditions and pressures, contributing to a hardened modernization drive which inflicted misery upon the common person.[113] It was the "liberal free-trade principles that had been imposed by Europe which prevented the reformers from providing the Ottoman infant industries with the protection they needed in order to survive."[114] From the perspective of the Young Ottomans, the Tanzimat administrative apparatus was guilty of functioning as an agent in the empire's progressive loss

---

[109] Haldun Gulalp, "Modernization Policies and Islamist Politics in Turkey," in *Rethinking Modernity and National Identity in Turkey* (Washington: University of Washington Press, 1997), 53.
[110] Mardin, *Religion and Social Change*, 9–12.
[111] Kasaba, *Rethinking Modernity*, 15.
[112] Mardin, *Religion and Social Change*, 9–12.
[113] Ibid., 9.
[114] Mansfield, *Middle East*, 69.

of national independence. The Tanzimat had become a "political machine whose function [was] that of maintaining order for the promotion of [European-Balkan Christian] interests which eventually became definitely non-Turkish."[115] Intellectually, the Young Ottomans responded to the impact of the "European culture of the Enlightenment" as "a view of stellar bodies in movement" projected "onto the understanding of the ... state [as] a machine," favouring "human networks" and "intimate, face to face relations" over "blocks" or "society and nation ... as real entities to which real persons were and should be subordinated."[116] The Young Ottomans—rejecting the mechanically formulaic view of nation-making—embraced the Enlightenment heritage on the level of immanence in the name of the multiple lifeworlds.

The call for a traditionally grounded modernization process was linked, in this sense, to a critique of the modern state politics of violence-truth in favour of open-ended creative civil society networks. While the Young Ottomans often criticized the state over specific instances of violence in police brutality, the effects of the tax burden on peasants, and the violent nature of the modernization process itself, there was also a more fundamental critique.[117] Namik Kemal argued that the 19th-century separation of religious criteria from government practices left no guiding ideology or ethical code beyond the sheer force of the state. In the view of the Tanzimat reformers the state worked according to the *laws of nature* and did not therefore require the framework of *traditional norms*.[118] The Young Ottoman response implied a democratic Enlightenment critique of state power embedded in a truth–violence Enlightenment compound claiming mono-vocal certainty. They questioned the possible democracy of an abstract system operating beyond the person with their specific lifeworld and values. The Young Ottoman–Tanzimat debate embodied the full complexity of varying constructions of violence in Enlightenment nation-making practices.

The Tanzimat administrative apparatus, then, embraced a specific Enlightenment discourse giving primacy to control over

---

[115] Berkes, *Secularism in Turkey*, 159.
[116] Mardin, *Religion and Social Change*, 10–12.
[117] Mardin, *Young Ottoman Thought*, 165.
[118] Mardin, *Religion and Social Change*, 10.

the general population, or a form of "enlightened despotism." Suppression of freedom to achieve the intended end was a simple matter of course. The state was the prime mover and the Young Ottomans—embodying resistance from civil society—upstarts who introduced difficulties onto the path of the reform project. The Tanzimat rulers belonged to the ideology of *devlet*, conceived on the model of 18th-century European cameralism which "saw government as a science of the state to be applied by technicians and managers."[119] In a correspondence between the Tanzimat statesman Mustafa Reshid Pasha (1800–58) and Sadik Rifat Pasa (1807–57), a clerk stationed in Vienna, we see their driving ideology. Reports sent from Vienna in 1837 correspond to reforms undertaken in the empire during the opening Tanzimat years. Sadik Rifat Pasa corresponded with and met Prince Metternich (1773–1859) while in Austria, and received advice on the means to salvaging the empire. This stressed the importance of "efficiency" over "liberty," and warned of the danger of "excessive freedom."[120] Metternich had urged the achievement of peace and prosperity through channelling disruptive human energies into productive behaviour to make controlled citizens.[121] This programme contained an authoritarian concept of modernization with the population the mere object of the state's modernizing designs.

This existed in tension with the dynamic and autonomous realm of an emerging limited Ottoman civil society breaking loose in multiple and mutating forms from the fixed pyramidic arrangement of the traditional Ottoman order, or the *Nizam*. The *Nizam*, conceived in the likeness of a body and unequal in its constituent parts, was composed not of individuals but positions grounded within an Islamic theological schema.[122] In the period of its decline we see the "drawing of both material and metaphorical boundaries, including territorial, national, ethnic, racial, cultural and religious," that is, the "formation of subjectivities" without antecedent existence.[123] The Ottoman state, in its

---

[119] Mardin, *Rethinking Modernity*, 68.
[120] Mardin, *Young Ottoman Thought*, 179.
[121] Ibid., 182.
[122] Berkes, *Secularism in Turkey*, 14–16.
[123] Cinar, *Bodies, Places and Time*, 34.

slipping power, demonstrated an increasingly excessive violence against the population as with the brutal suppression of the Bulgarians by irregular forces composed of embittered refugees in 1876.[124] The atrocities against the Bulgarians were not unlike the manner in which the European monarchies had abandoned the gentlemanly rules of 18th-century war in the summer of 1792 and treated the French as rabid dogs to be shot, instigating the popular crusade of a *nation in arms*. The violence of this period is comprehensible within larger patterns of nation-making and modernization occurring around the world under the pressures of globalizing capitalism.[125]

The problem—in its modern intensification—betrays a wider crisis of Ottoman Islamic political and cultural identity in terms of constructions of violence. The Ottoman worldview of Providence declined. At the 1571 Battle of Lepanto, Selim II (1566–74) had written that "War is uncertain in its result [because] Judgement belongs to God."[126] Criticism of this view emerged among 19th-century Ottoman administrative and military elites. Mahmud II persisted in viewing war as Providence, reproducing the myth of the Red Apple (*Kizil Elma*) where the Turks as "true Believers" were fated to conquer Christendom irrespective of armaments or military preparations on account of "divine destiny."[127] Although the 1828 Russian war closely followed the Janissary extermination, Mahmud insisted it necessary that reorganized troops rely on divine support for victory. Narrowly risking execution, the advisor Izzet Molla (1785–1820) replied by asking "whether this was a state of the Seriat or a state of reason." He argued that "military reforms having been undertaken on rational grounds, reason also had to be used in weighing the possibilities of success in warfare." The alternative, he insisted, would make "a travesty of religion."[128] He was subsequently exiled to Siwas.[129]

---

[124] Mansfield, *Middle East*, 72.

[125] Quataert, *Ottoman Empire*, 70.

[126] Mohammed Arkoun, *The Unthought in Contemporary Islamic Thought* (London: Saqi Books, 2002), 294.

[127] Berkes, *Secularism in Turkey*, 57.

[128] Mardin, *Young Ottoman Thought*, 172.

[129] M. Th. Houtsma, *E.J. Brill's First Encyclopaedia of Islam, 1913–1936* (Leiden: E.J. Brill, 1993), 571.

This dialogue demonstrates an autonomous political sphere or plane of immanence linked to a secular worldview as a practical imperative. Izzet Molla's dismissal scandalized the bureaucratic circles of the capital, showing the bureaucratic apparatus as a growing shaper of public opinion.[130] New conceptions of violence grew from these experiences, extending Ahmed Resmi's (1694–1783) 18th-century argument that "reason and experience" teach that violent conflict is determined by circumstance rather than Providence and peaceful reconciliation preferable when victory remains an unrealistic aim.[131] An emergent ethic of reconciliation is detectable in elite discourses.

Practical imperatives interfaced with multiple and contradictory discourses, both traditional and modern, as options in dealing with this crisis. The shift from Providence to historical consciousness—based on human agency—grew from efforts to mitigate the crisis of the long centrifugal moment. Ibraham Muteferrika's "Rational Basis for the Politics of Nations" (1731) divided the contemporary world into old and new, and argued that the success of the *Christian* world in conquering cities in China, India, and America was the result of navigation and other analytical-empirical methods.[132] A new focus on technology and power, evaluating ends and means in terms of observable material circumstance, came into force.

Vasif Efendi (d.1806) rebuffed a French officer's proposal in 1783–84 to train the Ottomans in modern methods of warfare saying that "success or failure depend upon the conduct of Almighty God." He spurned the new "doctrine of a school of philosophers according to whom the Creator has no role in particular matters" and in which "the side superior in material means of warfare becomes victorious over the other."[133] Vasif's rejection of the mechanistic strain in European Enlightenment derived from traditional denials in Islamic philosophy of an order of nature functioning independently of the will of God, following independent and fixed rules, as in mechanistic cosmologies. Ibn Rushd's (1126–98) self-moving nature met outcry while

---

[130] Mardin, *Young Ottoman Thought*, 161.
[131] Berkes, *Secularism in Turkey*, 57.
[132] Ibid., 43.
[133] Ibid., 66.

al-Ghazali's (1058–1111) rejection of Aristotelian cosmology or secular metaphysics met wide acceptance as affirming the unity of God through the synthetic unity of the universe. The universe as "a current of being emanating from an inexhaustible source ... spread out over everything outside God" implied Islamic natural law as the "revealed law of God" or "immanence of God in nature," and hence indistinguishable from the Seriat.[134] Politics as a "self-contained process with its own inner dynamic" was by extension unfeasible.[135]

Despite this weighty intellectual background, the opposite argument increasingly prevailed in 19th-century debates among Turkish ideologues in the Ottoman Empire. Singular occurrences as the area of human action where freedom exists to make decisions came to include not only military planning but also government measures aimed at national reform. This increased the burden of responsibility upon the deeds and decisions of statesmen. It made visible an empire whose future was increasingly uncharted, and whose ethical-legal framework for action as inherited from the past was fundamentally contested. Undefined political violence as requiring structuration through democratic institutions (i.e. as conflict resolution) was expressed by the Young Ottoman movement, who also paradoxically presented the strongest case for an Islamic modernization process. This story dismantles simple notions of a traditional and frozen Islamic essence confronting a homogeneous modernity. It refutes a *fundamental* or *ontological* difference imaginatively dividing Turkish and European experiences of modernity. It doesn't lessen the gravity of the many problems. The common history of modernity is a proliferation of context-specific problems whose flux and variation refuses to yield to the traditional logic of pure objects.

TWENTIETH CENTURY MUTATIONS IN THE OTTOMAN–TURKISH ENLIGHTENMENT

Contrasting the ambiguity and pluralism of the Young Ottomans, the Young Turks (founded 1889) shared a more unified ideological

---
[134] Mardin, *Young Ottoman Thought*, 89.
[135] Ibid., 84.

outlook. This partly reflected the Ottoman population homogenized through the territorial losses of war. Following the 1878 Treaty of Berlin—which confirmed Europe's almost arbitrary power to redraw Ottoman borders at will—the richest and most populous territory had been lost to the Ottoman Empire. In the remaining territories Muslims constituted a clear majority, where before the empire had been a highly rich mosaic of difference.[136] The leaders of the Young Turks—primarily army officers, doctors and teachers—came to reject the Young Ottoman theory of "Unity of Elements" (I'ttihad-i Anasir).[137] Three contending ideologies of salvation emerged at the close of the 19th century in Ottomanism, Pan-Islamism and Turkism.[138] In the 1880s a system of military schools was inaugurated with a student body of 8,000 by 1898. The new 1890s generation of reformers embraced a conception of social relations relegating human beings to an epiphenomenon of broader natural and social laws.[139]

A rising educated class indoctrinated in "popular materialist ideas created the conditions for an explosion of Ottoman materialist activity in the last two decades of the nineteenth century," which exerted a "profound influence over both the intellectual progenitors of the Young Turk Revolution and the founders of modern Turkey."[140] There was continuity between their worldview and that of the new bureaucrats of the Tanzimat reform. Yet the new generation, with deeper knowledge of geography, modern history and mathematics, embraced a new worldview based on laws abstracted from reality.[141] They revived and extended the Tanzimat view of society privileging "elements working beyond the person."[142]

The army officers leading the Young Turks were "no liberal democrats" and "detested Abdul Hamid's rule for its corruption and inefficiency rather than its despotism." Their overriding aim

[136] Mardin, *Modern State*, 200–201.
[137] Berkes, *Secularism in Turkey*, 329.
[138] Ayse Neviye Caglar, "The Greywolves as Metaphor," in *Turkish State, Turkish Society*, eds. Andrew Finkel, Nükhet Sirman (London: Routledge, 1990), 81.
[139] Mardin, *Religion and Social Change*, 10.
[140] Hanioğlu, *Ottoman Empire*, 101.
[141] Mardin, *Modern State*, 203–5.
[142] Mardin, *Religion and Social Change*, 12.

was strengthening the empire's defences. They derived selected practical components from the French Revolutionary experience while negating others. It had "welded the people of France into the potent force which overwhelmed the Revolution's enemies," and they hoped to use Ottoman citizens to similar effect.[143] They had an "ability to transcend the present and soar into the future" using an "abstracting, utopian and futuristic cast of thought."[144] There was mutation and continuity with the Tanzimat ideology in efficiency over liberty as the aim of a modernizing process. While claiming the Young Ottoman tradition—often reduced to a brief and innocuous *failed* antecedent—they dispensed with the elements of liberal institutions and Islamic religious values. Preserving the element of mass political mobilization in a modern and enlightened affirmation of the rule of force in human affairs, they created a new practical–discursive variation out of the multiple mutations in the Ottoman Enlightenment heritage.

Raised under Abdul Hamid II, where political discussion was prohibited and a crudely monolithic religious ideology prevailed, this was a generation of materialists who rejected any political horizon where religious ideas or values were permitted a role. They equated the prevailing state ideology with the full reality of Islamic tradition. While Abdul Hamid embraced science in its practical applications, he also sought to employ Islam as a lever to "instil some consciousness of a collective goal in his subjects" in a process of "consciousness building."[145] This technique, certainly resurrecting the Tanzimat collective identity project as a survival strategy, was now employed to authoritarian elite ends in nation-making from above. Increased literacy with "thousands of books, journals, newspapers and pamphlets" accompanied strict censorship. *Seditious* authors, including Namik Kemal, Rousseau and Voltaire, were banned.[146]

The Young Turk movement was divided between decentralization and centralization, and the supporters of the latter formed the 1906 Committee of Union and Progress. In 1909, just following the Young Turk revolution, the CUP still contained

---

[143] Mansfield, *Middle East*, 126–27.
[144] Mardin, *Religion and Social Change*, 120.
[145] Mardin, *Modern State*, 201–2.
[146] Shaw and Shaw, *Rise of Modern Turkey*, 251.

a diversity of ethnic groups. The Armenian Revolutionary Federation had helped the revolution to come to power. The second Constitutional Period began with the 1876 Constitution restored, a parliament set up, censorship abolished and Abdul Hamid's 30,000 spies disbanded.[147] Abdul Hamid's attempted counter-revolution a year later saw him deposed.

The multi-cultural discursive–practical formation of the 19th century had not been extinguished or superseded, but existed as a marginal tendency in a new economy of practices. The year 1908 saw the first working class movement, as a new class of industrial workers appeared in most towns.[148] The forms of organized labour were

> becoming very different [and] new kinds of labour organizations were appearing [including] mutual aid societies, syndicates and unions ... [in] the largest Ottoman cities ... [where] a real explosion in the number of these new organizations occurred during the 1908 strike wave, when workers often formed unions as they went on strike to express their grievances.[149]

Independent worker's movements and organizations often expressed continuity with the earlier multi-cultural ethic of the Young Ottomans, with minorities playing a crucial role in spreading socialist ideas.[150] The Salonica Workers' Federation of the early 1900s included several thousand supporters including Jews, Turks, Bulgarians, Serbs and Albanians, and was committed to defending "the integrity of the Ottoman Empire" against the "'bourgeois power' of the Young Turks." They published newspapers in a variety of languages.[151] Although this tendency

---

[147] Duncan Townson, *Dictionary of Modern History: 1789–1945* (London: Penguin, 1994), 931.

[148] Berkes, *Secularism in Turkey*, 273.

[149] Quataert, *State and the Subaltern*, 21.

[150] Feroz Ahmad, "Some Thoughts on the Role of Ethnic and Religious Minorities in the Genesis and Development of the Socialist Movement in Turkey," in ed. Mete Tuncay and Eric Jan Zurcher, *Socialism and Nationalism in the Ottoman Empire, 1876–1923* (London: I.B. Tauris, 1994), 13.

[151] Paul Dumont, "A Jewish, Socialist and Ottoman Organization: The Worker's Federation of Salonica," in *Socialism and Nationalism in the Ottoman Empire, 1876–1923* (London: I.B. Tauris, 1994), 49–75.

represented one stream and not the entirety of the early 20th-century Ottoman workers' movement, it demonstrates a clear alternative path in the politics of *consciousness building* at the level of emerging civil society.

The oppressive politics of the Hamidean period saw a radical rise in the idealization of the West. An imagined dichotomy between West and East increasingly framed the writings of dissidents throughout this period. Disgust towards tradition spread as Europe became glorified as the "land of the Enlightenment," and European literature was secretly consumed in as great a quantity as possible. This generation of intellectuals who were largely state officials had one "common thread running through them all—the denial of tradition." Their beliefs were an assortment of "rationalism, materialism, evolutionism and naturalism" which rejected traditional beliefs as absurd, superstitious and contrary to reason.[152] There was an "uncompromising opposition to what they saw as the useless remnants of the *ancien regime*," or a crude political ideal of "rupture" along French Revolutionary lines.[153]

Under the Hamidean regime "all literary and quasi-philosophical developments toward understanding European thought were stopped"; still, emblematic intellectuals such as Besir Fuad (1852–87) managed to take inspiration from the anti-religious messages of Diderot, D'Holbach, and D'Alembert "as the founders of modern realism and naturalism based in science."[154] The new Westernist point of view also found its intellectual articulation in Tevkit Fikret (1867–1915) who wrote that *Reason* is *the Light* while the traditional religious past "was nothing but a lie."[155] The emergence of *pure modernity* as a political mode of imagining is visible in these examples, with its missionary attitude and mythic qualities which elevate a dogmatic "universal" truth above considerations of freedom of conscience.

Although the 1908 revolution was essentially a coup staged by military officers, it was the sheer organizational scale that

---

[152] Berkes, *Secularism in Turkey*, 293.
[153] Mardin, *Modern State*, 203.
[154] Berkes, *Secularism in Turkey*, 294.
[155] Ibid., 301.

permitted the leaders to forcibly restore the Constitution. Propaganda, mass demonstrations and terrorism were used in the seizure of state power. From the hidden underground cells of the Hamidean era, hundreds of Society of Union and Progress branches established in every town permitted spontaneous national organization.[156] Slogans from Fikret's verses appeared in the pre-1908 period expressing the ideals of the generation, and testifying to the gap between leadership and masses.[157] Indeed, the Young Turks were concerned with "improving the administration of the realm and the power of the state rather than promoting democracy," and to this end oversaw the implementation of a "single party in power between 1924 and 1950" based on a "Rousseauist-Jacobin conception of the 'general will'."[158] They saw history in terms of "irresistible progress toward a 'positive' system relying on a reductionist dialectic made up of two antagonistic postulates, 'science' and 'reaction'."[159]

With the restoration of constitutional rule, the millet controversy persisted in complicating the national modernization movement as from its beginnings. Yusuf Akcura (1876–1933), a journalist of Russian origin, saw through the maze of disagreements to a single *ultimate* solution. He argued that the "trouble lay in the morbid nature of the Ottoman empire as a conglomeration of nationalities. The Young Turks were under an illusion. What was imminent was not a union of nationalities, but a fierce struggle among them." Thus, he articulated a national discourse where history is fundamentally a state of war. He published the following injunction from exile in Cairo: "Forget about being Ottomans—be Turks!"[160] With his influence—against the background of the Balkan Wars (1912–13)—the tide turned increasingly against the older Ottoman conception of multi-religious nationality. The specific circumstances which explain its failure were attributed to the nature of *reality* in ontological fashion,

---

[156] Feroz Ahmad, *The Young Turks: The Committee of Union and Progress in Turkish Politics, 1908–1914* (London: Oxford, 1969).

[157] Berkes, *Secularism in Turkey*, 301.

[158] Mardin, "Projects as Methodology: Thoughts on Modern Turkish Social Science," *Modern State*, 68–69.

[159] Ibid., 71.

[160] Berkes, *Secularism in Turkey*, 321–22.

rather than the history of foreign domination comprising external–internal manipulation and war.

In the struggle to conceive a modern ideal of belonging, dichotomous modes of imagining contained tacit practical violence. The most influential Young Turk intellectual, and the most esteemed modern Turkish thinker after Namik Kemal, was Ziya Gokalp (1876–1924). He became well known through his participation in the 1908 Revolution and involvement with the Party of Union and Progress. His work produced a new approach to the "fundamental problems which had become acute in Turkey following the restoration of the Constitutional regime in 1908." The ideas he articulated were "behind the main trends in Ataturk's drastic reforms," and he assisted in preparing the new constitution in 1924.[161]

Addressing the troubled legacy of the Tanzimat era, Gokalp saw a society riven by divided loyalties between tradition and the new European models. His solution was an Enlightenment discourse of radical nationalism where Reason transcends the individual and is identified with the nation. The creation of everyday democratic institutions was of secondary importance to revolutionizing social and cultural consciousness through a closed process of modernization. Deeply influenced by positivism, the nation for Gokalp represented a sociologically verifiable "independent social unity"—i.e. of a foundational or essential nature. The *pathological* and *irrational* past hangovers required elimination to restore the original *ethnic basis* of the Turkish people. Discursive formations, then, were employed from the authoritarian aspect of the Enlightenment heritage to meet the new exigencies of violently imposed demographic change and public terror of total foreign occupation.

In its elitist and anti-cosmopolitan ideals, however, the discourse traversed the frontier into counter-Enlightenment. The essentialism implied rejection of cosmopolitan ideals, to say nothing of minorities—only the "nation" was "real." Gokalp saw his theory as a normative discipline or positive science. His practical ideas centred the deeds of *great* and not *average* men. Evoking

[161] Ziya Gokalp, *Turkish Nationalism and Western Civilization* (London: George Allen & Unwin, 1959). From the introduction by Niyazi Berkes, 13.

rupture, he defined "social revolution" as the "creation of a New Life by discarding an older one."¹⁶² This *New Life* was "not a cosmopolitan but a national life."¹⁶³ It would succeed because "Turkish blood has remained rejuvenated and hardened like steel with the glories of the battlefield." This implied the violent means to this "social revolution." The nation discovers its true being as an "ideal" in moments of crisis and violence: "When a nation experiences a great disaster … individual personality disappears and becomes immersed in society [and only then does] the national personality live in the soul of the individual."¹⁶⁴ In these "ideal" moments "a general will becomes the only I in every consciousness."¹⁶⁵ Those lacking such "ideals" are "lost souls."¹⁶⁶ Gokalp's discourse shows that Enlightenment and counter-Enlightenment do not represent water tight opposites, but exist in a dangerous dialectical ambiguity. The Enlightenment and modernity are problems rather than finished objects.

This romantic nationalist outlook steered the Turkish national movement away from the cosmopolitan or multi-religious universalism defining the Young Ottomans into a narrow and intolerant identity politics. Gokalp celebrated the movement ontologically as an "awakening to identity," implying the antecedent existence of a historical national essence.¹⁶⁷ The notion that this was imaginary and contestable was not considered. The nation was evoked in terms of life and vitality and above all language, an "ethnic unity" with the "same consciousness" and "faith." It partook of a widespread contemporary Enlightenment-nationalist discourse, where in contemporary Europe "only those states which are based on a single-language group are believed to have a future." Gokalp could thus write: "all of us realize that the idea of a state or homeland supposedly common to diverse nationalities, is nothing but a mere concept, devoid of any zeal, enthusiasm, and devotion."¹⁶⁸

---

[162] Ibid., 56.
[163] Ibid., 58.
[164] Ibid., 67.
[165] Ibid., 68.
[166] Ibid., 82.
[167] Ibid., 70.
[168] Ibid., 80–81.

Such a vitalist outlook is dismissive of constitutional structures as merely cerebral while celebrating the visceral organically bound national community. Yet unquestionably Gokalp's writings affirm the need for modernization and the primacy of science. He ultimately influenced the emergence of the pan-Turanian movement, a call for the "union of all Turkish-speaking peoples; including those of central Asia."[169] Kemal Ataturk rejected this pan-Turanian perspective, remaining within the borders of the Turkish nation that he spent much of his early life fighting desperately to create. He was eager to be done with the bloody politics of empire, declaring that "We must put an end from now on to the delusion of imagining ourselves the masters of the world."[170] At the same time the politics he created within the new Turkish Republic harboured much from Gokalp's vision of the nation—itself embedded within a deeper heritage of discursive formations.

Ataturk envisioned an "organized, well-articulated, linear process of modernization through which the whole nation was going to move simultaneously and with uniform experience" to create the "end process" of a "militantly secular, ethnically homogeneous republic."[171] In his own words, he proclaimed teleologically that "There are a variety of countries, but there is only one civilization. In order that a nation advance, it is necessary that it join this civilization."[172] The flaw in Ataturk's ideological outlook as he sought to institute the norms of the new Turkish public sphere in the 1920s was the same as that of the French Revolution and dominant Enlightenment paradigm from which he drew inspiration: that there can be a total rupture in the history of the nation or the world, dividing it from its past and introducing an entirely new and "modern" future; and the linear vision of emancipation this entails, with the state as the causal instrument in a transformation of the people.

Kemalism functioned as a "monolithic force that tried to mold Turkish society and mentality."[173] In his famous 1927 speech

[169] Mansfield, *Middle East*, 128.
[170] Quoted Berkes, *Secularism in Turkey*, 460.
[171] Kasaba, *Rethinking Modernity*, 17.
[172] Cinar, *Bodies, Places and Time*, 5.
[173] Kasaba, *Rethinking Modernity*, 18.

Ataturk described the nation's problem in terms of "mental development."[174] In his manner of using the state as an agent of revolution from above—a representative of the "people" who does not consult them—Ataturk partook of the deeper tradition of Ottoman statesmanship going back to the 18th century and the Tanzimat reforms; it was not his invention. It broke with the tradition of the Young Ottomans as endeavouring to involve the public as a plural, growing and self-reliant entity in the process of modernization.[175]

The point is never to judge Ataturk as a man; he was doubtlessly a courageous individual with admirable ends on behalf of the Turkish people. He was committed to "complete independence" for Turkey after decades of damaging foreign domination.[176] What is interesting to consider is the means he employed. Indeed, he fostered a form of modernity in which "the breaking of traditional ties [was] so urgent a task that it seemed not to matter what methods were used to achieve that end."[177]

To achieve his ends, Ataturk "inherited a complete and ruthlessly efficient state apparatus, which [he employed] to effect a cultural revolution of sorts."[178] His thinking partook of several traditions—the French Enlightenment/Revolution, Positivism and the Ottoman Tanzimat statism. As an ideological framework of modernity, it saw no potential value in the traditional past and sought its destruction to make way for the modern. Ataturk believed in a "sharp break from the Ottoman past" to create a "brand new nation."[179] In a historicist intellectual posture he rejected the "backward Ottoman identity."[180] In passing the 1925 Hat Law, he defined the fez as sitting "on the heads of our nation as an emblem of ignorance, negligence, and fanaticism and hatred of progress and civilization."[181] It is as if the fez does

---

[174] Ataturk, *A Speech Delivered by Mustafa Kemal Ataturk, 1927* (Istanbul: Ministry of Education Printing Plant, 1963), 78.

[175] Samith Vaner, ed., *Modernisation Autoritaire en Turquie et en Iran* (Paris : L'Harmattan, 1991), 23–24.

[176] Ataturk, *A Speech Delivered by Mustafa Kemal Ataturk: 1927*, 9.

[177] Kasaba, *Rethinking Modernity*, 30.

[178] Zurcher, *Young Turk*, 61.

[179] Cinar, *Bodies, Places and Time*, 62.

[180] Ibid., 66.

[181] Kasaba, *Rethinking Modernity*, 25.

not have many potential and changing meanings, but is determined in a single meaning by the logic of *History*. Concerning the veil, Ataturk demanded: "can the mothers and daughters of a civilized nation adopt this strange manner, this barbarous posture? It is an object of ridicule. It must be remedied at once."[182] In certain aspects, Turkish women in the 1920s and 1930s had more rights than women in several European countries.[183] Yet because Kemalism conceived development as the negation of civil society it was never a question of asking women for their views on traditions such as the veil, but imposing the imperative of *History*. Hence, expressions of civil society such as the Women's Peoples Party formed in 1923 were promptly denied authorization to exist by the Turkish state.[184]

There was a binary conceived between the modern and the traditional with the state as the agent of the modern, in which the "new state itself acquired the role of the liberator who would guide the nation toward civilization."[185] Because of likely popular resistance of the "ignorant" masses, dictatorship was necessary over democracy until the "people" has been "remade." Even worse, certain cultures—such as the Kurds—were identified as belonging to this unwanted past and were presented with an option between assimilation and erasure. In this respect a "citizenship constituted foundationally around universally applicable civil rights never developed," and we see instead a "homogeneity deriving from ethnic unity, and this unity would be expressed in a single voice."[186] The predictable end of presenting sections of the population with such options was open violence.

This was a politics of violence based on a higher claim to a single truth based in the Enlightenment tradition. Ataturk insisted that the "consciousness of the new Turks was to be rooted in science ['Western civilization'] which [he] repeatedly mentioned

---

[182] Cinar, *Bodies, Places and Time*, 62.
[183] Ibid., 65.
[184] Ibid., 67.
[185] Ibid., 63.
[186] Caglar Keyder, "Whither the Project of Modernity? Turkey in the 1990s," in *Rethinking Modernity and National Identity in Turkey*, eds. Sibel Bozdogan and Resat Kasaba (Washington: University of Washington Press, 1997), 42.

as the source of all valid knowledge and behaviour."[187] The same ideas are described in Rousseau's *The Social Contract*. Rousseau's theoretical work, in one respect, attempted to overcome the problem of modern political violence in the era of emerging nation states; yet in the process he also lent himself to it a great deal. The military officers of Ataturk's generation enthusiastically read Rousseau, Montesquieu and Hugo, and studied the French Revolution.[188] An avid reader, Ataturk read Rousseau, Comte and Durkheim as well as biographies of Napoleon and other generals of the French Revolutionary period.[189] He did not simply use Rousseau's theory of the General Will as a theoretical inspiration; he also drew off vitalist tendencies and Bolshevik techniques that were current in the interwar period, among other elements, in pursuit of a national vision very much shaped by the political climate of the time.

The Turkish national revolution under Ataturk was a movement of final ends. In the period leading to the seizure of state power, this final end was kept quiet and the ideology remained shapeless. This was not because nation-making was conceived by Ataturk and his colleagues as an open ended development. It was rather so the movement could absorb the maximum population in the struggle, and when the battle was won, turn around and eliminate the *enemies*. Among *friends* later turned on as retrograde elements and enemies were the ulema and the Kurds.[190] The *founding moment* of national history was declared to begin on 1923, not 1920, because 1920 "consisted of elements of a much wider political spectrum, including Islamists, Ottomanists, and Kurdish nationalists as well as Bolshevists" while "1923 was much more homogeneously assembled around the principles of secularism and Turkish nationalism under Ataturk's unchallenged authority."[191] Violence and erasure were fundamental

[187] Mardin, *Modern State*, 211.

[188] Paul Dumont, *Mustafa Kemal invente la Turquie Moderne* (Paris: Editions Complexe, 1983), 43.

[189] Enver Ziya Karal, "The Principle of Kemalism," in *Ataturk: Founder of a Modern State*, eds. Ali Kazancigil and Ergun Ozbudun (London: C. Hurst and Co., 1981), 13.

[190] Alexandre Jevakhoff, *Kemal Ataturk* (Paris Talandier, 1989), 127; Kasaba, *Rethinking Modernity*, 22.

[191] Cinar, *Bodies, Places and Time*, 151.

tools in the Turkish national revolution, and this strategy of gaining power was only one expression of it.

It was certainly not the case that Ataturk was a rogue. At the Battle of Gallipoli (1915–16), where he gained fame as a military commander, the defeated enemy was impressed by Ataturk's chivalry. He was a man of high intelligence and high personal standards. It was a matter of his having adopted a discursive–practical assemblage where violence was the core means to social transformation. In 1927, Ataturk ridiculed the dialogic aspect of democracy as being "unnecessarily lost in a labyrinth of theories."[192] He dismissed the voices of opposition as "but an echo of the twaddle of misguided and ignorant brains."[193] At the National Assembly in 1922, Ataturk silenced opposing voices by declaring the irrelevance of "academic debate" to the functioning of politics. Sovereignty, he insisted, "is acquired only by force, by power, and by violence." He urged the "nation to revolt against the usurpers, to put them in their place, and to exercise the facts of sovereignty." His concluding threat was that "heads should roll" in the event of further disagreement.[194] The underlying worldview "believed that people were the product of nature," and that "life, in its deepest meaning, was a continual war with nature" in which the "most important factor is science."[195] *Science*, in this specific discursive construction, constituted a transcendental claim justifying political violence.

This ideology is derived from the French Revolution. The National Assembly was the single and only possible representative of the nation.[196] It represented a single will and indivisible sovereignty.[197] As an organic unity, it was considered to be above classes and social difference. The seizure of state power was the road to the new nation. Ataturk proclaimed himself "openly at the head and [assumed] the leadership of the entire national and military movement."[198] The nation's adversary was an endless

---

[192] Ataturk, *A Speech Delivered by Mustafa Kemal Ataturk, 1927*, 65.
[193] Ibid., 583.
[194] Mustafa Kemal Ataturk, *Memoires* (Paris: Coda, 2005), 125.
[195] Kazancigil and Ozbudun, *Ataturk*, 14–15.
[196] Jevakhoff, *Ataturk*, 259.
[197] Ibid., 300.
[198] Ataturk, *A Speech Delivered by Mustafa Kemal Ataturk, 1927*, 54.

resource of conspiracies and enemies driven by "fanaticism" and who needed to be "crushed," "destroyed" and "eliminated."[199] In the long line of conspiracies we find, for example, the assertion in 1925 by Ankara that the Kurdish nation did not exist. It was an invention of enemies, particularly the British, who sought to carve up the country.[200] In the same year, a gigantic political operation was put in motion by the Independence Tribunal in Ankara to try many of Ataturk's ex-colleagues from the CUP for a "conspiracy" during the War of Independence.[201] In effect this operation served as a cover for crushing all shades of political opposition.

The Ottoman past, which Ataturk identified with the Oriental side of the national culture, was a source of shame and needed to be gotten rid of. He proclaimed that "If our bodies are in the East, our mentality is oriented toward the West."[202] The Turkish people, he asserted, "need a modern education" and to "get rid of the oriental influences which weigh upon them."[203] That is why the seat of power was moved from Istanbul to Ankara: to show a nation turning its back upon the past and beginning anew upon a *tabla raza* where no important Ottoman monuments were on view.[204] This was also the logic for abolishing the Caliphate, which he called "a laughing stock in the eyes of the civilized world, enjoying the blessings of science."[205] No official days of commemoration referring to Ottoman events were permitted, and compulsory school textbooks negated the Ottoman past.[206]

In this nationalist programme based on rupture we see a shrinking of historical time from centuries to decades in a state-imposed amnesia, leaving the longer and complex Ottoman past a void to be later recuperated and deployed by the political Islamists.[207] This was committed in the name of the Enlightenment, although the Ottoman–Turkish Enlightenment was greatly more complex and

[199] Ataturk, *Memoires*, 83–86.
[200] Jevakhoff, *Ataturk*, 344.
[201] Ibid., 370.
[202] Cinar, *Bodies, Places and Time*, 5.
[203] Jevakhoff, *Ataturk*, 29.
[204] Ataturk, *Memoires*, 133.
[205] Ataturk, *A Speech Delivered by Mustafa Kemal Ataturk, 1927*, 10.
[206] Cinar, *Bodies, Places and Time*, 142/148.
[207] Mardin, *Modern State*, 200.

creative. Subsequent Enlightenment reforms or rapid drives to *modernize* the *public mentality* through enforcing public dress codes, forbidding *oriental music*, changing names and banning orders of monks and dervishes resulted in great anger and resistance.[208] Ataturk announced that these people are "not connected to the country or the Turkish Republic." He announced that "the objective of the reforms is the transformation of the people ... into a modern society, both in appearance as well as inside... The mentalities which do not accept this reality will be destroyed."[209] There was certainly no room, then, for negotiation about the meaning of modernity; the state had decided this in advance. The nature of this decision was made explicit by a reference in the civil code to the "family of modern civilisation" in which "there are no fundamental differences" and which was by implication Western.[210]

Ataturk also spoke often of History as if it were an authority and all-seeing judge rather than a humanly constructed memory or analysis of past events.[211] He proclaimed it "futile to try to resist the thunderous advance of civilization, for it has no pity on those who are ignorant or rebellious."[212] This view was influenced by a Comtean concept of universal history where religion belongs to a primitive phase and science promises a new world in the Religion of Humanity and a positive politics based on the physical sciences. These politics are to be implemented by the technocratic elite. What is central in Comte's metaphysical account of *science* is that it does not advance by accident, but constitutes a necessary movement toward an ideal world based on *Order and Progress*.[213] There is an inherent hostility to open or pluralistic democratic politics in a worldview based on *positive politics*. The temporal premise of democracy is that we know neither final answers nor the future—i.e. change and fallibility—and must therefore depend as far as possible on non-violent public debate.

[208] Jevakhoff, *Ataturk*, 435.
[209] Ibid., 354.
[210] Ibid., 359.
[211] Ataturk, *Memoires*, 66; Ataturk, *A Speech Delivered by Mustafa Kemal Ataturk, 1927*, 49/54.
[212] Kasaba, *Rethinking Modernity*, 26.
[213] Kenneth Thompson, *Auguste Comte: The Foundations of Sociology* (London: Nelson, 1976), 83–100.

The outcome of such uncoerced debate depends upon a myriad of ever-changing and specific factors and is regulated by a system of checks and balances. Science cannot answer certain questions of an ideological and religious nature on a public level to everyone's satisfaction. The final unification of the social sciences into a *complete theory* is inconceivable, for criticism is their very engine. Ataturk held a non-critical view of knowledge. Posted in Sofia, Bulgaria, in 1913, he wrote that "what counts in an idea is its capacity to be accepted as an absolute without being the object of criticism ... no other logic or judgement can unbalance it."[214] This youthful jotting reflects an almost romantic notion of epistemology that Ataturk seemed to harbour throughout his life, and exists in important streams of Western Enlightenment thought.

If the National Assembly acted upon the principles of science, translated into the pure service of the national will, then it need have "nothing to do with the vile interests of political parties."[215] The scientific basis of this political power was "according to the dominant principles of the age," or the "modern mentality" grounded in "the principles of knowledge, general science and progress" in their "march toward the future."[216] This march was violent: "The revolution changes existing institutions by violence."[217] It embraced a high-speed temporal horizon. Just as Zia Gokalp had urged that Turkey "skip five hundred years and not stand still," Ataturk insisted that "our standards should be based not on the lethargic mentality of the past centuries but on the concepts of speed and movement that define our century."[218] It was deemed necessary in the modernization programme to "act with the greatest promptness possible, burning up the steps and making jumps across time."[219] This principle of *speed* was later admired and imitated by the Shah of Iran in his own efforts to transform his people in revolution from above.[220]

---

[214] Jevakhoff, *Ataturk*, 28.
[215] Ibid., 140.
[216] Ibid., 163.
[217] Ibid., 418.
[218] Kasaba, *Rethinking Modernity*, 26.
[219] Dumont, *Turquie Moderne*, 164.
[220] Jevakhoff, *Ataturk*, 380.

The counterpart to this accelerated power based in *scientific* knowledge as a practical formation is the elitist discourse on "the ignorance of the population," cited as the reason for the government designation of members to the electoral college at the time of the 1919 elections.[221] In 1923 the Republic of Turkey was announced and by 1925 a single party regime had been established under the Republican People's Party. Kemal announced in 1926 that

> our people are not ready for a constitutional and democratic regime. We, the founders of the Republic, have to prepare them for this. For 10–15 years, it is us and us alone who must assume the affairs of state. After, the Turkish people will be authorized to form political parties to freely discuss political questions.[222]

In 1935, Celal Bayer, one of the principle architects of the regime's political economy, announced that "the new Turkey is in the process of applying a policy of statism."[223] The state is a causal instrument in the creation of the nation as a new world. Following the 1930 second attempt at a multiparty system, and seeing his designs rejected by the public, Ataturk quickly suppressed the elections arguing that "we must not sacrifice the authority of the state in the name of liberty."[224] In the first free elections in 1950 the Kemalist Party was roundly voted out of office by a popular grassroots movement clandestinely organized well in advance.

The French Revolutionary archetype of the *enemy* was evoked in the *Founding Moment* of 1923 when it was announced that the nation would be defended against its enemies by any means necessary.[225] The nation had been born in bloodshed. Earlier, when fighting the War of Independence, Ataturk had insisted that "the Assembly is not a theory, but a truth, and the greatest of truths. First, the Assembly, and then the army ... It is the nation that will

---

[221] Ibid., 156.
[222] Ibid., 349.
[223] Dumont, *Turquie Moderne*, 165.
[224] Jevakhoff, 404.
[225] Ibid., 328.

make up the army and the Assembly will be its representative."²²⁶ The mass mobilization necessary for the creation of the new Turkish nation was a massive act of violence under the banner of the highest truth in the nation. Yet while the population may have been indispensable in the quick seizure of power, they were having no role in it in the aftermath.

The nation state with its modernizing drive inevitably produced the very middle class who would come, in time, to challenge its complete hold on power. The contradiction is clear: a fixed and absolute idea—conceived in advance and therefore closed—as the basis for a national programme cannot be democratic; for democracy is by nature temporal, responding to change and multiple changing points of view. Turkey has become a democracy today in spite of the Kemalist ideology, through the energies and struggles of its people. The underlying democratic energies shaping the Turkish nation have their source in the struggles of the 19th century, and perhaps before.

The Ottoman–Turkish Enlightenment confronted the problematic nature of democracy as an experiment in the interwar years. After 1918, the 120-year movement met with the violent intersection of empires, nations and minorities in the interwar period. With the Treaty of Versailles (1919) Europe went from three to thirteen republics as the Russian, Austro-Hungarian, Hohenzollern and Ottoman empires collapsed. Like the Ottomans, these empires had faced the challenge of a "tangled mass of regional legal codes and conventions" in their attempt to create a national body of law, or to rationalize power.²²⁷ These empires had based their legitimacy on the principle of dynastic loyalty, and so a German could rise to a high position in the Tzarist administration. The populations were mixed and the dockworkers of Ottoman Saloniki routinely spoke six or seven languages.²²⁸

The Paris peace treatises extended national self-determination principles to central and eastern Europe's complex and overlapping ethnic mosaic. As this concept of sovereignty was based on the *people* defined as a specific nation, the presence of other

---

²²⁶ Ibid., 187.
²²⁷ Mark Mazower, *Dark Continent: Europe's Twentieth Century* (New York: Vintage, 1998), 9.
²²⁸ Ibid., 44.

ethnicities within the borders gave rise to the minority problem and the new democracies were often exclusionary and antagonistic in ethnic relations. Minorities in the interwar period were often seen as a danger and fifth column. In this context, where 2,500,000 people had suddenly become minorities, the imagined utopia of the pure nation was taken for *underlying* reality. The Greek scholar Kambouroglou wrote that "on Greek soil there should be nothing that is not Greek."[229] Minority rights policy was a response to this crisis. The political logic took the form of massive population exchanges between nations, notably Greece and Turkey, where "thousands of Turkish-speaking Orthodox villagers from Asia Minor were expelled to Greece ... while Greek Muslims ... embarked for Turkey" with "homes and property abandoned, friends left behind."[230]

At the heart of these politics was a doctrine of assimilation traceable to the French Revolution. The formation of the French Republic had been a long process of destroying difference and gradual assimilation of the population from above. As late as 1863 an official tally in France indicated that one-fifth of the population did not speak the language, and the figure was probably higher.[231] The paradigm of assimilation had found its way into 19th-century liberal thought in John Stuart Mill's claim that "free institutions are next to impossible in a country made up of different nationalities."[232] This was a discursive formation embraced across a wide spectrum, with grave practical consequences.

This view on assimilation was a consensus verging on dogma in the interwar period. The New States Committee in Paris, prompted by US President Wilson, "dismissed Jewish demands for national autonomy for the Jewish minority in Poland" on the grounds that it was undesirable "to forestall the process of assimilation which was still believed to be the desirable long-term outcome." The British Foreign Office issued a statement

---

[229] Ibid., 42.

[230] Ibid., 62.

[231] Eugen Weber, *Peasants into Frenchmen: The Modernization of Rural France* (Stanford: Stanford University Press, 1976), 310.

[232] John Stuart Mill, "Considerations on Representative Government," in *On Liberty and Other Essays*, ed. John Gray (Digireads.com Publishing, 2010), 235.

that minority treaties were hindering the process of assimilation. Carl Schmitt (1888–1985), a leader in Germany's conservative revolutionary movement of the 1920s, argued that modern mass democracy presupposed "first homogeneity and second—if the need arises—elimination or eradication of heterogeneity." Lenin had argued that to oppose assimilation is to "turn back the wheel of history" because the "process of assimilation of nations by capitalism means the greatest historical progress."[233]

Lenin's outlook changed with the Bolshevik nationalities policy that exerted a powerful attraction over the minorities of central and Eastern Europe—Macedonians, Belarusians, Jews and Ukrainians—in the interwar period as they faced the dangerous consequences of the Versailles nation state policy. Minorities celebrated the downfall of the Polish Republic and the arrival of the Red Army into the Western Ukraine in 1939.[234] Yet whatever its federal appeals, the Soviet practice of suppressing political liberty as a matter of ideological policy quickly instilled in these minority groups a sense of brutal disillusionment. It is within this broader international context that we may clarify the nationality criterion in the Turkish Republic in terms of the Turkish language, and the refusal to recognize even the very existence of other ethnicities. The reconstruction of national history and memory occluded a rich and creative local Enlightenment heritage. The natural next step was attempted forcible assimilation by the state.

---

[233] Mazower, *Dark Continent*, 49–57.
[234] Ibid., 51.

6

The Heritage of Non-violence in the Nehru Period: The Ethic of Reconciliation in Nation-Making

Jawaharlal Nehru's first major Assembly speech in 1946 proclaimed India an "independent sovereign republic," invoking Gandhi's legacy and the "great past of India" as well as "modern precedents such as the French, American and Russian revolutions." His speech affirmed a new Enlightenment confluence, the two rivers of the Western Enlightenment tradition and the Indian contribution of a mass movement based on the philosophy and practice of non-violence.[1] Nehru's upbringing had been in the Enlightenment tradition, his father Motilal Nehru being "a product of that late Victorian, free-thinking rationalism, which had learnt to dispense with divine explanations of the working of the universe" and "pinned its faith on human intellect and on science to lead mankind along endless vistas of progress." Motilal also belonged to the composite tradition of Indian culture, avowing "his love of Persian classics and Urdu poetry."[2]

The Raj had proven untenable faced with the Indian population as an increasingly ungovernable force throughout the 1940s. An empire of two centuries was hastily undone within a period of two months, suffering conditions of scarcity, religious riots, mass refugee resettlement, class conflict and intransigent local vested power interests. Since the late 19th century the three alternatives of secularism, Hindu nationalism and Muslim separatism had aimed at uniting "either the entire population of the country or one of the two largest segments ... into united wholes to contest

---

[1] Ramachandra Guha, *India after Gandhi: The History of the World's Largest Democracy* (London: Picador, 2008), 106.
[2] B.R. Nanda, *Jawaharlal Nehru: Rebel and Statesman* (New Delhi: Oxford University Press, 1998), 98/118.

for power."³ With the partition of British India, India chose a secular constitution while Pakistan chose to be an Islamic Republic. In Pakistan, Nehru saw the communal ideological drive to "differentiate and create two classes of citizens ... the latter having some kind of inferior status and less opportunities."⁴ Because Maulana Abul Kalam Azad, one time President of the Indian National Congress (1940–45), was a deeply religious Muslim, while the founding father of Pakistan, Mohammed Ali Jinnah, hardly practiced at all, we see that broader principles of justice and power were at stake than simply one's religious identity.⁵

The Congress conception of justice had been shaped by the Gandhian ethic of reconciliation, and Nehru's own notions of secular democratic justice were profoundly conditioned by his relationship with Gandhi which began in 1919–20. Nehru became gradually convinced that "what had kept India going was ... a varied and tolerant culture."⁶ We see this influence in the shift in Nehru's thought from the austere socialist historicism of the *Autobiography* (1934–35) to the rich historical pluralism of *The Discovery of India* (1944). When Gandhi resolved the 1936 Congress crisis between liberal and socialist wings and avoided the impending split, it had a "chastening effect upon Nehru [who] decided to subordinate ideological considerations to ... Gandhi's leadership and to the Congress party as the chief instrument of the anti-imperialist struggle."⁷ Nehru wrote, at this time, that Gandhi "knew how to make the most of the objective conditions" while "[Left] groups with a more advanced ideology functioned largely in the air."⁸ Although Nehru was a radical socialist

---

³ Paul R. Brass, *The Politics of India since Independence* (Cambridge: Cambridge University Press, 1990), 228. We also must note the central and tragic importance of Sikh separatist politics at Partition in the Punjab.
⁴ Nehru, *Letters to the Chief Ministers, Volume 3* (New Delhi: Oxford University Press, 1989), 439.
⁵ Amartya Sen, "Secularism and its Discontents," in *Secularism and its Critics*, ed. Rajeev Bhargava (New Delhi: Oxford University Press, 2009), 467–68.
⁶ Nanda, *Jawaharlal Nehru*, 99.
⁷ Ibid., 188.
⁸ Bipan Chandra, Mridula Mukherjee, Aditya Mukherjee, Sucheta Mahajan and K.N. Panikkar, *India's Struggle for Independence* (New Delhi: Penguin, 1989), 299.

and agnostic, Gandhi chose him as his political successor because "he felt sure of a deep ethical streak" and for reasons of democratic principle: "My own feeling is that Jawaharlal will accept the decision of the majority of his colleagues."⁹ A commitment to structural-institutional aspects of democratic nation-making and context-specific logics of modernization underlay their bond, and rejection of magical fictitious Hegelian universalisms.

Nehru consistently affirmed the Gandhian heritage, saying during the Chinese Premier Zhou Enlai's (served 1949–76) visit to India in 1954 that "peaceful struggle for independence under Gandhiji's leadership ... had conditioned us" and India's "policies had developed from that struggle and we propose to follow them."¹⁰ He wrote that for the "first time in the world's history ... we saw a great political mass movement wedded to [non-violent] ideals," and contrasted Soviet and Chinese communism as based on "class conflict, hatred and violence" in terms of means—though not ends in broad economic and political justice.¹¹ Nehru suggested that the violent means had "distorted the ends" in the communist approach to social transformation in these countries.¹² By contrast, India had "won our independence through a bloodless revolution in conditions of honour and dignity both to ourselves and to the erstwhile rulers of our country. We in India today are children of this revolution and have been conditioned by it."¹³

The Nehruvian temporal horizon was a pragmatic historicity, and rejected ideological historicism. He said in 1955: "the problems that confront us today had never come up before any communist countries [which] adopted totally different methods to solve them that we do not like."¹⁴ In a world polarized between Marxist–Leninist and liberal capitalist Enlightenment ideologies, Nehruvian Enlightenment politics were innovative, creative and unique. Gandhian modifications of the received Enlightenment

---

⁹ Nanda, *Jawaharlal Nehru*, 100/48.
¹⁰ Nehru, *Letters to the Chief Ministers*, 3, 590.
¹¹ Nehru, *Letters to the Chief Ministers*, 4, 535.
¹² Nehru, *Letters to the Chief Ministers*, 3,583.
¹³ Jawaharlal Nehru, *Selected Works*, Vol. 36 (New Delhi: Oxford University Press, 1984–1991), 491.
¹⁴ Nehru, *Selected Works*, Vol. 28, 3.

paradigm were transferred to India's post-independence politics. Gandhi was never an absurd absolutist, conceding that even violence is a matter of condition and context, as during Quit India in 1942. Pakistan invaded Kashmir using Pathan tribesmen in 1947 to prevent the Kashmiri population from deciding between joining India or Pakistan, and Gandhi supported the Indian troop intervention into Srinagar to roll back the aggression.[15] He recognized coercion and hierarchy in some form as indispensable in human society, and aspired to tame the phenomenon using ethical norms implicit in cultural institutions. This was implied in his conviction of the limits of reason and the imperfection of humankind. The acknowledgement of moral ambiguity—in contrast to philosophical utopia—means that no society exists beyond power, and the labour of maintaining justice through struggle this condition implies.

Post-independence Indian state institutions—inspired by the broader mode of imagining state structure—embedded the political history of the independence struggle and its central ideas. It also reflected sets of traditions and practices both initiated and innovated during this period. As well as being "one of the most democratic in the world by most conventional measures of political participation," it is also the case that "India's political system is unique."[16] We may explain this in terms of specific discursive and practical formations linking the pre- and post-independence experiences. The post-independence Nehru period (1947–64) shows the heritage of non-violence as an underlying principle employed to stabilize the complex turmoil of events following World War II. The bid among numerous Congressmen for a strong centralized Indian state reflected atrocious communal violence in 1946 with estimated one to two million dead. Stability was a key issue as the population grew faster than efforts to create jobs and provide education.[17] A shift had occurred in the global power balance following World War II. The Atlantic Charter's guarantee of the right to self-determination expressed a condemnation of imperialism reflecting the trauma of anti-Nazi

---

[15] Bipan Chandra, Mridula Mukherjee, Aditya Mukherjee, *India since Independence* (New Delhi: Penguin, 2008), 94.
[16] Brass, *Politics of India*, 364–65.
[17] Chandra, et al., *India since Independence*, 135.

struggle. Although empire had ceased to be considered morally defensible, India's foreign policy of non-alignment met with the Cold War ire of the United States which started arming Pakistan in 1954.

India's insistence on the "right to consider each international issue as it arose on its merits" expressed the National Movement principle of context-sensitivity to conditions. This rejected the fixed ideological commitments—or Manichean fantasy for many—prevailing at the global level.[18] Nehru stated that non-alignment reflected a "national way of thinking with its roots in the long past"—that is, a determination to retain an independent viewpoint consolidated during the national struggle for independence.[19] Nehru spoke in terms of conditions, not essences, following discursive formations founded during the Independence struggle.[20] Nehru warned of the "danger" in "metaphysical generalizations" which "though seeming to embody higher truths, do not help us very much in our daily tasks."[21] He rejected doing violence to the "traditional past" in the name of "reason," saying "we cannot uproot all our history just because some abstract logic requires it."[22] Rejecting the metaphysics of rupture as the blueprint for nation-making, the Nehru government emphasized the institutionalization of democracy in the everyday life of the Indian people. This approach drew on the plurality of national traditions while remaining critical of traditional aspects conflicting with the projected democratic framework of an equal and egalitarian Indian society. There existed no formulaic solution: it had to be pragmatic and dialogic. Nehru said, in 1953:

> To be able to understand a problem, we have to talk to one another and argue and discuss, for merely learning by rote cannot help us to understand the crux of the problem....

---

[18] Nanda, *Jawaharlal Nehru*, 63.
[19] Rudra Chaudhuri, "Why Culture Matters: Revisiting the Sino-Indian Border War of 1962," *Journal of Strategic Studies*, 32 (December 2009), 850.
[20] Nehru, *SW, 28*, 4.
[21] Nehru, *SW, 9*, 107.
[22] Nehru, *Letters to the Chief Ministers, 3*, 568.

How are we to integrate these [innumerable forms and differences] while retaining their beauty?[23]

Nehru conceived India's independent future in terms of a "desire for synthesis between the old world and the new."[24] While seeking to reform many customs, he did not undertake a project of violently *transcending* India's past traditions. Through a dynamic and creative perspective on traditions he wrote that they "have to be accepted to a large extent and adapted and transformed to meet new conditions and ways of thought."[25] Tradition required proximate rather than ultimate re-evaluation, or everyday over metaphysical, that is, in terms of temporality. Describing much contemporary religion as a "husk and a ritual [without] content," Nehru yet asserted that "in its wider and deeper conception [religion] can be something of great value to life."[26] He saw religion as variable and without fixed essence, multi-definitional and compatible with progressive change no less than socially reactionary politics. This conceptual pluralism expressed the legacy of Gandhi if we conceive non-violence as a broader intellectual worldview concerned with the creation of value. Rather than framing a general picture of reality that determines the ultimate definition of things within it, Nehru considered how existing beliefs might operate effectively in terms of the practical problems of emerging democratic Indian society.

The Nehru era saw the non-violence principle shift from a mass movement (claiming to represent the nation) to a political party (within the competitive arena of a democratic political system). This involved shifting to specific policies and political tactics demonstrating Nehru's preference for pluralist and non-interventionist solutions to the myriad centre–state and civil society dilemmas of the early Indian republic. Linguistic, regional and minority conflicts were resolved through pluralistic mechanisms, suggesting the many-sidedness of truth. The state adopted an arbitrating and mediating role, in an endorsement

---

[23] Nehru, *SW*, 23, 67.
[24] Nehru, *The Discovery of India* (New York: Penguin, 2004), 41.
[25] Ibid., 47.
[26] Nehru, *SW*, 9, 106.

of self-reliance and the ethic of reconciliation.[27] Nehru was a rare non-interventionist statesman. He set a world precedent with the "biggest experiment in democracy in human history"—universal adult suffrage with a largely illiterate population (1951 16.6 per cent literate)—upon the highly fragmented and culturally heterogeneous space of newly independent India.[28] Indeed, it was the "most culturally diverse country in the world."[29]

Nehru's statesmanship coped with this great complexity through pragmatism and close attention to conditions rather than historicist abstractions, following the Gandhian legacy of a multi-centred nationalism without essence. When Nehru stated in 1952 that India "consists of you and me and the millions like us" and is "not something separated from us," he extended the Gandhian conviction that the nation is the everyday world of ordinary people and their common efforts rather than a transcendent entity.[30] There was no notion of pure or total truth above politics and the existing circuits of power, but democratic values. Power, never seized by the elite, required constant negotiation among multiple centres after independence. The predominance of Hindu Brahmins in the Congress was offset by adult suffrage extended to intermediate castes and the power and economic effects of Zamindari abolition.[31] The bourgeois class, too weak to undertake industrialization on its own, lacked the strength to seize control over the state.[32] On the international front, following the devastating 1962 war with China, Nehru continued to maintain that "We should not ... think in terms of permanent enemies and we should always leave the door open for friendship"—extending the Gandhian logic of nationalism without enemies.[33]

In Nehru's policy, the ethic of reconciliation generated under Gandhi's leadership applied to the multiplying difficulties of

[27] See Brass, *Politics of India*. Sometimes this had negative consequences in terms of the protection of minority rights at the state and local level.

[28] Guha, *India after Gandhi*, 147 ; Chandra, et al., *India since Independence*, 184.

[29] Brass, *Politics of India*, 65.

[30] Nehru, *SW*, 19, 71.

[31] Brass, *Politics of India*, 247–48.

[32] Baldev Raj Nayar, *Globalization and Nationalism* (New Delhi: SAGE, 2001), 73.

[33] Nanda, *Jawaharlal Nehru*, 205.

the domestic sphere. The politics of pluralism in the new Indian Republic were exemplified in the language policy, the process of linguistic state reorganization, the tribal policy, the Constitutional and federal structure, the national elections, all of which presented a complex and multi-sided interaction of popular movements, civil society, and ruling/opposition parties within a broad national context comprising both rural and urban areas. Nehru stated that "this is too large a country with too many legitimate diversities to permit any so-called *strong man* to trample over the people and their ideas."[34] Nehru understood liberty not as a single metaphysical reality based on a system of interlocking rights—corresponding, for example, to self-interested values as uniquely rational, or a *scientifically* determined uniform quantity of public pleasure capable of displacing the false cultural baggage thrown up by history (Utilitarianism). Such concepts assume a single destiny in nation-making, and the marginalization of all others. Nehru understood liberty as multiple, conflicting, and sometimes mutually subverting freedoms that require constant negotiation via a democratic and secular institutional framework and the participation of broad and diverse sections of the population. This is part of a political ethic of reconciliation.

In the 1950s, for example, the right to property conflicted with Zamindari abolition and agrarian reform; reservations for Scheduled castes and tribes conflicted with rights to equality; rights to free speech conflicted with security for minorities under the duress of hate speech in the shadow of the Partition massacres. The adoption of Assamese as the official language of Assam provoked counter-movements among Bengali speakers and smaller tribal groups, in a frequent pattern reflecting competition over access to job, educational, or political opportunities. The just resolution of such intractable conflicts required the constant defining and redefining of the relationship between individual rights and social good, openness and adaptability to changing conditions, and sensitivity to changing context.[35] These claims were made democratically through the courts or other public channels—of course slowing down reforms—in a way inconceivable for an authoritarian state unilaterally unfolding

---

[34] Chandra, et al., *India since Independence*, 226.
[35] Ibid., 59.

a programme grounded in a blueprint of epistemic certainty. The multi-centred democratic aspect of independent India constrained or negated any universal development plan based on a pure Utilitarian calculus, and imposed from above.[36]

These various freedoms, moreover, included concerns over what *we are*: character, selfhood, loyalty and the entire range of different values and qualitative heterogeneity in worldviews these existential issues imply. Nehru was aware, for example, of the social prestige of powerfully landed elements and the positive value social groups invested in their religious identities even as he struggled democratically to remould these elements of society in conformity with his Enlightenment vision of justice.[37] This was reflected in the extended struggle over the 1951 Hindu Code with its gradual piecemeal implementation, and in the retention of personal law for Muslims in order to avoid frightening the minority traumatized after Partition.[38] A strict fact–value dichotomy in broaching such everyday world issues was democratically untenable, and Nehru argued that development should "not be separated from values."[39] Nehru's vision of freedom was closer to Amartya Sen's concept of freedom as capabilities, not only "being well-nourished" but also "having self-respect [and] being able to take part in the life of the community."[40]

Nehruvian pluralism grounded in the ethic of reconciliation was distinct from the Utilitarian single definition of *interest*, implying two different visions of Enlightenment and modernity. Nehru believed it "was not possible to mobilize a large majority around a clear-cut, structured, ideological definition of socialism. A large majority could be mobilized only by uniting diverse

---

[36] Partha Chatterjee has portrayed Nehruvian development as "premised upon one consciousness and will—that of the whole" based on a Hegelian "universal rationality of the state"—implying this universal structure to be identically underlying every national development project and rendering their differences insignificant. See Partha Chatterjee, "The Nation and its Fragments," in *Omnibus* (Oxford: Oxford University Press, 2007), 204.

[37] Chandra, et al., *India since Independence*, 226.

[38] Ibid., 182–83.

[39] Nehru, *Letters to the Chief Ministers*, 5, 178.

[40] Quoted Hilary Putnam, *The Collapse of the Fact/Value Dichotomy and Other Essays* (Cambridge: Harvard University Press, 2002), 57.

interests and multiple views and ideological strands around a common socialist vision or framework."[41] Nehru stood on the middle road separating *pure* (i.e. uncritical) claims to "being" (Heideggerian communalism) and *pure* claims to *modernity* (absolute knowledge and tradition dichotomy; rupture), recognizing value in both *being* and *becoming* as a matter of state policy within a *critical* democratic framework. As Gandhi had maintained, no issue of *being* (i.e. religious doctrine or identity) may override a humanist consideration of democratic justice. Thus, we see categorical measures such as the abolition of untouchability in 1955, but wider latitude of negotiation on most life world-value-related problems.

The most visible example of Nehru's vision of freedom might be in his perception of the 400 different tribal peoples spread all over India (and a majority in the north-east) with their distinctive languages and cultures. Seeing the impossibility and undesirability of isolating them from changes in Indian society, nor did Nehru wish to see them "engulfed by the masses of Indian humanity" as such assimilation would destroy their unique identities and virtues.[42] In a rejection of historicist assumptions of succession, he deemed it *absurd* to use the term *backward* for India's tribal people.[43] His tribal policy aimed at "integrating the tribal people … even while maintaining their distinct identity and culture."[44] Nehru wrote of the tribal people in 1952 that "we have to take special care not to impose ourselves and our ways on them" or "allow them to be exploited by others."[45] He warned against any politics contributing to their becoming "drab imitations."[46]

Thus, we see that Nehru respected their *being* while hoping to involve them in the ongoing changes in the mode of self-reliance. Needed changes in modern medical facilities, agriculture and education would be "worked out by tribals themselves."[47] There

[41] Chandra, et al., *India since Independence*, 226–27.
[42] Ibid., 137–38.
[43] Nehru, *Letters to the Chief Ministers*, 3, 148.
[44] Chandra. et al., *India since Independence*, 108.
[45] Nehru, *Letters to the Chief Ministers*, 3, 26.
[46] Ibid., 248.
[47] Chandra, et al., *India since Independence*, 137.

should be no compulsion from the outside, and no outsider should be able to take possession of tribal lands. Nehru articulated his thinking on this question in 1950:

> Culture ... is an inner growth; it cannot be imposed from outside. That inner growth can be influenced greatly, more especially in early childhood, by the environment, by educational processes .... But whatever the means adopted, the growth must come from the inside. To tell a man ... to change his culture appears to me to have no meaning. The only thing we can do is to produce conditions which gradually influence him in the direction of changing his cultural outlook.[48]

Thus, rejecting coercion in the face of the Naga language movement in the north east, Nehru said that "the moment we try to put pressure, everything will be ruined."[49] Nehru's conception of modernity had a place for movements and mobilizations based on issues of *being* (language, identity, etc.) within the limits of non-violence (i.e. excluding religious or other forms of secessionism). Groups were permitted to promote, retain and protect their cultural life, language and script.[50] Culture was neither a pure tensionless éssence to be left undisturbed (the fantasy of the *fragment* and *innocence*) nor the refuse of history to be abolished as has tragically often been the case in modernist discourses.

Given these multiple influences nation-making was comparatively open or non-linear, but the process centred the non-negotiability of secularism—for the pluralism of the system could not be possible in its absence. Secularism, its meaning constantly debated in the Nehruvian period, was in practice the institutional expression of the politics of non-violence. Nehru insisted during the first national elections (1951–52) that the basic struggle of the time opposed secular and communal forces, arguing that

---

[48] Nehru, *SW*, 15, 83.
[49] Nehru, *SW*, 23, 61.
[50] Brass, *Politics of India*, 12. Compare to Ataturk, who believed the Kurdish language and culture to be a throwback, and in the historical inevitability of its destruction in the name of modern progress.

"we stand till death for a secular State."⁵¹ Explicit attempts were made to drag secular public debate within the limits of a discursive universe, as when the RSS speaker Swami Karpatriji Maharaj challenged Nehru to publically debate the Hindu Code in terms of Shastric merits rather than its implications for women's rights and children's protection.⁵²

During the campaign Nehru spoke to peasants, miners, factory workers, agricultural labourers and women of all social classes at 300 mass meetings—about 20 million people.⁵³ About 60 per cent of registered voters exercised their franchise—more workers than middle class people.⁵⁴ A Turkish journalist who witnessed the election expressed admiration for Nehru having not developed a "dictatorship with centralization of power and intolerance of dissent." The American ambassador claimed to have abandoned his conviction about the need for a benevolent dictator to prepare the masses for democracy in a poor country.⁵⁵ Their tacit assumptions were destabilized by this alternative practice. A horizon of ultimate synthesis was rejected in favour of a temporal horizon envisioning a continuing pluralism.⁵⁶ The politics of secularism aimed to preserve a public space for multiple points of view and lines of action—or, the open space based on the non-violent ethic of reconciliation opened up by Gandhi during the national movement for independence.

The pluralistic nature of political developments was structured within the framework of the 1950 Constitution in another instance of the ethic of reconciliation. Based on the ideology and values of the national movement, the Constitution aimed to create the widest possible consensus rather than to impose a uniform will. The Constitution represented freedom not as a seamless metaphysical web but as the on-going *maintenance* of conflicting and mutually subverting freedoms: between a fixed principle of individual liberty (in Fundamental Rights) and a dynamic principle of social

---

⁵¹ Chandra, et al., *India after Independence, 1947–2000*, 133.
⁵² Guha, *India after Gandhi*, 233.
⁵³ Ibid., 141.
⁵⁴ Ibid., 144–45.
⁵⁵ Ibid., 148–49.
⁵⁶ The pluralism was sometimes a weakness, as in failure to protect local minority rights by the centre.

change (in the Directive Principles). The Fundamental Rights guaranteed traditional civil rights—freedom of speech, assembly, etc.—intended to protect the individual citizen from violence from the state/others *in every case*. These had long-term consequences in terms of protecting the autonomy of multi-centred civil and oppositional sources of power—universities, the media, trade unions, parties, etc. which were essential to the functioning and survival of Indian democracy. This guaranteed a fixed foundation for public expression of multiple points of view.

The Directive Principles were the new economic and social rights that could not be guaranteed immediately but only in the course of economic and social development: these represented the dynamic element of longer term social transformation. This system acknowledged the unforeseeable paths of these transformations over time and the effects of diverse sources of civil and political intervention: the *specific content of each case*. The driving principle was that economic development and political freedom are inextricably joined in democratic nation-making and cannot be legitimately separated. Nehru acknowledged that "in the process of dynamic movement certain existing relationships are altered, varied or affected" and that there "is a certain conflict in the two approaches."[57]

The 1950 Constitution attempted a middle way between "diversity as well as the requirements of unity."[58] The writing of the Constitution involved years of debates within the Assembly that included Muslim members of diverse viewpoints, women demanding "equality of status" and "justice" and Untouchables including Ambedkar.[59] Between the fundamental rights and the directive principles we have a "curious amalgam of contending pulls."[60] The Indian constitution's wide frame of inclusiveness corresponded to the latitude of participation in the national

---

[57] Quoted in Chandra, et al., *India since Independence*, 46.

[58] Ibid., 109.

[59] Guha, *India after Gandhi*, 103–23; Partha Chatterjee, "Secularism in India: The Recent Debate," in *Secularism and its Critics*, ed. Rajeev Bhargava (New Delhi: Oxford University Press, 2009), 361. Ambedkar resigned in 1951 over the Hindu Code Bill controversy (see Christophe Jaffrelot, *Dr. Ambedkar and Untouchability: Analysing and Fighting Caste* [New Delhi: Permanent Black, 2005], 116–17).

[60] Guha, *India After Gandhi*, 109.

movement: the contributions of women, the propertyless and the illiterate entitled them to enfranchisement.[51] At least 40 per cent of eligible women voted in the first national elections, reflecting the expanding patterns of participation inherited from the independence struggle and ongoing changes in the structure of family relations.[62]

Where the urban-based organs of civil society were often beyond the reach of the rural poor, their mass participation in elections became their instrument for impacting events.[63] Nehru said, in 1955: "We took a bold step in India by adopting a democratic Constitution and adult suffrage .... It demonstrated our faith in our own people."[64] This remark expresses the sense of pragmatic hope and experiment, rather than a dogmatic worldview, which inspired the politics of the Nehruvian period. Nehru articulated this sensibility: "I do not despair. Although sometimes I feel a little angry at our failings and weaknesses, I have faith in our people and in the future of India, and also in a better ordered world. It is because of this faith I carry on."[65]

India's distinctive tradition of democratic national development as multi-centeredness may be contrasted to the dominant tradition of the General Will as inherited from the French Revolutionary experience. This contrasts with India's universal adult suffrage *prior* to national development. Consensus was not taken for granted as an ontological point of departure, but was envisioned as a provisional end of the democratic process. These present two distinct temporal horizons in nation-making. Nehru called for the "broadest national point of view and not the narrow party point of view," meaning not the singular *general will* but a point of view grounded in a multi-centred source of power.[66] He argued that conditions "differ so much in various parts of the country that any rigid rule or attempt at uniformity does not appear to be desirable."[67] On the grounds that "one pattern is

[61] Chandra, et al., *India since Independence*, 39.
[62] Ibid., 134.
[63] See Brass for account of how rural political conditions often became democratically derailed.
[64] Nehru, *SW*, 28, 4.
[65] Nanda, *Nehru*, 206.
[66] Nehru, *Letters to the Chief Ministers*, 3, 501.
[67] Nehru, *Letters to the Chief Ministers*, 5, 266.

unsuited to another place" he insisted on the "absolute importance of self-reliance."[68] In Nehruvian multi-centeredness democracy under the rule of law implied a state monopoly on violence *but not on truth*. The strength of the public sphere was that it remained plural, open and contested in a "balance of recognition," rather than a declaration of supreme national identity.[69]

Nehru defined democracy as "a manner of thinking, a manner of action, a manner of behaviour to your neighbour and to your adversary and opponent," that is, as a dialogic principle and respect for the person.[70] Affirming self-reliance, he hoped to "unleash forces from below among our people."[71] Rather than direction from the top, a variety of popular social movements played a formative role in shaping the direction of this evolving national policy. This is demonstrated in the accession of the Princely States and the formation of Linguistic States. With the 1947–48 accession of the 56 autocratic Princely States (40 per cent of the territory at independence), a popular movement for Indian integration in Mysore saw 3000 people court arrest; in Orissa and Kathiawar protestors took over courts, prisons and government offices. In Junagadh, where authority staunchly resisted public pressure to join India until 1948, a popular movement finally forced the ruler to take flight. In Hyderabad, the large Muslim population of the state took part in the movement for union with India.[72] The Congress used the power of these popular protests—often focused on a desire for political rights—to pressure rulers to allow their publics a plebiscite choosing between accession to either India or Pakistan. Within two years, largely through non-violent negotiation, these centres of rural autocracy had been converted into 14 new democratic administrative units.[73] There was also a popular movement against continued Portuguese rule in Goa that helped unseat the colonial power.

---

[68] Nehru, *Letters to the Chief Ministers*, 5, 157.
[69] Brass, *Politics of India*, 153.
[70] Chandra, et al., *India since Independence*, 175.
[71] Ibid., 186.
[72] Ibid., 95–96.
[73] Guha, *India after Gandhi*, 42–44; Chandra, et al., *India since Independence*, 90–93. The most tragic of these cases was Jammu and Kashmir.

We see a similar dynamic with the formation of linguistic states, where "the central government recognized most of the large language groups among whom major mobilizations developed for the creation of separate linguistic states."[74] Public protest over the 1952 Andhra controversy (including the fast-unto-death of Potti Sriramula, who died after 58 days) resulted in the government yielding to the demand for a separate linguistic state, and a rash of subsequent demands erupted for altered boundaries on a linguistic basis.[75] The resulting States Reorganization Commission of 1953 underwent a two year process of reckoning with these issues, faced with demonstrations, strikes and other agitations and in 1956 the States Reorganization Act was introduced creating new states along linguistic lines with several exceptions. This was widely accepted by the population.

Yet where severe disagreement continued, notably in Maharashtra, powerful and broadly based opposition movements formed and a protest vote in the 1957 elections only narrowly let the Congress Party pass. Popular agitation continued a further five years and in 1960 the government yielded and divided the state of Bombay into Maharashtra and Gujarat. We regularly see a concession by government to the pressures of public opinion when a negotiated general satisfaction among the varying participants was a possibility. As late as 1964 massive student demonstrations, riots and self-immolations in Tamil Nadu resulted in the Official Languages Act of 1965, assuring that Hindi would never be imposed upon non-Hindi speaking states and preserving English as an additional official language for inter-state communication.[76] However, in a further 1956 incident in Punjab the demand for a separate linguistic state took on overtly communalist overtones. When the Akali Dal and the Jan Sangh, respectively, representing Sikh and Hindu communal political interests advanced this campaign, Nehru and the Congress leaders categorically refused to concede to the demands.[77]

---

[74] Brass, *Politics of India*, 153.
[75] Guha, *India after Gandhi*, 188.
[76] Brass, *Politics of India*, 166.
[77] See account in Chandra, et al., *India since Independence*, 129.

New states were also "carved out in response to tribal demands."⁷⁸ This policy led to a "balance in centre–state relations," in which the Centre avoided confrontation with emerging popular groups while mediating and arbitrating between contending linguistic and cultural forces according to the criteria of secularism, national unity and non-violence. The guarantee of minority rights within these new states became an issue, reflecting the sometimes weak linkage between state and centre that also explained unevenness in education and land reform projects. Within this context, the state sought to establish a balance between protecting the existence of minorities and curbing separatist impulses that created serious conflict within the new states. Ultimately, the creation of a diversity of linguistic states served to consolidate rather than divide the Indian nation. The success of these experiments in establishing an enduring democratic system was very likely based in the prior extended struggle to ground enduring democratic sensibilities (i.e. Gandhi's values of self-reliance, secular justice and non-violent resistance) among the Indian masses during the national struggle for independence.

A request in 1946 by the Constituent Assembly for submissions from the public at large resulted in hundreds of responses touching on issues of ill treatment of low caste people, demands by linguistic minorities for freedom of speech in the mother tongue, and protection for religious minorities, testifying to the "precocious existence of a rights culture among Indians."⁷⁹ Arguments overemphasizing the supposed tendency of the masses to see in Gandhi and Nehru only living gods on earth, implying an essentialized religious perception, lose sight of the dynamic and dialogic transformation of popular political (or religious) consciousness involved in the long term social movement. The theoretical reliance on a disjunction between mobilization and statecraft fails to explain the rugged persistence of Indian democracy over time, and is often linked to prophecies of disintegration based on comparisons with Yugoslavia or the Soviet Union—where hegemony did not take root through a prolonged

---

[78] Brass, *Politics of India*, 169.
[79] Guha, *India after Gandhi*, 105.

national movement.[80] During the independence struggle, tens of thousands of cadres in both urban and rural areas had popularized notions of parliamentary democracy, republicanism, civil liberties and social–economic justice at the grassroots level.[81] The partial failure of the Indian national movement to achieve this across the full spectrum of the population was a factor in the Partition. Moreover, in the princely states where the national movement was unable to take root we observe notable differences in the depth of a rooted democratic sensibility and practice at the time of independence.[82]

We see serious challenges to the early Indian Republic that confirms its hegemonic hold over important parts of the Indian masses. Following the transfer of Hyderabad to India an interval of uncertainty permitted communists to assume control of the Telengana region where there were food shortages and unrest among farmers. Weapons abandoned by the retreating Razakar forces were used by communists to destroy the homes of landlords, to redistribute land among peasants and to enforce law and order. This success inspired the vision of an India-wide peasant revolution. In Calcutta, 1948, the road was declared open to "freedom and real democracy" by way of the "spirit of revolution among the masses," and Nehru's Anglo-American puppet government would soon be "collapsing like a house of cards."[83]

Following Mao Tse-tung's example in neighbouring China and Russian theorists comparing the Nehru government to the Kuomintang, the communists declared open war on the Indian state. A military and propaganda offensive ensued in which the Indian state used village and pantomime dramas to dramatize the conflict, and the membership of the communist party dropped by about 70,000 members within two years. This experience revealed the lack of popular empathy for ideologies or strategies of unbridled revolution and the depth of hegemonic hold of the Congress over much of the Indian population.[84] Widespread and growing participation from both urban and rural areas in

---

[80] Brass, *Politics of India*, 21.
[81] Chandra, et al., *India after Independence*, 20.
[82] Ibid., for detailed account of these geographic differences.
[83] Guha, *India after Gandhi*, 96–97.
[84] Ibid., 97–99.

the universal suffrage elections of 1952, 1957 and 1962 ratify the ongoing hegemony of the ruling Congress Party.

Indian politics remained pluralistic. In 1957, the Communist Party of Kerala, following Khrushchev's endorsement of a peaceful socialist transition and denunciation of Stalin, won local elections on a campaign of new industries, food production, wage increase, educational reform and housing construction.[85] The Communist Party took the opportunity to work within the framework of the Indian Constitution. Communist policies in Kerala produced more effective measures in agrarian reform and agricultural labourer welfare than many other parts of India where landed interests remained (i.e. Rajasthan).[86] Unfortunately, the Communist Party conflicted with the Church over control of education that resulted in serious violence and civil unrest, forcing the Indian state to eventually intervene in Kerala and unseat the existing government.

In these experiences, multiple lines of power came from different class, regional and cultural levels within the new Indian society. We see attention committed to the institutional aspects of the democratic system and efforts to embed public habits within the parliamentary process. Centring self-reliance and maximum popular participation, Nehru said in 1957:

> [I]f there is real democracy in India, we have to involve the maximum number of people in the task of decision-making and implementation.... The modern nations in particular cannot grow unless the responsibility is delegated to the people.... Democracy is not a matter of passing laws, it has to take roots among the people.[87]

He said that "democracy is not merely a question of elections" but the "democratic spirit" which "we hope will grow with outward forms of democracy."[88] Nehru's notion of democracy differed from the conventional liberal ideal; it was closer to Dewey's concept of deliberative democracy, which is focused less

[85] Ibid., 288–89.
[86] Brass, *Politics of India*, 279.
[87] Nehru, *SW*, 36, 73.
[88] Ibid., 286.

on periodic elections than the on-going practices of the everyday (i.e. lifeworlds).

The drive for industrial development during the Nehru period, in contrast with the West European experience and other post-colonial societies, was undertaken in a democratic state with universal adult franchise. India was developing "within a democratic framework, maintaining individual liberty [which had] not been attempted in any other country on such a large scale" — Nehru called this an "experiment" without "parallel anywhere in the world."[89] This posed questions about the interplay between planning and democracy: "How to combine this democracy with socialism is the question before us."[90] In 1957, Nehru described socialism as "a growing conception, as a thing that is not rigid, as a thing that must fit in with the changing conditions of human life and activity in every country."[91] Socialism for Nehru was not a rupture with the past, and nor was it universal in the sense of a pattern transcending India's specific conditions (i.e. "in the air"). Nehru's socialism, context-specific and immanent, did not centre the historical conquest of utopia to be attained by any means. He specified that the means had to be democratic: "We have definitely accepted the democratic process.... We think that in the final analysis it promotes the growth of human beings and of society.... We want the creative and adventurous spirit of man to grow."[92]

These comments make clear that development for Nehru was a human process in which growth was itself the end, not some ultimate horizon, and this is why the process had to be democratic. Growth is an alternative temporal horizon in nation-making to rupture. The state was an instrument of *maintenance* in the everyday rather than the *conquest* of the absolute. Thus, Nehru emphasized temporality: "this process of bringing socialism in India ... by the democratic way, will take time." Nehru contrasted this with countries such as the Soviet Union and China which

---

[89] Nehru, SW, 28, 32.
[90] Nehru, SW, 36, 286.
[91] Ibid., 284.
[92] Ibid., 285. The mistakes in the Five Year Plans concerned miscalculations of resources and savings, but did not reflect any intellectual dogma about a unique historical path.

industrialize far more quickly with authoritarian states.[93] He said: "It is not enough for us merely to produce the material goods of the world [and] to have high standards of living ... at the expense of the spirit of man."[94] Development and freedom were interwoven: "we seek free discussion and consultation as well as the willing and active cooperation of our people in the implementation of the Five Year Plans."[95]

It follows that Nehru's concept of socialism did not concern improvement as the discovery of universal historical laws. Such an epistemic view disregards the need of democracy as embodying the flawed *subjectivity* of the common people, and is prepared to employ violence to attain the higher end grounded in the certainty of delivering a better world. Nehru accepted fallibility, indicating "plenty of failings in the Congress."[96] He urged that "no plan is static and we must keep wide awake all the time in line with changing conditions." It was an issue of *character* (integrity and being awake to the environment) as much as "intellectual understanding."[97] Nehru perceived the link between dogmatic certainty and political violence, noting that "in the Soviet Union and China, there is only one line to follow [and] people are not free to criticize it" and thus "human beings cannot develop fully."[98] The methods these societies "adopted were usually violent [and] wrong means would not lead to good results."[99] Democracy, he maintained, "means peaceful method of working" and being "open to free discussion" where "minorities, religious or otherwise, must have their say."[100] Nehruvian nationalism broke from the pattern of internal homogenization and outer sovereignty but functioned by way of multiple inner autonomies relating to the centre based on a principle of non-violence.

In his discussion of the *scientific temper*, Nehru warned experts in community projects that they must take a humble and respectful approach to the villagers because "the average farmer knows

[93] Ibid., 285.
[94] Ibid., 286.
[95] Ibid., 492.
[96] Ibid., 286.
[97] Ibid., 290.
[98] Ibid., 75.
[99] Nehru, *SW*, 9, 464.
[100] Nehru, *SW*, 36, 76.

much more than you [from] the experience of generations."[101] That is, Nehru affirmed the modesty of thought. Science, technology and economic development were intended for the broad public welfare on a material level; they did not represent a *whole* claim to metaphysical truth on a supposedly higher level than *ordinary* worldviews (as in the Positivism that inspired the violent Kemalist Westernization drive). Nehru regularly argued that "forced imposition of ideas on any section of the population is bound to fail."[102] In this sense Nehru's outlook departed quite radically from what had prevailed in most Enlightenment thought until this time.

The Nehruvian experience of national autonomy differed from the influential view in Ernest Gellner's *Nations and Nationalism*. Gellner uncouples nationalism from the Enlightenment. Yet the sociological claims made by Gellner concerning the function of language and communication do not preclude the existence of a larger multi-religious and multi-linguistic national experiment modelled on the ideals of Enlightenment. The Indian experience contradicts the tacit pessimism in Gellner's conclusion on nationalist politics as exclusively wedded to assimilation, exclusion and violence. Gellner posits inherent links between nationalism and violence as a world of "rival cultures struggling to capture the souls of men" in a "period of transition ... bound to be violent and conflict ridden."[103] Nationalism is a politics of cultural *homogenization* in which most "cultures are led to the dustheap of history by industrial civilization without offering any resistance" or dissolve "into the wider culture of some new national state."[104] This point of view is advanced as an ontological claim about the "inescapable logic" of the "nationalist imperative."[105]

The post-independence Indian experiment in democracy did not, however, affirm Gellner's definition of the "nationalist principle," in which the "territorial political unit" must "become ethnically homogeneous" through some strategy that "either kills, or

---

[101] Nehru, *SW*, 19, 83.

[102] Ibid., 84.

[103] Ernest Gellner, *Nations and Nationalism* (New York: Cornell University Press, 1983), 40.

[104] Ibid., 47.

[105] Ibid., 100.

expels, or assimilates all non-nationals"[106] and according to which two men "are of the same nation if and only if they share the same culture."[107] Gellner openly deems it irrelevant to consider nationalist ideas as such, as they are *a priori* forms of "false consciousness" or self-deception, and the actors "almost without exception ... fail to understand what it is that they do."[108] The Industrial Revolution itself, the alleged original fountainhead of the nationalist structural metamorphoses, was born out of the fundamental blindness of human experience and will never be fully comprehended even as it is persistently imitated.[109] It is sometimes difficult to identify whether Gellner's account of modernity is driven by a sombre realism or a mood of pessimism regarding the possibility of human agency. Gellner does not give any account of the important range of degree in the democratic character—or lack thereof—of a given nationalist ideology, movement or political order. This is the problem with essentialist explanations based on inner logic rather than comparative studies examining the overlapping complexity of linkages (Wittgenstein's "family resemblances") in temporally conditioned experiences. As Hegel showed using dialectics, they fall apart through tensions in the contained stability of their own logic.

The secular element being at the core of Nehruvian universalism, we might reflect on the charge that a secular politics of the nation is a derivative form of Western politics and ideology constituting an inherent violence against Indian cultural, social and historical autonomy. This view on the Enlightenment and the nation is expressed by Partha Chatterjee from a post-structuralist or subaltern perspective. Following Ranajit Guha, whose disillusionment with Soviet politics prompted "a deeper questioning of an entire mode of modern knowledge [placing] enormous value on technological mastery over nature" and inspired by "Heidegger," Chatterjee's is a totalizing critique championing an abstraction in the "fragment."[110] Chatterjee unites Said's

---

[106] Ibid., 26.
[107] Ibid., 7.
[108] Ibid., 35.
[109] Ibid., 19.
[110] Ranajit Guha, *The Small Voice of History: Collected Essays* (Ranikhet: Permanent Black, 2009), 16. From introduction by Partha Chatterjee.

Orientalist critique and Foucauldian genealogy to a concern with authentic origins—yet Foucault rejected the problem of origins.[111] His refusal of the category of *authenticity* was the grounds for his opposition to Sartre's philosophy.[112] Chatterjee's project seeks to go *outside* (striking a Bachelardian–Althusserian theoretical pose) of both nationalism and the Enlightenment presumably to a more *authentic* form of social and political organization entirely beyond the epistemic and political legacy of European colonialism and grounded in *community*. Substantial suggestions for practical politics, such as intracommunity normative institutions as an alternative to the state, have been very thin.[113] Chatterjee advances his most forceful arguments on theoretical terrain.

Yet the nationalist discourse to emerge from the Nehru period does not, upon close examination, conform to the *derivative* paradigm of the nation as evoked by Chatterjee. It displays its own qualities that combine both Indian and non-Indian traditions (that is, it is closer to Amartya Sen's concept of "components"). Above all, it is characterized by the core tenet of a non-violent ethic of reconciliation extending from the National Movement to the Nehru period as a guiding principle. Chatterjee describes the Nehru period as driven by the "ambit of bourgeois-rationalist thought," and so victim to the "lack of autonomy of nationalist discourse itself."[114] Embodied in the "universal ideal" of the "Enlightenment" as the "implantation into new cultures of an alien framework," our own unreflected ideas become our prison.[115] For Chatterjee, following a Foucauldian line, knowledge amounts

---

See also Ranajit Guha, *History at the Limit of World-History* (New York: Columbia University Press), 79.

[111] This is made clear in Michael Foucault, "Nietzsche, Genealogy, History," in *The Foucault Reader*, ed. Paul Rabinow (New York City: Pantheon Books, 1984).

[112] Foucault, "On the Genealogy of Ethics: An Overview of Work in Progress," in Foucault *Ethics: Subjectivity and Truth, Volume I* (London: Penguin, 1997), 262.

[113] See Chatterjee's essay in *Secularism and its Critics*.

[114] Chatterjee, *Nationalist Thought and the Colonial World* (New Delhi: Oxford University Press, 1993), 10–11.

[115] Ibid., 27.

to domination.[116] He seeks to overcome the Western—sometimes evoked as colonial, sometimes as capital—dominance which "remains on the epistemic plane."[117] The villain is in the unconscious mind: the "intellectual premises of modernity," or "epistemic privilege" as "the last bastion of global supremacy" in the wake of only superficially successful anti-colonial movements.[118]

A pure Western episteme remained unscathed, lurking beneath the surface of consciousness, throughout the entire historical passage of India's struggle for independence—using Gandhi like an innocent puppet for the purpose of winning the approval of the religious masses—only to then openly spread its wings in the post-independence Indian state once the door was firmly locked on the unsuspecting population. India remains subjected to this day, like a somnambulist taking dreaming for the world, and awaiting Chatterjee's awakening intervention. Armed with the *analytical tools* in post-structural theory required for unmasking this predicament, Chatterjee reveals those believing themselves as India's freedom fighters to be its prison wardens.

This outlook is closer to the romantic politics of paranoia and pessimism that we find in Heidegger's lamentations of a lost authentic being than anything in the Marxist tradition. There is the uncritical adulation of community (the "struggle between community and capital"[119]) that both Gandhi and Nehru saw the need to avoid. Ultimately, the whole discourse of the *derivative* rests on the tacit and seductive idea or promise of an authentic Indian being or community glowing somewhere beyond the "cunning of reason" or the prison of modernity. In this sense Chatterjee's ideas have the attraction of a utopian allure in a world where we long for a change in the way things stand, but very little of practical value beyond that. The tendency to submerge the complexity of multiple experiences under such a blurred notion as "bourgeois-rationalist thought"—as if the experiences of India and Turkey might be an essentially identical "structure" on this

---

[116] Foucault, "Nietzsche, Genealogy, History," in *The Foucault Reader*, ed. Paul Rabinow (New York: Pantheon Books, 1984), 95.
[117] Chatterjee. *Nationalist Thought*, 17.
[118] Ibid., 31/17.
[119] Partha Chatterjee, *Omnibus*, 238–39.

"level"—does a disservice to political experiences of difference and so finally to the endeavour of historical reflection itself. The argument, moreover, is meant to be taken on such a broad level: "the theoretical structure of my argument must stand or fall at the general level, as an argument about nationalist thought in colonial countries."[120]

The Indian National Movement and the Nehru period were based on forms of Enlightenment universalism; but this was not the universalist assumption that *we* can understand any and all *alien beings* in order to assimilate them to our *rationality*. It was rather a context-specific universalism grounded in respect for difference—i.e. immanence—without the need to necessarily *understand* it. Hence, the centrality of dialogue linked to belief in the practical imperative of non-violence rather than universal epistemic finality. This demonstrates the pluralistic and sometimes conflicting nature of the Enlightenment as a political and intellectual heritage in modern nation-making. It suggests the significant link between politics based on the non-violent ethic of reconciliation and the creation of modern democratic societies.

---

[120] Chatterjee, *Omnibus*, 50.

7

Iranian Enlightenment: Struggle for Multi-Cultural Democracy and Its Demise

MOHAMMED MOSADDEQ'S WORLDVIEW WITHIN THE EMERGENT IRANIAN ENLIGHTENMENT

Behind the Iranian Constitutional Revolution (1906–11) there was a complex multi-part historical evolution. The Constitutional Revolution formed around political principles and intellectual concepts identifiable with democratic Enlightenment, but was simultaneously specific to Iran's particular historical and cultural situation. It was a

> reaction to failures of plans and actions toward the reforms in the second half of the 19th century [and was driven by the] rise of new thoughts and ideas in the academic and practical areas of judicial system, extension of economic and cultural interactions between Iran and European countries, and unaccountability and brutality of the political leaders.

The struggle "led to establishment of a new legal base for judicial organization, and passing of the judicial regulation in judicial committee of the newly established parliament."[1]

The Constitutional Revolution—one moment in the Popular Movement—contained diverse and often contradictory threads. It had broad multi-class support: "Almost all merchants, artisans and shopkeepers, most of the *ulama* and religious community, many if not most of the landlords and nomadic chieftains, most of the ordinary urban public, and the entire modern intelligentsia

---

[1] Majid Mohammadi, *Judicial Reform and Reorganization in 20th Century Iran. State-Building, Modernization and Islamicization* (New York: Routledge, 2008), 55.

either actively or passively supported it."² It involved a series of largely non-violent, mass based and multi-class political experiments grounded in an ideal of national independence and constitutional democracy. Facing emerging problems specific to Iran, the Popular Movement "did not begin with an established theoretical framework."³ It started *practically* with the Tobacco Revolt of 1890–91 and culminated in the popular National Movement of the post-Reza Shah period (1941–53) under Dr. Mohammed Mosaddeq (1882–1967). It reached its abrupt and inglorious end with the 1953 CIA-organized coup.

The Popular Movement was broadly based upon the pluralistic terrain of emergent civil society. Mosaddeq described its means-ends scheme in terms of "political parties" and a "popular base" as the "prerequisite of a constitutional system." It included "a number of people who shared common ideas and interests [and so] set up a society or association [that] could unanimously agree on a given policy and defend political freedom." It was an activist movement, where "some of these people lost their lives ... and sacrificed everything for their faith and conviction."⁴ At the global level, Mosaddeq argued, the precondition for building Iranian democracy was full independence from foreign imperial domination: "as long as foreign powers operated Iran's oil resources. [it] would never see the face of freedom and independence."⁵ He argued that "traditional politicians had jeopardized Iran's very existence with their misguided policy of 'positive equilibrium' and 'capitulating' to the great powers. Such a policy, he warned, prompted other powers to demand equivalent concessions, endangering national sovereignty."⁶

Domestically, Mosaddeq favoured "peaceful means to move the society" (i.e. non-violence) and "gradualism" having "regard for the nature of the Iranian society, and its national and religious

---

² Homa Katouzian, *Iranian History and Politics: The Dialectic of State and Society* (London: Routledge, 2003), 144.

³ Homa Katouzian, *Musaddiq and the Struggle for Power in Iran* (London: I.B. Tauris, 2009), 95.

⁴ Mohammad Musaddiq, *Musaddiq's Memoirs* (London: JEBHE, 1988), 135.

⁵ Ibid., 353.

⁶ Ervand Abraham, *A History of Modern Iran* (Cambridge: Cambridge University Press, 2008), 114.

traditions" (i.e. ethic of reconciliation). He opposed "illegal means to bring down the establishment in its entirety" (power seizure).[7] His practices embodied this ethic of reconciliation. To create a middle way with opposition, his 1951–52 cabinet purposefully included outsiders.[8] He opposed the banning of any political party from electoral participation, rejecting the Shah's 1951 bid to exclude the Tudeh Party.[9] While opposing British domination, he retained cordial working relations with the South Persian Rifles (SPR) but officially refused their recognition.[10] In a moral battle with them over the confiscation of a Shiraz landowner's farm (to be turned into an SPR race course), he used the pressure of non-violent persuasion to settle the conflict to everyone's mutual satisfaction.[11]

Mosaddeq's vision was both cosmopolitan and rooted in Iranian traditions. He affirmed grassroot democracy and an ethic of reconciliation, rejecting violent modernization from above—the discursive–practical formation advocated by important contemporaneous Iranian intellectual currents. Mosaddeq's critical embrace of modernity and respect for Iranian tradition provided an alternative to the dogmatically Eurocentric modernist discourses of *rupture* based on Auguste Comte or Stalinist communism. Both of these urged postures of capitulation to British imperialism and the Soviet Union respectively. He condemned *superficial* supporters of *modernism*, seeing that modernity creates new possibilities both for democracy and new regimes of absolute power more dangerous than traditional ones.[12] Mosaddeq and his Iranian opponents adopted opposed discursive aspects of the Enlightenment heritage, between the immanence of civil society and the transcendental vision of total state authority.

Mosaddeq argued that "democratic government was itself an evolving system" (an ongoing means, not a final end).[13] He recognized the danger in the transition to a democratic society

[7] Katouzian, *Musaddiq*, 218.
[8] Ibid., 113.
[9] Ibid., 119.
[10] Ibid., 15.
[11] Musaddiq, *Memoirs*, 219.
[12] Ibid., 128.
[13] Katouzian, *Musaddiq*, 26.

in imperialism's alignment with traditionally vested power interests. Accordingly prioritizing the proper legal framework, he realized that it could function effectively only given adequate time for public democratic practice to take root.[14] Of utmost priority was that "people take part in their own affairs" and that "elections should be free," for "no one would serve the people's interest better than the people themselves." This view privileged moral virtue or practice over higher knowledge: "No one could benefit from public institutions even if they were staffed by the best educated personnel, until such times as the people became interested in social issues and partake in public affairs."[15] Mosaddeq's thought linked Montesquieu's concern with institutions to Emerson's valuing of self-reliance at the level of mass mobilization as an open temporal horizon.

Mosaddeq therefore opposed authoritarian power concentration to the independent multi-centredness of civil society. A "monopoly of politics by the government ... prevent independent political analysis and criticism [from the public]." It was only "freedoms [i.e. direct action from the masses] which had enabled the country to regain its freedom and independence."[16] This entailed a critical public ideal. The press must not be

> afraid of censureship, or arrests, for criticising either my own conduct or the conduct of my government ..., so that if their criticisms were reasonable, I would try to make my decisions consistent with public opinion.... Freedom of expression and of the press is one of the basic pillars of the constitutional system.[17]

It follows that Mosaddeq held a secular reformist vision of Islam. He opposed still comparatively minor mobilizations to purge Iran of alien influence and to *restore Shi'i purity*. In his 1914 *Iran and the Capitulation Agreement*, he argued that "it is an affront to a people as well as their religion for foreign residents in their country to be immune from their laws," while demanding the

---

[14] Musaddiq, *Memoirs*, 116–18/132.
[15] Ibid., 339/350/149.
[16] Ibid., 370.
[17] Ibid., 193.

"reform of existing laws [that] the European powers would agree to their citizens being subjected to Iranian law." Insisting that the Shari'a is historically "flexible and adjustable," he compared reforms in traditional states ranging from "Turkey and Tunisia to Japan and Bulgaria."[18] The ideas of Edmund Burke provided a point of analysis. Mosaddeq expressed a compound of discursive and practical Enlightenment ideals focused on development as freedom.

At only 24, Mosaddeq participated in the Constitutional Revolution. Born into old regime Qajar court life, he was appointed Khorasan province treasurer at 15 following his father's death, the treasurer general. He thereby gained practical insight into the workings of government. His generation was the first to attend the newly opened School of Political Sciences, Tehran, whose members formed the leaders in the *bastnishini* at the British delegation in 1906. Elected to the first national Parliament in the same year, he was refused the seat because of his young age. In 1909, he attended the Ecole des Sciences Politiques in Paris where he completed a Swiss doctorate in law. Upon his return to Iran, Mosaddeq taught at the School of Political Sciences. After 1919, he held the highest posts including minister of justice, finance, foreign affairs and was governor of Fars and Azerbaijan.[19]

The background to Mosaddeq's intervention was 19th-century Iran's experience of pressures under the consolidating global imperialist framework. The Qajar state undertook several modernization experiments to either break free or—more likely—to guarantee advantage for the ruling Iranian elite within the new global order of power. Qajar Iran contained social complexity and regional diversity: with a population largely fragmented by the geographic terrain into isolated villages, towns and tribes, there were multiple languages including Persian, Armenian, Arabic and Turkish among others. Considerable religious difference existed between Muslims, Nestorian/Catholic Christians, Jews and Zoroastrians. Muslims were divided between the Shi'i and Sunni branches, and the Shi'i majority was split between the

---

[18] Katouzian, *Musaddiq*, 10–11.

[19] Roy Mottahedeh, *The Mantle of the Prophet: Politics and Religion in Iran* (New York: Pantheon, 1985), 114–16.

official Mujtahedi Twelvers and smaller groups, schools and sects scattered throughout the country.

Discursive formations specific to traditional Iranian Shi'i Islam have been identified with the logic of the *precipice*, where the future is conceived as open and unmade in relation to a fixed moment in the future.[20] This mode of thinking lent itself to revolt against the status quo and tended away from teleological schemes. It has multiple roots: following the declared occultation of the Twelfth Imam in 874 the "ideal truth is beyond men's reach in the present era of occultation" and "God has a kind of suspended decision."[21] Thus, the Ismailis conceived religion through historicity rather than fixed doctrines, implying concern over the welfare of the people of the specific time. The philosopher Mulla Sadra (1571–1641), combining various Muslim philosophical traditions, deepened this tendency in his doctrine of "substantive movement."[22] Rejecting the historical determinism of orthodox theologians (*fuqaha*), he articulated a vision of existence among philosophers and mystics (*urafa*) where movement occurs in the substance and qualities of things. Mulla Sadra thereby introduced a more humanist worldview in progressive evolution towards perfection, excluding knowledge as given in its entirety. This angered the orthodox theologians who fought to retain their monopoly on public meaning through waves of public persecution against *urafa*.[23]

During a period of disorder the Qajars (1794–1925) obtained power and never entirely consolidated their position.[24] From as

[20] Reza Baraheni, "Bridging the Gap or Filling the Precipice. The Poetics of Passage in Contemporary Persian Literature" (unpublished lecture given at New York University, 2010).

[21] Mangol Bayat-Philipp, "Tradition and Change in Iranian Socio-Religious Thought," in *Modern Iran: The Dialectics of Continuity and Change*, eds. Micheal E. Bonine and Nikki Keddie (Albany: State University of New York Press, 1981), 38–39.

[22] Ibrahim Kalin, *Knowledge in Later Islamic Philosophy: Mulla Sadra on Existence, Intellect and Intuition* (Oxford: Oxford University Press, 2010), 207.

[23] Christian Jambert, *The Act of Being: The Philosophy of Revelation in Mulla Sadra* (New York: Zone Books, 2006), 12–23.

[24] David Morgan, *Medieval Persia, 1040–1797* (London: Longman,, 1988), 158–59.

early as 1800 European imperial rivalry impacted Iran. Napoleon contemplated using the country as an alternative to Egypt for an invasion of British India. These developments led to Russian invasion and the humiliating Treaties of Golestan (1813) and Torkaman (1828) where Iran both lost considerable territory and had to award capitulations to Russia. Fearing an expansionist Russia as a threat to the Indian Empire, Britain invaded Iran from the south. The 1857 Treaty of Paris secured the kingdom of Afghanistan as a barrier to French, Russian and possible Iranian designs on the Indian Empire.[25] This afforded the Qajars international recognition as the legitimate Iranian rulers while forcing commercial capitulations to Britain in return. Iran's fate was linked to India in the global history of imperialism.[26] Foreign economic penetration patterned future commercial and political relations between Iran and the European powers. During the 19th century, the total volume of foreign trade increased by as much as eight times.[27] The importation and consumption of luxury products by a small minority coexisted with declining local industry, depleted welfare and dislocation for the majority.[28] Among other privileges, foreign merchants were exempted from the jurisdiction of shari'a law courts. Iranian independence became, between Britain and Russia, largely a fiction as "the mutual desire to forestall control of Iran by the other party was the most important factor in maintaining Iran's formal independence."[29] Under the last Qajar Shahs, royal authority barely extended beyond Teheran and Tabriz—suggesting the restricted limits of the centralized state apparatus compared to Ottoman developments at the same time.[30]

[25] Peter Mansfield, *A History of the Middle East* (New York: Viking Penguin, 1991), 140–42.
[26] See Willem Floor and Edmund Herzig, eds., *Iran and the World in the Safavid Age* for a detailed account of Persian, Indian, Ottoman and European linkages in the early modern period.
[27] Ervand Abrahamian, *Iran Between Two Revolutions* (Princeton: Princeton University Press, 1983), 51.
[28] Homa Katouzian, *The Political Economy of Modern Iran, 1926–1979* (New York: New York University Press,1981), 50.
[29] Nikki R. Keddie, *Modern Iran: Roots and Results of Revolution* (New Jersey: Yale University Press, 2003), 34.
[30] Eric J. Zurcher, *The Young Turk Legacy and Nation Building: From the Ottoman Empire to Ataturk's Turkey* (London: I.B. Tauris, 2010), 61.

The context for the Constitutional Revolution was a globally inflicted crisis. The impact of rising

> industry and empire in Europe jolted the Iranian economy out of its traditional equilibrium and opened it up more than before to international trade such that it tended to export cash crops and import manufactured products. Apart from that, loss of territory reshaped the map of the country, robbing it (sometimes) of some of its best natural and human resources, diminishing both its productive capacity and its internal market, and reducing its military and political power.[31]

Nineteenth century Shi'ism developed two major schisms in Shaykhism and Babism, presenting the gravest challenge to established power in the early century. In the 1840s, Ismaili and then Babi revolts broke out, led by the *Bab* (1819–50) or gateway to the divine truth.[32] These movements contained great diversity of belief. An 1863 Babi offshoot, the Baha'is, introduced a "cosmopolitan, pacifist and liberal doctrine."[33] Shaykhism drew off Sufi concepts in viewing the "community ... in constant motion toward improvement," echoing Mulla Sadra and implying social progress. A later offshoot, by contrast, denounced reform and insisted upon submission to the state.[34] The founder of Shaykhism, Shaikh Ahmad Aha'i (1753–1826), contested the orthodox *ulama* in the name of Hurqalya or the Realm of Images, a hierarchic system of interworlds accessible only to the imagination and beyond the reach of rational abstractions.[35] These struggles over power and meaning demonstrated re-evaluations of old certainties faced with political and social disorder under new international imperial pressures.

In the later 19th century, a group of educated men—including Mirza Malkom Khan (1833–1908) and Mirza Aqa Khan Kermani (1854–96)—distinguished itself from the *ulama* and the

---

[31] Katouzian, *Iranian History*, 143.
[32] Mansfield, 143.
[33] Abrahamian, *Two Revolutions*, 48.
[34] Ibid., 14–15.
[35] Mangol Bayat-Philipp, *Modern Iran*, 42–43.

urafa class on explicit Enlightenment grounds. Inspired by the "antitheologicial, antimetaphysical philosophers of eighteenth century Europe," they privileged the "pragmatic solution of particular problems" over the "mystery of life." This group's discourse showed interacting components. Continuities existed with the *urafa*, in Kermani's notion of religion as a "pragmatic, useful instrument" following the Isma'ili, Shaikhi and Babi idea of Revelation evolving to a "constantly changing, progressing, world." His anti-*ulama* stance reflected the *urafa* tradition no less than Voltaire. He broke with Sadra's vision of "yearning for divine love" in favour of "man's thirst for knowledge and social progress" in a secular scientific moment. Shi'i mystical ecstasy turned to an ideal of national social action in a still "traditionally monist view" and "passionate longing to discover one unitary truth."[36] Kirmani studied the works of Descartes, Rousseau, Voltaire, Montesquieu, Spencer and Darwin.[37] The European turn did not represent an uncovering of naked reality, but entry into a new discursive universe—this time inspired by the socio-political aftermath of the 17th-century Scientific Revolutions.

This heritage of diversity, new ideas and increasing change under global imperialist pressures—exacerbating multiple centrifugal pressures within Iran—is the background for the project of modern nation-making undertaken with the 1906 Constitutional Revolution. A new movement of political creation and experimentation changed people's everyday lives and attitudes through an open secular democratic vision of Iran's situation. As distinct from a single party or programme, this was a plural movement from below linked to multi-faceted changes in vision and habit rather than a single ideological line. The larger stakes were the power sharing arrangement in the emergent modernizing state. Mosaddeq urged that it be "opened to all individuals, groups, and parties ... ready for struggle and self-sacrifice to overthrow the colonial apparatus, and every effort ... be made so that those who seek the freedom and independence of Iran are brought

---

[36] Ibid., 47–51.

[37] Ali Mirsepassi, *Intellectual Discourse and the Politics of Modernization: Negotiating Modernity in Iran* (Cambridge: Cambridge University Press, 2000), 61.

into the circle of activists."[38] While a national movement, it was constituted of mutations rather than a continuous line of identity. The optimism created for many Iranians by the Constitutional Revolution, however, was extinguished by the brutal reality of civil war and then World War I.[39] A new romantic intellectual vista opened as German philosophy gained popularity. Unlike Britain and Russia, it was not an imperial power in the Middle East.[40] The 1917 Russian Revolution—an inspiring call to change—saw Russian imperial presence subside but permitted Britain a freer hand.

Reza Khan (1878–1944) ended the Qajar Dynasty in the 1921 coup, promising order after years of insecurity and posting proclamations on the city walls reading "I command."[41] He established the first modern dictatorship (as Reza Shah) linked to the global imperial context. Mosaddeq recognized this, arguing in perhaps overstated fashion that as the 1919 Agreement "was not acceptable to the Iranian people, and met with their strong protest [Britain] decided to resort to a coup d'état [1921] to put a government in power that would be in complete command of the country's affairs."[42] Other modernist Iranian intellectuals, meanwhile, saw in the 1921 coup an opportunity to achieve emancipating rupture with the past.[43] Reza Shah "sought to modernize from above" following Mustafa Kemal Ataturk in Turkey.[44] He similarly followed a violently assimilationist cultural politics, closing the schools of Jewish, Christian, and Baha'i minorities.[45] There was a single line of identity affirmed, and identified with the state in a "new national cult of monarchy."[46] In the 1921 coup a fixed programme and single power block—linked to imperialism—predominated over the myriad threads of the growing Popular Movement which had posed an increasingly self-conscious

[38] Katouzian, *Musaddiq*, 237.
[39] Patrick Clawson and Michael Rubin, *Eternal Iran: Continuity and Chaos* (New York: Palgrave, 2005), 51.
[40] Katouzian, *Musaddiq*, 8.
[41] Mottahedeh, *Politics and Religion*, 57.
[42] Musaddiq, *Memoirs*, 289.
[43] Mottahedeh, *Politics and Religion*, 57.
[44] Clawson and Rubin, *Eternal Iran*, 53/56.
[45] Mottahedeh, *Politics and Religion*, 68.
[46] Ibid., 311.

challenge to foreign domination and domestic power monopoly. The democratic movement in the mode of opening possibilities yielded to an authoritarian programme from above with a charted course.

Emerging Iranian modernity therefore involved two opposed and rival visions of secular Enlightenment: one authoritarian, elitist and Eurocentric, with a closed vision of the future, and the second pluralistic, democratic and with an open vision of the future in the making. Each was a distinctive temporal horizon in modern nation-making linked to the heritage of Enlightenment in its multiple components. The boundary dividing them, where agency interacted with the tacit dimension, was potentially ambiguous. In the 1941–53 interim these divisions became increasingly visible in a national hegemonic struggle where leadership deployed discursive–practical formations in a deciding conjuncture for the country's future. Inspired by India's independence and Nehru's non-alignment movement, the distinctive contours of a broadly based and peaceful movement committed to democratic ends became visible as an available alternative to Stalinism's iron historicist necessity and violence in national liberation movements. Khalil Maleki (1903–69), who had led the split in the Tudeh Party that helped form the National Front, theorized this as "socialist roads to progress, which were independent from the Eastern bloc and discovered by each country on the basis of its own culture and historical experience."[47]

THE POPULAR MOVEMENT (1891–1953): EARLY INTELLECTUAL INFLUENCES

The Popular Movement was a wide and complex public reaction to Nasir al-Din's (ruled 1848–96) 19th-century modernization efforts, aspiring to a more democratic road to national modernity. At the popular level, *democracy* signified non-violence and self-protection. At the elite level, the spectrum of meanings was a wide variety of means-ends templates linked to emergent discursive formations. The 19th-century modernization bid—beginning with Fath' 'Ali Shah (ruled 1797–1834) and Muhammad Shah

---

[47] Katouzian, *Musaddiq*, 100–101.

(1834–48) — struggled with new destabilizing global conditions. It pursued administrative and military security through a functioning state-wide bureaucracy and effective standing army. Nasar al-Din alternated between timid reform efforts and violent reaction as the dangers of an emergent self-conscious Iranian public opinion became manifest. A government printing office — deriving an Enlightenment narrative for modernization and survival — published translations of Voltaire's essays on Peter the Great.[48]

Modernization was initially the collaboration of the new intellectual elite and the regime. Inspired by Iran's new *enlightened* intellectual movement, Nasir al-Din modelled administrative and military reforms on the Ottoman Tanzimat example. He founded the Ecole Polytechnique in Tehran. In 1872, fatally undermining foreign concessions for modern military building — most famously to Baron Julius de Reuter in 1873 — began to compromise Qajar sovereignty. Lord Curzon (1859–1925), British Viceroy of India and Foreign Secretary, described "the most complete surrender of the entire resources of a kingdom into foreign hands that has ever been dreamed of."[49] The Qajar regime self-stabilized through collaboration with foreign powers at the general population's expense in a relation of dependence.[50] The peasant majority were most heavily taxed to pay for the increased purchase of foreign goods such as tea, sugar, tobacco and textiles.[51] Absolutely no political rights were extended to the peasantry, who worked merely to survive.

With the failed 1876 Young Ottoman constitutional revolution and Abdul Hamid II's 1878 autocratic reversion, Nasar al-Din abandoned his liberal reformist experiments.[52] The 19th-century Qajar political regime was linked to the Ottoman Empire at the discursive–practical level in its parallel strivings for security and independence through the hazards of inter-imperial power politics. Thus, we see state formation grounded in an Enlightenment discursive–practical basis — very often authoritarian — across the 19th-century Middle East. The early 20th-century Popular

[48] Abrahamian, *Two Revolutions*, 58.
[49] Keddie, *Iran*, 54.
[50] Abrahamian, *Two Revolutions*, 52.
[51] Keddie, *Iran*, 51.
[52] Mansfield, 143.

Movement, as a mass movement grounded in everyday life, far outstripped most efforts by contemporary Iranian intellectuals to conceptualize it. The creation of a public consciousness out of Iran's ethnic, religious and geographical dispersal involved multi-centred global dimensions. Firstly, European economic penetration threatened the urban bazaars and fostered the coalescing of scattered commercial interests into a cross regional traditional middle class which for the first time took consciousness of its common problems. Identity, under imperial pressures, was a problem; not an inanimate reality like a stone.

Secondly, the creation of modern educational systems intended to overcome national weakness introduced new concepts and produced a new professional middle class or the intelligentsia. With this the Enlightenment discourses of liberalism, nationalism and socialism entered Iran and the words nationality, the people, feudalism, parliament, despot, democrat and aristocrat entered the modern Iranian vocabulary. Yet these terms adopted specific Iranian nuances.[53] Sometimes terms combined with already existing Iranian discourses such as the anti-state Shi'i ideas of the traditional middle class. This held that "the practical leadership of the Islamic community had been *usurped*" and "the state [was] itself symbolic of the usurpation of the kingdom of God on earth."[54] Enlightenment was never a simple one-directional projection from West to East, but the interaction of multiple components.

Thirdly, at the more popular level, Iranian merchants and workers travelled to India, Russian Transcaucasia and Turkey. They witnessed reforms and heard liberal or radical ideas concerning government and social reforms that might free the country from foreign control.[55] It suggests a geographic decentredness in the formation of Enlightenment. This experience was linked to the Iranian socialist movement, "among the oldest not only in the Middle East but in Asia," joined to a "working-class trade union movement [among whom] were Iranian labourers working in the Russian Caucasus." From 1906–37 we see the

[53] Katouzian, *Musaddiq*, 73.
[54] Abrahamian, *Between Two Revolutions*, 50–51; Katouzian, *Political Economy*, 61.
[55] Keddie, *Iran*, 58.

growth of a "militant, revolutionary communist movement with strong ties to the emerging working class and an emphasis on trade unions."[56] The political trajectories of late 19th- and early 20th-century Iranian reform thinkers reveal an array of international dimensions illustrating growing public consciousness of national existence within a wider constellation of state and civil forces of power.

What is striking about the story, for example, of Sayyid Jamal al-Din "al-Afghani" (1839–97) is less the Pan-Islamic call for the adaptation of the *umma* to the scientific and technical realities of the modern world in a rationalization of the Islamic faith — though this is striking in pointing to the range of contention being publicly voiced merely over the definition of Islam — but rather in suggesting the globally interconnected, interactive and overlapping nature of the process of nation-making itself. It was not a matter of straight historical lines. Al-Afghani searched for answers to the threat of imperial domination of Iran. He came from a family of Azeri-speaking landowners and received a Shi'i education in the rationalist philosophical tradition of Avicenna.[57] He became interested in unconventional subjects such as Shaykhism and Babism, and eventually grew fascinated by modern sciences.

Around this point he claimed to have "obtained nothing from traditional learning" (i.e. rupture).[58] Going to India on a quest to discover the modern sciences, he arrived in Bombay in 1857 and witnessed the Indian Revolt. The experience marked him deeply, for he saw both the potential power of popular religion linked to political action and the defeat of this mass uprising by the power of modern technology. He thus concluded that if the Middle East was to resist full colonization, it was necessary to both fully adopt modern technology and mobilize the latent powers of popular religion against imperialism. In India al-Afghani participated in polemics with religious and antireligious Muslims seeking to overcome the religious and non-religious dichotomy from a basically pragmatic perspective. He criticized Muslims refusing to

---

[56] Mirsepassi, *Intellectual Discourse*, 161.
[57] Keddie, *Iran*, 60.
[58] Abrahamian, *Between Two Revolutions*, 62.

participate in the common struggle for national liberation out of a sense of separate religious identity.[59]

Al-Afghani subsequently spent time in Afghanistan as a guest at the royal court. He then lived in Istanbul where he gave a now famous lecture at the newly created House of Sciences (*Dar-ul-funun*) at its 1870 opening ceremony. This institution was established by readers of Voltaire and Diderot with iconoclastic Enlightenment ideas of their own.[60] Yet al-Afghani reportedly caused a scandal by arguing that human progress depends upon science, technology and reason, and implying autonomy for rational human existence from the Shari'a and God's will. In his lecture, al-Afghani "presented a thesis which had been well refuted since the time when *kalam* triumphed over philosophy" in traditional Islamic thought.[61] Exiled from the Ottoman Empire in 1871, he subsequently lived first in Egypt and then Paris.

In 1886, Nasar al-Din showed interest in al-Afghani's reformist and pan-Islamic writings and invited him back to Iran as an honoured member of the Royal Council. In 1890, al-Afghani led the popular denunciation of the British tobacco concession and was deported yet again. Despite this, his powerful influence in Iran persisted and in 1896—supposedly under his suggestion—an unemployed trader and disciple assassinated Nasir al-Din at the shrine of Shahzadeh Abd al-Azim. This murder set in motion the final decline of the Qajar monarchy.[62] From whispering in the king's ear as royal intellectual, to mass agitator, to inspiration for assassinating the royal head of state—al-Afghani ran the gamut of Enlightenment activist profiles.

Al-Afghani's final years were in Istanbul as an honoured guest for the autocratic regime of Abdul Hamid II. His *Refutation of the Materialists*, written previously in India in 1878 against philosophical naturalism, became the confirmation of the "wisdom of [Abdul Hamid's] persecution of the constitutionalists."[63] At the time of his death al-Afghani expressed hope, believing that

---

[59] Ibid., 63.
[60] Niyazi Berkes, *The Development of Secularism in Turkey* (Montreal: McGill University Press, 1964), 178.
[61] Ibid., 188.
[62] Keddie, *Iran*, 63.
[63] Berkes, 267.

the "stream of renovation" from West to East would destroy the "edifice of despotism." He expressed regret for insufficient time spent sowing "the seeds of [his] ideas on the fertile ground of the people's thoughts."[64] The constant careful weighing of the balance of opposing political forces throughout his life expressed the outlook that dominated al-Afghani's worldview: that "power is the manifestation of life and of existence .. and power is never manifest and concrete unless it weakens and subjugates others."[65] He saw the struggle for existence pervading human history, in the post-Renaissance adulation of force that has sustained much Enlightenment and Romantic thought. There has been an overlap on this issue, as though it were nothing more than common sense.

Al-Afghani's story demonstrates the imperialist horizon and matrix of plausible political action, and the intertwinement of contested power relations with problems of the Enlightenment, science, democracy, and cosmopolitanism. The multicentred reality of the political debates and events from Bombay to Istanbul demonstrates this in a way that al-Afghani's remark about the one-directional "stream of renovation" from the West fails to appreciate. Such a one-directional perspective has also been voiced by some of the major historians of the Constitutional Revolution, as when Morteza Ravandi identifies a *causal* relation between the "awakening"(*bidari*) and the introduction of European culture.[66] This is essentially the *impact–response* thesis based on the predominant inside-out mode of imagining modernity. In fact, the underlying pluralistic reality of the period of Constitutional struggle is in contradiction with the homogeneous and narrowly Eurocentric discourse of the nation that came to predominate with the victory of the Constitutional Revolution. Practice was far ahead of theory, reflecting a crisis of intellectual and political leadership.

The West-centric or impact–response thesis fails to do justice to a more pluralistic and multicentred phenomenon. Amartya Sen's conception of mobile and interacting components functions more appropriately as a model of change. Firstly, political

---

[64] Abrahamian, *Between Two Revolutions*, 65.

[65] Aziz Al-Azmeh, *Islams and Modernities* (London: Verso, 1993), 83.

[66] Morteza Ravandi, *Social History of Iran, Volume 3* (Tehran: Amire Kabir Publisher, 1975), 541; Mirespassi, *Intellectual Discourse*, 57.

events in Japan, particularly the constitutional Meiji Revolution (1889) and the defeat of Czarist Russia by a nationalist Japan in the Russo-Japanese War (1904–05) had important influence on Iranians undertaking the struggle against absolutism and seeking a constitutional government. The news of Japan's constitutional movement reached Iran through the Iranian constitutionalists' largest Persian language newspaper which was based and published in Calcutta. Similar Persian language newspapers were also being published in Egypt at this time. Secondly, the internal forces driving the Constitutional movement were neither ethnically nor religiously homogeneous, with minority groups such as Jews, Armenians, Zoroastrians, and Babis participating actively. Finally, other significant actors in the movement had lived in Russia and the Caucasus where they were deeply influenced by the circulation of revolutionary socialistic ideas. Still others derived their understanding of modernity from writings and journals being published inside the Ottoman Empire.[67] Only a great feat of metaphysical contortion could identify a universal Western impulse at the root of these multiple instances in their various mutations and unfoldings.

Among the most representative of 19th-century Iranian intellectuals in foreshadowing what became the dominant Eurocentric ideology of the Constitutional Revolution is perhaps Malkom Khan (1833–1908). An Armenian who received a French Catholic education in Isfahan and was awarded a state scholarship to study engineering in France, Malkom Khan embraced Saint Simon's positivism and Comte's Religion of Humanity. Following Condorcet, these discourses teach the inevitable growth of scientific knowledge and the final perfection of a universal human nature. The newspaper *Qanun* (Laws) that he published from exile in London at the end of his life—its mere possession in Iran a state crime—was later "hailed as a major factor in the outbreak of the Constitutional Revolution." This newspaper demanded a "national consultative assembly" with the "full authority to formulate laws that would initiate social progress."[68] The call for institutional reform combined with an imagined historical

---

[67] Mirsepassi, *Intellectual Discourse*, 59–61.
[68] Abrahamian, *Between Two Revolutions*, 68–69.

vista deriving from one stream of the European Enlightenment heritage.

Like al-Afghani, Malkom Khan's active political life involved a search for solutions to Iran's dilemma spanning several continents. A committed constitutionalist, he wanted to transform his country in order to rescue it from foreign domination. But his activist life alternated between attempts at change from above though the Iranian administrative system—finding the way every time blocked—and the impotence of repeated exile abroad. Shaken repeatedly between these poles, he was eventually pushed from cautious administrative reform to inciting revolt through appeal to the anger of the Iranian masses.

Yet Malkom Khan mistrusted the public which, through organized popular uprising, formed the only viable road to the realization for his plans. He believed in the necessity for "Iran's capitulation to Western values" based on the "acquisition of Western civilization without Iranian intervention."[69] This outlook, typifying many intellectuals of the Constitutional period, partook of a broader discursive formation spanning the Asian continent. This resulted partly from the fact that "France served as the Mecca of modern intellectual and political thought." Iranian intellectuals "were very much interested and affected by the experience of the French Revolution, and ... felt a great deal of sympathy for its principles and aims."[70] One historian of Qajar Iran cites each intellectual with "a book about the French Revolution and [yearning] to play the role of Dante [and] hot with fiery words." This generation celebrated French thinkers such as Descartes, Rousseau, Voltaire and Montesquieu.[71] Under Malkom Khan's influence, there was an intellectual drift toward dreams of rupture.

Gaining Nasar al-Din's interest in his ideas, Malkom Khan drafted the first systematic reform proposals in 19th-century Iran with his Ottoman Tanzimat-inspired Book of Reform (*Daftar-i Tanzimat*). The work posed two alternative futures for Iran: either European domination or emancipation through a new legal

---

[69] Mirsepassi, *Intellectual Discourse*, 62.

[70] Ibid., 60.

[71] Mahdi Quli Khan Hidayat, *Khatirat va Khatarat, Memories and Dangers* (Tehran, 1950), 9; quoted in Mirsepassi, *Intellectual Discourse*, 60.

system. He promoted secular law distinct from the Shari'a and centred on public welfare and civil equality, envisioned within an administrative and military reform framework including education, taxes, banking and transport. This vision of nation-making from above—envisioning justice for the population without participation—formed an already publically available and widespread Enlightenment discursive formation.

The favour and influence that Malkom Khan enjoyed in Nasar al-Din's court was short lived. The monarch's initial enthusiasm turned when an aristocratic and clerical backlash condemned the reform ideas as heresy. Malkom Khan was exiled to the Ottoman Empire. In 1871 Nasar al-Din again pursued a reformist course and invited him back in a special advisory capacity. Following reforms in the court budget and the separation of executive and legislative branches, the clerical and aristocratic opposition again objected. The reforms halted and Malkom Khan was sent to London as an ambassador.

From London Malkom Khan persisted in urging the Iranian court to follow a path of reform until losing his ambassadorship in 1889. He subsequently transformed into a furious and radical journalist calling for Iranian modernization on the basis of a partnership with the *ulama* that he had previously denounced. The newspaper *Qunan* became his weapon in cloaking the ideas of Comte and Saint Simon in respectable Islamic terminology—showing in effect how superficially he viewed both the Iranian masses and popular religion as a force to be manipulated on the road to *universal ideas*.[72] Like al-Afghani, he saw the value-laden lifeworld beyond changing relations of force as something essentially artificial or relative—and therefore to be manipulated creatively at will. Malkom Khan hailed the outbreak of the Constitutional Revolution and was considered by its leaders as a mentor, but was unable to return to Iran and participate. He died in exile in 1908 as civil war was breaking out in Iran.

Malkom Khan's commitment to liberal institutions and rule of law was a vision of Iranian national emancipation, but the West-centric core of his thought amounted to the uncritical acceptance of a static paradigm of universal modernity. Hardly conducive

---

[72] Abrahamian, *Between Two Revolutions*, 67. At a public lecture in London in 1889 Malkom Kahn proclaimed this as his aim.

to the vigour and spontaneity of the mass political movement already underway, this epistemic dogma made headway among the intelligentsia grown from an abyss of mistrust dividing leaders and the broader Iranian public. While only one among competing intellectual threads seeking to articulate the Constitutional Movement, this ideology finally achieved dominance and manifested itself in a programme of modernization from above in the period of Reza Shah (1926–41). Here it revealed itself in collusion with foreign domination.

THE TOBACCO CRISIS (1891–92) AND THE CONSTITUTIONAL REVOLUTION (1906–11)

The major 19th-century landmark in Iranian politics—expressing the emergence of the Popular Movement as a pluralistic mass phenomenon—was the Tobacco Crisis of 1891–92. We see, "for the first time in memory, the state ... compelled to bow to popular opinion in response to widespread urban rebellion."[73] This event prefigured and displayed many of the main elements of the Constitutional Revolution of 1906–11 at the level of non-violent practice grounded in everyday life. A local revolt transformed into a general rebellion, indicating the growing awakening to a national consciousness and power. In this instance the intelligentsia and the traditional middle class effectively worked together. Above all, we see that the Qajar regime incapable of resisting the force of public opinion organized as a nation-wide mass movement.[74]

This intervention of the popular Iranian urban masses showed modes of resistance grounded in traditional and largely non-violent practices. Although no organized ideology of non-violence found articulation among the leaders, these active expressions of popular discontent largely remained within non-violent limits until intense threshold moments of state provocation. Simultaneous acts of assassination by individuals remained undenounced by popular leaders. In short, the self-protective political activities of the broad population, grounded in traditional forms of protest,

---

[73] Katouzian, *Political Economy*, 53.
[74] Abrahamian, *Between Two Revolutions*, 73.

harboured a potential that the ideological leadership seemed frequently blind to. A non-violent discursive formation was lacking among intellectuals. The practical formation had a deeper existence in collective Iranian modes of self-protection through traditional lifeworlds.

The Tobacco Crisis started when Naser al-Din sold still another concession in a 50 per cent monopoly over distribution and exportation of tobacco to an Englishman named Major Talbot. A liberal Iranian newspaper published in Istanbul, *Akhtar* (Star), charged that because of the concession the vast majority of tobacco profits would henceforth remain with the English company and that large numbers of Iranians would lose their employment.[75] The popular action began in Shiraz, the main tobacco growing region, with a shutdown of the bazaar upon the arrival of the company agents in 1891. By way of the new telegraph system the shutdown spread into a general strike of the leading bazaars including Isfahan and Tehran. A religious fatwa at this point also contributed to a state-wide consumers' boycott. Further demonstrations followed on the streets of Tehran, and support was expressed from afar by Jamal al-Din in Istanbul and Malkom Khan in London. Nasar al-Din was forced to retreat and cancel the concession. Iran was henceforth involved in a struggle from multiple sides over the future political shape of a nation in the making based on this powerful practical precedent. The Tobacco Revolt showed the legacy of a popular mass movement grounded in everydayness and civil society, demanding national independence and constitutional government, and based in existing popular traditions of practice that only figures such as Mosaddeq and Maleki were to fully appreciate as leadership possibilities and at the intellectual level.

In the aftermath of the Tobacco Crisis Nasar al-Din shunned reform to follow a course of resolute political repression. He sought to repress expressions of emergent civil society in newspapers, schools and scientific societies, even resorting to the closure of tea houses (evidently unnerved by public gatherings). He attempted to seal the country from European influences—restricting travel abroad and requesting ministers "who did not know

---

[75] Ibid., 73.

whether Brussels was a place or a cabbage."[76] Having witnessed the force of the united efforts of the population, he aspired to undermine national unity by manipulating inter-communal rivalries and making scapegoats particularly of Babis. This repressive politics failed in its aims, culminating in the assassination of the last effective Qajar ruler in 1896.[77]

Nasar al-Din set a strategic modernization from above precedent in the most brutal terms. Following his assassination, Muzaffar al-Din Shah (ruled 1896–1906) combined the unlikely policies of unpopular economic measures and a relaxation of political repression. The infamous D'Arcy concession of 1900 granted a British company a monopoly on Iranian oil exploration and production until 1960. This set an imperialist-client state pattern for much of the 20th century. The 1908 Anglo-Persian Oil Company sent 51 per cent of its shares to the British government.[78] Iranian state policy therefore fanned resistance against a state perceived as having failed to protect the country's independence and using the narrowly distributed fruits of that subordinate position as its own lifeline.

Multiple organized particles emerged united in the aspiration to create a plateau for a functioning civil society out of a condition of official lawlessness. Iran's civil society network expanded rapidly, expressing the continuity of the Popular Movement. Numerous important opposition parties or clandestine organizations appeared, including the Social Democratic Party, the Society of Humanity, the Revolutionary Committee, the Secret Centre and the Secret Society. These had their foundations largely in the modern intelligentsia, though some (such as the Secret Society) were formed of the traditional middle class. Not all of them grew from an emergent and bemused bourgeoisie. Some were of a socialist orientation, such as the Social Democratic Party which worked with migrant workers in the Baku oil fields organizing strikes, eight hour work days, pension plans and so on.

This self-protective Enlightenment current of radical socialist politics—the ancestor to the highly popular and powerful inter-war Tudeh Party—emerged in the north and fell at varying

---

[76] Abrahamian, *Between Two Revolutions*, 74.
[77] Katouzian, *Political Economy*, 53.
[78] Ibid., 67.

moments on either side of the divide between a nationalist politics committed to Iranian autonomy and an *internationalism* on behalf of Soviet Cold War political aims. This political contradiction, coupled with an openly anti-religious discourse (based on an imagined temporal horizon of secular exorcism), contributed much to the marginalization and ultimate downfall of a broadly based politics of the Left in Iran.[79] The Society of Humanity, heir to Malkom Khan, followed the radical positivist teachings of Saint Simon and Auguste Comte, focusing more on legal equality and social engineering as a means to national development. The Society of Humanity adopted ceremonial secrecy from the European Freemasons as a shield against the authorities and the religious masses. Other groups sought links with the urban masses based on a mix of religious and secular principles while embracing more radical tactics, as with the Revolutionary Committee which was devoted to the "overthrow of despotism."[80]

Iran's first state-wide stock company was founded "to preserve the country's independence by fostering such modern industries as textiles [and] by protecting the traditional handicrafts, particularly the miniature arts."[81] Sayyid Hassan Taqizadeh, who played an important role in the Constitutional Revolution, published a new Persian-language journal called "Treasure of Knowledge" (*Ganjeh-i Fonun*). Taqizadeh adopted a West-centric line, arguing for "absolute submission to Europe, and the assimilation of the culture, customs, practices, organization, sciences, art, life, and the whole attitude of Europe, without any exception save language."[82] Thus, we see the discursive formation of rupture as a distinctive temporal horizon in the ideological politics of Iranian nation-making. There are the first rumblings of an information war over the shaping and reshaping of national memory.

Ideological perspectives in this register made the Constitutional Revolution a *narrow prism* upon the past at the intellectual level, encouraging a view of it as "nothing but a corrupt state (*dawlat*) oppressing the people (*mellat*)." The past was described as "a shameful age of dogmatism, fanaticism, and rampant clericalism"

---

[79] Mirsepassi, *Intellectual Discourse*, 159–79.
[80] Abrahamian, *Between Two Revolutions*, 75–79.
[81] Ibid., 75–79.
[82] Mirsepassi, *Intellectual Discourse*, 54.

and an "embarrassing prelude to the revolution" (i.e. rupture).[83] Hardly pragmatic or conciliatory, so reductive and categorical a rejection of Iran's pluralistic past projected only the most thinly abstract, uncompromising and singular vision of the *secular* future. The politics of modernity excluding the ethic of reconciliation in favour of totality shows itself. The tension between such a dogmatic *modern* outlook and the mutual intransigence in conservative religious elements contributed eventually to violently splitting Iranian national politics along *religious* lines. Fatally, this introduced an imaginary road to *authenticity* into popular politics at the expense of democracy as a *derivative* idea. Neither closed homogeneous authenticity nor the codified Shari'a as the base for an Islamic state had precedent in Islamic history, showing the character of this ideology as a significantly modern reaction to its perceived adversary in the *modernists* themselves.[84]

At the Constitutional Revolutionary stage no authentic–inauthentic binary had yet been conceived. Instead national development discourses with cosmopolitan dimensions underlay the proclamations of influential religious figures of the time. A National Library and private secondary schools were opened by a popular Shi'i preacher who proclaimed that only education "separates humans from animals … generates light in an environment of intellectual darkness … and shows us how to build power plants, steam engines, factories, railways, and other essential prerequisites of modern civilization." He hailed Japan as being able to "transform itself in one generation from a backward nation into an advanced powerful nation."[85] His integrity as a good Muslim was not questioned by any sizeable part of the population because of these Enlightenment-developmental discourses. Political and economic restructuring inevitably posed a potential threat to the *ulama* as a traditional vested interest (i.e. in terms of an independent modern judiciary, or in education), but the ideology of authenticity had yet to gain the popular ground of the 1960–70s. By then, it was an imaginative modern ideology hybridized with Marxist and Existentialist elements (i.e. Heidegger) and targeting the newly educated modern middle class.

---

[83] Abrahamian, *Between Two Revolutions*, 10.
[84] Aziz Al-Azmeh, *Islams and Modernities*, 31.
[85] Abrahamian, *Between Two Revolutions*, 76.

By 1905, Iran was entering a revolutionary conjuncture within the international and domestic configuration. The Russian Revolution of 1905 inspired hope in popular power to subvert a powerful absolutist state and momentarily removed the ever-present threat of Russian intervention to prop up the Qajar regime. Trade was disrupted in the north by these events and prices rose sharply, inducing further unpopular state economic measures as the Qajar state snatched at the population's resources to regain its balance. A bad harvest contributed to the country's economic crisis, so that the "government's financial and moral bankruptcy was absolute."[86] Conditions were set for the nation-wide hegemonic struggle that followed.

The Constitutional Revolution involved people "from all walks of urban life except for the military-bureaucratic establishment." The peasant class, however, "were neither specifically represented in the objectives of the revolution nor autonomously took part in it," doing so only when "mobilized and led by their own landlords."[87] The Iranian public, as before, took a line of largely non-violent civil disobedience to voice demands for reform to the state. These were grounded in various types of traditional Iranian popular protest such as religious processions and the *sit-in* (*bastnishini*). This suggests that force of public opinion as expressed through a growing mass movement was significantly constrained by the ethical framework of popular religious traditions of resistance, and the task of the leaders (whether the modern intelligentsia, the traditional middle class, or the *ulama*) was to find modes of organizing these largely spontaneous upsurges at the national level. As previously noted, important national leaders viewed political change in terms of a pure play of force, universalist abstractions, or certain pre-set narratives. They failed to take seriously constraining ethical frameworks as containing value or meaning in their own right.

Secondly, and relatedly, the problem of violence was tacitly at the core of the Constitutional Revolution. The concept of the constitution was not borrowed wholesale from Western political experience. The word *mashruteh* means *conditioned* or *constrained*, and the principle demand of the Revolution was "the

---

[86] Mottahedeh, *Politics and Religion*, 52.
[87] Katouzian, *Political Economy*, 60.

establishment of a constrained or qualified monarchy." This aim was counter-posed to the existing "rule of force," as in traditional Shi'ism the state embodies the "rule of force," or pure violence without spiritual guidance. In combining this traditional view with modern constitutionalism (as two components), the revolutionaries sought to abolish the violence and danger of an organized and official lawlessness by restructuring absolute state power into a government legitimized by popular consent.[88]

Thirdly, the paradigm of the French Revolution or Enlightenment failed to apply to the Iranian Constitutional Revolution: i.e. the secular wing opposing its religious antithesis with religion an inherent force of reaction and enemy of open society. In the Constitutional Revolution religious institutions, groups and individuals played a complex and ambiguous role on various sides of multiple political divides. Indeed, without the "total support to the revolution" given by the three most eminent Shi'ite leaders of the holy city of Najaf, Iraq, through "edicts and public statements, communicating with religious and other leaders of the revolution, sending acrid letters and telegrams to the Shah," the "revolution could not have succeeded when and how it did."[89]

During the early stage of the Revolution a general consensus prevailed as merchants, lower administrative ranks, landlords, noblemen, common preachers and theological scholars all participated "with the single unifying aim of destroying despotism and replacing it by a constitutional government."[90] This *consensus* was not based on a shared terrain of abstract ideological assumptions concerning the merits of democratic over despotic political systems. The collective movement was primarily protective. In popular imagination, the regime's hegemonic crisis was juxtaposed with existing practical alternatives. The Enlightenment ideal of an internationally strong and domestically secure constitutional state was available as a model in Japan and Russia as new nation-making experiments, in addition to core capitalist powers in Western Europe and North America.

The Iranian public consensus converged upon the rule of law and bespoke a concern with *material* conditions. This is why—in

---

[88] Ibid. Part One for detailed account.
[89] Ibid., 56–64.
[90] Ibid.

contrast to earlier 19th-century revolts of the Babi and Shaikhis—there was no significant demand for religious doctrinal change. Rebellion obtained force through deliberate coincidence with a public religious temporality. Specific issues concerned religious sensibilities. The use of religious terms and temporality, however, were mainly symbolic in promoting modern democratic political ends. The struggle—"fought by all classes and individuals who hoped to gain from its results"—was conceived upon a convergent field of secular interests without direct bearing on the status of a person's belief.[91] This secular popular politics concerned issues of perceived social and political justice (i.e. self-protection), and was hardly a derivative imposition despite discursive–practical links to the European Enlightenment heritage.

The second aspect of the *consensus* was the common desire for mastery of the laws, the economy, and so on, faced with open intervention and domination by foreign powers. This was the soil for nationalist discursive constructions. The molecular political processes shaping the Constitutional Revolution were simultaneously and unconsciously carving out a secular space for thought and action in the emerging Iranian national context. Mostashar ad-Dowleh (?–1895) was a deeply religious middle-level civil servant who worked in St. Petersburg and Bombay. His writings and ideas expressed this 'consensus'. He wrote that it is

> self-evident that in the future no nation—Islamic or non-Islamic—will continue to exist without constitutional law …. The various ethnic groups in Iran will not become one people until the law upholds their right to freedom of expression and to the opportunity for education.[92]

Inevitably, constitutional reorganization and dismantling of the traditional hierarchic order would entail multiple points of negotiation arrayed across a field of dangerously conflicting interests and viewpoints. It does not follow that Mostashar ad-Dowleh's

---

[91] Ibid., 60–64.
[92] Quoted Mottahedeh, *Politics and Religion*, 52; Mehrdad Kia, "Constitutionalism, Economic Modernization and Islam in the Writings of Mirza Yusef and Khan Mostashar od-Dowle," *Middle Eastern Studies*, 30, No.4 (October 1994).

view of an Iranian democratic modernity conflicted inherently with Shi'ism or religion *as such*, unless we take freedom itself to mean a metaphysically defined entity with religion as its sworn enemy on some epistemic battlefield linking truth and virtue.[93]

The 1905 Constitutional Revolution began from below with three public protests. The first took place during the month of Muharram and was integrated with the traditional Shi'i ceremony of mourning. A protest spokesman demanded that the government "reverse its present policy of helping Russians at the expense of Iranian merchants, creditors and manufacturers" and "protect our businessmen."[94] A traditional spiritual structure was employed as a modern political instrument to achieve secular ends (i.e. the ends to be achieved were independent of religious doctrines and practice). It took place as a procession by two hundred shopkeepers and moneylenders requesting the repayment of loans borrowed from them and the dismissal of the Belgian director general of customs. Shops were closed and photographs of the director dressed as a mulla at a fancy dress party were distributed. A congregation gathered at the sanctuary of 'Abdul 'Azim. Muzaffar al-Din Shah responded with finally unkept promises to meet the demands. The second protest occurred later the same year, multiplying the demands. When a 79-year-old sugar importer who had financed the repair of the central bazaar and several mosques was publicly charged with speculation and ordered to lower prices, he argued that high import prices were linked to the disorder in Russia. The governor of Tehran—ostensibly in an effort to lower sugar prices—ordered that he and another sugar importer be publicly beaten on the soles of their feet. For much of Qajar history such a punishment would have been, however much regretted by the public, a matter of course. On this occasion, the public reacted with absolute condemnation

---

[93] Or the creatively formulaic conception of secularism, here presented as the root of all ills, in Ashis Nandy. Nandy tends to turn words like "modernity" and "secularism" into puppets to be beaten in juxtaposition with other puppets to be praised such as "innocence." A form of provocative and interesting word-game theatre, it seems to be too essentialist to have substantial bearing on the complexity of actual events.

[94] Abrahamian, *Between Two Revolutions*, 81.

as stores and workshops closed throughout the bazaars and the protesting crowds filled the main mosques.

A public demand was made for the establishment of a House of Justice (*Idalat-khaneh*).[95] There was a series of "street demonstrations, mosque meetings, political leaflets and proclamations, and *sit-ins* in sanctuaries (*bastnishini*)."[96] The government initially countered—employing counter-Enlightenment discourse—that a House of Justice would destroy all ranks "even between princes and common grocers."[97] The general strike in Tehran lasted for one month before the government yielded to the pressure, and the crowds returned from the *sit-in* shouting "Long Live the Nation of Iran" (*Mellat-i Iran*). It was reportedly the first time this phrase was used. Both the government's taunt and the shouting of the street procession indicate the emergence of modern political stakes articulated within a secular conceptual framework and vocabulary imbued with Iranian nuance.[98]

The third protests began in 1906 when a local preacher was arrested for his public charge that *backwardness* was the result of "autocracy and injustice and the want of laws," and his condemnation of the government as "a parasite."[99] The subsequent shooting of a theology student who happened to be a sayyid (descendent of the Prophet) during a mass student demonstration outside of a police station resulted in thousands of students, shop keepers and guild members proceeding from the main bazaar to the central mosque in a public funeral procession. The issue at stake was articulated in terms of the right to protection from arbitrary arrest—yet strikingly we see no divorce between ethics and politics, as would later characterize the discourses of both Comte and socialist inspired politics in their claims to a value free *scientific universality* in politics.

When attacks by the Cossacks resulted in 22 deaths the two largest scale *bastnishini* to date were simultaneously organized with the aim of paralyzing the country on both the legal and

---

[95] Keddie, *Iran*, 67.
[96] Katouzian, *Political Economy*, 59.
[97] Abrahamian, *Between Two Revolutions*, 82–83.
[98] Katouzian, *Musaddiq*, 30 for a discussion of these nuances in words such as *mella*.
[99] Abrahamian, *Between Two Revolutions*, 82–83.

commercial levels. Muhammed Sadeq Tabatabai (1841–1914), one of Tehran's more respected mujtaheds, led a group of religious notables, their families, and 2000 religious students to perform a *bastnishini* at the holy city of Qom. He wrote in an open letter, "Do not hold captive the needs of 30 million people for the despotism of one person."[100] As a result of this popular intervention, Tehran was to be left without judicial actions and legal transactions until the shah met the popular demands. Thus, we see self-organizing civil society undertake a non-violent and popular hegemonic battle to remove the power basis from the existing state.

Simultaneously, two merchants of the Secret Society led the second *bastnishini* at the British legation. This crowd was largely merchants and craftsmen from the bazaar organized by guild elders, putting Tehran business at a standstill.[101] Numbering 14,000, the sit-in was non-violent and almost nothing was damaged except the flowerbeds. Teachers from the polytechnic and the newly opened schools of agriculture and political science arrived and gave lectures on constitutional government, reportedly transforming the gathering into "one vast open-air school of political science."[102] These 1906 events "brought honor and fame to the supporters of the new education" in introducing a new Enlightenment political vocabulary to the urban masses.[103] Women's demonstrations were also organized outside the legation, a "new feature of the period" being "the entry of many women into the political arena."[104] A committee was organized to transfer money from wealthier merchants to poorer workers who could not afford to keep up a prolonged strike.[105] This finally successful political movement, aiming for the realization of secular goals, was grounded in a participatory and self-reforming sense of community carried along by a common secular objective. The movement subsequently spread to the provinces, with particular force in the relatively prosperous and progressive province of

---

[100] Sayyid Muhammad *Unpublished Memories* (Tehran: Nashr' Abi Publishers, 1382 A.H /1962 C.E.), 21–23.

[101] Keddie, *Iran*, 67.

[102] Mottahedeh, *Politics and Religion*, 53.

[103] Ibid., 54.

[104] Keddie, *Iran*, 71.

[105] Abrahamian, *Between Two Revolutions*, 34–35.

Azerbaijan. General attitudes hardened among the leadership as demands shifted from simply a House of Justice to a Constitutional government and a National Assembly (*Majles-i Melli*).[106] In August 1906, the encircled and outmanoeuvred government yielded to the pressure of the general strike as news started to circulate of coming defections among the Cossacks and telegrams arrived from Baku and Tiflis threatening to send armed volunteers.[107]

The subsequent preparation of electoral law and formulation of the National Assembly showed great creativity in the wider emerging Iranian public sphere. Political organizations favouring the constitution multiplied in the form of professional associations and ethnic clubs for Zoroastrians, Armenians and Jews. The circulation of newspapers also leaped from 6 to over 100 during a 10-month period following the triumph of the Revolution with names such as *Unity*, *Awakening* and *Progress*. The old order had been overturned by a co-operation among merchants, street peddlers, wholesale dealers, shopkeepers, science and theology students, *ulama*, civil servants and members of numerous religious groups. When the National Assembly opened in October 1906 its social composition reflected the dominant role of the traditional middle class in being composed of 26 per cent guild elders, 20 per cent clergy men and 15 per cent merchants. It was made up of three groups in the Royalists (princes, nobles, landowners), the moderates (led by the merchants who had led the *sit-in* linked to the *ulama*) and the liberals (led by Taqizadeh and other intelligentsia).[108]

A process of interaction among diverse and potentially conflicting forces was behind the formulation of the new Iranian constitution. Power was disproportionately invested in Tehran, holding 60 seats to only 96 for all of the provinces combined. Basing itself on the Belgian Constitution, the National Assembly declared itself "the representative of the whole People."[109] Sovereignty was declared to be derived from the people and not God. The shah's real powers were stripped away. Under

---

[106] Katouzian, *Political Economy*, 59.
[107] Abrahamian, *Between Two Revolutions*, 85.
[108] Ibid., 85–88.
[109] Ibid., 88.

economically most oppressed in the absence of any politics on their behalf within the National Assembly.

At this conjuncture Muhammad Ali Shah—apparently fallen by the political wayside—emerged from his isolation and made steady headway in the modern political game of gaining public support. Underclass suffering from bad harvest, high inflation on food products and continued foreign subjection, manifested itself in hostility for the deputies of the National Assembly. A quiet recruitment programme began in the poorest quarters of the capital aiming to mobilize counter-revolution with promises of national independence, dignity, traditional continuity and food for the hungry. The seminal Shaykh Fazallah Nouri (1843–1909)—a respected and conservative mujtahed who had participated in the 1906 protest—joined these efforts in reaction to the hard anti-religious line of the radical Liberal wing. He represented some mullahs, who, having supported the revolution, now "saw that a constitution on a foreign model and ideas of justice not traditionally accepted in Shiah Islam had been pushed forward by the secular constitutionalists" and experienced a certain doubt about its implications for Shi'ism.[125] Attacking emergent civil society formations, Shaykh Fazallah declared journalists "non-Muslims for their support of the Assembly."[126] Yet he did not represent an "Islamic norm", for he also "met with the hostility of his own fellow *ulama*."[127]

Shaykh Fazallah argued that a human institution designed for legislative purpose offended Islam as "the Prime Legislator had already spoken" (i.e. the Qur'an).[128] In place of a Parliament, he promoted an assembly to implement the Islamic injunction "to command the good and forbid the evil."[129] Constitutional forms of government were inherently inauthentic, as were the Iranian constitutionalists for introducing "the customs and practices of the abode of disbelief."[130] This totalizing new vista countered

---

[125] Mottahedeh, *Politics and Religion*, 224.

[126] Ibid., 222

[127] Fakhreddin Azimi, *Iran: The Crisis of Democracy* (London: I.B. Tauris, 1989), 3.

[128] Mottahedeh, *Politics and Religion*, 132.

[129] Ibid., 222.

[130] Ibid., 221.

the historical Shari'a as the "nominal umbrella of a variety of different things [which] is by no means univocal."[131] It relinquished the *ulama*'s "independent power and prestige precisely because of their usual lack of direct association with the despotic apparatus."[132] The claim to *authenticity*, others quickly realized, could be levelled from all sides. Shaykh Fazallah was officially *unfrocked* and excommunicated by the Shi'ite leadership in the holy city of Najaf—to whom he had appealed for support—who supported the Constitutional Revolution.[133] This suggests that he was no traditionalist, but an innovator and renegade.

Shaykh Fazallah founded the 1907 Society of Mohammed to oppose the "heathen" constitutionalists. Encouraged by Muhammad Ali Shah, he led several thousand mullas, theology students, peasants, unskilled workers, and craftsmen to Cannon Square to a sermon denouncing "the concept of equality as an alien heresy."[134] The Liberal wing (he argued), like the French Jacobins, was paving the way to nihilism. Such a "metaphysic of decline," linked to the "irreducible essence of Islam," is a modern messianic package linked to categories of the European political imagination.[135] Underlying his counter-Enlightenment discourse was the fundamental opposition between *Mashru'eh* (Islamic law) and *Mashruteh* (constitution) that had earlier been introduced by Muhammad Ali Shah, with whom he hoped to share power in a future post-constitutional state.[136] Arousing the assembled crowd to the pitch of passion with his sermon, he intended to lead a march upon the National Assembly.

However, massive public support for the National Assembly turned the march back as a general strike ensued and 100,000 citizens appeared in the streets to defend it.[137] A foreign observer described the diversity of the crowd that rallied to defend the National Assembly. It included:

---

[131] Al-Azmeh, *Islams and Modernities*, 94.
[132] Katouzian, *Political Economy*, 63.
[133] Ibid., 64.
[134] Abrahamian, *Between Two Revolutions*, 95.
[135] Al-Azmeh, *Islams and Modernities*, 137.
[136] Katouzian, *Political Economy*, 63.
[137] Abrahamian, *Between Two Revolutions*, 95.

Europeanized young men with white collars, white-turbaned *mullas*, Sayyids with the green and blue insignia of their holy descent, the *kulah-nomadis* (felt-capped peasants and workmen), the brown *'abas* (cloaks) of the humble tradesfolk; all in whose hearts glowed the sacred fire gathered there to do battle in the cause of freedom.[138]

The description clearly shows the gravity of the mistake in imagining this seminal event in modern Iranian history as a perennial clash of *Islam* against *freedom* (i.e. in the monolithic caricatures of Bernard Lewis or Samuel Huntington in certain works).

Muhammad Ali Shah again retreated, swearing renewed loyalty to the constitution. Secretly his efforts persisted and he gained the financial support of a magnate threatened by new parliamentary budget cuts, as well as the backing of regional tribes unhappy with the power sharing arrangement under the new constitutional order.[139] Using the Russian-led Cossack brigade he newly assaulted the National Assembly in 1908, and carried out a successful coup d'état. Many leaders of the Constitutional movement were poisoned, strangled, tortured and banished. The sudden violent seizure of state power, however, proved inadequate. Masses of armed volunteers rose up in Tabriz, Isfahan and Rasht, followed by resistance in other cities and finally erupting in Tehran. The population was not prepared to lose the political gains of the Constitutional Revolution.

The Azerbaijani Provisional Government, standing in for the National Assembly, largely carried the ensuing civil war. Within a month the royal position had deteriorated and a new Grand Assembly convened in Tehran following the convergence of two rebel armies upon the capital. In the aftermath, a new electoral law was passed that reduced property qualifications and reduced Tehran's allocation from 60 seats to 15 as the government sought to reward those who had brought victory in the civil war.[140] By the end of 1908 the constitution had been secured. Evidence of partial popular support for the royalist cause during the civil war, however, demonstrated that the National Assembly—with

[138] Ibid., 95.
[139] Ibid., 96.
[140] Ibid., 101.

its neglect of social rights and rejection of tradition in favour of European modernity—had been partly unsuccessful in winning broad public hegemony. This discursive conjuncture reveals the gravity of ideas in the hegemonic struggle. One council member noted that while the traditional urban middle class had remained committed to the constitution, the "slums had been turned into hotbeds of reaction."[141] Shaykh Fazallah was hanged as a traitor following the Constitutional victory in 1909. His memory was later revived as a symbol of *authentic* resistance to *Occidentosis* in one of the seminal Iranian texts of the 20th century.[142]

BETWEEN DICTATORSHIP AND DEMOCRACY (1926-41)

The Reza Shah Pahlavi period (1926–41) derived ideologically from the extreme elements in the Liberal wing of the Constitutional Revolution. The nation-making path entailed elimination of the local, *freedom* from religion in favour of Aryan pre-Islamic heritage, contempt for the superstitious masses and the creation of modernity from above grounded in a single national identity conceived along *Western* lines. Reza Shah's bid for power was supported by "Iranian nationalists and modernists of various descriptions," and some *ulama*.[143] Support for his 1926 coup was grounded in disillusionment with the constitutional experiment, an outlook exemplified in historian and linguist Sayyed Ahmad Kasravi (1890–1946): "After twenty years of constitutional government [we] now know that that the blame [for backwardness] rests not with the rulers, but the ruled."[144] Beyond Kasravi's critique of popular superstitions and practices (which he eventually paid for with his life), there were strong new economic motivations.[145] The new middle class, expanded after World War I, applied pressure

[141] Ibid., 98.
[142] Jahal Al-e Ahmad, *Occidentosis: A Plague from the West* (Berkeley: Mizan Press, 1984), 27.
[143] Katouzian, *Musaddiq*, 25.
[144] Abrahamian, *Between Two Revolutions*, 126. There is a discussion of Kasravi in Mottahedeh Chapter 3.
[145] The Fedayan-e Islam, a small group of minor clerics and bazaar apprentices, demanded strict application of the Shari'a and in 1946 hacked Kasravi to death for his historical books criticizing Shi'ism.

the instigation of a group of mullahs a "supreme committee" of *ulama* was appointed to scrutinize all laws being passed in terms of their compatibility with the Shari'a—reproducing what is the traditionally consultative but not legislative role of the Shi'i *ulama* in relation to political power.[110] The shari'a was traditionally "a body of narratives relating to precedents to which is ascribed a paradigmatic status ... and have parallels ... in other traditions" rather than (as modern Islamists insist) a "code."[111] It was this traditional understanding of the shari'a that made possible the ambiguity of the "gospel of Shi'ism [being] incorporated into a modern structure of government derived from Montesquieu."[112]

In 1907, the Anglo-Russian Entente settled their differences over "Tibet, Afghanistan and Iran" by dividing Iran "into three spheres," with Iranians "neither consulted on the agreement nor informed of the terms when it was signed."[113] Muzaffer al-Din Shah had meanwhile sealed the Revolution by ratifying the constitution only days before his death, and the majles (Parliament) was to function within grave limits "as a guardian against certain foreign encroachments."[114] The constitutional struggle with royal authority, however, was only at its beginning. Muhammad Ali Shah (ruled 1907–09) began his short-lived reign determined to undo the Revolution's achievements and restore the style of rule from the reign of Nasar al-Din. His 1908 Russian-backed coup d'état—though provisionally successful—ended badly when was driven into exile by the Bakhtiari tribal and northern revolutionary Mujahidin forces.[115]

THE DISCURSIVE SHIFT TO COUNTER REVOLUTION

This brief 1908 episode concealed dramatic ideological and discursive transformations in the emerging Iranian public sphere.

---

[110] Mottahedeh, *Politics and Religion*, 221.
[111] Al-Azmeh, *Islams and Modernities*, 25.
[112] Abrahamian, *Between Two Revolutions*, 89–91.
[113] Keddie, *Iran*, 69–70.
[114] Ibid., 71.
[115] Ibid., 70.

Muhammad Ali Shah confronted the National Assembly by launching two consequential new lines of debate. Firstly, he replaced the liberal prime minister with a conservative premier who, having spent time in Japan, now believed that social reform could only be achieved by an autocratic central state. From this perspective, the constitution presented an obstruction to the goal of swift national unification and development.[116] Secondly, he tried to change the dominant terms of the constitutional–royalist debate. The true conflict was not between *constitutionalism* and *despotism*, but *constitutionalism* and *Islamic law*. He thereby created the grounds for identifying constitutionalism with an alien and hostile culture, i.e. as *inauthentic*.[117] Often viewed as a *return* to tradition, it was a strategic political construction in the modern state-power struggle.

These new and divisive political arguments—anticipating the modern romantic Islamism of Egyptian Sayyid Qutb (active as Islamist in the 1950–60s)—would have an afterlife in Iran well beyond Muhammad Ali Shah's ill fated reign, as surely as would the legacy of the Constitutional Revolution itself. The new categories twisted the struggle over the constitution and divided mullahs along previously concealed or non-existent lines, making it "wrong ... to characterize the mullahs at any period as either for or against the constitution."[118] The 1908 episode also revealed the population's capacity to employ effective non-violent public practices developed as a coordinated movement during the Tobacco and Constitutional revolts. Muhammad Ali Shah's initial challenge was his refusal to ratify the new Constitution on the grounds that he wished—citing the German constitution—to keep control over the armed forces. He rejected the guarantees of "citizen equality before the law, protection of life, property, and honor, safeguards from arbitrary arrest, and freedom to publish

---

[116] This view exists among contemporary historians to this day. It is sometimes tacit in Clawson/Rubin. Indeed, it was a predominant concept of development through much of the twentieth century across the political spectrum.

[117] Abrahamian, *Between Two Revolutions*, 89–91.

[118] Mottahedeh, *Politics and Religion*, 222–23.

newspapers and to organize associations" as well as the division of powers reducing royal authority to insignificance.¹¹⁹

The popular response was immediate and widespread public protest as the major cities conducted new *bestnishini* and strikes that paralyzed important sections of the economy including the telegraph offices. Numerous provinces, notably Azerbaijan, threatened to secede should the constitution not be ratified. The various associations also swiftly united in the Central Society to mount a general strike in the main bazaar and the government bureaucracy accompanied by a meeting of 50,000 and 3,000 armed volunteers to defend the National Assembly. These events culminated in the assassination of Prime Minister Amin al-Sultan, who had argued the unique legitimacy of an autocratic development path.¹²⁰ Muhammad Ali Shah retreated and agreed unconditionally to the National Assembly demands, even joining the Party of Humanity with a court entourage to demonstrate sincerity. The balance of power was profoundly reversed in terms of multiple organized elements of civil society functioning at a broad national level.

However, the National Assembly united front unravelled over several points, lending unexpected strength to the royalist political wing. This was hastened by Iran's division into British and Russian zones in anticipation of the coming struggle with imperial Germany. Coupled with still deepening economic crisis, it dampened the spirits of both Constitutional leaders and the general public. Many of those believing that Britain supported Constitutional aims, following the British legation *sit-in*, were disillusioned.¹²¹ This unhappy contingency fostered a public mood of persecution. It provided a fertile ground for politically harvesting the authenticity discourse introduced by Muhammad Ali Shah opposing constitutionalism and the Shari'a, or the *West* and the *East*. We have to understand this significant discursive shift at the national level in terms of precise conjunctures (i.e. changing attitudes to Britain, failures of the Constitutionalist discourse regarding the new urban poor), and not posited eternal

---

¹¹⁹ Abrahamian, *Between Two Revolutions*, 89.
¹²⁰ Ibid., 91.
¹²¹ Mansfield, 146.

essences where scholarship reproduces the imagined ideological terms of given strategic agents.[122]

The National Assembly faced a forking policy path between assimilation or pluralism, centralized or federalized power and the proper latitude of public inclusiveness for a democratic political system. These secular-institutional issues constitute the Enlightenment terrain of conflicts and differences. Debates addressed the Liberals' proposed electoral reform measures: the Moderates objected that in a largely illiterate country universal male suffrage constituted a dangerous opportunity for manipulation by forces of reaction; secondly, expanded representation for religious minorities was accused of subverting the Shari'a; and finally the enlargement of representation for provincial regions threatened national division and anarchy. The tensions over these issues were further aggravated by articles published outside of the Parliament by the more radical wing of the Liberal faction blaming the *decline* of the Middle East on "clerical ignorance, superstitions, petty-mindedness, obscurantism, dogmatism, and insistent meddling in politics."[123] The legitimacy of the Supreme Committee was thus attacked. The simultaneous founding of a girl's school provoked outrage among the religious conservative element, further triggering a deadlock. As a result important projects envisioned by the makers of the Constitutional Revolution, such as a free public education programme, were prevented from being carried out.[124]

Such policy conundrums corresponded to anomalies within clashing worldviews. The Liberal faction advocated universal suffrage while promoting the abolition of false popular religious beliefs, discursively grounded in pristine universal *human nature* awaiting emancipation beyond religious superstition. The Moderate faction aimed to represent the Iranian people while stratifying the diverse population to privilege the religion and language of the majority. Both wings, largely ignoring the issue of social rights, invited a rival political force to stand up for the

---

[122] This was Furet's critique of scholarly conventions on the French Revolution, but can be applied elsewhere.

[123] Abrahamian, *Between Two Revolutions*, 93.

[124] Keddie, *Iran*, 91.

The Reza Shah regime's ambition to reproduce the French and Turkish *universal* road to modernity was not adopted as a pure episteme, but was given ambiguous colour by multiple contemporary ideological cross-currents. In a journal describing the outlook of pro-Reza Khan reformers, *Iranshar* (Country of Iran), we find a celebration of pre-Islamic Iran and Voltaire's anticlericalism, Gobineau's racism, and Gustave le Bon's studies of the *irrational mob*. It was argued that the French Revolution provided a model on how to "liberate the *common masses* from clerical domination. The 7th-century Arab invasion explained Iran's *backwardness*. The country could never progress until freed from the "shackles of the superstitious and religious clergy." The journal cited the harmful effects of ethnic diversity, demanding the elimination of "local sects, local dialects, local clothes, local customs and local sentiments." On this basis it will be possible to "form a centralized state and a unified national identity."[170]

The campaign, according to *Iranshar*, envisioned "extending the Persian language throughout the provinces; eliminating regional costumes, destroying local and feudal authorities; and removing the traditional differences between Kurds, Lurs, Qashqayis, Arabs, Turkomans, and other communities that reside within Iran." This discourse of forced assimilation as the basis for nation-making was legitimized by such modern historical precedents as Germany, Italy, Poland, Rumania and the Ottoman Empire. The policy toward the tribes was also conceived on the basis of achieving "one people, one nation, one language, one culture"; viewed as part of a "primitive state of nature," they were disarmed, conscripted and forced into "model villages."[171] There was no natural or inevitable logic to this nation-making scheme, however numerous the precedents. It was a discursive formation taken for the unique road to modernity.

It follows that provincial territories suffered under Reza Shah's regime, and Azerbaijan—that had contributed perhaps most to the pluralistic heritage of the Constitutional Revolution—experienced hardship during this 15-year period. The period of *one man rule* ended when Reza Shah was toppled from power by the 1941 Allied Occupation, fleeing into South African exile

---

[170] Abrahamian, *Between Two Revolutions*, 123–53.
[171] Ibid., 123–53.

where he died three years later. Britain's prior conviction—that Reza Shah's "remarkable hold over his people warranted his retention"—had dwindled, and his refusal to expel his Axis nationals on command provoked mistrust. The time came to remove him. He was removed.

The 1941 invasion saw widespread panic as Tehran experienced "sporadic bombing" and the "speedy disintegration of the army which flooded its streets with 50,000 shabbily dressed and hungry conscripts." The hegemonic dimension was the regime's undoing. We can explain "Reza Shah's astonishing loss of nerve in the face of the Allied invasion only in terms of his complete lack of any popular power base."[172] The country found the despotic machinery empty and the Parliament—functioning as a rubber stamp—once again became a meaningful centre of power. The suppressed ministers and political leaders returned from hiding to shape the country's future following years of political repression under a dictator's will. In this moment independence and democracy were the most popular political demands in the country and it appeared briefly—before falling to Mossadeq and the National Front—as if "the Tudeh Party would be the organizer and standard bearer of the Popular Movement."[173]

Iranian civil society newly awoke as workers unions were formed, new political parties organized, and the print media revitalized. The number of Iranian periodicals in publication leaped from 41 to 582 after the fall of Reza Shah. There was a swift renewal of guilds, associations and other voluntary societies. Out of numerous labour organizations the Council of United Workers was formed by the summer of 1942 representing over 26 industrial, craft and white collar unions. By 1944, the Central Union of Federated Trade Unions of Iranian Workers and Toilers had been formed, and British foreign office documents record the number of union members at 75 per cent of the total industrial labour force in Iran.[174] Political parties became, for the first time, the "dominant forms of political participation and citizen involvement in national affairs."[175] The National Front, the Tudeh Party,

---

[172] Azimi, *Crisis of Democracy*, 36–37.
[173] Katouzian, *Musaddiq*, 43.
[174] Mirsepassi, *Intellectual Discourse*, 67–68.
[175] Ibid., 67–68.

the Democratic Party of Iran, the Democratic Party of Azerbaijan and the Democratic Party of Kurdistan were the most prominent among an ever changing and chaotic labyrinth of political parties and organizations. The historical interval of the post-Reza Shah period therefore presented a "rare historical opportunity to construct the democratic political structure and secular pluralist culture that the country had strived for so long to achieve."[176]

In the period between "1941 and 1951, [before] Mosaddeq became prime minister, cabinets generally did not last more than a few months, and there were revolts in the provinces and destructive conflict within the Majles itself."[177] During this transitional interval, Iran bordered on an open conflict situation. The strong incentive to participate in the run-up to elections did not translate into stable peace in their aftermath. Iran found itself in a situation of dual sovereignty between the revived Parliament and the new monarch Muhammed Reza Shah Pahlavi (1941–79) who enjoyed neither "the backing of the Allies nor any sustained domestic support."[178] Although he had inherited a drastically shrunken version of his father's absolute power, a nationwide struggle over political power was in the making. Five poles of contending national power existed: the court, the Parliament (*Majles*), the cabinet, the foreign embassies and the fragmented general public, with each centre containing its own multiple inner conflicts.[179] The suppressed national tensions of the Reza Shah period materialized upon two plateaus: severe class antagonisms within the towns and ethnic rivalries in the countryside.[180] The post-dictatorial development power landscape was dangerous regional and class inequality where the "upper and new middles classes became increasingly Westernized and scarcely understood the traditional or religious culture of most of their compatriots."[181] This cultural and class gulf—the contingent creation of the modernization scheme in population

---

[176] Ibid., 66.
[177] Mark J. Gasiorowski and Malcolm Bryne, eds., *Mohammed Mosaddeq and the 1953 Coup in Iran* (Syracuse: Syracuse University Press, 2004), 3.
[178] Azimi, *Crisis of Democracy*, 37.
[179] Abrahamian, *Between Two Revolutions*, 170.
[180] Ibid., 172.
[181] Keddie, *Iran*, 111.

restructuration—became a powerful axis for politicization under the nostalgic banner of *tradition*.

Ahmad Qavam (1876–1955), a constitutional monarchist dubbed the *old fox* for his political cunning, became premier in 1941. Aspiring to severe Muhammed Reza Shah from the military, he was soon confronted with the Azerbaijan crisis. The Azerbaijanis, being a Turkic-speaking people, were angered by the Aryanisation policy under Reza Shah which forbade them (following Ataturk's minority policy) "to learn to read and write their own mother tongue."[182] Meanwhile, the Soviet Union remained in northern Iran following Allied departure. It was viewed with admiration by many Iranians for its heroic struggle against fascism during World War II. Its oil concession demand in Azerbaijan raised the boundary problem between Iranian national autonomy and Soviet interests. Following the violently homogenizing national politics, the regional provinces (i.e. Azerbaijan and Kurdistan) sought greater political autonomy with the sympathy of progressive opinion in Tehran.[183] The Democratic Party of Azerbaijan became entangled in the Soviet occupation and the fate of the Tudeh Party.

The Tudeh Party, a powerful nationwide political organization, was founded in 1941 as "a coalition of radical and progressive Iranians" who were "initially committed to Iranian national independence" while applauding "the Soviet Union as the champion of anti-fascist struggle and an ally of the Third World and colonized countries."[184] The Tudeh Party was critical in spreading an ideal of social rights among the Iranian masses. It upheld the

> general conviction that the state had the moral responsibility to provide citizens with basic necessities [with the popular slogan]: 'Work for All, Education for All, Health for All.' Rights became associated more with social democracy than with laissez-faire liberal democracy [and] it introduced into politics the demand for land reform and for root-and-branch transformation of landlord–peasant relationships.[185]

[182] Katouzian, *Musaddiq*, 59.
[183] Katouzian, *Political Economy*, 150.
[184] Mirsepassi, *Intellectual Discourse*, 69.
[185] Abrahamian, *Modern Iran*, 113.

for investment and modernization, the development of a national market and central control over the provinces.[146] Following a successful campaign of intimidation against parliamentary deputies, only four voted against deposing the Qajars to clear the way for Reza Shah's rise to power.[147]

Mosaddeq, one of them, voiced resistance on the eve of Reza Shah's seizure of power in parliamentary speeches: "If they cut off my head and mutilate my body, I would never agree to such a decision. After twenty years of blood-letting [for freedom and democracy] do you now believe that someone should be both shah and prime minister and ruler?"[148] The means employed in Reza Shah's new road to national *regeneration* from above were violence and the crushing of civil society—that is, of the very texture and ground of the Popular Movement. In this period the Parliament was reduced to a merely "ceremonial function," all independent newspapers were closed down, political parties destroyed and all trade unions banned.[149] Strikes were outlawed and low wages were the rule.[150] It was superficially a period of political quiet and order, concealing an inferno of hidden internal conflicts beneath an iron fist. Mosaddeq described this as the moment where the "imperfect freedom" of the Constitutional era was "destroyed."[151] Initially, certain radical secular nationalists and women's rights advocates willingly endured Reza Shah's complete power monopoly, persuaded via prevalent discursive constructions that the ends justified the means.[152]

Reza Khan seized power in early 1921 voicing his aims in strong nationalist terms. The oil industry continued at this point to "have little effect on Iranian socioeconomic life" and remained an isolated enclave controlled by the British.[153] This British influence on the oil-producing regions persisted and Britain did not

---

Ervand Abrahamian, *A History of Modern Iran* (Cambridge: Cambridge University Press, 2008), 116.

[146] Keddie, *Iran*, 87.
[147] Ibid., 86.
[148] Katouzian. *Musaddiq*, 25.
[149] Abrahamian, *Between Two Revolutions*, 138–39.
[150] Keddie, *Iran*, 94.
[151] Musaddiq, *Memoirs*, 434.
[152] Keddie, *Iran*, 88.
[153] Ibid., 86.

object to the coup.¹⁵⁴ Reza Shah promised to "initiate an age of national revival by ending internal disagreement, implementing social transformation, and saving the country from foreign occupation."¹⁵⁵ In 1925, he deposed the Qajar dynasty and took the imperial throne. From 1925 to 1941, we see "the partial fulfilment of a far larger modernization program than had ever been attempted in Iran."¹⁵⁶

Reza Shah implemented an ambitious national development programme without freedom. New national roads laid the infrastructure for economic and particularly industrial development. State administration was developed in the urban sectors by raising revenue from the rural masses, and state power was extended to the remotest towns. Between 1925 and 1941, the annual allocations for education increased twelvefold. The intelligentsia was transformed from a narrow stratum into a modern middle class. A modern working class was created largely out of the developing oil industry.¹⁵⁷ Reza Shah changed the law, introducing a version of the French Civil Code. The *ulama* were stripped of traditional land and power.¹⁵⁸ From 1925 to 1930, a uniform school curriculum was introduced on the French model. The armed forces—the main public expenditure—and the bureaucracy grew in the centralization campaign along with the size of Tehran's population.¹⁵⁹ In the rural provinces, 95–98 per cent of the agricultural population remained landless even into the dynamic growth period of the 1930s.¹⁶⁰

Reza Khan was unable to fulfil his national independence promise. He cancelled the D'Arcy concession in 1932 but signed an equally unfavourable agreement the following year, threatened with losing Iran's foreign assets. The AIOC "had not only turned an important part of the country into an almost autonomous colony, but [it] indirectly ran the country as well,"

---

¹⁵⁴ Stephen C. Poulson, *Social Movements in Twentieth Century Iran: Culture, Ideology and Mobilizing Frameworks* (Lanham: Lexington Books, 2006), 140.
¹⁵⁵ Abrahamian, *Between Two Revolutions*, 118.
¹⁵⁶ Keddie, *Iran*, 89.
¹⁵⁷ Abrahamian, *Between Two Revolutions*, 137–47.
¹⁵⁸ Ibid., 140.
¹⁵⁹ Keddie, *Iran*, 89–92.
¹⁶⁰ Ibid., 96.

practicing discrimination in pay, conditions and services against Iranian workers and refusing "to show its accounts to the Iranian government."[161] Reza Khan's autocratic development scheme, therefore, depended upon continued Iranian subordination to foreign power interests.

Liberal Enlightenment reforms followed an autocratic logic in envisioning an ideal with neither public choice nor participation (i.e. suppression or control of civil society). Reza Khan's long-range goal of rebuilding Iran culturally modelled on *Western* modernity followed Ataturk's discursive–practical precedent.[162] He imposed the wearing of European brimmed hats as "international" headgear, with the aim of eradicating visible ethnic difference. Reza Shah would "inaugurate a reform a year or two after a nearly identical one had appeared in Turkey."[163] In raising the status of women, Reza Khan did not give them the vote but opened access to higher education. The veil was outlawed unilaterally without regard for the public perceptions as a matter of *higher knowledge*.

The modernization programme included a limited hegemonic campaign. There was discursive grounding in a partial Enlightenment horizon—widespread at the time—of rebirth from above. Reza Khan initially used "the army, through a policy of national conscription, to indoctrinate young Iranian men with the concept of Iranian nationalism" increasingly "influenced by fascist doctrines espoused by the Germans."[164] New 20th-century counter-Enlightenment discursive components therefore interacted with the received authoritarian Enlightenment horizon. Violence, according to this scheme, was par for the course as opponents were systematically jailed and terrorized. Reza Shah's path to power was "paved not simply by violence, armed force, terror, and military conspiracies, but by alliances with diverse groups inside and outside the Fourth and Fifth National Assemblies" (1923–24) including the Reformers' Party, the Revival Party, the Socialist and the Communist Parties. These collaborators—including conservatives and reformers, radicals

---

[161] Katouzian, *Musaddiq*, 64.
[162] Abrahamian, *Between Two Revolutions*, 121–44.
[163] Keddie, *Iran*, 92.
[164] Poulson, *Social Movements*, 141.

and revolutionaries—ideologically embraced the discursive construction of a rapid and effective road to national unification and empowerment. This scheme required a *revolutionary dictator* to forcibly liberate the ignorant masses. Violence was sublimated through dimensions of the Enlightenment heritage combined with other discursive components. In the Fifth National Assembly the Revival Party, formed of "young Western educated reformers who had previously supported the Democrats," held a majority under Reza Khan's guiding hand.[165] Classes benefitting included "government employees, army officers, students, professionals and merchants" while the conditions of the poor deteriorated.[166]

However, Reza Khan successively alienated the majority of his traditional middle class and later modern middle class supporters through concentrating power within his own hands and wealth largely within the court, and by his continued servile relation to Britain in seeking these ends. Into the 1930s, "Britain continued to reap huge profits and pay low royalties" and remained "economic masters [in] the oil industry."[167] The modernization drive reflected personal arrogance. An astronomically expensive North–South Trans-Iranian Railway was built through regressive taxes that overwhelmingly hurt the poor, but which was less useful or practical than a cheaper national road system.[168]

The open deployment of violence—as discursively justified—widened the gulf between Reza Shah and the Iranian population. Authoritarian development confronts the structural conundrum of creating a civil society while striving to dominate it. His politics of "often-forcible suppression of discussion and opposition and the neglect of the rural and tribal majority" were an ideological option—echoing the French and Turkish *universal* experience—based on violence in his programme to "modernize a society with so many divisive centers of power."[169] Even his closest subordinates suffered. Taqizadeh—an early enthusiast for total *Westernization*—lost his ambassadorship in Paris and through a string of excuses remained there in eternal exile.

---

[165] Abrahamian, *Between Two Revolutions*, 121–44.
[166] Ibid., 92.
[167] Keddie, *Iran*, 101.
[168] Ibid., 93.
[169] Ibid., 103.

This outlook was increasingly stifled in the contradictory maze of Cold War politics and ideologies. In 1943, the Tudeh Party would grant no further concessions to any foreign power. Yet, when the Soviet Union demanded its oil concession the following year the Tudeh Party extended full support on *ideological* grounds. The Tudeh Party evolved towards a Stalinist pro-Moscow Party, ultimately losing much public support. International political pressures transformed "the Tudeh party [into] the local evangelical force of the Stalinist faith by 1949."[186] The Final Revolution was constructed as a mesmeric loyalty obligation with the force of monotheist Judgement Day, and only obedience to the Soviet Union placed one upon the right side of a totalizing impending historical divide.

The political nuts and bolts were inevitably less luminous than this heady Enlightenment prophecy. When Azerbaijani autonomy was bloodlessly seized by the Azerbaijani Democratic Party in 1945, it was done under Soviet military protection. In 1946, the Qavam–Sadchikov agreement granted the Soviet Union a 50-year concession for north Iranian oil in return for leaving Iranian territory. Azerbaijan was subsequently invaded by Iranian troops and a massacre ensued. These events explain Mosaddeq's rise as the dominant nationalist leader after 1949. He embraced Enlightenment values while rejecting the heritage's dogmatic and violent epistemic dimensions. His National Front organization offered an Iranian alternative to the many Left-inclined individuals disillusioned with the Tudeh Party following the Azerbaijani crisis. Mosaddeq noted the common end and differing vision, saying the "Tudeh party and the National Front were, and still are, opposed to the dictatorial regime, each from a different angle, and for different reasons."[187] This happened upon the post-Reza Shah power terrain involving a struggle between "the battered forces of despotism and the anti-despotic forces of both left and right: landlords and big businessmen belonged to the *conservative,* and the middle merchants, retailers, artisans, workers, younger intellectuals and students to the *radical,* wing of this broad anti-despotic tendency."[188]

---

[186] Katouzian, *Musaadiq,* 50.
[187] Musaddiq, *Memoirs,* 430.
[188] Katouzian, *Political Economy,* 165.

The Tudeh Party split in early 1948, producing an alternative socialist movement linked to the National Front led by Khalil Maleki (1903–69).[189] Maleki explained that communism had come to constitute a "faith" and the Soviet Union a "centre of power."[190] He argued that the Soviet Union had "destroyed economic, political and personal freedoms in Russia," and called for a Third Force committed to a "socialist approach which is consistent with the progressive tenets of European democracy." Reacting to the Soviet takeover of Czechoslovakia, Indian independence and Nehru's non-alignment, and revolutionary movements against imperialism in Vietnam and China, Maleki defined the Third Force as a coalition united in building "an independent road to socialism on the basis of each country's peculiar culture and traditions." He urged the masses of "Asia, Europe, Africa and elsewhere" to reject the bipolar Cold War and "co-operate with each other" while protecting *"their own national and social character and identity."*[191]

Maleki revived the democratic pluralist discourse of the Popular Movement in response to the lessons of the Constitutional Revolution, Reza Shah and new global events. His conviction, shared in acknowledged fashion with the Indian national movement, concerned the necessary linking of development and freedom, and socialism and democracy. These were learnings, not doctrinal dogmas. Mosaddeq articulated this conviction in affirming that "technical and economic progress must involve the people's consent," with "freedom, law and democracy" being more important than "technical progress." Rejecting modernist rupture, he spoke of *Iraniyat va Islamiyat* (the Iranian and Islamic way of life).[192] Yet he kept sight of this as a global and democratic process, with "people everywhere [in the world] rising up to bring down despotic regimes, and establishing constitutional governments in their place."[193] Notably, there was no illusion that

---

[189] Homa Katouzian, ed., *The Political Memoirs of Khalil Maleki* (Tehran: Enteshar, 1988).
[190] Katouzian, *Musaddiq*, 97.
[191] Ibid., 101–03.
[192] Ibid., 28.
[193] Musaddiq, *Memories*, 309.

rule of law is merely a *bourgeois* prejudice to be dispensed with on the road to an inevitably greater reality through dictatorship.

Mosaddeq's political vision centred an ethic of inclusiveness and reconciliation. Deploring exclusion, he argued that "the root of every discontent in society is discrimination."[194] He envisioned a widely pluralistic organization as the basis for the national movement, arguing that "Iran, with its many conflicting groups, does not need a disciplined party with a precise program. On the contrary, Iran needs a loose coalition of organizations in a national front with a general and broad program." On this basis he refused "to establish yet another political party."[195] Yet he was also a nationalist who aspired to "speak for the nation as a whole," with the obvious idea that this was not possible through one supreme or dominant voice.[196] From the outset Mosaddeq appeared opposed to an ideologically monistic political structure based in a completed or fixed idea of nation-making and adopted an ideologically heterogeneous approach. At the same time, he had political tactics for struggle, i.e. means, which were non-violent, rooted in civil society, and sometimes leaned upon a form of populism or the *general will* which in one instance appealed to the masses above the formal institutions of government.

The National Front was formed in 1949 following the swift seizure of power by the Shah through a policy of martial law following the assassination attempt on his life. This restored powers, on the eve of the 16th *Majles* elections, similar to the pre-1941 period. The Left-migration to the National Front included several main organizations. Firstly, the Iran Party shifted from a pro-Tudeh to a pro-Mosaddeq position between 1947–49, retaining its socialist ideology and professional middle class base in engineers, university students, government ministers and modern educated women. It called for national independence and the creation of a socialist society. Citing Montesquieu, it aspired to a constitutional monarchy. It promoted neutralism in international affairs and non-violent means in ousting the aristocracy within the framework of constitutional law. It also opposed "atheistic

---

[194] Ibid., 365.
[195] Abrahamian, *Between Two Revolutions*, 225.
[196] Ibid., 253.

international communism" in the name of the "legitimate rights of religion and national identity."[197]

Secondly, the Toilers Party, composed largely of shopkeepers and students, was also led by a defector from the Tudeh Party. It also called for national independence and expressed opposition to "all forms of imperialism, including Russian imperialism." The party adopted a universalist outlook, claiming to "identify with the peoples of Africa, Asia and Latin America, with the democratic movements in Europe, with the rank and file of the Tudeh dissatisfied with pro-Russian undemocratic leadership." It published critical essays on the writings of figures such as Richard Wright, Karl Marx, Andre Gide and Bertrand Russell and on movements such as the Chartists or Yugoslav workers' control. It declared a "respect for Islam because it is the religion of our people."[198] Though not resembling any dominant model for a political programme along the conventional modernity-tradition binary, its sometimes contradictory ideological configuration matched the aspirations of much of the growing Iranian popular movement at this time. These movements rejected the ideology of the Reza Shah period. They deemphasized "ancient Iranian empires" and were not anti-Islam, anti-Arab or anti-Turk. Nor did they plan to recover lost Iranian territories which were now either independent or within the Soviet Union. The more extreme nationalist fringe of the Nationalist Front umbrella, including youth groups who dabbled in forms of fascist politics, were forced to modify their aims or leave the Popular Movement.[199]

Mosaddeq's thought and practice was a context-specific and pragmatic Iranian variant on the tradition of universal Enlightenment. He was viewed as "an educated man who was deeply rooted in Iranian traditions."[200] He gained "prestige and popularity" through "his championing of causes likely to benefit the entire nation, and particularly its middle and lower classes," a line of action which "distinguished him from the bulk of the Iranian ruling class."[201] It was his "charisma and lifelong cour-

[197] Ibid., 253–57.
[198] Ibid.
[199] Katouzian, *Musaddiq*, 89.
[200] Katouzian, *Political Economy*, 148.
[201] Azimi, *Crisis of Democracy*, 259.

age and honesty [that] made him vastly popular with most Iranians."²⁰² Mosaddeq's programme, which "threatened the traditional configuration of clan politics and alarmed the Court and the pro-British elements," consisted of "only two points: implementation of the oil nationalization law and the utilization of revenues for the improvement of the economy; and reform of the parliamentary and municipal electoral laws."²⁰³

Mosaddeq stood uncompromisingly for Iranian national independence, as his financially reasoned 1944 parliamentary speech on the robbery of Allied occupation encapsulated.²⁰⁴ In response to the Tudeh argument that the Soviet oil monopoly functioned as a countervailing force against British power in Iran, Mosaddeq called this analogous to asking "a person one of whose hands has been amputated to have the remaining hand cut off."²⁰⁵ He claimed that "the moral aspect of oil nationalization is more important than its economic aspect."²⁰⁶ He viewed the AIOC as an "exploitative and iniquitous enclave with a revenue exceeding the earnings of the Iranian Government," and which had "led to the moral decay of Iranian politicians, the corruption and dependency of their governments and the destitution of the people." Recognizing the "importance of oil revenues for welfare and economic development, he also believed that if necessary it was better for Iran to be poor and independent than to tolerate the survival of the AIOC and remain under British domination."²⁰⁷

Mosaddeq's political framework was a moral rather than epistemic universalism, or nationalism without essence. This extended as well to his critical reconstruction of the received nationalist paradigm within Iran as inherited from the Iranian Constitutional Revolution. He moved beyond the construction of Iranian historical memory as merely dogmatism and fanaticism to be transcended, and sought to make it a resource for a progressive national political movement. His vision was of self-reliance among the people. He promoted the "spread of literacy and

---

²⁰² Keddie, *Iran*, 126.
²⁰³ Azimi, *Crisis of Democracy*, 259.
²⁰⁴ Katouzian, *Political Economy*, 143.
²⁰⁵ Ibid., 154.
²⁰⁶ Katouzian, *Musaddiq*, 92.
²⁰⁷ Azimi, *Crisis of Democracy*, 260.

education in the rural areas" to provide peasants the autonomy to "press for laws which they realize to be in their interest."[208] He did not seek to dictate their interest to them based on a master development plan.

Mosaddeq emphasized the urgency of social rights in nation-making, explaining the spread of communism in terms of "the obscene gap in the living standards between the few and the many" and the "disillusionment of patriotic people arising from the collusion of imperialist powers [with] corrupt and dishonest individuals."[209] He has been described as "the lightening rod that lay both chronologically and intellectually at the center of Iranian politics of the twentieth century," and as the leader who came "closer than anyone else to ending the tradition of [Iranian] monarchy" before the 1979 Revolution.[210] His politics, however, were not utopian, and unlike many of his contemporaries he was not fixated on the ideal model of the French Revolutionary legacy at any price. His priority being freedom, he observed that there were "many republics which lack freedom, and many constitutional monarchies which enjoy complete freedom and independence."[211]

Despite the new shape Mosaddeq gave to Iranian popular politics, he viewed himself within the tradition of the Iranian Constitutional Revolution and saw his political work as the "completion of the Constitutional Movement."[212] He mobilized a different and opposed aspect of that heritage to the Reza Khan authoritarian stream. Rejecting epistemic totality-based authoritarianism, he championed rule of law and public liberty. In 1925, he had stood among the few to openly challenge Reza Shah's rise to absolute power, arguing in the Parliament that if "we take this retrograde step and say he is king, prime minister, ruler, everything, this is nothing but reaction and autocracy."[213] He condemned the shah's development plan as grandiose and

---

[208] Musaddiq, *Memories*, 441.
[209] Ibid., 442.
[210] Mottahedeh, *Politics and Religion*, 115–16.
[211] Musaddiq, *Memoirs*, 354.
[212] Abrahamian, *Between Two Revolutions*, 190.
[213] Mottahedeh, *Politics and Religion*, 124.

ill-suited to the country's specific needs.²¹⁴ In the wake of this he spent much of the Reza Shah period either in prison or under house arrest, using his time in the 1930s for sugar beet cultivation, well drilling, opening a primary school and running a medical dispensary out of his home.²¹⁵

Mosaddeq attempted to seriously engage the problem of creating a space for reconciling Iranian traditional Shi'i law and modern constitutional law. This was in part the subject of his 1914 doctoral thesis. Running against "a thousand years of Shiah thought in asserting the superiority of reason to other sources of law," he "developed a historical scheme that completely justified his turning the tradition upside down."²¹⁶ Mosaddeq therefore engaged the Enlightenment heritage in an open, critical and non-dogmatic way. He identified the historical epoch following the Constitutional Revolution as one in which law is no longer a stationary entity to be *discovered* in conformity with religion but rather something to be *made* within the specific context of evolving modern conditions. At the same time he promoted a consultative role for jurisconsults versed in Shi'i legal tradition. In this way, he preserved a vision, grounded in historicity and not historicism, of the future as open and needing to be made.

This amounted at the epistemic level to the argument that legislation is not the "search for a reading of God's mind detached from cultural and social circumstances" but a flexible and adaptive endeavour dedicated to a democratic politics and without final ends.²¹⁷ He in this way attempted to give the Shari'a a modern temporal political basis adapted to democratic conditions of ongoing multi-perspective negotiation and social reform. These efforts reflected Mosaddeq's conviction that Shi'a Islam is "one of the most important parts of the cultural and social world of Iranians." Arguing that "Iranian solutions must take heed of Shiah beliefs," he opposed the idea of modernization as a politics of "imitating Europe."²¹⁸

---

[214] Musaddiq, *Memoirs*, 435.
[215] Mottahedeh, *Politics and Religion*, 124.
[216] Ibid., 119.
[217] Ibid., 120–21.
[218] Ibid., 121.

THE INTERREGNUM 1941-53 AND THE IRANIAN POPULAR MOVEMENT (NEHZAT-E MELLI)

In 1941 Mosaddeq emerged from his political exile a man "proven 'pure' in motive by his consistency through long life experience," having "fulfilled an essential moral drama that Iranians expect to see performed on the political stage."[219] This suggests the importance of moral virtue in the hegemonic struggle. In the early forties he fought against concessions through the parliament, passing a bill in 1944 forbidding the Cabinet to even discuss concessions with foreigners.[220] In the late forties following the declaration of martial law he undertook the leadership of the main opposition movement to the Shah deriving political legitimacy from the tradition of the Constitutional Revolution. Public support for the Shah was very low at this time because his recent political coup evoked dark memories of the dictatorial period of his father; newspapers were suppressed and the Tudeh Party had been banned. The Shah's unwillingness to confront Britain over the oil controversy undid any national credibility as a nationalist leader he might otherwise have had.

Mosaddeq's politics created him dangerous enemies. The opposition was composed largely of "conservative, unpopular and discredited elements ... directly or indirectly in contact with the British Embassy," some of whom were "purely opportunist" while others "conceived of Iranian interests along the same lines as the British." They considered it *naïve* to believe it possible to prevail over Britain and establish full sovereignty over Iranian oil, and saw Mosaddeq's policy as "paving the way to Soviet penetration."[221] The Soviet Union, and therefore the Tudeh Party, interpreted the nationalization of Iranian oil as a conspiracy cemented between Mosaddeq and the United States.[222] It was Mosaddeq's refusal to take coercive action against these adversaries, permitting free reign to all movement within civil society even at the height of his emergency powers, which partly explains his undoing. It was because the banning of any political

---

[219] Ibid., 125.
[220] Ibid., 126.
[221] Azimi, *Crisis of Democracy*, 265.
[222] Katouzian, *Musaddiq*, 115.

party would have been inconsistent with Musaddiq's political ideals that his government failed to "prevent campaigns of defamation, disruption and destruction against itself." [223] This partly explains why his political leadership did not survive the fatal challenges of the early 1950s.

In late 1949, prior to the Shah's US trip in search of foreign aid, Mosaddeq led a large procession of politicians, university students and bazaar traders into the palace gardens to perform a *bastnishini* in protest against the lack of free elections. This action applied enough force to make the court promise to end electoral fraud and led to the formation of the broad coalition of the National Front (*Jeb'eh-i Melli*). Within the tradition of the Constitutional Revolution, the movement was launched with a non-violent protest. The National Front put forward three demands: "honest elections, lifting of martial law and freedom of the press."[224] The National Front—as with the Constitutional Revolutionary tradition it extended—faced the uncharted contradictions and ambiguities in creating a modern civil society rule of law based on parliamentary democracy and full national independence. These contradictions were the result of differences between the modern and the traditional middle classes in terms of—for example—ideals of state development versus free trade, or the Napoleonic code versus the Shari'a as the principle component of legitimate law.[225] These contradictions had serious practical consequences in terms of, for example, the movement to extend suffrage to women. Yet for all the tensions resulting from these sometimes incompatible elements, the practical framework encasing the Constitutional Revolutionary heritage was adequate to unite the modern and traditional classes at least during the period of common struggle—i.e. a representative parliamentary body unifying the Iranian nation on the basis of the rule of law. Consensus was a provisional end, not an ontological point of departure.

Mosaddeq's leadership of the National Front was an experiment in creating a political force capable of reconciling these social elements within the framework of a democratic political

---

[223] Ibid., 114.
[224] Abrahamian, *Between Two Revolutions*, 252.
[225] Ibid., 259.

organization at a time when Iran knew a "relative invisibility of religious politics" in terms of any call for an anti-secular religious dictatorship.[226] It is for this reason that the Iranian popular movement, in spite the weaknesses which partly explain its final undoing by its opponents, is a fascinating and worthwhile experiment to consider as a case of concrete mass political action on a national scale. In 1950, the 16th *Majles* began stocked with royalists installed illicitly through the Shah's increasing power monopoly. Taking up the court on its promise to end electoral fraud, the National Front sponsored candidates in the main cities as well as functioning through the civil network of the populace. There was a multi-centred mobilization. It organized guild strikes against proposed tax increases on tradesmen and craftsmen and mobilized protests among bakers against government inefficiency in delivering wheat. A series of public meetings in the university and the bazaars culminated in a rally of 12,000 outside of the parliament building. These events climaxed with the assassination of the court minister Abul Hussein Hezhir by the Fedayan-e Islam, a small group of religiously driven minor clerics and bazaar apprentices, on the supposed grounds that he was a "secret Bahai."[227]

Under this fierce public pressure (combining semi-organized popular non-violent practices and uncontrolled violent acts by organized minority groups) new elections in Tehran were ordered by the prime minister in which Mosaddeq and seven of his colleagues won. Although this was merely eight out of the already installed 130 deputies, the subsequent months showed that "the eight, supported by the middle classes, could shake not only Parliament but also the shah and the whole country."[228] The parliament took on an increasingly volatile continuity with popular activity in the streets. This opening moment typified the entire approach of the Iranian popular movement of the late 40s and early 50s under Mosaddeq's leadership.

With the aim of creating an independent and democratic Iranian society based on the rule of law, Mosaddeq consistently

---

[226] Mirsepassi, *Intellectual Discourse*, 68.
[227] Abrahamian, *Modern Iran*, 116.
[228] Abrahamian, *Between Two Revolutions*, 261.

drew from the nationalist passion of the masses as if seeking to drive the state by the force of these elemental energies. In 1951 he "turned to the people" when his "national loan scheme was not well received by the rich."[229] The Parliament followed the popular sentiment manifested on the street, with mass demonstrations in 1951 being "so marked that the majles turned completely to a pro-Mosaddeq position" on the oil question under their influence.[230] Seeking to pursue the policy of an "oil-less economy" following failed negotiations with the World Bank in 1952, Mosaddeq refused further aid from the United States when pressured to commit himself to defence of the "free world." This involved, as well, his objection to a reference to "backward countries" in the provision for aid payment, saying he felt "ashamed to hear it being said that backward nations must be helped."[231]

Mosaddeq sought to undertake the democratic transformation of the Iranian society on the basis of sheer popular momentum from within. He argued that other "nations [also] bore heavy costs for freedom and independence until they realized their goals," yet unlike many nations Iran in this instance attempted this transformation under an emerging democratic system with full civil rights that was riven with lines of a merciless power struggle.[232] As poverty increased due to lost oil revenues, it was the "government's great popularity which enabled it to take such unpopular measures without provoking a backlash of public opinion against itself."[233] The mass movement was embedded in the new communication possibilities created by modern technology. Mosaddeq was the "first Middle Eastern leader to create a vast following by using the radio."[234] This exemplifies the populist or voluntarist current in Mosaddeq's outlook, which would ultimately prove compromising to his simultaneous lifelong legalist or constitutionalist ideals. The newly installed National Front declared that "although its delegation was small its voice would be clear and loud since it represented the whole nation."

---

[229] Azimi, *Crisis of Democracy*, 280.
[230] Keddie, *Iran*, 124.
[231] Azimi, *Crisis of Democracy*, 280–81.
[232] Musaddiq, *Memoirs*, 359.
[233] Katouzian, *Musaddiq*, 155.
[234] Mottahedeh, *Politics and Religion*, 127.

Mosaddeq charged the existing Constituent Assembly, filled with royalists from trumped elections, to be "fake and illegitimate." He argued that the "country belongs to the people and the people have the right to choose their representatives" and that only the people "have the right to change the constitution."[235]

Yet almost immediately the different elements within the National Front were pursuing differing paths to national reconstruction. These differences generally concerned the degree of bureaucratic intervention in the project of national development and the role of Islamic law within the legal system. But the overall outlook of the National Front was expressed by Ayatallah Abul Qassem Kashani (1885–1961), a leading political mujtahed, when he warned that "a nation that has willingly spilled its own blood to obtain the constitution will never again fall victim to despots and dictators."[236] When in June 1950 the government submitted a proposal to the parliament for revising the 1933 Anglo-Iranian Oil Company Agreement, the National Front denounced this highly unpopular proposal and called for the nationalization of the oil company. This bid for complete national independence marked "the high point of support for the National Front."[237] They did so on the grounds that

> so long as a large and powerful foreign company owned the country's most important modern industry, effectively controlled one of its provinces, and interfered in its politics to defend and promote its own interest, it would not be possible to establish either sovereign or democratic government.[238]

This unprecedented radical move—which reached the point of no return within the framework of international power relations—was met by a passionate outpouring of popular support from the streets as the "AIOC was seen as a major cause and channel for British influence and control over Iran."[239]

---

[235] Abrahamian, *Between Two Revolutions*, 262.
[236] Ibid., 263.
[237] Poulson, *Social Movements*, 172.
[238] Gasiorowski and Bryne, *Mohammed Mosaddeq*, 5–6.
[239] Keddie, *Iran*, 124.

Mosaddeq viewed the action as a moment of public empowerment, noting that "after the nationalization of the oil industry, [the public] did not miss any opportunity to display interest and emotion about their country's affairs."[240] This action had long-term influence in the politics of nationalist struggle, particularly with Nasser (1918–70) and the nationalization of the Suez Canal.[241] Around this time Mosaddeq passed through Egypt on route to Iran to a "tumultuous welcome by the Egyptian people," which "was noted by the British Foreign Office" as further evidence of the need to unseat him from power.[242] Although launched by peaceful means, the movement was quickly spurred along by individual acts of public violence designed to inspire terror. The assassination of a pro-British politician led the Shah to appoint General Razmara (1901–51) as prime minister. This powerful personality, embodying a different Enlightenment discourse, tried to quickly implement the proposals while avoiding public notice and trouble. A self-styled *nationalist* determined to "save the country from chaos and backwardness," Razmara held a Eurocentric modernization ideal and felt "natural distaste for democracy." His reforms included "removal of street vendors from around the Tehran bazaar" and the "imposition of a fine for appearing outdoors in pyjamas."[243] He would neither threaten landlords nor the international arrangement that secured the Shah's lifeline.[244] Yet by initiating peasant land reforms, promoting provincial assemblies and easing Tudeh Party restrictions, he perhaps intended to create a veil for pushing through the oil proposals. His politics met with a highly violent reaction among much of the mistrustful general population.

The National Front launched an attack on the grounds that full national independence should precede domestic reform. Mosaddeq addressed a Tehran rally of 12,000 to voice this message. Mass public demonstrations climaxed in Razmara's assassination in 1951 (again, by Fedayan-e Islam)[245] followed by

---

[240] Musaddiq, *Memories*, 319.
[241] Mottahedeh, *Politics and Religion*, 127.
[242] Katouzian, *Musaddiq*, 119.
[243] Ibid., 78–79.
[244] Katouzian, *Political Economy*, 165.
[245] Abrahamian, *Modern Iran*, 116.

widespread rejoicing in the streets.[246] Razmara's death pushed a radical change of outlook within the parliament among deputies previously loyal to the Shah's designs. Sensing the gathering storm of public anger, many conservative state ministers backed Mosaddeq and the National Front in its outlook and plans. There was an overall shift towards radical solutions, with the resurgent strength of the Tudeh Party (outlawed since the 1949 assassination attempt) acting through strikes and demonstrations, and the obstinacy of the AOIC pushing even Iranian moderates to favour nationalization.[247] As Mosaddeq explained it, "The National Front was not a party [but] a Majlis minority which enjoyed the support of the people solely because it took its inspirations from them. My government which had been formed by the support of public opinion had to respect public opinion."[248] Following Razmara's death in 1951 the bill to nationalize the British oil company was passed and two months later Mosaddeq was voted prime minister against the shah's chosen candidate.[249] Within this political climate of extremes, Mosaddeq deliberately included outsiders in his cabinet to *reassure* conservatives and *minimize trouble*.[250] His ethic of reconciliation, in fact, put him in danger. In response to the shah's expressed fears that a republic was being established, Mosaddeq suggested that he nominate the chief prefect of police himself.[251]

Following the 1951 Iranian oil nationalization, the United States surprised Iran by joining Britain's worldwide gunboat-enforced embargo. The British attempted recourse to the International Court at The Hague failed when the Court ruled the matter within Iranian law and Iran's right to nationalize with compensation.[252] Iran subsequently faced a crisis graver than in the post-war years through the deliberate animosity of a declining empire. Between 1952 and 1953 Iran broke diplomatic relations with Britain. These conditions intensified the battle of dual-sovereignty within Iran.

---

[246] Abrahamian, *Between Two Revolutions*, 265.
[247] Keddie, *Iran*, 124.
[248] Musaddiq, *Memories*, 334.
[249] Keddie, *Iran*, 124.
[250] Katouzian, *Musaddiq*, 113.
[251] Ibid., 114–15.
[252] Keddie, *Iran*, 125.

The hostile world-context introduced disruptive violence and provincial election rigging by the shah and Tudeh forces into the impending Seventeenth Majles elections. Mosaddeq and the shah both "wanted to send their own candidates to the chamber; Musaddiq, by the people's free vote, the shah, mainly by direct and indirect interference." The anti-government provincial magnates "would interfere in the elections with the aid and support of the provincial army and gendarmerie chiefs who still took their orders from the shah."[253]

Open civil society under violent conflict conditions and potential state collapse can be manipulated in violent and harmful ways. There was therefore minimum reform in the early Mosaddeq period. We see "popular unrest was organized into different movements" by opposition linked to British interests, seeking to thwart any reform efforts just as pressure for reform mounted and the "majles had increasingly to heed the demands of the people."[254] The shah advocated that "Musaddiq's reputation should be totally destroyed before his fall," adding that "the British also wanted to see him 'discredited' first."[255] The stakes of this battle were increasingly viewed in terms of hegemony, public opinion and information war, taking into account a perceived world opinion and future historical memory. With the 1951 elections the "Popular Movement candidates won in almost all the large cities and towns," with the Tudeh Party's vote considerably lower and the conservatives in last place. Provincial towns and rural areas saw vote rigging and violence, with the government forced to stop an election in Abadan despite imminent victory for the National Front candidate.[256] Seeing the opposition poised to illicitly take the majority of the provincial seats, Mosaddeq stopped the voting upon election of the parliamentary quorum of 79 deputies.[257] This electoral non-completion constituted a setback for opposition forces linked to Iran's undemocratic traditions from the shah to local powers, and designs for reinstating imperial domination. Disruptive manoeuvres, however,

---

[253] Katouzian, *Musaddiq*, 119.
[254] Keddie, *Iran*, 126.
[255] Azimi, *Crisis of Democracy*, 283.
[256] Katouzian, *Musaddiq*, 120.
[257] Abrahamian, *Between Two Revolutions*, 269.

continued into 1952 and prevented the Majles from undertaking its projected work.

The opposition, Mosaddeq announced, was "prepared to see Iranian national aspirations defeated so that they could cling for a few days longer to their privileged position." He declared sabotage futile for "the Iranian nation is wakeful and, whether this government remains or falls, the previous situation will never be restored."[258] The state apparatus, however, was irreconcilably divided from within. During the 1951–53 period Mosaddeq was in charge of only one state organ while the "rest of the state apparatus was still in the hands of despotic agents and institutions."[259] While Mosaddeq and his colleagues adhered to parliamentary democracy with a lenient policy towards "illegal campaigns against," the opposition of both Left and Right embraced the tradition of "the politics of elimination."[260]

From this point on Mosaddeq used the streets of Tehran like the rudder of a ship to steer the parliament his way, going repeatedly over the heads of the ministers to appeal directly to the general public. One of the ministers protested that statecraft "has degenerated into street politics."[261] In the growing conflict with the active royalist and pro-British elements dispersed throughout the national state apparatus, Mosaddeq sought to increase the pressure by removing the disqualification on illiterates in the electoral system. A coalition of royalist, military and tribal leaders managed to thwart this effort. No doubt seeing this opposition in the countryside as the work of vested landed interests, the National Front undertook a "propaganda war against the landed upper class."[262] Mosaddeq demanded the shah transfer his unconstitutional command over the armed forces to the parliament. He sought to remove the instrument permitting the route to power through unlimited violence. Arguing that short of this "the struggle started by the Iranian people cannot be brought to a victorious conclusion," he resigned his premiership. The shah replaced him with Qavam who made an inflammatory public

---

[258] Azimi, *Crisis of Democracy*, 285.
[259] Katouzian, *Political Economy*, 164.
[260] Gasiorowski and Bryne, *Mohammed Mosaddeq*, 19.
[261] Abrahamian, *Between Two Revolutions*, 267.
[262] Ibid., 270.

radio broadcast promising to "court martial" opponents and to "prevent the spread of superstition and retrogressive ideas."[263]

In the following days, the *bast* of the Popular Movement deputies and a press campaign targeting the shah with unprecedented directness prepared for a general strike.[264] With the support of the semi-legal Tudeh Party, strikes and mass demonstrations erupted spontaneously in all of the major towns in favour of Mosaddeq's reinstatement in the July Uprising. Although the peasants as a class did not participate in these uprisings, much of the population was capable of adequate self-organization to function as a fighting force to decide crucial national issues. Five days of rioting followed the shah's calling in of the military. People fought "tanks and bayonets with bricks, stones and bare hands."[265] Some military officers joined the demonstrations. Violent clashes occurred in the drapers', grocers' and metal workers' sections of the bazaar and in the working class districts on the eastern side of the city near the railway workshops and industrial plants. The city was ultimately occupied by protestors as military commanders, fearful of flagging troop loyalty, ordered their forces back to their barracks.[266] Terrorized by the scale of the disorder, the shah yielded and requested that Mosaddeq return to office to form a new government. He returned to power "with a greater prestige and popularity than ever before."[267] Mosaddeq's restoration was a "sign of new strength and determination by the nationalist coalition, and the signal for some serious reforms."[268] This victory for the National Front became known as *Siyeh-i Tir* (July 21).

As is axiomatic, the mobilization of popular violence had pushed the situation beyond the limits of reasonable control. Under the looming shadow of civil unrest, Mosaddeq used emergency powers. He struck against the court, excluding royalists from the cabinet. Encouraged by some followers to take revenge through imprisonment of prior opponents, he refused and instead set about using his new power "to bring about his programme of

---

[263] Katouzian, *Musaddiq*, 124.
[264] Ibid., 124.
[265] Katouzian, *Political Economy*, 176.
[266] Abrahamian, *Between Two Revolutions*, 272.
[267] Katouzian, *Musaddiq*, 121.
[268] Keddie, *Iran*, 126.

reform."²⁶⁹ He enforced tax collection and reduced the landlord's share of the crop, launched irrigation dam projects and rural development programmes. Import limitation and government planning produced the first post-war expansion of industry in sugar, textiles, dried fruit and cement.²⁷⁰ The military was placed under civilian rule. Evidence of Mosaddeq's persisting ethic of reconciliation was demonstrated in his "'horror' at the suggestion that most army generals should be dismissed." He finally permitted "many of them [to be] retired on full pension."²⁷¹ Royal lands were seized to finance a Health Ministry.

By 1953, the Shah was stripped of all of the powers he had fought to recover, though "treated with magnanimity" by Mosaddeq who could have used the moment to remove him politically altogether.²⁷² Land reforms were introduced to increase the peasant's share in annual produce and shift the burden of taxation away from low income sections of the population.²⁷³ There was an "increase in the educational budget, a five-year plan for road construction, rent controls, the nationalization of telephone installations, ... the creation of a uniform bus service in Tehran" and a "comprehensive scheme for workers' social insurance introduced."²⁷⁴ When these measures met with significant obstruction by remaining conservative sections of the parliament, Mosaddeq dissolved the parliament in 1953 and called for a national referendum to gage the degree of public support for his line of social reforms. Government opponents within the Majles had adopted a tactic of deliberately paralyzing the government, and conspired in the murder of the government's newly appointed police chief in 1953 while using parliamentary immunity to avoid trial. Mosaddeq's action expressed a shifted

---

²⁶⁹ Azimi, *Crisis of Democracy*, 294.
²⁷⁰ Keddie, *Iran*, 127.
²⁷¹ Katouzian, *Musaddiq*, 131–32.
²⁷² Ibid., 125. In fact, Musaddiq wanted a constitutional monarchy and not a republic.
²⁷³ Abrahamian, *Between Two Revolutions*, 273.
²⁷⁴ Azimi, *Crisis of Democracy*, 294–95.

dimension in the Enlightenment discursive–practical complex, from formal institutions to general will. He announced that if

> the government is compelled to spend all of its time on countering the disruptive activities of the opposition, it would by no means be able to accomplish reforms ... I must say with the utmost regret that this Government ... has no choice but to appeal to the people themselves for the solution of this difficulty.[275]

The general will tactic was rationalized in saying the population must be "powerful in will so as to carry out their discernment."[276]

The Mosaddeq–shah struggle, the Tudeh Party resurgence amidst socio-economic crisis, the Britain–US subversion schemes, and expanding popular National Front demonstrations inspired the confidence for Mosaddeq's move.[277] The murder of the police chief hurt both the National Front and to its opponents, as a massive popular attendance appeared for the police chief's funeral procession in confirmation of the government's continued legitimacy.[278] Mosaddeq announced that the "people of Iran – and no one else – has the right to judge on this issue [because] it was the people of Iran who brought into existence our fundamental laws, our constitution, our parliament, and our cabinet system."[279] The popular referendum, though conducted with notable flaws, came out in favour of Mosaddeq's action and within days the royalist coup was set in motion.[280]

The following months saw the traditionalist wing of the National Front start to break off. Many among them accused the government of using class war tactics and opposed the nationalization of key industries (communications, transport), complaining that Iran "would end up like the Soviet Union." The move to enfranchise women provoked opposition. At the end of

---

[275] Quoted Azimi, *Crisis of Democracy*, 323.
[276] Mottahedeh, *Politics and Religion*, 129.
[277] Keddie, *Iran*, 128.
[278] Azimi, *Crisis of Democracy*, 320–21.
[279] Abrahamian, *Between Two Revolutions*, 274.
[280] Katouzian, *Musaddiq*, 187–88.

Mosaddeq's six-month emergency powers period, he requested another year to complete the wave of social reform and received the charge from the traditional wing of "transforming Iran into a vast prison."[281] In fact, the government "was highly sensitive to the charges of dictatorship" levelled against it by the opposition press, and sometimes reproduced its arguments in pro-Government newspapers. By adhering to "legal and civil standards the Government had left matters to be dealt with by the existing legal processes which were inefficient, susceptible to pressure [and] often corrupt"; the Government showed itself not effectively "in control of the state apparatus or the army." This, coupled with its ideal of political lenience, resulted in its being vulnerable to the point that "those accused of murdering (the Police Chief) Afshartus ... continued to abuse the government and even tabled a motion of interpellation against it."[282] A pervasive politics of violence, grounded in authoritarian vested interest and foreign power, began to gain ascendancy over the National Front project of dialogic and multi-cultural democracy.

THE COUP AND ITS AFTERMATH

It is well known that the political experiment of the Iranian Popular Movement was cut short by the coup d'état conducted by a group of foreign and domestic forces, in large part organized and funded by the C.I.A. from the basement of the US embassy in Tehran. The final success of the 1953 coup restored to Muhammed Reza Shah dictatorial powers that would last until the 1979 Revolution. It was preceded by two other attempts in which the popular masses intervened and thwarted the takeover, in the second instance forcing the shah to flee into exile. In the first of these on 28 February 1953 a band appeared at Mosaddeq's home and attempted to assassinate him. A crowd attacked the band outside of the gates of his house, led by the celebrated writer and translator Jalal Al-e Ahmad (1923–69), who was leading the Third Force Party (an offshoot of the Toiler's Party).[283] The Third Force called

[281] Abrahamian, *Between Two Revolutions*, 275/276.
[282] Azimi, *Crisis of Democracy*, 328.
[283] Katouzian, *Political Economy*, 177.

for women's suffrage and further land distribution.²⁸⁴ In the subsequent and more serious attempt the coup was again foiled by mass public reaction causing the shah to flee to Baghdad. The event was followed by several days of highly destructive rioting. In the final attempt, a section of the army and a group of paid rioters including prostitutes and mobsters led from the red light district by Sha'ban the Brainless managed to capture and loot Mosaddeq's home and force him into temporary hiding until his capture.²⁸⁵ It is reported that after two days of hiding in a cellar, when one of Mosaddeq's minister's said "How badly it all turned out!" Mosaddeq replied "And at the same time how really well it turned out, how really well!"²⁸⁶ It implies that there existed for him some appeal in the tragic.

The project of constructing secular politics and cultural pluralism endured a fatal blow with the successful coup d'état of August 1953 as the returning Shah's regime undertook the systematic limitation and destruction of all forms of democratic and secular political organization and institutions including trade unions, student organizations, political parties and associations, and parliament. In the final two decades of the Shah's reign "no legal opposition political parties or organizations existed in the country" and even underground opposition was effectively crushed.²⁸⁷ Thus, under the post-coup regime of state-driven *Westernization* from above, the only political spaces for dissent emerged in the mosques, seminary schools, bazaars, universities and groups in exile, structurally contributing to the desecularization of Iranian politics.

Iranian intellectuals in the post-coup period have evoked it as a time of *strangulation, loneliness, darkness, fatigue* and *nothingness*.²⁸⁸ It was within this atmosphere that in the late 1960s Ahmed Fardid (1912–94) was appointed professor of philosophy at Tehran University. Fardid is well known for having introduced

---

²⁸⁴ Abrahamian, *Between Two Revolutions*, 277.
²⁸⁵ Katouzian, *Political Economy*, 179.
²⁸⁶ Mottahedeh, *Politics and Religion*, 133.
²⁸⁷ Mirsepassi, *Intellectual Discourse*, 70.
²⁸⁸ Ibid.,76.

German philosophy into Iranian intellectual circles.[289] At the time of the Constitutional Revolution, German philosophy had enjoyed the least popularity in comparison with that of France and England.[290] Fardid was a particular authority on Heidegger, the interwar German thinker whose famous *Being and Time* (1926) revolted against empty Enlightenment universalism in defence of local cultural authenticity or *being*, and who was later embroiled in controversy over his involvement in the Nazi regime. Fardid derived from Heideggerian historicism a notion of history as a fluid field of competing understandings of truth in which one is eclipsed by another in an ongoing power struggle at a given time.

Fardid interpreted the Western Enlightenment as the historical advent of truth interpreted as material *reality* triumphing over the authentic "true spiritual essence" of Islam and the "East." Once again reproducing Heidegger's historicist argument, he argued that the core of Western scientific truth is the drive to world domination while in Islamic spirituality we find benevolence and compassion. The earlier discourses of authenticity articulated by Muhammed Ali Shah and Shaykh Fazallah were thus given a substantiated metaphysical basis in the Western philosophical *ontological turn*, i.e. Heidegger's rejection of the entire Western metaphysical tradition stemming from ancient Greek origins. Fardid in this way concluded that Iran must abandon the dominance of the West (*Gharb*) in order to once again *find itself*. Fardid's rather obscure ideas were "warmly received by an important segment of the community of Iranian intellectuals eager to reassert their own identity."[291] The same Al-e Ahmad who had fought to defend Mosaddeq against the conspiracy, a once but subsequently violently disillusioned member of the Tudeh Party, picked up on Fardid's discourse and produced the most influential book of the 1960s and 1970s with his *Gharbzadegi* (1962) or *Occidentosis*. It represented a complete turnaround from his earlier ideals grounded in a radical universalism through the embrace of a *local* and *authentic* solution. In arguing that Iranian modernization was a disease from the West and that Western

---

[289] Mehrzad Boroujerdi, *Iranian Intellectuals and the West: The Tormented Triumph of Nativism* (Syracuse: Syracuse University Press, 1996), 63.
[290] Mirsepassi, *Intellectual Discourse*, 60.
[291] Boroujerdi, *Iranian Intellectuals*, 64–65.

ideas were inherently complicit in imperialist power, he hailed Nouri as a martyr in his struggle against the Constitutional Revolution. He called for an *authentically* Iranian road. His book was published one year after the death of Ayatollah Boroujerdi, the end of the relatively subdued period of the clerics.

Ayatollah Khomeini (1902–89) began in this same interval to mobilize the Shi'i establishment to radical political ends.[292] Al-e Ahmad's book, together with the slightly later work of Al-e Shari'ati (1933–75), created a fashionable modern ideology. It drew nearly an entire generation of the modern Iranian middle class and the youth into complicity with an emergent religious mass movement. This reacted against a *Westernizing* regime that had, by its tyrannical hold on power and severely uneven development project, succeeded in alienating all but the entire Iranian population. In this intellectual climate, many convinced themselves that the earlier Constitutional Revolutionary struggles and the Popular Movement had been nothing more than meaningless and misguided flights of *inauthenticity* derived from a culturally alien Enlightenment.

[292] Mirsepassi, *Intellectual Discourse*, 107.

Conclusion

VIOLENCE

This study investigates the link between violence and change at the historical core of Enlightenment and nationalism. The problem of violence was central—in diffused and tacit way— to Thomas Hobbes' and Max Weber's analyses of modernity, Hegel's historical "slaughter bench," and Fernand Braudel's conception of modern history as the "violent division of the world."[1]

HISTORY AS A MAZE

The maze is the most apt metaphor for writing history today, in the wake of Emmanuel Levinas' (1906–95) assertion that History constitutes the imperialism of the same, a titanic mode of imagining in Universal History as assimilation. This was a critique of Hegelian totality under Heideggerian inspiration with the aim of finding a *way out*. It would seem that modern universalism, by trying to break the walls between people, created even more—a conundrum made much of in the modern literature.

It is detectable already in Christopher Marlowe—Faustian self-destruction as the central modern archetype and knowledge as the abyss from which it flowers—whose unsolved and politically dubious murder invited this comment in 1593: "I find the matter as in a labyrinth: easier to enter into it than to go out."[2] Since Dostoyevsky declared a wish to send "all systems and theories to the devil," there have been many trying to find a *way out* along a romantic road.[3] It has often fostered a mood of nihilism. Melville's Captain Ahab said regarding the white wall of the absolute—a multiple metaphor from ontological emptiness to

---

[1] Fernand Braudel, *La Dynamique du Capitalisme* (Paris: Flammarion, 2008), 94.

[2] See the epigraph to Charles Nicholl, *The Reckoning: The Murder of Christopher Marlowe* (Chicago: University of Chicago Press, 1995), 5.

[3] Ian Hacking, *The Taming of Chance* (Cambridge: Cambridge University Press, 1990), 146.

American Manifest Destiny as historical fanaticism—that "sometimes I think there's naught beyond."[4]

In the 20th century, the conceptual maze produced the confusion of a false identity between liberation and agitation. It refers to the confluent confusions of the unthought. This was exemplified in Claude Levi Strauss' hailing of Louis-Ferdinand Céline's *Journey to the End of Night* (1932) as a "revolt against all forms of oppression and injustice" and an ally of the Left in its opposition to a common bourgeois enemy. The novel was perhaps the greatest literary expression of anti-democratic counter-Enlightenment in the 20th century. The underlying reality of the world is meaningless horror, which is periodically manifested, and all of the rest is empty words.[5] Céline's nihilistic hate of the bourgeoisie appealed to the Left. His rejection of egalitarian values appealed less to them—but this could pass as a healthy loathing for bourgeois institutions. They failed to see that it portended his collusion with the Vichy government during the World War II German occupation of France.[6]

This confusion between emancipation as political liberty and cultural authenticity was expressed in Michel Foucault's praise of the 1979 Iranian Islamist revolution. He would hardly have welcomed such a movement in France. Orientalist fascination fused with longings for the "death of man" must have contributed to his readiness to celebrate the Iranian *exception*.

This confusion traces the fault line of a modern intellectual paradigm crisis. The great attraction of disillusioned Left thinkers to Heidegger (Ranajit Guha, Partha Chatterjee, Talal Asad or the 1960s French poststructuralists) exemplifies it. The dominant representations of modernity as an infallible monolith prepared to inflict cosmic justice—linked to power configurations—are not least to blame for the predicament.

Is historical imagination as much a straitjacket as Levinas implied in saying to approach the other we must be uprooted

---

[4] Herman Melville, *Moby Dick* (London: Wordsworth, 1993), 136.

[5] Louis-Ferdinand Céline, *Voyage au bout de la nuit* (Paris: Gallimard, 1952), 14–15.

[6] Levi Strauss, *Voyage au bout de la nuit de Louis-Ferdinand Céline Critiques 1932–35* (Paris: Imec, 1993), 176.

from history as a totality?⁷ Levi Strauss' call to "dissolve man" because human rights are merely West-centric embraced cultural relativism.⁸ But Levinas, devastated by experiences of totalitarianism, was concerned with an ethical critique of politics permitting each to live their life as a "secret" — something not to be known, dominated and controlled by power as an object in the name of higher claims to truth.⁹ Such a concern with human autonomy and respect for the other has its prerequisite in a notion of universal reason and recognition of historical truth — as a human capacity for ethical and practical problem solving on dialogic grounds.

As Levinas implied, alternative modes of historical imagining to a totalized synthesis exist. We should beware of Heideggerian *ontological* generalizations about knowledge as *essentially* the domination of the other, where "nothing is any longer able to withstand the business of knowing, since technical mastery over things bears itself without limit" — even as this tendency may be included among the multiple potentials recognized through a critical evaluation of knowledge production.¹⁰

HEIDEGGERIAN HISTORICISM AND THE 20TH-CENTURY LEFT

Heidegger, like Céline, came of age on the bloody European battlefields of World War I and this trauma formed his worldview. Politically, he declared modern democracy the "moribund semblance of a culture" and liberalism "the slavery of contingency."¹¹

---

⁷ Robert J. C. Young, *White Mythologies: Writing History and the West* (New York: Routledge, 1991), 43–44.

⁸ Richard Wolin, *The Seduction of Unreason. The Intellectual Romance with Fascism from Nietzsche to Postmodernism* (Princeton: Princeton University Press, 2004), 5.

⁹ Emmanuel Levinas, *Ethique et Infini* (Paris: Fayard, 1982), 69–75. He was a Jewish Lithuanian child refugee during World War I, lived the Russian Revolution, and lost much family while imprisoned by the Nazis during World War II.

¹⁰ Martin Heidegger, "On the Essence of Truth," in *Basic Writings* (San Francisco: Harper Collins, 1993), 129.

¹¹ Heidegger, *The Cambridge Companion to Heidegger* (Cambridge: Cambridge University Press, 1997), 277; Wolin, *The Politics of Being: The*

A Nazi collaborator during World War II, he never renounced these views. Philosophically, he has often been celebrated as the champion of a new pluralism. His thinking, however, was deeply essentialist.

Heidegger's revolt against modernity affirmed the cultural authority of community. This grounded his naïve embrace of Nazism as German national salvation under the *alien* Weimar Republic. *Modernity* is a unified, pervasive and tacit worldview, controlling people unwittingly.[12] An authentic connection to *being* is consequently lost: "inauthentic historical existence (is) burdened with a legacy that has become unrecognizable to it."[13] A unified public meaning, based on the "loyalty of existence to its own self," the "sole authority that a free existence can have," where "everything good is a matter of heritage" — could restore authentic roots.[14] At best, Heidegger urged a world of mutually respecting *pure* fragments.

Heidegger's (often tacit) followers — while celebrating his supposed pluralism — have inherited his philosophical essentialism. Chatterjee's structuralist notion of Enlightenment as a "thematic," for example, presupposes a single worldview invested with essentialist limits: "the stricter definition of scientific truth is now contained within the wider notion of rationality as an ethic" linked to "epistemic privilege as the last bastion of global supremacy." It is a "seduction" and "prison" which negates the "symbolic orderings" of "non-scientific cultures" and their "pre-theoretical practical" orientations in "everyday life."[15] Historical actors are often represented as little more than discursive structure puppets.

This Heideggerian analytic of the unthought, projects the principle characteristic of the "post-Enlightenment worldview" as an "entirely new idea of man's *control* over nature." This

Political Thought of Martin Heidegger (New York Columbia University Press, 1990), 25.

[12] Martin Heidegger, *An Introduction to Metaphysics* (New Haven: Yale University Press, 2000. 23–39).

[13] Heidegger, *Being and Time* (Albany: State University of New York Press, 1996), 358.

[14] Ibid., 351/357.

[15] Chatterjee, *Nationalist Thought and the Colonial World* (New Delhi: Oxford University Press, 1986), 16–17.

anti-modernism, linked tenuously to Marx in the "rational conception of society" as imposed upon the "relations between man and man," ultimately entails a romanticization of *community* in a pattern of imaginatively fabricated essentialisms buried under *discourse analyses*.[16] Capital is the Manichean antithesis of community.[17]

The only glimmer of hope within this totalizing and Kafkaesque purview—oppressed by an all-pervasive and hidden *alien worldview*—is a mysteriously utopian *outside*. Chatterjee evoked a "new beginning" where the "old problematic and thematic (is replaced) with new ones."[18] It is a variant on the totalizing Heideggerian "other thinking" or "other beginning."[19]

John Dewey addressed the being–becoming conundrum that was also Heidegger's obsession, but from the immanent view of a self-transforming Enlightenment heritage. Dewey wrote, "The idea of a whole, whether of the personal being or the world, is an imaginative, not a literal, idea."[20] The conundrum of the maze is, in important ways, imaginary between these dialectical poles of black and white, totality and fragment, and new and old worlds. The impassioned rejection of the world on any fixed essentialist premise undermines the very hope and wakefulness required for changing it. For essentialism never sees the immanent world, only the totalizing transcendental vista projected beyond it.

We may alternatively open our eyes to multiple forking paths as suggested in Dewey's philosophy of conceptual pluralism: in post-traditional societies no single set of truths can serve exclusively for understanding the world. Yet this is an opening for more ethical and creative ways of imagining social life in a centreless environment of multiple histories. The achievements of science hold great promise as well as tragic risk. That is, the pluralistic consequences of modernity—for all of the colossal challenges they present—should not be pinned down philosophically

---

[16] Ibid, 14.
[17] Ibid. 169–170.
[18] Ibid.
[19] Heidegger, "Letter on Humanism," in *Basic Writings*, 231; Michael Inwood, *A Heidegger Dictionary* (Oxford: Blackwell Publishers 1999), 6–7.
[20] John Dewey, *A Common Faith* (New Haven: Yale University Press, 1962), 18.

by any pessimistic or closed ontological totalization, i.e. it is only on the opposite side of the total grave of *capitalism* imagined as a seamlessly unified juggernaut that value in science, knowledge, politics and existence (i.e. as absolute realities) may be retrieved.

The essentialist attitude presents a stubborn and closed politics of *loyalty* to an Idea, an empyrean fantasy, rather than the open and imaginative analytic vista required for elucidating the multiple practical and ethical problems presented by global capitalism as a varied and changing interplay of forces implicated in massive structural violence.

Regarding history and the imagination, Collingwood writes: "the underside of this table, the inside of an unopened egg, the back of the moon. Here again the imagination is *a priori*: we cannot but imagine what cannot but be there."[21] History, he says, is a critical activity of going beyond what the authorities say, a rediscovery of what is forgotten or occluded, a constructive practice based on evidence. The *a priori* imagination, as such, remains neither real nor unreal upon the threshold of a universe that is unfinished.

This is unthinkable without the principle of intellectual autonomy basic to the democratic Enlightenment tradition. There is grave responsibility in historical writing without metaphysical guarantees of unity or closure. The renunciation of history as a "white myth" does a disservice to the democratic heritage of Enlightenment. David Irving was ready to bury the historical memory of the Holocaust on Nazi methodological grounds (his rejection of the Enlightenment heritage), and thus became unacceptable to the social science community.[22]

The Enlightenment is not an objective reality, but a tradition based on provisionally accepted, continuously contested, values and meanings. This implies methodology as responsible allegiances within civic institutions where adjustment of standards through multiple crosschecks is always possible. It is a practical and self-protective ethic, rather than a claim to being. The Left

---

[21] R.G. Collingwood, *The Idea of History* (New Delhi: Oxford, 2000), 242.

[22] Had he been a Nazi, but disinclined to purposefully distort evidence to a higher end, the issue would have been different. But then, he would not have been a Nazi except in name.

paradigm crisis of the late 20th century produced maze-like conceptual wanderings into arcane questions of *being*. For Foucault, the "being of language" had been "forgotten since the sixteenth century," and might presumably be revived with the "death of man."[23]

THE SECULAR AND THE COMTEAN LEGACY

The secular is proposed as a limit, not a totalization. Cautious of such steps as already taken by Spinoza (collapsing God into nature) and later taken by Hegel (collapsing God into man)[24] in their tacit granting that every human action is thereby permitted, Kant posited a limit—concerned fairly directly with the problem of constructing violence—in refusing any guarantees of ultimate reconciliation, i.e. non-closure.[25]

The secular signifies one departure from multiple discursive religious universes in the linking of *truth* to *evidence* rather than authority (belief may be self-certain but lack evidence). This is a historical learning, not a truth of the universe. It has critical ethical implications (i.e. Saint Thomas Aquinas: heretics must be "shut off from the world by death" as an institutional ethic).[26] It does not follow that the secular must make substantive truth claims about the world intended to *necessarily* supersede other worldviews as the seal of metaphysical propositions. This *seal* was the implication of Comtean positivism, a mode of imagining highly influential—though in differing degrees—to the cases in this study.

A self-proclaimed "heir to the French Revolution," Comte (1798–1857) considered his influential positivist philosophy to be the constructive force of world regeneration in the wake of the necessary destructive work of the Revolution. Considering

[23] Michel Foucault, *The Order of Things. An Archaeology of the Human Sciences* (New York: Vintage, 1973), 44/387.
[24] Technically, Feuerbach did this in Ludwig Feuerbach, *The Essence of Christianity* (Cambridge: Cambridge University Press, 2012), 30.
[25] Lilla, 170–211.
[26] Walter Kaufmann, *Critique of Religion and Philosophy* (New Jersey: Princeton University Press, 1958), 149.

his writings, the "final study of social phenomena" and part of a "final condition of which nothing can halt the great evolution," he declared "no further systems possible." He had unveiled "the true and definitive nature of modernity." He declared "politics and (his) philosophy" to be a part of one "inseparable universal system," an "objective criteria of social reconstruction," prepared to collapse the barrier between "public and private life" in a "final institution" based on the "true totality of human existence." His single "regenerative doctrine" suggested a single universal path to national modernity.[27] Such a *seal* must be rejected for reasons of democratic principle—it violates the freedom of thought secularism was intended to gain.

It follows the Cartesian paradigm where a *natural inner light* opposes belief radically to knowledge. It bore the potentially totalizing implication that habit and tradition unfounded in reason must be eradicated. Comte made an explicit horizon target of what Descartes had rather deliberately left tacit.

Michael Polanyi, like Céline and Heidegger, came of age through the World War I trauma.[28] Polanyi's "tacit dimension"—in contrast to them—self-consciously and critically upholds the Enlightenment heritage. It is an imaginative horizon invested scientifically in—while seeing ethically beyond—the human dialectical attitude of unceasing transcendence in the cognitive mastery of ever new beings. It concedes and respects the other as stranger in principle. The belief realm of our practical and everyday relation to the world, in so far as temporality links meaning to inner experience, has an "inexhaustible profundity."[29]

We see that Levinas, Heidegger, Polanyi and Dewey were struggling within a roughly shared conceptual problematic. In varying ways, they either reconstructed or rejected the dominant Enlightenment paradigm. The answers they produced have radically differing practical and ethical implications.

---

[27] Auguste Comte, *Discours sur l'Ensemble du Positivisme* (Paris: Flammarion, 2008), 18–32.
[28] Both Polanyi brothers served in the Austro-Hungarian army.
[29] Polanyi, *The Tacit Dimension* (New Delhi: Penguin Books, 2009), 68.

TRANSCENDENT AND IMMANENT

Geographically, the Enlightenment is conceived in terms of Braudel's contention that, beyond the Orientalist and other culturally essentialist modes of imagining, we are really talking historically about the interactions of a common Eurasian space.[30] The suggestion is an interrelated web of varying historical–temporal structures including economies, technologies, institutions, populations, discourses and languages—in sum, the complex of mobile and semi-stable forms. This implies a multi-centred theoretical lens reflecting the methodological achievements of the Annales School of history under the influence of Emile Durkheim (i.e. his notion of the complex causational situation).[31]

This differs from the distinct spirit, or *essence*, investing ethical life, state, culture and religion, forging a distinct destiny, as we find in Hegelian teleology. It follows a neo-Saussurian or Wittgensteinean conception of identity/meaning as relational or comparative rather than transcendental. This immanent methodology parts with the classical opposition between the universal and the particular. Identity is not essence but relations constituting individuation without hidden metaphysical places.[32] This is also the non-essentialist pattern by which Sen's ideational and cultural components interact and mutate.

The assumption of abstract form following a mathematical paradigm—where the starting and terminal points as a sequence are interlocked in necessity and there is no option of variance in the outcome except in error—is inappropriate as a metaphor for problem solving in a history of ideas (i.e. the metaphor of the crossword puzzle). Following the interventions of Bachelard, Saussure and Nietzsche, it is hard to take seriously the totalizing premise of continuity–narrative that underpinned the Western philosophical tradition going back to Plato's metaphor of the cave, i.e. knowledge as a universal dualism dividing night and

---

[30] Fernand Braudel, *Capitalism and Material Life: 1400–1800* (London: Weidenfeld and Nicolson, 1973).

[31] Fernand Braudel, *Ecrits sur L'Histoire* (Paris: Flammarion, 1969), 41–85, for Braudel's theory of temporal multiplicity.

[32] Ferdinand de Saussure, *Cours de Linguistique Générale* (1916) (Paris: Payot, 2005), 1–32.

day. Its historicist heir imaginatively projects a totalizing system (i.e. chronologically, thematic categories, divisions of reality and objects of study, origin–essence–identity claims linked to a narrative such as the Gibbon–Hegel Athens–Jerusalem–Rome triangle[33]) as an inviolable scientific postulate rather than tools or modes of imagining.

The diverse roots of modern democratic ideas are traceable through multiple "constitutive elements" in many civilizational-cultural traditions—intermingled with undemocratic elements and requiring differentiation—and not to some unitary civilizational-cultural *whole*. What follows from Sen's fluid, molecular and demonstrable conception of ideas and identities is *ambiguity* rather than *essentialism* (to describe in fixed terms of one definition, or one origin). We find that multiple traditions exist in *dialectical* relation to one another rather than any distinctive identity reducible to *substantive* definition (in the Aristotelian tradition). This would affirm Weber's neo-Kantian notion that *disenchantment* shows a dialectical or overlapping quality between the religious and the secular, and is not merely the unpeeling of *false consciousness* in a secular discovery of the world as *it really is*.

Seyla Benhabib has argued that the feminist project becomes impossible once the entire tradition of Western philosophy as a universal project of emancipation is deemed worthless as a discourse.[34] This logic applies equally to historical and contemporary civil and human rights efforts, national independence struggles and labour politics. To say the opposite is rather like Margaret Thatcher's famous quip that she owes nothing to the tradition of feminism.

Yet despite the important contribution of Western philosophy to such democratic struggles, notably in the principle of rational autonomy from dogmatic belief, the Enlightenment as a tradition far exceeds Western philosophy in dimension and scope. John Dewey noted this, with particular reference to the limits of Eurocentric thought "it shows a deplorable deadness of imagination to suppose that philosophy will indefinitely revolve within

[33] Lilla, 190.
[34] Seyla Benhabib, "Feminism and the Question of Postmodernism," in *The New Social Theory Reader*, ed. Steven Seidman and Jeffrey C. Alexander (Noida: Routledge, 2008), 156–62.

the scope of the problems and systems that two thousand years of European philosophy have bequeathed to us." He argued "the whole of Western European history is a provincial episode."[35]

For this reason Dewey argued that it was time to be done with finished philosophical edifices. He presents a valuable conceptual framework on the meaning of democratic change in relation to the hegemonic Enlightenment. He articulated persisting tensions between Eurocentric limitations and emancipatory promise. The present project intends to push the conception of the Enlightenment tradition beyond its Eurocentric limits simply on the basis of an empirical history that respected historians including Gertrude Himmelfarb have—to all appearances—preferred to ignore.[36] This intention is very far from the essentialist declaration of Enlightenment as the enemy of either *innocence* or *community*, as we see in Nandy and Chatterjee, respectively. The champions of Eurocentrism and the non-Western fragment both stand on transcendental ground, which gives their arguments an atemporal, fixed and fanciful quality.

JOHN DEWEY AND CENTRE-LESS TEMPORALITY

Dewey's centre-less temporality is summed up in two passages. Concerning methodology, he wrote that concepts concerning social phenomena are "means for determining a non-recurring temporal sequence." It corresponds to his notion of temporality: "life is no uninterrupted march or flow. It is a thing of histories, each with its own plot, its own inception and movement toward its close, each having its own particular rhythmic movement; each with its own repeated quality pervading it throughout."[37] It is a historical–sociological–conceptual equivalent to Joseph Conrad's subjective–ephemeralist remark, "it is impossible to

---

[35] John Dewey, *The Philosophy of John Dewey* (Chicago: University of Chicago Press, 1981), 13.

[36] Gertrude Himmelfarb, "The Illusions of Cosmopolitanism," in *Martha Nussbaum with Respondents, For Love of Country* (Boston: Beacon Press, 1996), 74–75.

[37] Dewey, *The Philosophy of John Dewey* (Chicago: University of Chicago Press, 1973), 410/555.

convey the life-sensation of any given epoch of one's existence — that which makes its truth, its meaning — its subtle and penetrating essence."[38] This might refer to the cumulative qualitative substance of civil society formation as a many-sided and open-ended collective experience.

Dewey addressed totalizing concepts with similar concerns to Foucault, without retreating into the fragment: "Philosophy forswears inquiry after absolute origins and absolute finalities in order to explore specific values and the specific conditions which generate them."[39] Embracing modern scientific achievements, Dewey criticized the dominant metaphysical narrative of scientific Enlightenment manifested in movements proclaiming a new universal truth. He described Comtean positivism as the "division into a superior true realm of being and a lower illusory, insignificant or phenomenal realm."[40]

It is false, in light of this, that Dewey did not recognize the tragic. He affirmed its inevitability linked to the irreducible fact of difference in ways of being and seeing the world: "To deny this qualitative heterogeneity (on the basis of claims about ultimate reality) is to reduce the struggles and difficulties of life, its comedies and tragedies, to illusion: the nonbeing of the Greeks or to its modern counterpart, the 'subjective'."[41] The tragic, for Dewey, meant that "experience means primarily not knowledge, but ways of doing and suffering."[42] It was a temporal condition that — rather like the *episteme* or the *tacit component* — could not be overcome: "in the end what is unseen decides what happens in the seen" and "when all is said and done, the fundamentally hazardous character of the world is not seriously modified, much less eliminated."[43]

Dewey saw in the world an "inextricable mixture of stability and uncertainty," and pervasive "ambiguousness."[44] He affirmed centre-less multiple histories, or temporality. Again,

---

[38] Joseph Conrad, *The Heart of Darkness* (London: Penguin, 1973), 39.
[39] Dewey, *Philosophy*, 38.
[40] Ibid., 289.
[41] Ibid., 66.
[42] Ibid., 77, 78.
[43] Ibid., 280.
[44] Ibid., 281.

like Foucault, he reflected upon the pluralistic consequences of modernity rather than its closure. He rejected pure reason, seeing reason as having "a real, though limited, function, a creative, constructive function."[45] This Deweyan concept of temporality is heir to the Kantian temporality of non-closure and belief reconstruction intended to render the conflict resolution path non-violent. Kant's tacit non-violence was made explicit by Dewey, who denounced the "tradition of violence" or "dogma of dependence upon force."[46] Instead, he called for "a wider and fuller union of individual efforts in accomplishment of common ends."[47] This suggests multiple civil society formations as studied in this book.

In sum, one tradition of Enlightenment can be traced centring the building of a political order grounded in an ideal of non-violence. This includes among its most important figures those who sought freedom in Enlightenment terms from secular and religious violence of every ideological variety, as well as the large scale structural violence produced by the predatorial logic of unrestrained capitalism.

Dewey's Enlightenment concept of temporality contains a radical self-critical component, for he was committed to democratic humanist values and a modest notion of progress far from phantasms of total change. Foucault, by contrast, viewed politics as a condition where "humanity installs each of its violences in a system of rules and thus proceeds from domination to domination," erasing the distinction between democratic and authoritarian regimes. It makes a democratic mass movement pointless and inherently oppressive as compared to politics of the self.[48]

The mass democratic movements in this study—selected for their intellectual and practical ambiguity upon the map of modernity as compared to the Russian or Chinese Revolutions—are closer to a Deweyan than Foucauldian vision (although we do find varieties of the politics of the self). They elude the

---

[45] Ibid., 50.
[46] Ibid., 649.
[47] Ibid., 651.
[48] Foucault, Michel. "Nietzsche, Genealogy, History," in *The Foucault Reader*, ed. Paul Rabinow. New York: Pantheon Books, 85. We should not forget, though, his frequent participation in political activism during his lifetime.

conventional conceptual pattern of modernity (modernity vs tradition, universal vs particular, etc.) derived largely from the constructed memory of the French Revolutionary experience. Dewey, unlike Foucault, would not have been enchanted by the 1979 Islamist turn in the Iranian Revolution as a "strange, unique road."[49] He was not seeking a 'way out' of modernity through any enchanted door (i.e. the "death of man").

Wittgenstein, in view of the often violent dogmatism of rational Enlightenment, would have preferred to leave religious traditions untouched and uncriticized in a spirit of pluralism and tolerance. Dewey also maintains that the complexity of religious traditions as human value/meaning resources be acknowledged. He never the less affirmed that a radical deconstruction of religious traditions—in light of scientific and democratic modernity—is irreversibly shaping the contemporary world in unfinished and undecided manner. From the perspective of the rights of the person, it must.

Dewey and Weber, in a post-foundationalist reformulation of the Kantian horizon, saw tragedy as a temporal mode flowing from the inescapable conflict of moral ideals in the world. Their tacit recommendation was that, without the make-believe of conflict-free society beyond all power, such conflicts can and must be resolved to the greatest extent possible non-violently through appropriate institutional arrangements. For Dewey, this entailed self-reliant mobilization of the population for whom they are intended in the mode of deliberative democracy. It is an immanent—not a transcendental—vision.

MULTI-CENTRED HISTORY

In the history of ideas, we cannot—except in bad faith or constrained by the moral dogma of the fragment—ignore the logical connections between thoughts: notably, the concept of an epistemic limit as the basis for an ethic of non-violence common to India and Europe visible in this study. This *universalism*, however,

---

[49] Ali Mirsepassi, *Intellectual Discourse and the Politics of Modernization: Negotiating Modernity in Iran* (Cambridge: Cambridge University Press, 2000), 1.

does not require or assume any fundamental ontological uniformity (i.e. of "structure" etc.), the historical *conditions* giving rise to the idea being comparable but also significantly different.

Secondly, in the history of ideas, we cannot assume merely a distinction between ideas, rather than an opposition: as if the different conceptions of Enlightenment held by the British Raj and the Indian national movement were merely *different*, and not *opposed*. At the level of analyzing ideas that flowered into political action, we see a *dialectical* relation. But we need not assume this relation is encased within an absolute or uniform principle of rationality (identity), implying a necessary process of succession with ultimate victory for the *most* rational idea in the Hegelian (or sometimes Weberian) sense of the highest plane of pure thought.

This is to invest rationality as a plural phenomenon with a homogenizing ontology, a religious notion of Providence—the very thing Dewey warned against in the name of responsible choice. The aforementioned Saussurian–Wittgensteinean notion of relational identity is itself dialectical in such an open way, just as we might point to Nagarjuna's dialectic of the void.[50] Opposed dialectical entities can co-exist without any eventual victory of one over the other: the most conspicuous case being Enlightenment and Romanticism.

This implies a Nietzschean conception of the pairing of necessity and chance, the genealogical tension in *The Birth of Tragedy* where at best we find an affirmation of contingency and so difference. But once the Nietzschean metaphysic of the Will to Power is introduced, we end up equating the pursuit of truth as well as meaning *merely* with the quest for domination—probably the root of the Heideggerian and poststructuralist attitude.

This was Foucault's slip in following the Nietzschean road far enough to assert that "all knowledge rests upon injustice" and that "the instinct for knowledge is malicious."[51] This view underappreciates not only the importance of argument and evidence in the cause of justice, as did Nietzsche himself (who cared nothing for it), but also the practical meaning of choice as ethical pluralism. Positivist historicity was methodologically wrong—from

---

[50] Jean-Marc Vivenza, *Nagarjuna et la doctrine de la vacuité* (Paris: Albin Michel, 2001), ch. 3.

[51] Foucault, Nietzsche, Genealogy, History, 95.

CONCLUSION

Condorcet to Saint Simone and Comte—to link scientific advance to inevitability as a prophetic discourse based on the innate goodness of the mind and projecting a utopia where all conflicting values are eliminated through *science* (or a technocratic elite).

Historical knowledge, as a negotiable and contested dialogic practice, constructs a public template for collective learnings. We are ethically responsible today, as an alternative with historically known consequences, for what Nietzsche could not have known in urging the political construction of a new aristocracy and disparaging Enlightenment principle (democracy, open scientific inquiry) as a modern slave mentality.[52] History is an organized knowledge construction combining inferential thought processes and evidence with ethical as well as scientific implications. In eradicating the moral value of truth as evidence, forgetting and repetition of past political tragedies become more likely. The traces of violence upon the victims can be erased by the perpetrators. There is a tacit conceptual complicity from those supposing nihilistically that rule of law is only "delight in the promised blood" (i.e. democratic and authoritarian systems are the same on a *basic level*).[53]

There is no methodological call for a *universal history* as in medieval Christian historiography, where the "historical process is everywhere and always of the same kind, and every part of it is a part of the same whole."[54] This is what the post-structuralist spirit rightly attacked. Any historiography modelled on this basis is another variation on Providence or an imagined unitary transcendent will, or history as a great plot—what Levinas warned against. Yet nor is its counterpart, say, a Greco-Roman oecumenical history revolving around a particularistic centre of gravity in Greece or Rome appropriate to the conditions of today's world: the sometimes tendency of national history as a unique inner impulse unfolding as a *narrative* in isolation from simultaneous

---

[52] In *Beyond Good and Evil*, several passages explicitly promote a political order of rank based on fixed difference to create a "higher man." This implies a criterion of truth in the service of this "higher" end. Irving's historical methodology would be a more recent equivalent. Nietzsche was far from a Nazi, but partook of an authoritarian epistemology where knowledge construction should serve higher 'aesthetic' ends.

[53] Foucault, Nietzsche, Genealogy, History, 85.

[54] Collingwood, *Idea of History*, 49.

events transpiring elsewhere, or the dogged insistence upon the micro-history as a principled revolt against the inevitable tyranny of every *holistic* claim.

Methodologically, neither can confront the crucial problem of linkages: say, the linkage between ex-Iraqi dictator Saddam Hussein and the US military–industrial complex in the eight-year-long Iran–Iraq War or the complex multi-agency conundrums linking Saudi Arabia, Pakistan and the Western powers upon the terrain of Afghanistan in its war against Soviet Invasion. This linkage network provides a more scientifically convincing explanation for the 9-11 attacks with their specific agents and discursive agenda. There was an intelligible context. In the absence of widespread public awareness of linkage systems, a metaphysical recourse to the *eternal essence* of Islam in Western media (suiting the illicit self-representative claims of the terrorists) endangered and maligned millions of Muslims.

To comprehend these many-sided situations—which after all are the shaping force in everyday life today—we require a multi-centred history.[55] This study, as a history of ideas, follows Chris Bayly's concern with the worldwide interconnectedness and interdependence of political and social changes. He analyzes the relations between the *core* industrial world economy and those events impacting back upon it to mould its ideologies and social/political conflicts, and how forms of human action come to resemble each other: a "complex parallelogram of forces."[56]

In the domain of a history of ideas, consider the impact of the American civil rights movement under Martin Luther King and the shaping influence of Gandhian practices and ideas upon America's political fate on the civil society level. It goes without saying that a discursive–practical study of the Enlightenment heritage focused on the United States offers a wealth of research domains (i.e. the American Civil War, the New Deal, the Civil Rights Movement). Conversely, the intellectual and political world of the American Transcendentalists—in their struggle against slavery and imperial wars of expansion—were among

---

[55] This, naturally, would be empty without micro-histories to construct it.

[56] C.A. Bayly, *The Birth of the Modern World: 1780–1914* (Malden: Blackwell, 2004), 7.

Gandhi's important influences. King's writings suggest the complex cosmopolitan overlapping and conceptual non-essentialism of these experiences and movements: "I had come to see early that the Christian doctrine of love operating through the Gandhian method of non-violence was one of the most potent weapons available to the Negro in his struggle for freedom."

King conceived his struggle in terms of the "common cause of minority and colonial peoples in America, Africa, and Asia struggling to throw off racialism and imperialism." The fundamental aim of his politics was to "enlarge democracy for all people." King contrasted democratic practice with violence:

> [T]he frequent method (of political change) that has been used in history is that of rising up against the oppressor with corroding hatred and physical violence. Now of course we know all about this method in Western civilization because in a sense it has been the hallmark of its grandeur, and the inseparable twin of western materialism.[57]

This represents an important discursive–practical formation that ruptures a tacit frontier of a long-held unthought. It transformed the discursive parameters of American politics.

We might also consider Norwegian John Galtung's influential theory of structural violence, derived from an interpretation of Gandhian thought. It effected the transvaluation in terms of seeing violence in patterns of hunger reflecting inequitable distribution of resources in everyday life. This is significant for institutional ethics. These instances affirm the democratic Enlightenment heritage while showing modernity as perpetually transforming energies and imagination free from any dichotomy between "reason" and "meaning," "West" and "East," or any such reductive binary.[58] We require a multi-centred history to understand and appreciate these moments, both critically and in terms of the lessons that they can impart to us. For example: Under what objective circumstances can a non-violent mass

---

[57] Martin Luther King, *A Testament of Hope: The Essential Writings and Speeches of Martin Luther King Jr.* (San Francisco: Harperone, 1990), 16–44.

[58] See Tim Jacoby, *Understanding Conflict and Violence. Theoretical and Interdisciplinary Approaches* (New Delhi: Routledge, 2008), 38–48.

movement actually succeed?[59] There is a multi-centred global basis for such a study, in the wake of recent decades from South Africa to Myanmar, Tunisia to Iran.

THE ENLIGHTENMENT

Conventional Enlightenment accounts begun and ended in 18th-century Europe, centred intellectually in France and politically upon the French Revolution. This is an exceedingly narrow view. This tendency has contributed to such frozen abstractions as the imagined anti-thesis between modernity–tradition that presumes religion to be the inherent enemy of modern progress, or that all traditional ideas and values must be excluded from participation in the democratic nation-making process. This project attempts to reveal the weaknesses of the dogmatic French Revolutionary Comtean paradigm, and where there are existing alternatives.

Significantly, in all Enlightenment movements prior to Gandhi, the problems of means and violence were overlooked—it was tacitly broached by natural rights theory and Locke in promoting tolerance and secular ideals but never became the focus of reflection. It remained in the unthought—scattered components lacking self-conscious assembly. Meanwhile, violence as a legitimate means was frequently taken for granted and sometimes affirmed in the name of larger metaphysical ideas and ends—it was imagined in direct linkage with an unfolding historical reason. Violence remained in the unthought, but was coded, patterned or structured via a narrative. This often had anti-democratic implications in the process of nation-making, forcing minorities into the framework of a larger *ideal* mould, and served to imaginatively justify colonial or imperial aggression. The Enlightenment heritage was linked to massive violence—whatever the motive complex may really have been—most conspicuously in American discourses justifying the Iraq War (2003–11). Today, 60–70 per cent of the child population suffers psychological problems after years of traumatizing daily violence.[60]

---

[59] By objective conditions, I have in mind a comparative study like James DeFronzo's *Revolutions and Revolutionary Movements* (1996).

[60] http://www.alertnet.org/thenews/newsdesk/IRIN/4ef14e3c0bd5ad74baf903a1b1ad849c.htm (accessed 25 December 2013).

CONCLUSION 359

It is doubtlessly in response to the many unresolved tensions—between authoritarianism and liberty, religion and secularism, nation and humanity, social justice and political freedom, reason and violence, etc., knotted at the heart of modernity—that the received understanding of Enlightenment underwent radical waves of reinterpretation throughout the 20th century. This represents the multiple invisible frontiers of the unthought, resoluble only through practice. Because of this, the project of modernity still evokes premonitions of danger and pessimism as often as optimism and hope.

We may say the Enlightenment itself has been a persistent site of changing hermeneutical interpretation over the meaning of modernity and various paradigms of the nation. Who does it belong to? Where does it begin and end? The traditional view of Enlightenment as a unitary phenomenon, as an entity called *the* Enlightenment, and an event which transpired largely in 18th-century France—in short the view of the Enlightenment as a completed historical project—has ceded increasingly to a radically alternative understanding of Enlightenment rather as a *process* or a *way of thinking* with ongoing and global implications and a highly pluralistic character.

The older and more conventional Enlightenment periodization conceives the departure point as 1715, the year of the sun king Louis XIV's death, and envisions a teleological progression involving the dominant French figures of Montesquieu, Voltaire and Rousseau culminating in the 1789 French Revolution. The Enlightenment period is presumed to end with the general disillusionment fostered by Napoleon's ascendancy to Emperor, sullying the values and promise in whose name the Enlightenment struggle had been fought. By this account the circuiting of ideas, across and within European societies, evolved through a predominantly intellectual and cultural movement. This movement self-consciously gave a label to the encompassing historical period, and was marked by historical events of which the movement was the author, culminating bleakly in the moment of *the Terror*.

Dorinda Outram's *The Enlightenment* (2005) contains a useful survey of the newer interpretative developments regarding the Enlightenment produced over the course of the 20th century. The leading pre-war interpretation articulated in Ernst Cassirer's 1932 *The Philosophy of Enlightenment* defined a period bounded by the lives of the two philosophers Gottfried Wilhelm Leibniz (1646–1716) and Immanuel Kant (1724–1804). The predominance of this model expressed the tacit assumption of Enlightenment as a primarily philosophical, if not even apolitical, movement, flying well above the disorder and conflict of immanent history. Such an intellectually elitist model restricted the fuller implications of Enlightenment in the politics of both everyday life and mass movements, the process of nation-making and lines of collective action via parties. It, hence, functioned as an unproductive barrier against reflection upon the full significance of Enlightenment for contemporary politics and culture in the world of *globalization*.

In the post-war period Cassirer's view of Enlightenment found an influential heir in Peter Gay's two volumes, *The Rise of Modern Paganism* and *The Science of Freedom*. Gay takes up the essentialist mantle in arguing that "there was only one Enlightenment." As the title indicates, for Gay the programme of Enlightenment is essentially hostile to religion as a new worldview intended to uncompromisingly supersede older ones. This implies the depth to which Gay's view of Enlightenment partakes of a preconceived interpretation, one based on the paradigm derived from the French Revolution. This reflects a narrow view of Enlightenment privileging particular discourses within the 18th-century French tradition, leaving others out of account. The historical construction lacks the degree of cultural diversity or the plural forms of rationality a multi-centred Enlightenment vista offers in changing ways of thinking and being.

It was not until the 1970s that a more complete picture of the Enlightenment outside Europe began to supersede the older model. H.F. May's 1976 *The Enlightenment in America* and A. Owen Aldridge's *The Ibero-American Enlightenment* both "made it impossible any longer to see the Enlightenment as a unified phenomenon, or one that was unaffected by geographical location."[61] Meanwhile, Franco Venturi identified Enlightenment as a force in Italy, Greece, the Balkans, Poland, Hungary and Russia, arguing that it was "precisely in these 'peripheral' areas where the stresses and strains within the Enlightenment could be

---

[61] Dorinda Outram, *The Enlightenment* (Cambridge: Cambridge University Press, 2005), 4.

best analysed."[62] This dawning recognition of the pluralistic character of Enlightenment hinges on the unveiling of a geographic problem which is also the undoing of European Empire.

In the wake of these studies, Outram writes that "We are now far more aware of the many different Enlightenments, whether national or regional, Catholic or Protestant, of Europeans and of indigenous peoples. This diversity mirrors the inability of eighteenth-century people themselves to make any single definition of Enlightenment."[63] Here we come upon the problem of the inherent pluralism of Enlightenment as a modern and global experience as it crashes against the long standing *essentialist* tendency in Western thought, a survival of Platonic Forms, which must insist that only a single definition is permissible as the *true* one for any particular subject and construct an ontological system toward establishing that certitude.

What we see in these interpretative developments is a temporal and geographical expansion and dispersal pointing to what Gramsci has called "a relation of forces in continuous motion and shift of equilibrium" rather than a reality that is "static and immobile."[64] The Enlightenment as an event ceases to be a monolithic block containing an essence and a teleological underpinning. It suggests what DeLanda has argued, that in order to "approach history in a non-teleological way," it is necessary to give up the idea "that human societies form a 'totality', that is, an entity on a higher ontological plane than individual institutions and individual human beings."[65] He argues that it is "crucial to emphasize (...) that the entire process does not emanate from some essence housed in people's heads, particularly not any reified essence such as 'rationality'."[66] Regarding modernity, he writes that "nothing intrinsic to Europe determined the outcome, but rather a dynamics bearing no inherent relationship to any one culture."[67] The very variety of interpretations of Enlightenment

[62] Outram, *Enlightenment*, 4.
[63] Outram, *Enlightenment*, 8.
[64] Antonio Gramsci, *Selections from the Prison Notebooks* (New York: International Publishers, 1971), 172.
[65] Manuel De Landa, *A Thousand Years of Nonlinear History* (New York: Swerve, 2000), 19/37.
[66] De Landa, *Nonlinear History*, 40.
[67] De Landa, *Nonlinear History*, 51.

suggests a hermeneutical problem, one subject to numerous interpretations each having a role in creating the very tradition itself. This already implies an inescapable condition of pluralism which de-centres the production of all closed systems.

In her own analysis, Outram locates the construction of the Enlightenment discourses in relation to the social and political crisis of the 17th century. Opposing the linear view of the Enlightenment as a mainly French phenomenon with a terminus in the French Revolution, she writes:

> A peaceful period called "Enlightenment" was *not* ended by a sudden upheaval called "Revolution". For most of Europe it is far truer to say that Enlightenment and Revolution proceeded side by side for much of the century. One could even say that the Enlightenment *began* with Revolution, that which occurred in England in 1688, which created the conditions for the emergence of the philosophy with which John Locke discussed new thinking about the relationship between ruler and ruled.[68]

Outram's view echoes the pioneering work of Paul Hazard, whose work "defined the modern, 'broader' notion of the Enlightenment" and was the first to "establish the beginnings of the Enlightenment proper in the seventeenth century."[69] Hazard contrasted the *stability* of the classical ideal to the *restless* character of Enlightenment thinking, and thereby argued for the importance of the Enlightenment as a particular *way of thinking* in response to the experience of modernity. In other words, Hazard conceived the Enlightenment in terms of a broader problematic of modernity, providing a more nuanced frame than the simplistic division between medieval and modern minds, or a clear frontier dividing these historical periods with the facile ontological clarity comparable to that often evoked as dividing the *East* and the *West*.

Hazard's *Crisis of European Consciousness*, moreover, shows to what extent the European Enlightenment constituted a set of social revolutions combined with a complex revolution in

---

[68] Outram, *Enlightenment*, 133.

[69] Peter Hulme and Ludmilla Jordanova, ed., *The Enlightenment and its Shadows* (London: Routledge, 1990), 3.

CONCLUSION

consciousness. This revolved around what we might call Europe's confrontation with an ontological vacuum. In the context of a worldview ontology gives an explicit account of what is *most real* independently of any mistaken interpretation and so assigns a clear hierarchy of value or significance to experience.

Ontology involves assertions about the nature of being. Such beliefs generally remain at an unconscious level. Assertions are not typically made—except in routine surface and self-reproducing manner—until a crisis situation renders explicit their problematic nature. Their *truth* value is then brought into collective question. The frontiers of the unthought are pushed at multiple points. Varying possible roads open up, implying collective commitments. The historian subsequently endeavours to analyze and *remember* these paths, thereby constructing discursive–practical horizons.

Such a crisis has been the subject of experiences of Enlightenment analyzed in this book. It has simply expanded the analytic space opened by Outram and Hazard, to discuss the experiences of non-Western societies. These are often consigned erroneously to a static condition out of laziness, prejudice or imitation or some combination of the three.

It is because we stand globally today in the midst of this discursive–practical paradigm crisis—and it impacts our everyday world—that we cannot afford to imagine the Enlightenment heritage as an event that is behind us. The crisis of consciousness is global, and there is no way out beyond the immanent horizon of our everyday struggles to live in mutual respect and dignity. Other alternatives—hierarchic and violent—certainly exist. We have seen them. The meaning of the Enlightenment heritage—among other things—is to self-consciously reject them because of the systemic violence they imply. It is in this light that we may look beyond the limits of the unthought, to recognize that the Enlightenment heritage has grown because of the Gandhi–Nehru paradigm.

Bibliography

INDIA

Primary Sources

Abul-Fazl, Allami. *The A-In-I Akbari*. Translated by H. Blochmann. New Delhi: Low Price Publications, 2008.

Akbar. *A Letter of the Emperor Akbar Asking for the Christian Scriptures*. Translated by Edward Rehatsek. *The Indian Antiquary: A Journal of Oriental Research in Archaeology, Epigraphy, Ethnology, Geography, History, Folklore, Languages, Literature, Numismatics, Philosophy, Religion, etc.* (April 1887), http://www.archive.org/details/indianantiquaryj266roya (accessed 25 December 2013).

Amit, Chaudhuri, ed. *The Picador Book of Modern Indian Literature*. London: Picador, 2001.

Bhagat, Singh. *Selected Speeches and Writings*. Edited by D. N. Gupta. New Delhi: National Book Trust, 2007.

Gandhi, M. K. *Hind Swaraj and Other Writings*. Cambridge: Cambridge University Press, 1997.

———. *The Collected Works of Mahatma Gandhi, Vol. 9*. New Delhi: Government of India, Ministry of Information and Broadcasting, Publications Division, 1996.

Christophe, Jaffrelot, ed. *Hindu Nationalism: A Reader*. New Delhi: Permanent Black, 2007.

Kabir. *The Weaver's Songs*. New Delhi: Penguin, 2003.

Nagarjuna. *The Fundamental Wisdom of the Middle Way*. Translated by Jay L. Garfield. New York: Oxford University Press, 1995.

Jawaharlal, Nehru. *Selected Works*. New Delhi: Oxford University Press, 1984–1991.

———. *Letters to the Chief Ministers*. New Delhi: Oxford University Press, 1989.

———. *The Discovery of India*. New York: Penguin, 2004.

Rabindranath, Tagore. *Rabindranath Tagore Omnibus III*. New Delhi: Penguin, 2006.

Sarvepalli, Radhakrishnan and Charles A. Moore, eds. *A Sourcebook in Indian Philosophy*. Princeton: Princeton University Press, 1957.

Tendulkar, D. G. *Mahatma*. New Delhi: Publications Division, 1992.

William Theodore de Bary, Stephen Hay, Royal Weiler and Andrew Yarrow, ed. *Sources of Indian Tradition*. New Delhi: Motilal Banarsidass.

Secondary Sources

Medieval and early Modern

Collections

Alam, Muzaffar, Francoise Nalini Delvoye and Marc Gaborieau, eds. *The Making of Indo-Persian Culture*. New Delhi: Manohar, 2000.
Irfan, Habib, ed. *A Shared Heritage: The Growth of Civilizations in India and Iran*. New Delhi: Tulika Books, 2002.
———. *Akbar and His India*. New Delhi: Oxford, 1997.
———. *Religion in Indian History*. New Delhi: Tulika, 2007.
Jha, D.N. and Eugenia Vanina, eds. *Mind over Matter. Essays on Mentalities in Medieval India*. New Delhi: Tulika Books, 2009.
Meenakshi, Khanna, ed. *Cultural History of Medieval India*. New Delhi: Social Science Press, 2007.

Historical Studies

Abraham, Eraly. *The Mughal World: Life in India's Last Golden Age*. New Delhi: Penguin, 2007.
Ali, M.A. *Mughal India: Studies in Polity, Ideas, Society and Culture*. New Delhi: Oxford University Press, 2006.
Andre, Wink. *Akbar*. Oxford: One World, 2009.
Irfan, Habib. *Essays on Indian History: Towards a Marxist Perception*. New Delhi: Tulika, 2007.
Harbans, Mukhia. *The Mughals of India*. New Delhi, Blackwell Publishing, 2004.
———. *Exploring India's Medieval Centuries: Essays in History, Society, Culture and Technology*. New Delhi: Aakar, 2010.
Jos, Gommans. *Mughal Warfare: Indian Frontiers and High Roads to Empire 1500–1700*. London: Routledge, 2002.
Neeru, Misra. *Sufis and Sufism: Some Reflections*. New Delhi: Manohar, 2004.
Prasannan, Parthasarathi. *Why Europe Grew Rich and Asia Did Not: Global Economic Divergence, 1600–1850*. Cambridge: Cambridge University Press, 2011.
Richards, J. F. *The Mughal Empire*. New Delhi: Cambridge University Press, 2008.
Sadia, Dehlvi. *Sufism: The Heart of Islam*. New Delhi: Harper Collins, 2009.
Saiyid, Athar and Abbas, Rizvi. *A History of Sufism in India: Volume I*. New Delhi: Munshiram Manoharlal Publishers, 1997.
———. *A History of Sufism in India: Volume II*. New Delhi: Munshiram Manoharlal Publishers, 2002.

Satish, Chandra. *Essays on Medieval Indian History*. New Delhi: Oxford, 2007.
———. *Medieval India from Sultanat to Mughals: Part I*. New Delhi: Har Anand, 2007.
———. *Medieval India from Sultanat to Mughals: Part II*. New Delhi: Har Anand, 2007.
———. *State, Pluralism, and the Indian Historical Tradition*. New Delhi: Oxford, 2009.
Shireen, Moosvi. *Episodes in the Life of Akbar: Contemporary Records and Reminiscences*. New Delhi: National Book Trust, 2007.
Sugata, Bose. *A Hundred Horizons: The Indian Ocean in the Age of Global Empire*. Ranikhet Cantt: Permanent Black, 2006.
Sumit, Guha. *Health and Population in South Asia: From Earliest Times to the Present*. Ranikhet Cantt: Permanent Black, 2001.
———. *Medieval India: The Study of a Civilization*. New Delhi: National Book Trust, 2007.
Sunil, Khilnani. *The Idea of India*. Farrar: Straus and Giroux, 1998.
Sunil, Sharma. *Amir Khusrau: The Poet of Sufis and Sultans*. Oxford: Oneworld Publications, 2006.
Wood, A.T. *Asian Democracy in World History*. London: Routledge, 2003.

Modern India

Collections

Bhargava, Rajeev, ed. *Secularism and its Critics*. New Delhi: Oxford University Press, 2009.
Wilkinson, Steven I., ed. *Religious Politics and Communal Violence*. New Delhi: Oxford University Press, 2005.

Historical Studies

Bandyopadhyay, Sekhar. *From Plassey to Partition: A History of Modern India*. New Delhi: Orient BlackSwan, 2009.
Basham, A. L. *A Cultural History of India*. New Delhi: Oxford, 1975.
Bondurant, J.V. *Conquest of Violence: The Gandhian Philosophy of Conflict*. Berkeley: University of California Press, 1965.
Brass, P. R. *The Politics of India Since Independence*. Cambridge: Cambridge University Press, 1990.
Chandra, Bipan Mridula Mukherjee and Aditya Mukherjee. *India since Independence*. New Delhi: Penguin, 2008.
Chandra, Bipan, Mridula Mukherjee, Aditya Mukherjee, Sucheta Mahajan and K. N. Panikkar. *India's Struggle for Independence*. New Delhi: Penguin, 1989.

Chandra, Bipan. *History of Modern India*. New Delhi: Orient BlackSwan, 2009.
———. *Ideology and Politics in Modern India*. New Delhi: Har-Arnand, 1994.
———. *Indian National Movement: The Long-Term Dynamics*. New Delhi: Vikas, 1989.
———. *Nationalism and Colonialism in Modern India*. New Delhi: Orient Longman, 2005.
Chatterjee, Partha. *Nationalist Thought and the Colonial World: A Derivative Discourse*. New Delhi: Oxford University Press, 1986.
Dalton, Dennis. *Gandhi's Power: Non-Violence in Action*. New Delhi: Oxford University Press, 1993.
David, Gosling. *Science and the Indian Tradition: When Einstein Met Tagore*. London: Routledge, 2008.
Guha, Ramachandra *India after Gandhi: The History of the World's Largest Democracy*. London: Picador, 2008.
Heimsath, C.H. *Indian Nationalism and Hindu Social Reform*. New Jersey: Princeton University Press, 1964.
Jaffrelot, Christophe. *Dr. Ambedkar and Untouchability: Analysing and Fighting Caste*. New Delhi: Permanent Black, 2005.
Metcalf, B.D. and T R. Metcalf. *A Concise History of Modern India*. Cambridge: Cambridge University Press, 2003.
Mukherjee, Mridula. *Peasants in India's Non-Violent Revolution*. New Delhi: SAGE, 2004.
Nanda, B.R. *Jawaharlal Nehru: Rebel and Statesman*. New Delhi: Oxford University Press, 1998.
———. *Mahatma Gandhi: A Biography*. New Delhi: Oxford University Press, 1958.
Panikkar, K.N. *Culture, Ideology, Hegemony: Intellectuals and Social Consciousness in Colonial India*. New Delhi: Tulika, 1995.
Parekh, Bhikhu. *Colonialism, Tradition and Reform: An Analysis of Gandhi's Political Discourse*. New Delhi: SAGE, 1989.
Parel, A.J. *Gandhi's Philosophy and the Quest for Harmony*. Cambridge: Cambridge University Press, 2006.
Poddar, Arabinda. *Renaissance in Bengal: Search for Identity*. Shimla: Indian Institute of Advanced Studies, 1977.
Rudolph, S.H. and L. I. Rudolph. *Gandhi: The Traditional Roots of Charisma*. New Delhi: Orient Longman, 1987.
Sharma, Jyotirma. *Hindutva: Exploring the Idea of Hindu Nationalism*. New Delhi: Penguin, 2003.
Singh, Yogendra. *Modernization of Indian Tradition*. Jaipur: Rawat, 2009.
Steger, Manfred. *Gandhi's Dilemma. Nonviolent Principles and Nationalist Power*. New York: St. Martin's Press, 2000.
Terchek, R.J. *Gandhi Struggling for Autonomy*. New Delhi: Vistaar Publications, 2000.

Journal articles and conference papers

Azizuddin, S.M. Dept. of History, Jamia Millia Islamia, New Delhi. "Legacy of Ibn-i-Sina (980–1037)." *Proceedings of Avicenna International Colloquium*, 1999.

Habib, Irfan. "Akbar and Social Inequities: A Study of the Evolution of his Ideas," *Proceedings of the Indian History Congress*, Warangal session, 1993.

Koch, Ebba. "The Intellectual and Artistic Climate of Tolerance at Akbar's Court." Unpublished paper from the Akbar Fourth Centenary Conference, 28–30 October, 2006. New Delhi: Indian Council of Historical Research.

Moosvi, Shireen. "Abu'l Fazl: A Sixteenth Century Spokesman for Science and Reason," unpublished paper from the Akbar Fourth Centenary Conference, 28–30 October, 2006. New Delhi: Indian Council of Historical Research.

Muzaffar Alam. "The Mughals, the Sufi Shaiks and the Formation of the Akbari Dispensation." In *Modern Asian Studies*, edited by Joya Chatterji. Cambridge: Cambridge University Press, 2008.

Rothermund, Dietmar. "Akbar and Philip II of Spain: Contrasting Strategies of Imperial Consolidation." Unpublished paper from the Akbar Fourth Centenary Conference, 28–30 October, 2006. New Delhi: Indian Council of Historical Research.

Theory

Mehta, V.R. *Foundations of Indian Political Thought: An Interpretation (From Manu to the Present Day)*. New Delhi: Manohar, 2008.

Sen, Amartya. *The Argumentative Indian: Writings on Indian Culture, History and Identity*. London: Penguin, 2005.

Chakrabarty, Bidyut and R.K. Pandey. *Modern Indian Political Thought*. New Delhi: SAGE, 2009.

THE OTTOMAN EMPIRE AND TURKEY

Primary

English

Ataturk, M.K. *A Speech Delivered by Mustafa Kemal Ataturk: 1927*. Istanbul: Ministry of Education Printing Plant, 1963.

Mithat, A.H. *The Life of Midhat Pasha: A Record of His Services, Political Reforms, Banishment, and Judicial Murder, Derived from Private Documents and Reminiscences.* London: J. Murray, 1903.
Ziya, Gokalp. *Turkish Nationalism and Western Civilization.* London: George Allen & Unwin, 1959.

French

Ataturk, M.K. *Memoires.* Paris: Coda, 2005.

Secondary

English

Collections
Atabaki, Touraj, ed. *The State and the Subaltern: Modernization, Society and the State in Turkey and Iran.* London: I. B. Tauris, 2007.
Bozdogan, Sibel and Resat Kasaba, eds. *Rethinking Modernity and National Identity in Turkey.* Washington: University of Washington Press, 1997.
Finkel, Andrew and Sirman Nukhet, eds. *Turkish State, Turkish Society.* London: Routledge, 1990.
Kazancigil, Ali and Ergun Ozbudun, ed. *Ataturk: Founder of a Modern State.* London: C. Hurst and Co., 1981.
Tuncay, Mete and E.J. Zurcher, ed. *Socialism and Nationalism in the Ottoman Empire: 1876–1923.* London: I. B. Tauris, 1994.

Historical Studies

Ahmad, Feroz. *The Young Turks: The Committee of Union and Progress in Turkish Politics. 1908–1914.* London: Oxford, 1969.
Barkey, Karen. *Empire of Difference: The Ottomans in Comparative Perspective.* New York: Cambridge University Press, 2008.
Berkes, Niyazi. *The Development of Secularism in Turkey.* Montreal: McGill University Press, 1964.
Cinar, Alev. *Modernity, Islam, and Secularism in Turkey: Bodies, Places and Time.* Minneapolis: University of Minnesota Press, 2005.
Cleveland, W. L. *History of the Modern Middle East.* Boulder, Colorado: Westview, 2004.
Clot, André. *Suleiman the Magnificent.* London: Saqi, 2005.
Finkel, Caroline. *Osman's Dream. The History of the Ottoman Empire 1300–1923.* New York: Basic Books, 2007.

Hanioğlu, M. Şükrü. *A Brief History of the Late Ottoman Empire*. Princeton: Princeton University Press, 2008.

Hasan, Kayali. *Arabs and Young Turks: Ottomanism, Arabism, and the Ottoman Empire. 1908–1918*. Los Angeles: UCLA Press, 1997.

Mardin, Serif. *The Genesis of Young Ottoman Thought: A Study in the Modernization of Turkish Political Ideas*. New York: Syracuse University Press, 2000.

———. *Religion and Social Change in Modern Turkey: The Case of Bediuzzaman Said Nursi*. New York: State University of New York Press, 1989.

Mansfield, Peter. *A History of the Middle East*. New York: Viking Penguin, 1991.

Pamuk, Sevket. *The Ottoman Empire and European Capitalism, 1820–1913: Trade, Investment, and Production*. Cambridge: Cambridge University Press, 1987.

Quataert, Donald. *The Ottoman Empire: 1700–1922*. Cambridge: Cambridge University Press, 2005.

Shaw, S.J. and E. K. Shaw. *Reform, Revolution and Republic: The Rise of Modern Turkey 1808–1975*, Vol. 2, History of the Ottoman Empire and Modern Turkey. Cambridge: Cambridge University Press, 1977.

Trencsenyi, Balazs and Michal Kopacek. *National Romanticism: The Formation of National Movements*. CEU Press, 2006.

Zurcher, E.J. *The Young Turk Legacy and Nation Building: From the Ottoman Empire to Ataturk's Turkey*. London: I. B. Tauris, 2010.

French

Dumont, Paul. *Mustafa Kemal invente la Turquie Moderne*. Paris: Editions Complexe, 1983.

Jevakhoff, Alexandre. *Kemal Ataturk*. Paris: Talandier, 1989.

Vaner, Samith, ed. *Modernisation Autoritaire en Turquie et en Iran*. Paris: L'Harmattan, 1991.

IRAN

Primary

Al-e Ahmad, Jahal. *Occidentosis: A Plague from the West*. Berkeley: Mizan Press, 1984.

Muhammad, Sayyid. *Unpublished Memories*. Tehran: Nashr' Abi Publishers, 1382 A.H./1962 C.E.

Musaddiq, Mohammad. *Musaddiq's Memoirs*. London: JEBHE, 1988.

Secondary

Abrahamian, Ervand. *Iran between Two Revolutions*. Princeton: Princeton University Press, 1983.
———. *A History of Modern Iran*. Cambridge: Cambridge University Press, 2008.
Azimi, Fakhreddin. *Iran: The Crisis of Democracy*. London: I. B. Tauris, 1989.
Boroujerdi, Mehrzad. *Iranian Intellectuals and the West: The Tormented Triumph of Nativism*. Syracuse: Syracuse University Press, 1996.
Clawson, Patrick and Michael Rubin. *Eternal Iran: Continuity and Chaos*. New York: Palgrave, 2005.
Katouzian, Homa. *Musaddiq and the Struggle for Power in Iran*. London: I. B. Tauris, 2009.
———. *The Political Economy of Modern Iran, 1926–1979*. New York: New York University Press, 1981.
———. *Iranian History and Politics: The Dialectic of State and Society*. London: Routledge, 2003.
Keddie, N. R. *Modern Iran: Roots and Results of Revolution*. New Jersey: Yale University Press, 2003.
Mirsepassi, Ali. *Intellectual Discourse and the Politics of Modernization: Negotiating Modernity in Iran*. Cambridge: Cambridge University Press, 2000.
Morgan, David. *Medieval Persia, 1040–1797*. London: Longman, 1988.
Mohammadi, Majid. *Judicial Reform and Reorganization in 20th-Century Iran: State-Building, Modernization and Islamicization*. New York: Routledge, 2008.
Mottahedeh, Roy. *The Mantle of the Prophet: Politics and Religion in Iran*. New York: Pantheon, 1985.
Poulson, S.C. *Social Movements in Twentieth Century Iran: Culture, Ideology and Mobilizing Frameworks*. Lanham: Lexington Books, 2006.
Savory, Roger. *Iran Under the Safavids*. Cambridge: Cambridge University Press, 1980.

Collections

Bonine, M.E. and Nikki Keddie, eds. *Modern Iran: The Dialectics of Continuity and Change*. Albany: State University of New York Press, 1981.
Floor, Willem and Edmund Herzig, ed. *Iran and the World in the Safavid Age*. (London: I. B. Tauris, 2012.
Gasiorowski, M.J. and Malcolm Bryne, eds. *Mohammed Mosaddeq and the 1953 Coup in Iran*. Syracuse: Syracuse University Press, 2004.

Papers and articles

Baraheni, Reza. "Bridging the Gap or Filling the Precipice. The Poetics of Passage in Contemporary Persian Literature." Unpublished lecture given at New York University, 2010.

Kia, Mehrdad. "Constitutionalism, Economic Modernization and Islam in the Writings of Mirza Yusef and Khan Mostashar od-Dowle." *Middle Eastern Studies*, 30, no. 4 (October 1994).

EUROPE

Primary

English

Bentham, Jeremy. *Selected Writings on Utilitarianism*. Hertfordshire: Wordsworth, 2001.

Cromwell, Oliver. *Speeches of Oliver Cromwell*. Edited by Ivan Roots. London: Everyman History, 1989.

Dewey, John. *The Philosophy of John Dewey*. Edited by John J. Mc Dermont. Chicago: University of Chicago Press, 1973.

———. *A Common Faith*. New Haven: Yale University Press, 1960.

Fontenelle, Bernard le Bovier de. *Conversations on the Plurality of Worlds* (1686). San Francisco: University of California Press, 1990.

Gramsci, Antonio. *Selections from the Prison Notebooks*. New York: International Publishers, 1971.

Hegel, G.W.F. *Phenomenology of Spirit*. Oxford: Oxford University Press, 1977.

Heidegger. *Basic Writings*. San Francisco: Harper-Collins, 1993.

———. *Being and Time*. Albany: State University of New York Press, 1996.

Hobbes, Thomas. *Leviathan*. London: Penguin, 1985.

Kant, Immanuel. *The Basic Writings of Kant*. New York: Modern Library, 2001.

King, Martin Luther. *A Testament of Hope: The Essential Writings and Speeches of Martin Luther King Jr*. San Francisco: Harperone, 1990.

Locke, John. *The Selected Political Writings of John Locke*. New York: Norton and Co., 2005.

———. *An Essay Concerning Human Understanding*. London: Penguin, 1997.

Machiavelli, Niccolo. *The Portable Machiavelli*. New York: Penguin Books, 1979.

Milton, John. *Political Writings*. Cambridge: Cambridge University Press, 1991.
———. *Prose Writings*. London: J. M. Dent and Sons Ltd., 1958.
Sieyes, E. J. *Political Writings*. Indianapolis: Hacket, 2003.
Smith, Adam. *The Theory of Moral Sentiments*. New York: Penguin, 2009.
Rousseau, Jean-Jacques. *The Social Contract*. London: Penguin, 1968.
Tolstoy, Leo. *A Confession and Other Religious Writings*. London: Penguin Books, 1987.
Weil, Simone. *An Anthology*. London: Penguin, 2005.

Collections of Primary Sources

Beardsley, Monroe, ed. *The European Philosophers from Descartes to Nietzsche*. New York: The Modern Library, 2002.
Buell, Lawrence, ed. *The American Transcendentalists: Essential Writings*. New York: Modern Library, 2006.
Curtis, Michael, ed. *The Great Political Theories: From the French Revolution to Modern Times*. New York: Harper Perennial, 2008.
———. *The Great Political Theories: From the Greeks to the Enlightenment*. New York: Harper Perennial, 2008.
Kramnick, Isaac, ed. *The Portable Enlightenment Reader*. New York: Penguin Books, 1995.
Selby-Bigge, Lewis Amherst, ed. *British Moralists: Selections from Writers Principally of the Eighteenth Century*. Oxford: Clarendon Press, 1897.

French

Comte, Auguste. *Discours sur l'Ensemble du Positivisme*. Paris: Flammarion, 2008.
Diderot. *Pensées philosophiques*. Paris: G. F. Flammarion, 2007.
Montesquieu. *De l'esprit des lois : I*. Paris: G. F. Flammarion, 1979.
Robespierre, Maximilien. *Robespierre: Entre Vertu et Terreur*. Edited by Slavoj Zizek. Paris: Stock, 2008.
Rousseau. *Discours sur l'origine et les fondements de l'inegalite parmi les hommes/Discours sur les sciences et les arts*. Paris: G. F. Flammarion, 1971.
Rouvillois, Frederic. *Les Déclarations des droits de l'homme*. Paris: Flammarion, 2009.
Saint, Just. *Œuvres Completes*. Paris: Gallimard, 2004.
Voltaire. *Dictionnaire Philosophique*. Paris: G. F. Flammarion, 1964.
———. *Lettres Philosophiques*. Paris: G. F. Flammarion, 1964.

Secondary

Collections

Glasius, Marlies, David Lewis and Hakan Seckinelgin, eds. *Exploring Civil Society: Political and Cultural Contexts.* New York: Routledge, 2004.
Hutchinson, John and Anthony D. Smith, eds. *Nationalism.* Oxford: Oxford University Press, 1994.
Perez, Zagorin, ed. *Culture and Politics from Puritanism to the Enlightenment.* Los Angeles: University of California Press, 1980.
Peter, Hulme and Ludmilla, Jordanova, eds. *The Enlightenment and its Shadows.* London: Routledge, 1990.

Historical Studies

Agnew, Jean-Christophe. *Worlds Apart: The Market and Theatre in Anglo-American Thought, 1550–1750.* Cambridge: Cambridge University Press, 1986.
Arendt, Hannah. *On Revolution.* New York: Penguin Books, 1990.
Ashley, Maurice. *England in the Seventeenth Century.* London: Penguin Books, 1961.
Bayly, C.A. *The Birth of the Modern World: 1780–1914.* Malden: Blackwell, 2004.
Beaud, Michel. *A History of Capitalism: 1500–2000.* New Delhi: Aakar Books, 2004.
Berlin, Isaiah. *The Roots of Romanticism.* London: Pimlico, 2000.
Borocz, Jozsef. *The European Union and Global Social Change: A Critical Geopolitical-Economic Analysis.* London: Routledge, 2010.
Braudel, Fernand. *Capitalism and Material Life: 1400–1800.* London: Weidenfeld and Nicolson, 1973.
Collingwood, R.G. *The Idea of History.* New Delhi: Oxford University Press, 2000.
De Landa, Manuel. *A Thousand Years of Nonlinear History.* New York: Swerve, 2000.
Diamond, Jared. *Guns, Germs and Steel: A Short History of Everybody for the Last 13,000 Years.* London: Vintage, 1998.
Doyle, William. *The Oxford History of the French Revolution.* Oxford: Oxford University Press, 1989.
Dunn, R.S. *The Age of Religious Wars.* New York: W. W. Norton and Company, 1979.
Elias, Norbert. *The Civilizing Process: The History of Manners and State Formation and Civilization.* Oxford: Blackwell, 1994.

BIBLIOGRAPHY

Foucault, Michel. *Security, Territory, Population. Lectures at the College de France 1977–78.* New York: Picador, 2007.
———. *Ethics: Subjectivity and Truth 1954–1984.* London: Penguin, 1997.
———. *The Order of Things: An Archaeology of the Human Sciences.* New York: Vintage, 1973.
Greif, Avner. *Institutions and the Path to the Modern Economy: Lessons from Medieval Trade.* Cambridge: Cambridge University Press, 2006.
Habermas, Jurgen. *The Structural Transformation of the Public Sphere: An Inquiry into a Category of Bourgeois Society.* Cambridge: MIT Press, 1991.
Hacking, Ian. *The Taming of Chance.* Cambridge: Cambridge University Press, 1990.
Hill, Christopher. *The Century of Revolution: 1603–1714.* London: Sphere Books, 1969.
———. *Milton and the English Revolution.* London: Penguin Books, 1977.
Himmelfarb, Gertrude. *The Roads to Modernity: The British, French and American Enlightenments.* New York: Alfred A. Knopf, 2004.
Hobsbawm, Eric. *The Age of Revolution: 1789–1848.* New York: Vintage, 1996.
———. *The Age of Capital: 1848–1875.* London: Abacus, 1975.
Holt, M.P. *The French Wars of Religion: 1562–1629.* Cambridge: CamMubridge University Press, 2005.
Howard, Michael. *War in European History.* London: Oxford University Press, 1976.
Ishay, M.R. *The History of Human Rights: From Ancient Times to the Globalization Era.* New Delhi: Orient Longman, 2004.
Israel, J.I. *Enlightenment Contested: Philosophy, Modernity, and the Emancipation of Man 1670–1752.* Oxford: Oxford University Press, 2008.
Jacob, M.C. *Scientific Culture and the Making of the Industrial West.* New York: Oxford University Press, 1997.
Kennedy, Emmet. *A Cultural History of the French Revolution.* New Haven: Yale University Press, 1989.
Kirchner, Walter. *Western Civilization from 1500.* New York: Harper Collins, 1991.
Koyre, Alexandre. *From the Closed to the Infinite Universe.* Baltimore, Maryland: John Hopkins University Press, 1968.
Kurlansky, Mark. *Non-Violence: The History of a Dangerous Idea.* London: Vintage, 2007.
Lefebvre, Georges. *The French Revolution.* London: Routledge, 2001.
Lewes, Henry. *The Life of Maximilien Robespierre.* Boston: Adamant Media Corporation, 2001.
Mazower, Mark. *Dark Continent: Europe's Twentieth Century.* New York: Vintage, 1998.

Outram, Dorinda. *The Enlightenment*. Cambridge: Cambridge University Press, 2005.
Pincus, Steven. *1688. The First Modern Revolution*. New Haven: Yale University Press, 2009.
Pocock, J.G.A. *The Machiavellian Moment: Florentine Political Thought and the Atlantic Republican Tradition*. New Jersey: Princeton University Press, 1975.
Polanyi, Michael. *Personal Knowledge: Towards a Post-Critical Philosophy*. Chicago: University of Chicago Press, 1962.
Polanyi, Karl. *The Great Transformation*. Boston: Beacon, 1957.
Rich, Norman. *The Age of Nationalism and Reform: 1850–1890*. New York: W. W. Norton, 1977.
Roberts, J. M. *The Penguin History of Europe*. London: Penguin, 1997.
Ronan, C.A. *Science: Its History and Development among the World's Cultures*. New York: Hamlyn, 1982.
Rude, George. *The Crowd in History*. London: Serif, 2005.
Soboul, Albert. *Understanding the French Revolution*. New Delhi: People's Publishing House, 1989.
Skocpol, Theda. *States and Social Revolutions: A Comparative Analysis of France, Russia and China*. Cambridge: Cambridge University Press, 1979.
Weber, Eugen. *Peasants into Frenchmen: The Modernization of Rural France*. Stanford: Stanford University Press, 1976.
Wedgwood, C.V. *The Trial of Charles I*. London: Penguin Books, 1983.
Woloch, Isser. *Eighteenth-Century Europe: Tradition and Progress: 1715–1789*. New York: W. W. Norton, 1982.

French

Braudel, Fernand. *La Dynamique du Capitalisme*. Paris: Flammarion, 2008.
———. *Grammaire des Civilisations*. Paris: Flammarion, 1993.
Chartier, Roger. *Les Origines Culturelles de la Révolution Française*. Paris: Editions du Seuil, 1990.
Chaunu, Pierre. *La Civilisation de L'Europe des Lumières*. Paris: Flammarion, 1982.
Furet and Ozouf. *Dictionnaire Critique de la Révolution Française: Acteurs*. Paris: Flammarion, 2007.
Furet, Francois and Mona Ozouf. *Dictionnaire Critique de la Révolution Française: Idées*. Paris: G. F. Flammarion, 2006.
Furet, Francois. *Penser la Révolution Française*. Paris: Gallimard, 1978.
Hazard, Paul. *Crise de la Conscience Européenne: 1680–1715*. Paris: Fayard, 1961.
Levinas, Emmanuel. *Ethique et Infini*. Paris: Fayard, 1982.

Articles

Steven, Pincus. "1688: A Fight for the Future," *History Today*, October 2009.

Other

Arkoun, Mohammed. *The Unthought in Contemporary Islamic Thought.* London: Saqi Books, 2002.
Aziz, Al-Azmeh. *Islams and Modernities.* London Verso, 1993.
Seidman, Steven and Jeffrey C. Alexander, eds. *The New Social Theory Reader.* Noida: Routledge, 2008.
Sen, Amartya. *Development as Freedom.* New Delhi: Oxford, 2000.
Rhodes, R.A.W., Sarah A. Binder and Bert A. Rockman, eds. *The Oxford Handbook of Political Institutions.* Oxford: Oxford University Press, 2006.
Wolin, Richard. *The Seduction of Unreason: The Intellectual Romance with Fascism from Nietzsche to Postmodernism.* Princeton: Princeton University Press, 2004.

Index

Abbas, Shah (1587–1629), 18
Abdu'l-Haqq, Shaikh, 48
absolute reality, xxv
Abul Fat'h, Hakim, 36
adultery, case of, xl
Aha'i, Shaikh Ahmad (1753–1826), 277
Akbar, Emperor. *See also* Mughal Empire under Akbar
   and bhakti saints, 40
   Dadu's influence on, 39–40
   interest in secularized knowledge, 36–37
   morality, 46
   nature of being human, 45
   as a state builder, 45
   Sufi Chishtiyya order, 23–27, 41–43
Akcura, Yusuf (1876–1933), 229
Alam-i Nau, 8
al-Basri, Al-Hasan, 24
Ali, Haidar (1761–82), 129
alternative modernity, xiv
al-Wahhab, Abd (1703–92), 131
American Civil Rights Movement (1955–68), xiii, 179
American War of Independence, 92
An-Naim, Abdul, xvii
Arabi, Ibn, 24, 34
Arendt, Hannah, xvii
Arkoun, Mohammed, xvii
Arminian-James I (1566–1625), 69
Arya Samaj, 132
Assembly Bomb Case, 171
assimilation, 242
Ataturk, 236–40
Augustine, St. (354–430), 65
Auliya, Nizamuddin, 29
Aurobindo, Sri, 116

Austrian succession (1740–48), 108
authoritarian development, xvii
Autobiography, 245
Azad, Maulana Abul Kalam, 245

Babi revolts, 277
Bacon, Francis (1561–1626), 69
Badauni, Abd-Al-Qader, 6
Badauni, Mulla, 16, 37
Balkan Wars (1912–13), 229
Barani, Ziauddin, 28
Battle of Chaldiran (1514), 13, 16
Battle of Gallipoli (1915–16), 236
Bayer, Celal, 240
Bayle, Pierre (1647–1706), 65
Bengal Renaissance, 1
   activists, 116–46
   British colonialism and, 108
   colonialism as a modernization process, 114
   English educational programme, role of, 112–15
   Naoroji's intervention, 112
Benjamin, Walter, xviii
Bentham, Jeremy (1748–1832), 159
Brahmo Samaj, 118, 129, 132, 137
Braudel, Fernand, xxxvii
British East India Company, 107
Bruno, Giordano (1548–1600), 74

Carlyle, Thomas (1795–1881), 174
Cartesianism, 56
18th-century civil society, 130
Chandavarkar, Narayan Ganesh (1855–1923), 128

Chatterjee, Partha, 266–68
Chattopadhyay, Bankimchandra, 114, 140–41
Chinese revolutions, xv

INDEX

Chishti, Khwaja Mu'inu'd-Din, 23
Christendom, 52
Christian priesthood, 68–69
CIA-organized coup, 1953, 271
Civil Disobedience Movement (1930–32), lvii, 173, 180–81
Collingwood, R. G., xx
colonialism, 111
Committee of Public Safety, 99
Committee of Safety under Robespierre, 103
Communist Party, 262
Comte, Auguste (1798–1857), 125
Comtean positivism, 346
Condorcet (1743–94), 82
Constitutional Revolution, xiv
Copernicus (1473–1543), 52
Crisis of European Consciousness, 362
Cromwell (1599–1658), 70–73
Cult of the Supreme Being, 104
cultural Westernization, xxvi

d'Alembert (1717–83), 82
Datta, Akshay Kumar (1820–86), 129
Declaration of the Rights of Man, 95
Delhi Sultanate (1206–1527), 39
democratic development, xvi–xvii
Derozio, Henry, 112, 116
  adherence to radical Enlightenment, 128
  on orthodox society, 126–27
Descartes (1596–1650), 56
Dewey, John, 54, 349–53, xiv, xvii, xx
Dhuhulow, Aisho Ibrahim, xl
Discovery of India, The, 245
discursive formations, xx
discursive–practical plane, xix–xx, xl, xxii–xxiii, xxxv
divine sanction, 66

Earl of Shaftesbury (1671–1713), 79
Eastern European revolutions, xv
Elias, Norbert, xxxv
Elizabeth I (1558–1603), 11
embeddedness, xxiv
Emerson, Ralph Waldo (1803–82), 159
Encyclopedie, 82
English Puritan movement, 68–69
  notion of Providence, 72
Enlightenment heritage, 358–63
  as capitalist expansion and exploitation of niche markets, xxv–xxvi
  elements of nation-making experiences, xiv
  Enlightenment democratic, xxxiii
  foreseeable events, avoiding, xxxiii
  and global wealth–poverty disparities, xvi
  heterogeneous experiences of modern nation-making and, xiii
  heterogeneous multiplicities of, xvii–xviii
  historical problem of, xxvi
  as a history of ideas, xix, xxxiv–xxxvii
  institutional carriers and their role in struggle, xxxv
  multi-centred modes of, xxvi–xxvii
  non-eurocentric interpretation, xxvii–xxxi
  as a philosophical problem, xiii
  as a political phenomenon, xxii–xxiii
  and principle of non-violence, xxxii–xxxiii
  reason, element of, xxxix

region of discursive–practical density, xix–xx, xxii–xxiii, xxxv, xl
in terms of revolution, xviii
in terms of violence, xxxi–xxxiv
20th-century, xv–xvi
European Enlightenment, 1, xliv
declining of feudal order and Papal jurisdiction, 63–64
ethic of reconciliation, 57
and everyday life, 58–62
modernity, xlvii–xlviii
modernization, 57
modes of imagining, xlv–xlvi
pluralism–acknowledgement mode of imagining, xlv
religion and civil society, link between, 76
religious pluralism, 65
scientific discoveries, xlvii–xlviii, 52–53
in terms of conflicting temporal horizons, 54–57
in terms of natural rights, 64–68, 74, 76
17th-century English Revolution, xlix, xlvii–xlviii, 68–81
18th-century French Enlightenment, xlvii, 62–68, 82
totality–assimilation mode of imagining, xlv
views of Europe's intellectuals, 81–89
European history, modern, xx

Fazl, Abul, 47, xliii
Foucault, Michel, xix, xx
Fredrick the Great of Prussia (1740–86), 83
French Revolution, 362
agrarian revolt against the seigneurial system, 95
civic rights, 91
concept of equality, 96
1789 Constituent Assembly, 96
at discursive–practical density level, xix–xx, xxii–xxiii
discursive–practical paradigms, 90–105
economic failure, impact of, 93–95
educational reforms, 91
French public literacy, role of, 92–93
as a history of ideas, xxxiv
Jacobin club, role of, 96–98
as a national mass movement, xviii–xix
notion of natural right, 93–94
press freedom, 91
Second Revolution, 99
French Revolutionary heritage, xxii
Fronde (1648–53), 68

Galileo (1564–1642), 52
Gandhian concepts
on change, 148
democratic Enlightenment values, 158
equal rights of untouchables, 149
Hinduism, 154
human solidarity, appeal to, 153
ideal of moral virtue, 149
ideal Swaraj, 157
mode of non-violent conflict resolution and political practice, 152
nationalism, 153–55
natural rights movement, 151
technique of nonviolence, 148
world view, 155–56
Gandhi–Nehru paradigm, xiii
Gellner, Ernest, 265–66
General Will, 82

INDEX

Ghose, Aurobindo (1872–1950), 170
Gokalp, Ziya (1876–1924), 230
Gokhale, Gopal Krishna, 116
Gramscian concept of hegemony, xxxvi
Grotius, Hugo (1583–1645), 64
Guha, Ranajit, 266

Haitian Revolution, 95
Hamidean regime, 228–29
Hamid II, Abdul, 226
Hamidu'd-Din, Shaikh, 23
Hapsburg Charles V, 10
Harley, Robert (1579–1656), 74
Heidegger (1889–1976), 177
Heideggerian historicism, 342–46
Henri IV (1589–1610), 10
Hindustan Republican Army, 171
historical contingency, xix
historical materialism, xxxii
Hobbes (1588–1679), 57

Indian National Movement, l, xxxiv. *See also* Gandhian concepts
  elements of tradition and modernity, 173
  Gandhian experience of, 147–58, liv–lvii
  Gandhian mobilization strategy, 174, 179–86
  Hindu–Muslim unity, 172, 183
  Home Rule Movement, 171
  Industrial Revolution and, 109–11
  intensification of dissident elite political movements, 175
  as a non-violent mass movement, 171–86
  peasant resistance, 174
  Satyagraha campaigns, 173
  as a self-conscious hegemonic project, xxxvi
Swadeshi Movement, 171
Indian nation-making experience, xxiii
Indian secularism, 187–95
Industrial Revolution, 109–10
inside–out identity paradigm, xxiv
invented traditions, 160–61
Iqbal, Muhammad (1875–1938), 132
Iranian Enlightenment, lxii–lxv
Iranian revolution
  1953 coup and its aftermath, 336–39
  Constitutional Revolution (1941–53), 324–36
  context for Constitutional Revolution, 277–80
  discursive transformations in, 301–8
  Iranian Constitutional Revolution (1906–11), 270
  Iranian modernity, emergence of, 280
  Mosaddeq, Dr. Mohammed (1882–1967), 271–75
  Popular Movement (1891–1953), 270, 280–89
  Reza Shah Pahlavi period (1926–41) and Constitutional Revolution, 305–23
  Tobacco Revolt of 1890–91, 271, 289–301
Islamicate world space, 11–12
Ismail, Shah, 25

Jinnah, Mohammed Ali, 245
Jones, William (1746–94), 123
Joseph II of Austria (1765–90), 83
Just, St. (1767–94), 94
  Report on the Police, 101
  view of a morally limitless, 103

Kakori Conspiracy Case, 171
Kant, Immanuel (1724–1804) xxxviii, 103

Kermani, Mirza Aqa Khan (1854–96), 277
Khan, Bairam, 4
Khan, Mirza Malkom (1833–1908), lxiii–lxiv, 277
Khan, Reza (1878–1944), 279
Khan, Sayyid Ahmed (1817–98), 132
Khomeini, Ayatollah (1902–89), 339
Khusrau, Amir, 29
Kirmani, Shah Ni'mat Allah, 42
Krishnavarma, Shyamji, 172

Lafayette (1757–1834), 92
Latif, Mir Abdul, 4
Law of Prairal, 104
Lenin (1870–1924), 176
Locke, John, xxxviii, 74–78
　concept of human nature as a blank slate, 80
　discourse of progress, 78
　discursive formation, 77–78
　Essay Concerning Human Understanding, 79
　idea in secularism, 103
　intellectual worldview, 78
　natural rights discourses, 76–77
　notion of the public, 76
Louis XV (ruled 1715–73), 83
Lovejoy, Arthur O., xx

Macaulay, Thomas, 115
Machiavelli (1469–1527), 60
Manning, Bradley, xl
Marat (1743–93), 97
Marxist Vietnamese Revolution, xv
Mill, J. S., 116, 152
The Mingling of Two Oceans, 48
Mirabeau (1749–91), 91
moderate Enlightenment, lii
modern history as a maze, 340–42
modernization process, xxi

Monserrate, Jesuit Father, 16
Montesquieu (1689–1755), 83
　debate between Voltaire and, 86
　secular ideal of institutionalized non-violence, 86
Mosaddeq, lxv
Mosaddeq, Dr. Mohammed (1882–1967), 271
Mughal Empire (1526–1857), 11
Mughal Empire under Akbar, xli
　agricultural reform, 21
　Akbarian court, xlii
　Akbar's relation to India, 5
　as beginning of modern age, 7–23
　Chishtiyya, influence of, 23–27
　cosmopolitan cultural zone, development of, 11–12
　decentralization of administrative order, 9
　early modern state, 15
　elite Mughal movement, 3
　ethical worldview, 6
　Hindu–Muslim marriages, 43–44
　Hindu–Muslim unity, 28–29
　humanitarian reforms, 24, 26–27, 37
　Ibadat Khana (house of worship), 3, 17, 25
　imperial military expansion, 14
　individual philosophies of spiritual salvation, 4–6
　Indo-Muslim tradition, 5
　Industrial Revolution, 10
　institution building during, xlii
　international level, xliii
　level of sovereignty, 12–13
　Mughal composite nobility, 14
　multi-religious considerations in policies, 23–28
　non-violence, xli

INDEX

pattern of emperor–noble relationship, 38–39
policy of tolerance, 17
public policies, 23–30
Rajput–Mughal marriages, 38
rationality of Universal Peace, xlii, 1–4, 11–12, 22
relation of Sufis to state builders, 41–43
secular-oriented reforms in education, 21
strategies of imperial consolidation, 14–15
system of coinage, 19–20
taxation policies, 9
technologies and scientific discoveries, 8–9
trade centres, establishment of, 17
urbanization, 9
multi-centred history, 353–58
Muslim state of Grenada in Spain, destruction of, 8

Nabi, Shaikh Abdun, 33
Naoroji, Dadabhai, 112
Naqshbandi movement, 47–48
Naqshbandi sect, 43
nation-making experiences, 60, xxv
  as capitalist expansion and exploitation of niche markets, xxv–xxvi
  dichotomy between social reform and political reform, 144–45
  European social-imaginary of, 61
  Fichte's views, 140–41
  in a framework of political violence, xxxi–xxxii
  state formation as a matter of survival, xxxv–xxxvi
  violence in, xxxvii–xl

natural right theory, 64
Necker, Jacques (1732–1804), 92
Nehruism, lxi, xvii
  centre–state relations, 260
  conception of modernity, 254
  concept of socialism, 264
  Constitution, 1950, 256–57
  Directive Principles, 256
  ethic of reconciliation, 250–51, 267
  formation of linguistic states, 259
  and Gandhian heritage, 245–46
  industrial development, 263
  institutionalization of democracy, 248
  liberty, 251
  multi-centeredness democracy, 257–58
  national autonomy, 265
  Nehruvian pluralism, 250–52
  nonalignment, 248
  notion of democracy, 262–63
  pluralist and non-interventionist solutions, 249
  post-independence Nehru period (1947–64), 247–48
  statesmanship, 249–50
  universalism, 265–66
  vision of freedom, 252–53, 255–56
  worldview, 249
  Zamindari abolition and agrarian reform, 251, 255
Newtonian universe functions, 56
Nicholas of Cusa (1401–64), 53
Non-Cooperation Movement (1919–22), lvii, 173, 179

Ottoman Empire, xiv, 12–13
Ottoman–Turkish Enlightenment, lviii
  Enlightenment discourses and context, 205–24

Kemalist revolution, 1923, 196–98
Mahmud II period (1808–39), lix
modernity struggle, 198–205
nature of democracy, issue of, 241
Tanzimat revolution, lix
Turkish national revolution under Ataturk, 235–40
Young Ottoman revolution, lix–lx
Young Turk Revolution, 224–43
Outram, Dorinda, 359–62

Paine, Thomas, 62
Paris peace treatises, 241–42
perfect institutions, xxv
Philip II's (reigned 1556–1598), 1
   Catholicism, 17
   early modern state, 15
   strategies of imperial consolidation, 14–15
Polanyi, Karl, xxii, xxxvi
Polanyi, Michael, xvii
post-Reza Shah period (1941–53), 271
pre-Gandhian Indian public sphere, 158–71
   Age of Consent Crisis, 166–68
   extra-constitutional dimension of protests, 163–65
   rise of individual terrorism, 168–71
Protectorate (1653–59), 69
Providence-based divine right theory, 66
public consent, 80

Qajars (1794–1925), 275

radical Enlightenment, lii–liii
Radical Puritanism, 68

Ranade, Mahadev Govind, 116, 135
   interpretation of Indian history, 136
religious sectarian massacre in Europe, 16
revivalist reformism, 131–32
Robespierre (1758–94), 57
Romanticism, 56
Rousseau (1712–78), 81
   civil religion, 87
   link between violence and sacred truth, 87
   political planning, 88
   slavery, 87–88
   state, 89
Roy, Rammohun, lii, 112, 114, 116–18, 143
   background, 117
   campaign against subjugation of women, 120
   on caste system, 118–19
   conception of immanence in political change and consciousness, 122
   concept of dharma, 121
   egalitarian religious ethics, 119, 125
   engagement with Western philosophies and religion, 118
   ideas and practices, 117–18
   insight regarding colonial power, 124
   on liberty and equality, 119–20
   mission in nation-making, 121
   opening of schools and colleges, 118
   Raj's vision of the past, 122, 124
   on secularism, 119
   on Sufi-Bhakti heritage, 125
   value of Christianity, 120
   vs orthodox Hindus, 120–21
Royalist–Puritan debate, 74

INDEX

Russian nihilism, 171
Russian revolutions, xv
Russo-Turkish War, 1877–78, xxiv

Sade, Marquis de (1740–1814), 105
Sadra, Mulla, 34, 275
Safavid Empire, 12–13
Saraswati, Dayananda, 110, 132
    vision of the modern nation, 135
Satyagraha, xxxiv
Schmitt, Carl (1888–1985), 243
secular, 346
secularism, xxxii
Sen, Amartya, xvii, xx, xxiv
    embeddedness, xxiv
    paradigm of a decentred world, xxv
Sen, Keshub Chunder, 112, 133, 137, 139
Seven Years War (1756–63), 108
Shari'ati, Al-e (1933–75), 339
Shikoh, Dara, 48
Shirazi, Fathullah, 37
Singh, Bhagat (1907–31), 169
Singh, Raja Sawai Jai (1681–1743), 130
Smith, Adam (1723–90), 80
social movement theory, xxii
Somalian Sharia court, xl
Sorel, Georges, lxvi
Spencer, Herbert (1820–1903), 125
Spinoza, Benedict (1632–77), 66
Stalin (1878–1953), 176
Stephen, Fitzjames (1869–72), 159
Sufi–Bhakti alliance, 43
Sultan, Tipu (1782–99), 129

Tagore, Dedrenath, 112, 137
Tagore, Rabindranath (1861–1941), 175

Taleb, Abu, 106–7
temporal monarchy, 46
20th-century nation-making developments, xv
17th-century Scientific Revolution, xliv
theory of conflict resolution, 67
Thirty Years war (1618–48), 66
Todorov, Tzvetan, xxxiii
Tonnerre, Clermont, 102
Treaty of Berlin, 1878, 225
Tse-tung, Mao, 261
Tunisian Jasmine Revolution (2010–11), 179

unconscious mental habits, xx
universalism, 353–54
universal modernity, xvii
universal religiosity of Akbar, xlii, 1–4

Varma, King Martanda (1729–58), 129
Varma, Rama (1758–98), 130
Vico (1668–1744), 56
Voltaire (1694–1778), 81, 83
    Christian history of Europe, 84–85
    ideal of progress and modernity, 84
    Lettres Philosophiques, 85

Wali-Allah, Shah (1703–62), 131
Weber, Max, xvii, xx, xxxv
Weil, Simone (1909–43), 176
Winstanley, Gerrard (1609–76), 71
world space transformations, xv

Yazdi, Mulla, 47
Young Ottoman movement, xxiv

About the Author

Tadd Fernée is currently a guest lecturer at the New Bulgarian University in Sofia, Bulgaria, where he leads seminars on Comparative History and the History of Ideas. The author completed a Postdoctoral Research Fellowship from Jawaharlal Nehru Institute of Advanced Studies, Jawaharlal Nehru University, New Delhi, in the year 2009–2010. The author has published the following books and articles: (co-authored with Ali Mirsepassi) *At Home and in the World: Islam, Democracy, and Cosmopolitanism* (April 2014); "Modernity and Nation-making in India, Turkey and Iran" in *International Journal of Asian Studies* (2012); "The Common Theoretical Terrain of the Gandhi and Nehru Periods: The Ethic of Reconciliation over Revenge in Nation-making" in *Studies in History* (2012); "Gandhi and the Heritage of Enlightenment: Non-violence, Secularism and Conflict Resolution" in *International Review of Sociology* (forthcoming); and "The American Civil War as a Social Revolution: The Enlightenment, Apocalyptic Imagination and Changes in Moral Perception" in the *International Journal of Interdisciplinary Studies in Linguistics, Political and Social Science, History and Philosophy* (forthcoming).